SOLDIERS IN THE ARMY OF FREEDOM

C&C

CAMPAIGNS & COMMANDERS

GREGORY J. W. URWIN, SERIES EDITOR

CAMPAIGNS AND COMMANDERS

Soldiers in the Army of Freedom

The 1st Kansas Colored, the Civil War's First African American Combat Unit

Ian Michael Spurgeon

University of Oklahoma Press | Norman

Library of Congress Cataloging-in-Publication Data
Spurgeon, Ian Michael, 1976–
Soldiers in the army of freedom : the 1st Kansas Colored, the Civil War's first
African American combat unit / Ian Michael Spurgeon.
    pages cm. — (Campaigns & commanders ; volume 47)
Includes bibliographical references and index.
ISBN 978-0-8061-4618-8 (hardcover) ISBN 978-0-8061-6879-1 (paper) 1. United
States. Army. Kansas Colored Infantry Regiment, 1st (1863–1864) 2. United States
—History—Civil War, 1861–1865—Participation, African American. 3. United
States—History—Civil War, 1861–1865—Campaigns. 4. African American
soldiers—History—
19th century. I. Title.
E508.51st .S68 2014
973.7'415—dc23
                            2014010474
*Soldiers in the Army of Freedom: The 1st Kansas Colored, the Civil War's
First African American Combat Unit* is Volume 47 in the Campaigns and
Commanders series.

The paper in this book meets the guidelines for permanence and durability of the
Committee on Production Guidelines for Book Longevity of the Council on Library
Resources, Inc. ∞

For Pierce, Karis, and Lillian

Contents

Illustrations

Figures

Maps

Acknowledgments

My first thought of writing a book on the First Kansas Colored Infantry emerged around 2002, well over a decade before the text finally made it to the publisher. Since that initial idea, countless people have played a role in creating this book. I would like to thank Governor Sam Brownback, who—as a senator and my boss in 2002—sparked my interest in this regiment by urging me to tell the story of fascinating Kansans of history. Alan Chilton of the National Park Service at Fort Scott opened his office and his schedule for much of my initial research, building the foundation of the book. Phil Reaka shared his expertise and photographs of Civil War and First Kansas Colored Infantry history related to his hometown of Paola, Kansas. Arnold Schofield and Chris Tabor, two outstanding scholars of Kansas Civil War history, have helped me, directly and indirectly, understand the regiment, its officers, and its battles. Tabor's work on the fight at Island Mound has been instrumental in teaching historians and the public about that important battle.

I must thank Robert Lull, descendant of the regiment's commander Colonel James M. Williams, who happily shared his knowledge of his ancestor and of American history with me; James "Jimmy" Johnson, who talked to me about his great-grandfather George Washington, an enlisted soldier in the First Kansas Colored Infantry; and my friend Bryan Cheeseboro, who spent many hours conversing with me about the United States Colored Troops and the Civil War.

A special thanks goes to Anita Tufts at the Hill College Historical Research Center, in Hillsboro, Texas, who helped me obtain historical material even while I was overseas and had difficulty accessing their physical records. I am grateful for the support from the Kansas State Historical Society, Bates County (Missouri) Historical Museum, the Carl Albert Congressional Research and Studies Center at the University of Oklahoma, the Fort Scott National Park office, the Mine Creek park office, the National Archives in Washington, D.C., and the Library of Congress.

In 2011 I was fortunate to have a chance encounter with Dr. Gregory J. W. Urwin. I complimented his outstanding work on the Civil War in Arkansas, the Battle of Poison Spring, and the First

Kansas Colored Infantry, and mentioned this writing project, which was about 75 percent complete at the time. He asked if I already had a publisher for it. I did not. So he described his role as editor of the Campaigns & Commanders series at the University of Oklahoma Press and told me to keep them in mind. With the knowledge that Dr. Urwin would be involved in the process, and seeing the high-quality books coming from OU Press, I put them at the top of my list. I am grateful that Dr. Urwin, Mr. Charles Rankin, and everyone else at OU Press, who accepted this manuscript and helped me turn a large electronic document on my computer into a well-produced book.

Much of this book was a family affair. My father, Larry, continues to be my closest associate on all historical writing and discussion. I cannot count the number of hours he has spent editing and reviewing drafts of my work, always giving me the right advice. That support is appreciated more than he knows. Besides being my computer and word-processing guru for preparing the final drafts, my mother, Debra, provides all the encouragement a mother can give. I would like to thank my father-in-law, Dennis Murphy, for the many trips to libraries and archives to hunt for bits and pieces of material while I was overseas. I greatly appreciate his encouragement and help in this project.

My greatest support, though, came from my wife, Jade, and our children. Jade helped me with many of the tedious duties of preparing the manuscript for print. But more importantly she provided the moral support (and patience—especially following me to all of those Civil War battlefields) required to create this book. My children, Pierce, Karis, and Lillian, are too young to understand what all of this work was about, but they inspired me nonetheless. This book is dedicated to them.

While this book could not have come to print without the help and work of the people mentioned above, and others, I take full responsibility for any errors, omissions, or discrepancies in the text. Furthermore, the views expressed in this book are solely mine and do not represent the Department of Defense.

SOLDIERS IN THE ARMY OF FREEDOM

PROLOGUE

O ver fence rails stacked to form a barricade, soldiers gazed at the peaceful landscape falling into shadows. It was beautiful country, typical of western Missouri, the stillness interrupted only by an occasional gust of wind. Yet in the timber behind the mounds to the south lay the enemy.

This was Union territory, but only in name. Most local residents, including Enoch Toothman, the owner of the farm the soldiers now occupied, were Southern sympathizers. Toothman's son, John, was, in the words of one federal cavalryman, "an unwilling guest of the guard house at Ft. Lincoln" for making war on the Union.[1] Enoch and his neighbors outside Butler, Missouri, were now the unwilling hosts to 250 Union soldiers from Kansas who had arrived two days before to kill or capture secessionist guerrillas. They had constructed a fortified camp on the farm, and now waited for the opportunity to scatter rebel Missourians.[2]

The opposing sides facing each other that October evening were a contrast in almost every way. The men in blue were formally trained infantry, marching and fighting in close formation, relying on discipline and strength in numbers. The Missourians were irregulars, conducting war on horseback, using speed and surprise to exact retribution on targets of opportunity. The Union soldiers carried secondhand Austrian and Prussian muskets, not the most reliable or accurate weapon available to Civil War soldiers, but serviceable for combat.[3] The large lead ball could bring down a man or a horse at one hundred yards or more, but the muskets were slow to load. A single infantryman could fire one shot every twenty seconds, leaving him vulnerable while he tried to ram powder and ball down the muzzle. The guerrillas carried shotguns and carbines, or short rifles, when available, but their weapon of choice was the revolver. Nearly worthless at more than thirty yards, handguns were ideal for guerrilla warfare. A mounted man could race to point-blank range, fire six shots at his victims, and then ride out of harm's way.

Yet the greatest divide between these combatants went deeper than arms, uniforms, or fighting style. The soldiers were not pawns in an abstract battle between rival governments—poor men fighting in a rich man's war, as some called it. The Union men on that Missouri farm were fighting a very real battle over slavery.

It was 1862, the second year of the Civil War. Kansans and Missourians had fought over slavery for almost a decade. The warriors of "Bleeding Kansas" used both ballots and bullets to decide the slaveholding status of Kansas in the 1850s. For proslavery men, the institution was an economic interest, a political principle, and a cultural symbol. For the free-state men, slavery was a corruption of American society and a blight on mankind. Only a minority of them were abolitionists, genuinely concerned about the welfare of the slaves. Yet virtually all of those involved in the fight over Kansas statehood in 1850s, on both sides, were white and free.

Most of the Union soldiers on the Toothman farm this night, October 28, 1862, were former slaves. Slavery had denied them legal rights and torn apart families. They had been treated as chattel. Now they wore the blue uniform of the Union army. They fought for their own freedom and for their families.

Across the field, the Missouri guerrillas looked for their opportunity to strike. Though not every guerrilla owned a slave, all of them quaked with rage, or fear, at the specter of black men carrying guns. They fought to preserve economic and social institutions; to protect their communities from change at the hands of Northerners. Even a large portion of Missouri Unionists, including the state's governor, Hamilton Gamble, wanted to maintain a racial status quo, which for them meant white supremacy.

The impending battle, though small by Civil War standards, would be historic. For the first time in that war an organized unit of black men wearing blue would strike a direct blow for freedom. This assignment, their first true test, had come about unexpectedly a few days before. For weeks the soldiers had been encamped at Fort Lincoln, a few miles north of Fort Scott, Kansas, guarding Southern prisoners and strengthening fortifications. False alarms and brief scouting expeditions had generated some excitement. Then, on Sunday, October 26, Major Benjamin S. Henning, the commander of Union forces at Fort Scott, received reports of Confederate guerrillas in the area. Union armies were engaging regular Southern forces much farther south in Arkansas. The soldiers under Henning's command aimed to protect supply lines along the Kansas and Missouri border. Lightning raids against wagon trains, federal encampments, and Kansas communities strained already overextended Union cavalry regiments patrolling the region. Infantry soldiers, not suited for this work, were ordered to fill the gaps. It was for this reason that Kansas officials turned to black men for military service.

Formation of the First Kansas Colored Infantry began only two months earlier and remained incomplete. Regimental officers still scoured Kansas communities looking for able-bodied men among the thousands of escaped slaves from Missouri to fill the remaining companies. And the regiment could not count on the Lincoln administration for support. The unit had not yet been mustered into federal service, but its political and military backers made sure the recruits wore the blue uniform of the United States military and carried the United States flag into combat.

Now they awaited their first test in battle. On October 29, the Confederates watched as a small group of First Kansas Colored Infantry soldiers marched out of their camp on the Toothman Farm to engage them. Two miles away they met. "Come on, you d—d niggers," the Rebels yelled.[4] The Battle of Island Mound—the first engagement in which a black regiment fought during the Civil War—had begun.

Few people today know of the First Kansas Colored Infantry. Even among many Civil War historians and enthusiasts the regiment merits little more than a footnote. Yet it was the first black regiment raised in a Northern state and, more significantly, the first black unit to see combat during the Civil War. Since the late 1980s the story of black soldiers in the Civil War has drawn increased interest in American culture, helped in no small part by popular films. The 2003 movie *Cold Mountain* accurately shows African American soldiers locked in a deadly struggle with Confederates at the Battle of the Crater, part of the siege of Petersburg, Virginia, in 1864 by Ulysses S. Grant's men. Stephen Spielberg's movie *Lincoln*, released in 2012, opens with a short and striking battle scene of the Second Kansas Colored Infantry engaging Confederate soldiers in another 1864 encounter, the Battle of Jenkins' Ferry in Arkansas. In both cases, the movies re-create battles in which black soldiers played an instrumental role. However, in both movies, African American soldiers are not the primary subjects. Viewers are left without a broader understanding of who the soldiers are.

The most influential portrayal of black Civil War soldiers is Edward Zwick's 1989 feature film *Glory*. The film portrays, with artistic license, the creation and first engagements of the Fifty-Fourth

Massachusetts Infantry. Raised in the early months of 1863, the Fifty-Fourth Massachusetts's ranks included sons of famed black abolitionist Frederick Douglass. It was commanded by the son of a wealthy and well-connected Massachusetts family and enjoyed support from Massachusetts's public and state officials. The regiment fought its most famous battle at Fort Wagner, a Confederate defensive position on the outskirts of Charleston, South Carolina, on July 18, 1863.

The movie received accolades for directing, cinematography, and musical score and for performances by Morgan Freeman and Denzel Washington; the latter won an Academy Award for Best Supporting Actor. Yet it helped perpetuate a mischaracterization of Civil War history. Many Americans now believe that the Fifty-Fourth Massachusetts was the first black regiment of the Civil War. This misconception is not surprising, given that the movie closes with the fighting at Fort Wagner and a brief written epilogue that reads, "As word of their bravery spread, Congress at last authorized the raising of black troops throughout the Union."[5]

To be sure, the sacrifices of the Fifty-Fourth Massachusetts furthered the cause of black military service and black rights in the United States. But that regiment had come into existence after, and largely *because*, President Abraham Lincoln and Congress had authorized raising black troops months earlier. Lincoln's Emancipation Proclamation went into effect January 1, 1863, and declared that African Americans "of suitable condition, will be received into the armed service of the United States to garrison forts, positions, stations, and other places, and to man vessels of all sorts in said service."[6] The same day that the Fifty-Fourth Massachusetts Infantry attacked Fort Wagner, July 18, 1863, the First Kansas Colored Infantry was marching victoriously off the field from Honey Springs, its fourth engagement.

This book does not mean to belittle the contributions of the Fifty-Fourth Massachusetts Infantry or any other black regiment; rather, it seeks to shed light on the relative anonymity of black soldiers from Kansas and to describe their contribution to Union victory in the Trans-Mississippi Theater of the Civil War. While at least a dozen books about the Fifty-Fourth Massachusetts are in print, this is the first widely published book about the First Kansas Colored Infantry. It is my hope that this book will bring long overdue recognition to those who broke a key color barrier in American society.

This story begins with the question, why Kansas? Why did the first black regiment to see combat in the Civil War come from a young state on the edge of the frontier in 1862? Today Kansas is best known for its unpredictable weather patterns, its flat landscape, and *The Wizard of Oz*. With an African American population of less than 6 percent, it is not known for racial diversity.[7] Indeed, its most notable role in the history of race and civil rights is as part of the U.S. Supreme Court case *Brown v. Board of Education of Topeka*. The 1954 decision held that segregated school systems, like the one in Kansas's capital, unconstitutionally denied black children equal opportunities in education. In that landmark event, a Kansas city was guilty of discriminating against African Americans. So why did a major advancement in black participation in the military occur in Kansas? The answer to that question may be found within the story of Kansas before the Civil War. The first two chapters set the stage by reconstructing the political, racial, and social realities of that time and place. The third chapter discusses efforts to raise black troops in Kansas in comparison to recruitment efforts in other Union areas. These early chapters explain how and why African Americans first entered military service during the Civil War. The subsequent chapters tell the story of the First Kansas Colored Infantry in military service, including battles in Missouri, Arkansas, and Indian Territory, and of the unit's struggles to achieve equality in the army and victory in the field.

Like their white counterparts in the war, the men of the First Kansas Colored Infantry overcame obstacles with pride and suffered from injury, disease, fear, and homesickness. Some deserted; some resisted military authority; and some served quietly with few records to distinguish them from any other soldier—black or white—during the Civil War. They were brave and afraid, sometimes capable of extraordinary feats but also of all-too-human frailties. Perhaps they fought with a tenacity that only ages of bondage can inspire. But the one thing that clearly separated them from white soldiers was the ever-present knowledge that if captured by Confederate forces they faced almost certain death or a return to slavery in Southern states.

They finished the war with a remarkable combat record, worthy of a place among the hardest-fighting regiments of the war. And they played a vital part in helping to begin the long and painful process of countering white prejudice by defying stereotypes. They simply wanted the opportunity to show that they were men—not property—and that was and remains the point. Too long overlooked, this is their story.

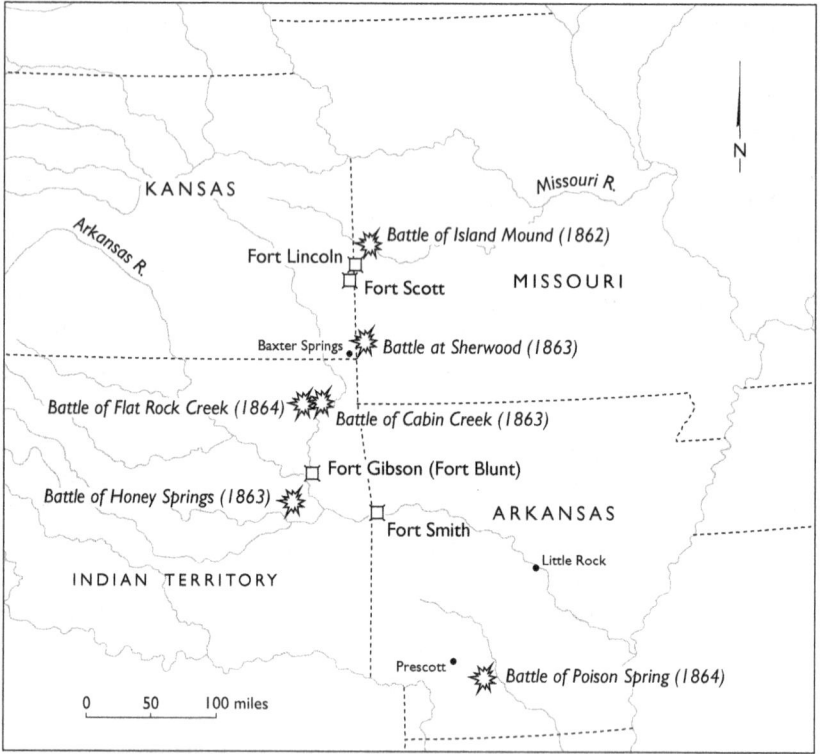

Map 1. Geographical Area of Operations. Map by Bill Nelson. Copyright ©
2014 by the University of Oklahoma Press.

CHAPTER I

BLEEDING KANSAS

The perplexing question will be *Negroes*.

The constitutional convention was in its second week. Much had been accomplished, a remarkable achievement given the vast differences among the thirty-six delegates. They had agreed that all political issues would be shelved until their common interest of securing Kansas as a free state in the Union was assured. Even so, one major obstacle threatened to derail the convention and the free-state movement.

"The perplexing question will be *Negroes*," a correspondent to the *New York Times* told eastern audiences from the rural territory of Kansas, "and I think the people will be called upon to vote directly on the issue of allowing *free blacks* to reside in the State."[1] All of the convention delegates opposed slavery, though for different reasons. The Topeka Convention was the Free State Party's attempt to form a state government, a rival to the proslavery administration in place at Lecompton, formed a few months earlier through voter fraud and ballot stuffing.

The Topeka Convention represented an effort to unite antislavery forces in Kansas. The delegates agreed that slavery should not be allowed in Kansas, but they could not agree on what to do with free blacks. The divide split New England abolitionists from midwestern conservatives. Some abolitionists wanted no race-based distinctions, but they were a distinct minority. Most free-state settlers had no concern for blacks. Migrants from the Midwest and Upper South exhibited a prejudice against African Americans surpassed only by their hatred of the institution of slavery. They supported the "black law," a prohibition against any black migration into Kansas. Another New York writer noted that many "who are known as Free-State men are not anti-Slavery in our Northern acceptation of the word. They are more properly negro haters who vote Free-State to keep negroes out, free or slave."[2]

The Topeka delegates were deadlocked over the "black law." And so, on this day, October 31, 1855, a commanding figure in the free-state movement took the floor to settle whether Kansas would open its borders to any black person. He stood about six feet tall and usually covered his lean body with ill-fitting clothes, sloppy by even the rough standards of the West. No one could call him attractive. His wild hair crowned a prominent forehead and intricately carved face with deep-set, piercing eyes. Eastern settlers in the Kansas Territory understandably found this strange man obnoxious, but no one denied his power as a public speaker. James Henry Lane was a forty-one-year-old former Democratic congressman from Indiana who came to Kansas to make his career in the territory's virgin political landscape. His quick rise to power in the free-state ranks was due to his experience in national politics and his stump-speaking abilities. He loved politics and thrived in an atmosphere of speeches and backdoor deals.

Many Kansans did not trust him. Abolitionists—those who opposed slavery for moral reasons and desired a proactive end to the institution—looked at his history and considered him a major contributor to the chaos in Kansas. In 1854, as a freshman member of the House of Representatives, Lane had voted for the Kansas-Nebraska Act, one of the most significant and controversial pieces of legislation in American history. It repealed a thirty-four-year-old law that prohibited slavery in western territories north of latitude 36°30"—a line extending from Missouri's southern border through the vast western expanses. The Kansas-Nebraska Act opened up all western territories to slavery, provided the residents approved. The new state's slaveholding status would be up for a vote. Supporters called this principle "popular sovereignty."

The Democratic Party promoted the concept as a truly democratic method of handling the question of slavery in the territories. Illinois senator Stephen Douglas wrote the Kansas-Nebraska Bill and used all of his political ability and force of personality to put popular sovereignty into action, not because he wanted to expand slavery, but to gain necessary Southern support for organizing the western territories for railroad interests.[3] The act sparked not only a tremendous upheaval in American party politics, but a transition in the battle over slavery from the legislative halls and courtrooms to the western plains. Anxious to determine Kansas's fate with ballots, and bullets if necessary, Northerners and Southerners began flocking to the territory in 1854. Lane, who declined to run for reelection in Indiana in 1854, was in Kansas by April 1855.[4]

The invitation for settlers to determine the slave issue in Kansas polarized the fledgling territorial electorate. With a sympathetic president, Franklin Pierce, in office, proslavery settlers established a territorial government in the town of Lecompton through voting fraud. Free-state settlers boycotted this government's activities and created a rival movement, claiming that they had the support of a majority of settlers, and represented the true interests of the territory and true popular sovereignty. This movement culminated in the creation of a Free State Party and a constitutional convention in Topeka in October. Now Lane was its president.[5]

As the *New York Times* correspondent noted, not all advocates for a free state of Kansas cared for black Americans. A large number of antislavery Kansans, and antislavery Americans, opposed slavery for reasons unrelated to the well-being of the slave. Some saw slavery as an impediment to regional and national development; others believed it promoted slothful behavior and crippled the work ethic seen by Northerners as necessary for a growing country. Some opposed it on the grounds that it harmed white Americans by limiting their options for economic advancement.[6] For most Northerners, however, that hostility did not translate into advocacy for the destruction of slavery. They were content to leave the institution alone as long as it, and blacks, remained in the South.

On the fledgling territory's eastern border was Missouri, a state that in 1850 had over 87,000 slaves. By 1860 that number had ballooned to nearly 115,000. As many as 20,000 slaves lived in counties that bordered Kansas during that period.[7] The boundary between Missouri and Kansas was an imaginary line, not a geographical feature. The realization that fugitive or freed slaves would seek refuge in a neighboring free state worried many Kansas settlers. An influx of blacks meant potential interstate conflict with Missouri slaveholders, racial competition for jobs, and the possibility of social interaction.

Long-standing presuppositions of black inferiority were common among settlers from the Midwest, a region heavily influenced by Southern culture and migration.[8] Even some Kansans who voiced sincere concern for blacks did not know how slaves would act if freed. "To any individual who would dare to utter or give vent to any Idea of the kind that the Negro is not of the human race," settler Robert Atkins Tovey declared, "in Short that he is not a man but that he distinctly & properly belongs to the baboon or monkey tribe to displace all this nonsense & trash from the rational mind it is only requisite to become a little a[c]quainted with them & you will not only find that they are men but many of them possessed of great Sagacity." Nonetheless, Tovey continued, "this the Author is ready to acknowle[d]ge that it is possible so to grind down, crush, Iron & whip the poor African that if he was to be set at liberty in that wretched state the good policy of such proceeding might be questioned. Let a poor fellow of that description look at once goaded laceratin [sic] & full of revenge he might become a terror to the neighborhood & an object of dread."[9] For many convention delegates, the best policy was to keep slavery and blacks out of Kansas altogether.

Antiblack attitudes were not powerful enough to push through a black exclusion law at the convention. Abolitionists stood in the way. To save the convention's efforts and promote the shared goal of creating a free-state constitution, Lane offered the following resolution: "That the Delegates nominated to this Convention, be and hereby are instructed to use their exertings to submit the question of excluding Free Negroes from the Territory, to the people of the Territory, on the day the constitution is submitted, their decision to operate as instructions to the first Legislature upon that subject."[10] If the delegates could not decide whether to exclude free blacks from Kansas, they could agree to let the white people of the state decide by popular vote. To save the convention from deadlock, Lane's resolution put the "black law" question to the masses. The resolution passed, so the voters of Kansas would decide the future of black residency in Kansas alongside their vote on the Topeka Constitution.

The concession was a bitter pill for humanitarian settlers to swallow. George W. Brown, editor of the *Herald of Freedom* acknowledged that "here we are willing our neighbors, who agree with us in the main, but differ on this question—and who we have conceded are in the majority—shall fix the matter up to suit themselves," but stated that he and his fellow easterners objected "to their placing us in a position which will require us to stultify ourself [sic], or give the lie to our entire past history."[11] Nonetheless, it was necessary for Free State Party unity.

On December 15, 1855, free-state Kansans went to the polls to accept or reject the Topeka Constitution and vote on black exclusion. Proslavery settlers generally boycotted the vote, leading to an absurdly disproportionate tally: 1,731 votes for the free-state constitution, 46 against. The referendum on the black law generated a bit more division but proved that antiblack sentiment was dominant in Kansas: black exclusion passed 1,287 to 453.[12]

The vote for the "black law" illustrated racial attitudes in territorial Kansas, although it had no practical effect on the African American presence there. For one, slaveholders who migrated to Kansas with their property ignored free-state efforts to enact territorial laws. After all, proslavery officials dominated the territorial government in Lecompton. Second, some militant abolitionists began raiding Missouri farms to help slaves escape into the territory. More importantly, the vote held no legal weight. The Topeka government would not officially exist unless both houses of Congress accepted the Topeka Constitution. Although Lane expressed confidence in gaining Northern Democratic approval, many powerful people in Washington considered the Topeka movement illegal. Indeed, Lane's attempt to personally petition the U.S. Senate to pass the Topeka Constitution in the spring of 1856 resulted in a humiliating defeat.[13] The Pierce administration and many congressional leaders recognized only the proslavery government in Lecompton, Kansas, as the territory's rightful authority.

The debate over black migration to Kansas in 1855 and 1856 was more about establishing a white society than about handling an existing migration problem. While some settlers did bring their slaves into the territory, and some abolitionists helped Missouri fugitive slaves into Kansas, estimates of African Americans in territorial Kansas were relatively small. In 1857, one source claimed there were less than 350 African Americans out of a total territorial population of over 47,000.[14] Another writer estimated that Kansas had 500 slaves in 1859.[15] The 1860 census listed 627 blacks in Kansas Territory, only 0.6 percent of the Kansas population.[16]

The "black law" never went into effect. Even if it had, it may have enjoyed only limited success. Antiblack laws in other Northern states, such as Indiana, Illinois, and Ohio, did not eliminate the presence of African Americans, though they did restrict black civil rights.[17] The referendum marked the height of antiblack sentiment in Kansas, for as the battle over slavery and Kansas statehood dragged on, the more radical free-state Kansans became.

During the summer of 1856 free-state and proslavery forces in Kansas waged a battle for control. Murders, ambushes, and military engagements earned the territory the moniker "Bleeding Kansas."

For some abolitionists, the violence was a necessary purging of the sins of slavery. Ohioan John Brown epitomized this fanaticism, personally carrying out one of the territory's most shocking atrocities in May 1856 when he and a handful of followers murdered five proslavery settlers.[18] Men like Brown helped sensationalize the conflict and inspired proslavery propaganda.

Most free-state settlers did not engage in a crusade to end slavery. They opposed proslavery rule in Kansas because it defied the antislavery majority. And they feared that the Lecompton government was kept in power by proslavery Missourians who invaded the territory to influence the political and military situation with no intention of settlement.[19] Still, these free-state Kansans separated themselves from abolitionism. "I know very well that numbers of kind hearted well disposed men at the north are made to believe that all the difficulties in Kanzas [sic] are caused by the factious movements of a party of 'fanatics,' 'abolitionists,'" one Lawrence, Kansas, resident wrote to his father. "This has been often true but is as often false. The fact is a majority of the citizens of Lawrence are western men, former democrats of the Pierce and Douglas stripe, which is true of a large majority of the inhabitants of the Territory, and where nothing but the 'Sack,' the 'Sword,' the 'Flamie' [sic] have dissevered from their strong party alliance."[20]

The conflict for Kansas statehood drew attention across the country and welcome support from Northern states. Public relations campaigns through letters, newspaper editorials, and speeches by leading free-state Kansans (Lane in particular) drew in financial, political, and manpower aid. During speaking appearances in the North in 1856, Lane emphasized the conservative nature of the Free State Party and argued that the interests of white men were at stake. In Cleveland, Ohio, he rallied a crowd of thousands into excitement by painting an image of slaveholders denying Northern white Americans justice in the territories. Slavery had to be opposed in Kansas, he said, to save the future of hardworking white men. "The laboring white man could not live in a Slave State," Lane told the crowd, "where the grades may be defined thus—1st, the slaveholder; 2d, the slave; 3d, the free negro; 4th, last and lowest, the laboring white man." In Lane's worldview, slavery elevated blacks above common white laborers.[21]

In Chicago, Lane attacked critics who claimed that free-state Kansans were abolitionists or "nigger worshippers." Holding aloft a copy of the Kansas territorial laws adopted by the Lecompton government, he read provisions dictating legal punishment for various crimes. "According to the Kansas code . . . if a person kidnapped a white child, the utmost penalty was six months in jail—if he stole a nigger baby, the penalty was *Death*. Who worshipped niggers, and slave nigger babies at that? To kidnap a white child into slavery—six months in jail—kidnap a nigger into Freedom—*Death!*"[22] This rhetoric appealed to an audience steeped in white supremacist ideology. Kansas was undergoing a battle over slavery, but African Americans were marginalized by both sides.

Still, conservative free-state settlers could not afford to disassociate themselves from abolitionists. Powerful northeastern groups helped the free-state cause with men, supplies, money, and weapons. Organizations like the New England Emigrant Aid Company, the Massachusetts Committee, and the New York Kansas Committee contributed thousands of dollars for rifles, most notably the new breech-loading Sharps rifle, which outmatched most muskets in both accuracy and speed of loading.[23] The weapons were shipped secretly to free-state communities, some marked in boxes labeled "books" or "Bibles." The alliance between New England and midwestern settlers did not change racial attitudes, but did contribute to a weakening in white supremacy rhetoric.

By 1858, it seemed clear that the U.S. Congress would never accept the Free State constitution. The proslavery Lecompton Constitution had strong support from the president and Democrats in the Senate, but failed to pass congressional muster, leaving the territory in limbo. Free State officials then arranged for a new convention in Leavenworth to approve a second constitution, one that would overcome the faults of the Topeka document.

The "black law" was noticeably absent this time.[24] Conservative delegates grew frustrated at the constitution's racial ambiguity. With no black exclusion, they worried that free blacks in Kansas would gain rights equal to white men. In particular, the constitution's section on "Elective Franchise" limited suffrage to males but made no racial distinctions. "I sign this Constitution under protest believing that a majority of my constituents are opposed to negro suffrage— under the article 'Education' which appears to permit coloured children to go to common schools with white children," delegate A. W. McCauslin declared. "On the subject of negro immigration I am not decided what is the will of my constituents." He then stated,

"The political exeigency [*sic*] of times imper[a]tively demand a new Constitution and una[ni]mity in the approval of the same, I regard as necessary to the welfare of the people of this Territory." Four other delegates united in a similar qualifying statement. "We sign this Constitution under protest for the reason that we believe a majority of our constituents are opposed to negro suffrage and the Emigration of free negroes to the State of Kansas." One delegate announced that he intended to interpret a restriction against black voting rights in the Constitution even though it lacked specific language: "I sign this Constitution believing that it does not extend the right of suffrage to negroes."[25]

Lane had embraced the "black law" three years before, and his views of black people had not changed. But he believed Free State success depended on drawing together a broad coalition of Kansans and that avoiding racial issues was necessary for that end. Unfortunately for Lane and supporters of the Leavenworth Constitution, many Kansans would not let those racial issues remain ambiguous. "Let the Convention pass this clause, and attempt to enforce their Constitution upon the people," the proslavery *Kansas Weekly Herald* told its readers, "and they will find the mass of the people are not prepared to allow a buck negro to walk up to the polls with a white man and vote."[26] Even with his legendary stump-speaking abilities, Lane could not win over an audience in Leavenworth, who ridiculed and booed his attempt to defend the proposed constitution.[27] Barely surviving a referendum in the territory, the Leavenworth Constitution limped into Washington, D.C., for congressional consideration and was promptly quashed.

As the 1850s came to a close, the territory remained firmly polarized on racial issues. The influx of fugitives from Missouri created conflict among free-state and proslavery advocates but also created collaboration among blacks and whites. On the extreme end of this cooperation were the few white abolitionists willing to actively free slaves in Missouri through violence or stealth. John E. Stewart, a former Methodist minister, described his preferred method of freeing Missouri slaves in a letter to abolitionist Thaddeus Hyatt:

> For I am in the habit of taking my team in Mo. [Missouri] under the pretense of buying something, say pigs, [illegible], potatoes, &c., &c., get into conversation with some slaves, find out some who wish to escape, appoint a meeting, show them in the bottom of the

wagon, give them some weapons to defend themselves with. And then put it through for life, & sometimes our success depends upon the fleetness of our horses, sometimes on a steady hand, when the revolver cracks.[28]

John Brown was the most famous abolitionist and raider. His reputation for violent opposition to slavery spread throughout the region, even among the slave community. In December 1858 a "negro man called Jim" risked his life to find Brown and begged for his help. Jim's wife and children, along with another slave, were about to be sold in Osage, Missouri. Brown rallied a group of followers to "forcibly liberate the five slaves, together with other slaves." In all, Brown's men freed eleven people from various farmsteads during that raid. The raiders also stole personal goods from Missourians and killed one of the white masters who tried to resist. All of this Brown accepted as perfectly justified. "Now for a comparison," he declared. "Eleven persons are forcibly restored to their natural & inalienable rights, with but one man Killed, & all 'Hell is stirred from beneath.'"[29]

These acts confirmed to proslavery Missourians the danger of Kansas falling into free-state hands. In previous years, numerous midwesterners agreed that activities against slavery threatened the peace and safety of the Union. Opposition to abolitionists in the Midwest had sometimes grown violent: for example, on November 7, 1837, in Alton, Illinois, abolitionist Elijah Lovejoy was shot and killed while trying to defend his printing press from a mob.[30] Now years of political and military conflict between antislavery settlers and proslavery forces in Kansas territory cracked this opposition. The struggle for Kansas did not generate concern for slaves so much as destroy whatever sympathy many settlers had for their slaveholding neighbors.

Among the most radical of these converts was James Montgomery, an Ohioan by birth but raised in slaveholding Kentucky. Moving to Missouri in 1854, he blamed his financial hardships there on the slaveholding economy and migrated to Kansas as a free-state man. Like other conservative free-state settlers, he had no love for black Americans, but proslavery attacks against his home in Kansas sparked a fiery rage that led to his reputation as one of the most dangerous militants in southeastern Kansas. Though he did not share John Brown's broader abolitionist goals, Montgomery worked with Brown to ignite a "reign of terror" in the region in late 1858. Montgomery's first efforts were directed toward proslavery settlers and officials in Kansas.[31] Yet he came to see slaves as valuable tools in his war. By early 1860, Montgomery carried out raids into Missouri to liberate slaves, more out of spite against their owners than humanitarian concern. He retained his view that blacks were repulsive, uncivilized, and far beneath white men. But he came to side with them and against the slaveholders during the struggle for Kansas.[32]

Raids into Missouri were relatively rare, although enough of a problem to alarm slaveholders who lived along the border. One newspaper writer claimed that "ten slaves are now stolen from Missouri to every one that was spirited off before the Douglas bill."[33] Yet most fugitive slaves reached Kansas territory through their own efforts. Some received information to guide them to friendly households, stops on the "Underground Railroad"—a nickname for the vast network of people helping slaves escape to freedom in the North. Lawrence, a town founded by New England abolitionists, unsurprisingly became an important center for runaways. "I am happy to inform you that a certain Rail Road has been and is in full blast," wrote Massachusetts native Samuel F. Tappan from Lawrence. "Several persons have taken full advantage of it to visit their friends."[34] Other runaway slaves knew little of what awaited them in Kansas. One old Missouri slave fled to Lawrence based on the *negative* comments his master had made about the town. Once there, he told abolitionist John Bowles that he "didn't know if all de peoples in disha town war debbils as ole massa had said or not," but that if he could get there, "old massa was afraid to come arter him, and if dey all should prove to be bad as ole massa had said he could lib wid dem bout as well as at home."[35]

Runaway slaves faced tremendous hazards. While slave owners usually wanted them returned alive and in good shape, runaways still risked being shot, beaten, or succumbing to any number of obstacles during their flight. One male slave from Missouri was shot during two different escape attempts, though he did manage to kill a pursuer in one instance. Still, he fled again and eventually helped dozens more slaves escape by leading them to safety or providing them necessary information for their own later ventures.[36]

Napoleon Simpson was another Missouri slave who made the passage between Kansas and Missouri on more than one occasion. In the fall of 1859 he learned that his master had sold him to a slave trader who planned to take him to the Deep South for resale. Desperate, Simpson fled the Jackson County farm before the transaction was complete. Outside Lawrence he stopped at the home of Joseph Gardner, a New England native and fervent abolitionist. The Gardner family helped prepare Simpson for the journey to Iowa, as they had for other fugitives, and sent him on his way. The following spring, Simpson returned to the Gardner home. He explained that he planned to rescue his wife from bondage. In fact, he had just tried but found her sick in bed and unable to travel. So he sneaked back to Kansas and asked Gardner for shelter while he waited a couple of weeks for her health to improve. Gardner agreed and even offered to openly employ Simpson as a laborer during his stay.[37]

At 1:30 A.M. on June 9, 1860, Gardner and his family awoke to the sound of dogs barking. Gardner rose from his trundle bed to investigate and saw the shadows of two men pass by a window. He hurriedly grabbed a revolver from his bedpost and sprang to the door. Just then someone outside grabbed the door handle. Gardner called out, "Who is there?"

"Open the door, sir," came the reply.

"What do you want?" Gardner asked and slowly opened the door. Standing on the doorstep were two men brandishing pistols. Gardner raised his .36-caliber revolver to the chest of the nearest man and fired. He slammed the door just as the second man ducked and fired into the house. The ball crashed through the wooden door and lodged in a wall. Gardner cracked opened the door, pointed his pistol outside, and fired blindly into the dark.

Theodore, one of Gardner's sons, peered out an upstairs window to see the silhouette of a man stumbling away from the house. The boy fired at the figure and then called for his father to "take a crack at him." The elder Gardner raced up the staircase and fired his pistol. Gardner's wife screamed at the sight of a man at the ground-floor window. As Gardner descended the staircase, the attacker unleashed a shotgun blast through the window. The buckshot missed Gardner by inches.

Simpson grabbed a Sharps rifle and fired at every moving object he could see from a window. After some moments the firing stopped. The men in the house cautiously peered out the windows but could see no one. Simpson stepped out the front door. Almost instantly he saw a figure crouching behind a well curb ten feet away and fired at the man, but missed. Simpson grabbed another cartridge and ducked to get out of the way but was hit in the shoulder and side from the blast of a double-barreled shotgun. He fell back into the house, crying out. Gardner ran to the dying man, now lying in a growing pool of blood. When asked what they could do for him, Simpson replied, "Fight! Fight hard!" "Talk about expressions of great generals on the field of battle," the humbled Gardner later told a Kansas audience. "A braver man never bled or died, nor fought in a better cause than that same Napoleon Simpson."[38]

The attackers heaped burning hay and straw against the house in attempt to set fire to the structure. A short rain shower frustrated those efforts, and the mysterious assailants eventually disappeared into the night, taking their casualties with them. Incidents like these created a bond between white abolitionists and fugitive slaves in the fight for freedom. Joseph Gardner championed the cause and sacrifice of Napoleon Simpson to fellow Kansans, and two years later he would again go to battle with black men, this time wearing the blue uniform of a Union officer.

The escalation of the political battle over slavery radicalized even some conservative free-state settlers. "There were a good many radical abolitionists that encouraged the slaves to run away and often helped them to get through on the underground railroad," recalled Indiana native Benjamin Van Horn of his time in territorial Kansas, "but the majority of us were more conservative and our principals [sic] were not to interfere with slavery where it then existed but that it must not go any further and especially not into Kansas." However, when two fugitive slaves sought refuge in a boarding house used by Van Horn, he aided in their escape. Like many midwestern natives, Van Horn considered blacks inferior to whites and regularly referred to them as "niggers" late into his life. His concerned centered on fairness among whites: "The government officials at Leavenworth often sent United States soldiers out to hunt for and capture runaway slaves, that, all of us objected to, from the fact that if our horses ran away or were stolen we had to get them ourselves or let them go, and we believed that the same principal [sic] should hold good with the slave owner and his slaves." Thus when a detachment of soldiers tasked with finding the fugitives approached the boardinghouse, Van Horn and other residents sprang into action. He later recalled the event:

The floor of the dining room was laid with loose boards not fastened down in any way, there had been two niggers there for two days. In the morning while we were eating breakfast some one reported that there were soldiers coming up the road, we all kn[e]w what they were after. Some one hollowed [sic] "what will we do," some one else hollowed "under the floor quick." We jumped from the table and raised some of the boards [and] the niggers crawled under. We replaced our chairs and proceeded with our breakfast. Thirty soldiers rode up, they left the regulation number to hold the horses and the balance formed round the house and sent two men in to bring out the niggers. They searched the house thoroughly but found no niggers. We were very busy eating, not a man cracked a smile, and we ate an uncommonly hearty breakfast that morning and were a long time at it, we extended it until the soldiers left and were out of sight down the road.[39]

By 1859, free-state forces firmly held Kansas. Migrating slave owners, determined to keep their property, chose other locations for settlement. When Kansas residents held the next, and final, constitutional convention in Wyandotte, the only significant question over slavery was whether it would be outlawed the day Kansas attained statehood or whether slaveholders would be given time to remove their slaves. Only a minority group actively pressed for total exclusion of African Americans from Kansas. The final draft of the constitution passed 34 to 13, without a "black law."[40]

On January 29, 1861, Kansas officially became the thirty-fourth state. The antislavery side had prevailed. For many Americans, black and white, Kansas stood as a symbol for abolition and freedom. The struggle for its statehood foreshadowed the national divide over slavery, now coming to a head following Abraham Lincoln's election to the presidency in November 1860. When Kansas's first congressman and senators—which included the triumphant James H. Lane—arrived in Washington, D.C., in early 1861 to take their seats, several Southern states had already seceded from the Union, and the first shot of the Civil War was but a few weeks away.

CHAPTER 2

SECESSION AND WAR

This is a white man's war.

Abraham Lincoln's election as president in November 1860 brought decades of sectional tension to its zenith. Powerful leaders from increasingly defensive slaveholding states whipped up fervor against abolitionist agitation. Southern "fireaters" had advocated Southern independence for years. Growing antislavery sentiments in Northern states seemed to vindicate their warnings, as a Northern party—the Republicans—had taken the presidency with an outspoken opponent of slavery. Though Lincoln did not threaten to end slavery where it existed in the South, he steadfastly opposed its extension west. Having lost Kansas to free-state settlers, many Southerners saw the elevation of antislavery interests to the country's highest office as a confirmation that Southern society was in immediate danger.

Southerners wanted to maintain their carefully crafted society, so strongly dependent on slavery. "Under the mild and genial climate of the Southern States and the increasing care and attention for the wellbeing and comfort of the laboring class, dictated alike by interest and humanity, the African slaves had augmented in number from about 600,000, at the date of the adoption of the constitutional compact, to upward of 4,000,000," stated Jefferson Davis in April 1861, shortly after taking office as president of the Confederate States of America. Further illustrating the vital importance of slavery to the South and the paternalistic ideology of slaveholders, Davis declared:

> In moral and social condition they had been elevated from brutal savages into docile, intelligent, and civilized agricultural laborers, and supplied not only with bodily comforts but with careful religious instruction. Under the supervision of a superior race their labor had been so directed as not only to allow a gradual and marked amelioration of their own condition, but to convert

hundreds of thousands of square miles of the wilderness into cultivated lands covered with a prosperous people; towns and cities had sprung into existence, and had rapidly increased in wealth and population under the social system of the South; the white population of the Southern slaveholding States had augmented from about 1,250,000 at the date of the adoption of the Constitution to more than 8,500,000 in 1860; and the productions of the South in cotton, rice, sugar, and tobacco, for the full development and continuance of which the labor of African slaves was and is indispensable, had swollen to an amount which formed nearly three-fourths of the exports of the whole United States and had become absolutely necessary to the wants of civilized man.[1]

Davis added that with "interests of such overwhelming magnitude imperiled, the people of the Southern States were driven by the conduct of the North to the adoption of some course of action to avert the danger with which they were openly menaced."[2] The chosen course of action proved to be secession.

Southern leaders argued that all white Southerners, even those without slaves, benefited from the institution. "The color of the white man is now, in the South, a title of nobility in his relations as to the negro," South Carolinian John Townsend wrote in an 1860 pamphlet titled *The Doom of Slavery in the Union*. Despite any financial or educational advantages a black man may have over a poor white in the South, Townsend continued, "the poorest non-slaveholder, being a white man, is his superior in the eye of the law; may serve and command in the militia; may sit upon juries, to decide upon the rights of the wealthiest in the land; may give his testimony in Court, and may cast his vote, equally with the largest slaveholder, in the choice of his rulers." Conversely, Townsend stated, "the status and *color of the black race* becomes the badge of inferiority, and the poorest non-slaveholder may rejoice with the richest of his brethren of the white race, in the distinction of his color."[3]

The disruption of slavery would mean a collapse of Southern society. Two centuries of slavery had come to reinforce a belief among white Americans that African Americans lacked self-discipline and good order—at least without careful and stern guidance from a superior race. Thousands of hardworking and determined free blacks in Northern and Southern states belied these beliefs daily. Yet most white Americans ignored their accomplishments. Jabez L. M.

Curry struck fear in the South with predictions of millions of freed blacks, unbound by the constraints of perpetual bondage and white patronage, falling into "poverty and vice." An Alabama secessionist, Curry told his fellow Southerners, "The white man is stimulated to labor by its returns. The black man will not work save by compulsion, and pauperism and crime are the results of his unhindered idleness."[4] Fear of homeless black vagabonds and criminals worried white Northerners as well as Southerners.

Governor Joseph Brown of Georgia foresaw bitter competition among blacks and poor whites in the wake of abolition. "The negro has only been accustomed to receive his victuals and clothes for his labor. Few of them, if free, would expect anything more," Brown wrote in the wake of Lincoln's election. "It would therefore be easy to employ them at a sum sufficient to supply only the actual necessaries of life." This meant a severe blow to wages for laboring whites, Brown told his constituents. "The negro comes into competition with the white man and fixes the price of his labor, and he must take it or get no employment."[5]

With such interests at stake, many Southerners saw secession as a means to prevent the ultimate destruction of slavery and breakdown of Southern society. On the other hand, disunion presented another element of uncertainty. "We have anticipated this evil— made ourselves miserable over it—and cannot be much if any worse off whether it happens or not," an article in the *St. Louis News* read, adding that "everyone prays sincerely to have the dark shadow removed from our country, and the 'glorious Union' gallantly preserved!" But, the author asked, "can Mr. Buchanan, or Mr. Lincoln, or any body, or any power prevent it, if the Southern States desire it? We answer *no.*"[6]

By early April 1861, seven states of the Deep South had chosen secession. They formed the Confederate States of America, a new republic with a constitution modeled on the old one, except for a few key details—including direct and strong protections of slavery.[7] Frustrated with the federal government's refusal to recognize its independence and remove United States soldiers from key military installations in the South, the Confederacy opened fire on federal troops at Fort Sumter in Charleston Harbor on April 12. The next day, the garrison surrendered. The Civil War had officially begun.

With only a small standing army gutted from widespread resignations by Southerners, President Lincoln issued a call for 75,000 volunteers to put down the rebellion. The Northern states responded enthusiastically, flooding military enlistment offices with volunteers. Several states of the Upper South, teetering on the balance of secession, tipped in favor of the Confederacy. Arkansas, Tennessee, Virginia, and North Carolina added strength, size, and confidence to the new Southern country. The remaining Southern states—Missouri, Kentucky, Maryland, and Delaware—were torn between secessionist and Unionist sentiments.

Historians have recognized an association between secessionism and slaveholding demographics. According to historian James McPherson, 37 percent of the white families in the Deep South owned slaves, compared to 20 percent of white families in the Upper South. Furthermore, slaves made up 47 percent of the total population in the Deep South, as opposed to 24 percent in the Upper South.[8] Generally, the farther north one traveled through the South, the weaker the institution—and support for secession—became.

Anticipation for war streamed through the American population. "I never knew what a popular excitement can be," one Northerner wrote. "The whole population, men, women, and children, seem to be in the streets with Union favors and flags."[9] White recruits flooded Northern enlistment offices. A week after the Lincoln administration requested thirteen regiments from Ohio, Governor William Dennison, Jr., wrote to the president that "without seriously repressing the ardor of the people, I can hardly stop short of twenty regiments."[10] The young state of Kansas passed its own militia law authorizing the governor to raise two infantry regiments, three cavalry companies, and two artillery batteries to support the Union war effort.[11] In mid-1861, acquiring uniforms and weapons for the growing Northern army proved more difficult than finding recruits. Indeed, Lincoln's July 4 message to Congress stated that "one of the greatest perplexities of the government, is to avoid receiving troops faster than it can provide for them."[12]

Nonetheless, Northern communities continued to encourage military volunteerism—that is, among the white population. Northern newspapers celebrated locally raised European ethnic militia units for patriotism to their adopted country. The *Leavenworth Daily Times* championed the efforts of both French and German immigrants to raise independent military units for Kansas. "The adopted citizens are zealous and earnest in their support of the government," the editor wrote about the Germans. "And it is natural that they should be. If our republic is not preserved, with it will perish the hopes of the brave defenders of free institutions, throughout the world. Hence, sympathy with the land of his nativity, as well as the land of his adoption, lends the foreign born citizen to be loyal and faithful to the Union."[13]

Abolitionists and African Americans—free and slave—saw opportunities for action and progress. American armies of the past had enlisted blacks, often for manual labor, but occasionally as fighting men. The patriot forces at Bunker Hill in 1775 included blacks, and New Jersey officials had considered enrolling black men into a home guard regiment in 1776. In 1779, the Continental Congress urged South Carolina and Georgia to bolster their regiments with slaves—even proposing to compensate the Southern slave owners as much as one thousand dollars per man provided. But these opportunities of black service proved fleeting. Less than a month after the battle at Bunker Hill, George Washington's headquarters forbade further enlistment of African Americans.[14] The plan in New Jersey fizzled, as John Adams warned a proponent, "Your Negro Battallion will never do. S. Carolina would run out of their Wits at the least Hint of such a Measure."[15] And despite the Continental Congress's offer for compensation, slaveholders in Georgia and South Carolina refused to entertain the idea of black soldiers, objecting to both the concept of arming their enslaved servants and the promise of emancipation the Congress had included to attract African American loyalty.[16]

African Americans served within some American units during the War for Independence and in a battle against British troops almost forty years later with Andrew Jackson near New Orleans during the War of 1812.[17] These examples proved that, fueled by desperation, white military commanders would give a black man a gun. And, in each case, black men performed well. But as each crisis ended the black volunteers had been quickly dismissed—sometimes with an expression of appreciation, sometimes not—and race relations within American society increasingly tipped toward federal and state enforcement of white supremacy.

With the new fervor for war in 1861, African Americans volunteered to fight, hoping that white officials would accept their services in the rapid militarization. Their offers were not well received. Jacob Dobson, a free black employee on the grounds of the U.S. Capitol in Washington, D.C., wrote to Secretary of War Simon Cameron on April 23 informing him of "some three hundred of reliable colored free citizens of this City, who desire to enter the service for the defence of the City." Cameron replied that his War Department had "no intention at present to call into the service of the Government any colored soldiers."[18]

Most government officials believed there simply was no need for black soldiers. A majority of white Northerners had no intention of letting the war alter the social or political landscape. When free black residents and businessmen of Cincinnati, Ohio, attempted to organize a home guard unit, local police forced one recruiting office to remove its American flag from display and exclaimed to other organizers, "We want you d—d niggers to keep out of this; this is a white man's war."[19]

Some African Americans tried to enlist in white units. Men with light complexions attempted to hide their African heritage. On arriving in New York from Valparaiso, Chile, sailor Joseph T. Wilson and two Spaniards volunteered for federal service. During his third day in camp, an old black cook recognized Wilson and greeted him enthusiastically, drawing attention from a corporal. Wilson later noted that "before I could give the cook the hint, he was examined by the officer of the day." His African lineage now known, Wilson was escorted out of camp. "I was a negro, that was all." He was honorably discharged, yet received no recognition of his enlistment or brief service.[20]

A similar story occurred in the First Kansas Infantry (white) shortly after its creation. The volunteer found his stay cut short once his fellow soldiers learned of the impromptu integration. "We have no objection to endure all the privations we may be called upon to endure," a petition from men of Company G read, "but to have one of the company, or even one of the regiment, pointed out as a 'nigger' while on dress parade or guard, is more than we like to be called upon to bear."[21]

A few individuals did manage to don the blue uniform of the federal army by attaching themselves to sympathetic—or at least apathetic—white units. Nicholas Biddle, a sixty-five-year-old runaway slave who had spent years in Pennsylvania, joined the Washington Artillerists days after Lincoln's call for volunteers. When the unit marched through Baltimore on its way to defend Washington, D.C., Southern sympathizers harassed the troops and targeted Biddle in particular. Some shouted, "Nigger in uniform," while at least one voice called out for someone to "Kill that ——ed brother of Abraham

Lincoln." Tension grew until the verbal taunts turned to physical violence. An object flew from the crowd and smashed Biddle's face, splitting the skin and muscle to the bone. He staggered and nearly fell before a white lieutenant rushed to his aid. The regiment continued its journey and eventually arrived in Washington.[22]

The war's objective for the Lincoln administration and most of the Northern population was to maintain the old Union. It was not a war to end slavery. Congress spelled out this conservative goal in July 1861, led by John J. Crittenden of Kentucky and Andrew Johnson of Tennessee. Their resolution declared:

> This war is not prosecuted upon our part in any spirit of oppression, nor for any purpose of conquest or subjugation, nor for the purpose of overthrowing or interfering with the rights or established institutions of those States, but to defend and maintain the supremacy of the Constitution and all laws made in pursuance thereof, and to preserve the Union, with all the dignity, equality, and rights of the several States unimpaired; that as soon as these objects are accomplished the war ought to cease.[23]

Passage of the Crittenden-Johnson Resolution was not unanimous. Three radical Republicans voted against it, and more than twenty congressmen withheld their vote.[24]

In the summer of 1861, Northern communities sent eager young white men into military ranks, confident of a short, glorious war. The young men had romantic ideas of combat, where they would surely meet honor and victory on the battlefield. These grand illusions began to crumble soon as the reality of a prolonged conflict emerged. In early May, after suffering through two weeks of poor weather, monotonous camp life, and widespread diarrhea, members of a Michigan militia unit learned that their regiment would be accepted into federal service for three years, rather than the three months they had expected. Sergeant Charles B. Haydon wrote in his journal, "There is a good deal of reluctance to enlist for the war or three years. There are all manner of doubts & excuses raised." He estimated that only half of his unit would agree to such a commitment.[25]

Weeks after the attack on Fort Sumter, Northerners voiced frustration with their government's apparent inaction. Commenting on a military procession in a Fourth of July celebration, a writer for the *New York Tribune* lamented, "Fine as the march of twenty thousand men was, it stirred no enthusiasm and commanded no pleasure. They were headed toward the Capitol when they should have been in Richmond." The writer focused on the Union's highest general, Winfield Scott, and explained, "The people have a trustful faith in Gen. Scott. They know his genius, and so does the world. They believe in his patriotism, but they are weary of his delay; and that weariness will become a stronger feeling with the waning days in which we wait for something to be done."[26]

Among the most fervent voices for action was James Henry Lane, a freshly elected senator from Kansas. Enraged at Southern secession and the attack on Fort Sumter, which he believed to be an ultimate act of treason, Lane had taken the initiative to raise a temporary unit of volunteers among other politicians and government employees in the capital to guard the White House until federal reinforcements arrived to defend the city; Lane himself served as captain, of course. This "Frontier Guard" served more as a morale boost for President Lincoln and nervous government officials than as a serious military force. But it revealed to the president Lane's dedication to the Union and willingness to lead in the field. "Now in my opinion is the time for a *Coup de etats* [*sic*]," he wrote to Lincoln, as his ragtag volunteers encamped in the White House, barely a week after the fall of Fort Sumter. "Could ever one as humble as myself have authority I believe I could precipitate upon this city from the North *through Maryland* such a force as would secure Washington & the Country."[27] The brash senator even led "several scouting expeditions into Virginia," one newspaper reported, "during one of which he captured a secession flag."[28]

Lincoln declined Lane's request to lead a campaign. But the president was impressed enough with Lane's assertiveness that on June 20 he told Secretary of War Cameron, "We need the services of such a man out there at once" and instructed Cameron to "appoint him a brigadier-general of volunteers to-day, and send him off with such authority to raise a force . . . as you think will get him into actual work quickest." Lincoln emphasized his wish for action: "Tell [Lane] when he starts to put it through. Not be writing or telegraphing back here, but put it through."[29]

Lincoln's remark reflected an early frustration with military commanders calling for more men, more supplies, and more time. The army's senior commander, Winfield Scott, was too old and obese to lead in the field. Command of the Union army in northern

Virginia fell to Irvin McDowell, a former staff officer. McDowell balked at the push for battle, arguing that he could not organize, train, and send into combat the amateur soldiers all at once. By late June, Lincoln recognized that delay benefited Confederate armies as much the federal recruits. He ordered McDowell to begin a campaign into Virginia, stating, "You are green, it is true; but they are green also; you are all green alike."[30]

Lane, on the other hand, proved all too eager to "put it through." The same day that Lincoln authorized Lane to raise soldiers, the senator sent a message asking the president to accept two Kansas regiments. The War Department approved the request.[31] "An insurrectionary war, commenced by rebels, in defiance of patriotism and duty, has now approached our border," he told his constituents, referring to the contentious line between Kansas and Missouri. Not to fear, he continued, for Lincoln "has been pleased to place in my hands the honor of leading the gallant sons of the youngest State of the Union to victory in defense of the Union of which it has so lately become a part."[32]

Before Lane could march Kansas troops into battle, his new senatorial duties in Washington, D.C., beckoned. He was in the capital city when excitement of McDowell's impending clash with Confederates in northern Virginia drew hundreds of spectators to the fields near Manassas in late July. Lane joined the procession, along with Senators Benjamin F. Wade and Henry Wilson, to see the promised victory. When musket and artillery fire announced the commencement of hostilities, Lane rode toward the front. A Union officer warned him of the dangers. Unperturbed, the Kansas senator —a combat veteran of the Mexican War and Bleeding Kansas— exclaimed that he wished to take part in the fighting. Reminded that he was not armed, Lane replied, "I can easily find a musket on the field." He had been in battle before, he told the officer, "and know that guns are easily found where fighting is going on."[33]

Following near success in the field, Union forces were stopped cold by Brigadier General Thomas Jackson's brigade on Henry Hill, earning Jackson the nickname "Stonewall." A Confederate counterattack shattered McDowell's army, sending it streaming to Washington. The Union officer who warned Lane of danger later recalled that during the retreat, "Lane was the first to pass me." The Kansas senator rode "an old-flea bitten gray horse," across its harness "a musket which, sure enough, he had found." Lane's long legs spurred the horse, "kicking far back to the rear to urge his old beast to greater speed, and so he sped on."[34]

The defeat stunned the North. Within a week Lincoln signed two bills authorizing the enlistment of one million men. Again enthusiastic white volunteers flooded recruitment offices throughout.[35] Lane saw the defeat at Bull Run as only a setback. He raced to Kansas in August, determined to carry out his own war against secessionists, setting his sights on Missouri. While that state had not formally seceded, its government and population were split in loyalty between the old Union and the Confederacy. One of the toughest Union commanders in the region, General Nathaniel Lyon, had fallen in battle against Confederates in Missouri at Wilson's Creek on August 10. Kansans feared an invasion from their eastern and southern borders and wanted action. Lane was ready to respond. His appointment from Lincoln had focused on recruitment, and Lane had denied to critics that he had surrendered his seat in the Senate to accept a brigadier general commission.[36] But since June, Lane had claimed a vague authority to lead men into combat. In the wake of recent Union defeats in the east and west, and a vacuum of military authority in Kansas, Lane stepped into a command position over three regiments—the Kansas Brigade.[37]

Lane did not wish for his brigade to stand idly by in Kansas. He advocated an advance into Missouri to keep the danger far from Kansas homes. Small companies of cavalry carried out guerrilla raids into Missouri throughout August, killing suspected secessionists and confiscating Rebel property, including slaves. These actions inflamed tensions along the border and set Kansas governor Charles Robinson into a frenzy. A long-standing political opponent of Lane, Robinson professed to Major General John C. Frémont, commander of the Western Department, "We are in no danger of invasion, provided the Government stores at Fort Scott are sent back to Leavenworth and the Lane brigade is removed from the border." The bigger fear, Robinson argued, was Lane's aggression. "But what we have to fear, and do fear, is that Lane's brigade will get up a war by going over the line, committing depredations, and then returning into our State."[38]

General Frémont sympathized with Lane's radicalism. A celebrity for his exploration of the western frontier before the war and his 1856 run as the Republican Party's first presidential candidate, Frémont faced a complex task in his new position as commander of the Western Department. Primarily responsible for military operations in Missouri, Frémont had visions of a grand campaign of his own, down the Mississippi River. After the Confederate success at Wilson's Creek, which threatened the rest of Missouri (and Kansas), Frémont shocked both North and South with a bold military order. On August 30, citing the "disorganized condition" and "helplessness of the civil authority, the total insecurity of life, and the devastation of property by bands of murderers and marauders, who infest nearly every county of the State," Frémont declared martial law in Missouri. He threatened severe punishment, including execution, to men found guilty of carrying arms in federally controlled areas and authorized the confiscation of rebel property. Frémont's proclamation included the additional, almost parenthetical, detail: "and their slaves, if any they have, are hereby declared freemen." The other details of the proclamation were white noise compared to the bombshell of emancipation. In barely ten words, Frémont shocked the nation and immortalized himself in Civil War lore.[39]

This was not the first effort to take slaves from secessionists. In May, Massachusetts politician turned Union officer, Benjamin Butler, had taken a novel step to confiscate slaves while occupying Fortress Monroe in Virginia. Three slaves employed by Confederate forces to construct nearby earthworks escaped into his lines. When a Confederate officer, under flag of truce, appeared and demanded the return of the slaves under U.S. law, Butler retorted that as Virginia and its residents claimed to be out of the Union, the Fugitive Slave Law did not apply. Butler then declared that his federal troops were confiscating the three slaves as "contraband of war."[40] It was a technical move that appeared to fall within the strict lines of military law. After consideration, Lincoln nodded in approval. Butler's actions drew praise among even some conservative Northerners, if nothing more than as a finger in the eye to Confederates who proclaimed independence, but still sought constitutional protection when it suited their interests. Among Northerners, the term "contraband" became synonymous with fugitive slave.

Butler's "contraband" policy was limited, though. First, it dealt with slavery on an individual level: it only concerned slaves who fell into Union lines. Furthermore, Butler did not officially declare the fugitives free men. The escaped slaves remained in legal limbo. Two months after his initial confiscation of "contrabands," Butler still did not know what to do with the increasing number of desperate black Americans fleeing into his lines. In the meantime he put them to work. "I had employed the men in Hampton in [improving] intrenchments, and they were working zealously and efficiently at that duty, saving our soldiers from that labor, under the gleam of the mid-day sun," Butler informed Secretary of War Cameron in late July. "The women were earning substantially their own subsistance [sic] in washing, marketing, and taking care of the clothes of the soldiers, and rations were being served out to the men who worked for the support of the children." Butler counted more than nine hundred fugitive slaves in his lines in Virginia and asked Secretary Cameron: "What shall be done with them? and, Second, What is their state and condition?" Butler looked for basic advice from the Lincoln administration. "Are these men, women, and children, slaves?" he asked. "Are they free? Is their condition that of men, women, and children, or that of property, or is it a mixed relation? What their status was under the Constitution and laws, we all know. What has been the effect of rebellion and a state of war upon that status?"[41] Neither Secretary Cameron nor President Lincoln provided answers.

The following week, on August 6, Congress passed a confiscation bill that authorized Union forces to free slaves actively used by secessionist forces. This was the foundation for Frémont's proclamation in Missouri, but his proclamation went further. The Confiscation Act was limited to freeing slaves employed in the Confederate war effort.[42] Frémont's proclamation made no such distinction. It declared freedom for all slaves of Missouri secessionists. President Lincoln quickly attempted damage control. Forced emancipation would "alarm our Southern Union friends, and turn them against us—perhaps ruin our rather fair prospect for Kentucky," he believed. He requested that Frémont tailor his proclamation to match the limits of Confiscation Act of August 6.[43]

The backlash from Southern Unionists, and Kentuckians in particular, panicked many Northerners. Inflammatory letters and complaints flooded the Executive Mansion. Frémont ignored Lincoln's letter, choosing instead to send his wife to persuade the president of the proclamation's value. The lobbying failed. Lincoln formally ordered Frémont to rescind his emancipation edict. A short time later, he removed Frémont from command.[44] Abolitionists derided the president for counteracting a significant blow to slavery, but this criticism had no effect: the administration and the majority of white Northerners were not yet ready for emancipation.

As these matters of policy played out, General Sterling Price's Confederate army moved north through Missouri toward Kansas City. Lane organized his forces and pushed them into Missouri. A portion of his brigade ran into Price's Confederates at Dry Wood Creek near Fort Scott on September 2. After a short engagement, the Kansans withdrew from the field in the face of a reinforced Southern advance.[45] Lane fired off messages to the commanding officer at Fort Leavenworth reporting the situation and calling for support, declaring, "In twelve hours after being re-enforced I can be upon them, give peace to Kansas, confuse the enemy, and advance the cause of the Union."[46] Kansas military forces were already stretched thin, and the border with Missouri spanned two hundred miles, approximately the same distance as from Washington, D.C., to North Carolina. Lane's call for more men and supplies went unheeded.

Fortunately for Lane, a climactic battle with Sterling Price did not materialize. Kansas scouts reported the enemy marching away from the Kansas border, and a Southern deserter said that Price's chosen target was Lexington, Missouri, near Kansas City. Still, Lane believed the maneuver was "for the purpose of crossing over to the north side of the Osage" to attack Fort Scott and Barnesville. Should the Confederates indeed push for Lexington, Lane planned to "annoy them as far as my forces and the protection of Kansas will admit of."[47]

Price did not intend to attack Kansas. As the deserter had disclosed, the Confederate army marched north to Lexington. By the time Lane realized Price's true objective, the Kansas Brigade was too far behind to seriously interfere with his campaign. Cavalry detachments from the brigade gave chase, but succeeded only in claiming a herd of cattle and liberating several Missouri slaves as "contraband."[48] Standing up to a large Confederate army in a conventional fight had not been a realistic objective for the Kansas Brigade. Lane's tiny army was outnumbered and too undisciplined to do much more than irritate Price's units. But the Kansans were well suited for an aggressive raid on Missouri towns. Without a large Confederate force in the way, Lane's men set across the Missouri countryside. At Morristown and Papinsville the Kansans chased away local and Confederate resistance and confiscated or destroyed property, earning a reputation as ruthless raiders and thieves.[49]

Lane attempted to make a distinction between the property of secessionists and Unionists. In early September, he issued an order that the rights and property of "the loyal citizens of other states must be sacredly observed," and he directed that confiscated secessionist goods must be turned over to federal quartermaster officials for proper disposition.[50] Enforcing those orders was another matter. For one, Lane intended that his brigade live off the land during its short campaign into Missouri. Second, raiding homes for supplies and booty proved too tempting for those who saw possibilities of profit. "These men who have heretofore been so violently opposed to Jay Hawking are as a general rule if not more, the most unscrupulous of all Jay Hawkers when they can have a share of the profits," wrote one Kansas soldier under Lane.[51] When incidents of theft accelerated to widespread looting, and stories of excessive foraging drew disapproval from Kansas residents, Lane lectured his men. "The thieves of this command have had their day. This is the last appeal that I shall make to you. After this I shall visit upon you the severest penalty of the law."[52]

It was with deep regret, he stated in a September 19 proclamation to Missourians, "that unwarranted excesses have been committed upon your property, by persons professing to belong to the United States army." Lane argued that those crimes were not by his men. "We are *soldiers*, not thieves, or plunderers, or jay hawkers. We have entered the army to fight for a peace, to put down a rebellion, to cause the stars and stripes—your flag as well as ours, once more to float over every foot of American soil." He encouraged Missourians to "reopen your courts, your schools, your churches. Restore the arts of peace. In short act the part of good, loyal, peace-loving American citizens; and the better to prove your claims as such, run up the American Flag before your doors." Should the people of Missouri recognize federal authority, "I promise you that the flag which has protected American citizens on every sea, shall be your protection; that this patriotic army of mine, which you so much fear, shall be to you what the strong hearted man is to the delicate woman by his side, a shield and a support. I will protect you against lawless plunderers and marauders from your own State, from Kansas, from anywhere."[53]

"Should you, however, disregard my advice," Lane warned Missourians,

the stern visitations of war will be meted out to the rebels and their allies. I shall then be convinced that your arming for protection is a sham; and rest assured that the traitor, when caught, shall receive a traitor's doom. The cup of mercy has been exhausted. Treason, hereafter, will be treated as treason. The massacre of innocent women and children, by black-hearted traitors lately burning a bridge on the Hannibal & St. Joseph Railroad, has satisfied us that a traitor will perpetrate crimes which devils would shudder to commit; they shall be blotted from existence, and sent to that hell which yawns for their reception.[54]

Lane did not wait long to back his threats. On September 22, the Kansas Brigade marched on Osceola and earned lasting enmity in Missouri for generations to come.

Osceola, a small town with less than three hundred residents, hardly seemed a significant objective for the Kansas Brigade. Yet its placement on the Osage River was an important landing spot for goods shipped up the river. Lane believed that secessionist forces used the town as a supply depot, particularly for ammunition.[55] The Kansas troops chased away a small band of militia on the outskirts of town and then confiscated several wagonloads of goods, before watching much of the town burn.[56]

The pillaging and destruction of Osceola not only inflamed emotions in Missouri but also brought condemnation from Lane's critics in Kansas. "What kind of property was this?" asked Governor Robinson, one of Lane's chief critics in Kansas. "Was it contraband of war—arms, ammunition, shot, shell, or cannon? No, it was the clothing, bedding, food and shelter of women and children, every dollar of which will have to be paid back by the General Government as soon as peace is restored."[57] Later writers and historians condemned the Kansas Brigade's actions at Osceola. Albert Castel believed that the "truth of the matter is that Lane's Brigade was an irresponsible mob which looted and burned Osceola out of a wanton lust for plunder and a self-righteous desire to injure the Missourians." Castel ridiculed the idea that the campaign into Missouri and against Osceola was "to suppress secessionist sentiment in Missouri and hamper Price's operations." Instead, he argued, Lane's "actual objective, besides plunder, was to give a practical demonstration of what he had told the Senate in July—that slavery could not survive the march of the Union armies."[58]

Castel exaggerates Lane's interest in striking against slavery. Lane had indeed spoken against the institution in the U.S. Senate in July 1861, blaming the "slave oligarchy" for trampling the rights of Kansans during the fight for statehood and now threatening the very existence of the country. And he predicted that "the institution of slavery will not survive in any State of this Union, and I thank God it is so." But this prediction was not from humanitarian principles. Lane freely acknowledged that he and his constituents "would have stood by the compromises of the Constitution, and would not, by word or act, have disturbed slavery in the States where it existed." The battle over slavery in the United States had not remained a political compromise. Slavery's proponents, he argued, had trampled the spirit of brotherhood and had inflicted on Kansas free-state men depredations for the expansion of African servitude. "I respect the gentlemen who represent the slave States on this floor," he had told his fellow senators, "but I say the institution of slavery requires of its devotees that kind of devotion which makes fiends of men. There is no crime that the devotees of slavery will not commit in maintaining or extending it." In regard to the matter of secession, Lane was very clear: "They have forced upon us this trouble, and I, for one, am willing it shall be followed to its logical conclusion."[59]

Unlike Frémont, Lane did not advocate an emancipation policy. He believed slaves would be freed as a matter of course, as a natural by-product of Union victory. During the same Senate discussion above, Lane asked a colleague, "Should the armies of the Union march into the slave States, and the slaves themselves should get up an insurrection, as I believe will be the case, and flee to the armies of the Union, or march out by the roads that Union armies march in, will the Senator, under such circumstances, expect the people of the North, or the armies of the North, to become the servants of the traitors, and return those slaves to their traitorous masters?" For Lane, the answer was a resounding no. "I disavow any intent upon the part of the Government or its Army to war against the institution of slavery," Lane stated. "I said that the effect of marching an army on the soil of any slave State will be to instill into the slaves a determined purpose to free themselves; and, in my opinion, they will crush out everything that stands in the way of acquiring that freedom." Lane envisioned that "there would be a colored army marching out of the slave States while the army of freedom was marching in," and during the expected insurrections and exoduses by enslaved blacks, he professed, "I do not propose to make myself a slave catcher for traitors and return them to their masters."[60]

The Kansas Brigade sought to accomplish several objectives, from distracting Sterling Price's army, to destroying Confederate supplies, to punishing secessionist Missourians. But the September raid into Missouri underscored Lane's arguments. Several slaves, including twenty-five from one farm, escaped from their masters and joined the brigade's procession back to Kansas.[61]

After the Kansas Brigade returned to its home state, Lane disputed accusations that his men liberated Missouri slaves with abandon. "Before I left Washington, I stated in a speech made in the United States Senate," he acknowledged to a crowd in Leavenworth in early October, "which was published in the papers, that slavery could not survive the march of the Federal army; that while an army of one color was marching into the Rebel States, another army of another color would march out." He clarified, however, that his men were careful to consider the loyalty of Missouri slaveholders. "No pains are spared to extend every protection to the property and persons of loyal citizens. If their slaves run away and come into our camp they are permitted to come and reclaim them if they can. The army is not allowed to interfere in the least, on either side." Even slaves of Missourians who sympathized with the secessionists but "stay at home and attend to their ordinary business, refusing to take up arms against the Government[,] are not molested." However, "the negroes, persons and property of armed rebels are seized wherever found. The slaves are set at liberty." Of course, several slaves of loyal Missourians successfully escaped into Kansas lines before the owners could retrieve them. Lane had an answer for that. "If a loyal citizen loses a slave on account of the army, we give him a certificate to that effect, and when the troubles are over the Government can make good his loss if it sees proper."[62]

These words hardly soothed the minds of his Kansas and Missouri critics. Lane knew as much. In fact, he accused Governor Robinson and other detractors of sympathizing with the enemy.

Why is it that these complainers have not a word of sympathy for the loyal citizens and families, which have been robbed, plundered and driven from their homes in Missouri? Thousands of them have sought refuge in Free Kansas, and will be dependent on our bounty during the coming winter. Oh, the miscreants! No concern for these, but if a Traitor's slave shall fall into the wake of the Kansas Brigade and regain the natural rights of man, then the vengeance that is breathed against Jim Lane is only equaled by the wail of distress and sympathy that is extended to the slave master.

Lane ridiculed the thought that his men would exert themselves chasing runaway slaves. "Should I say to Col. Blunt, Col. Ritchey, or any other officer or man in the Brigade, 'Go in search of this man's runaway.' Do you think they would obey? No, sir; they would first surrender their swords and commissions." Lane asked if another military officer ordered his soldiers "to go out into the streets of Leavenworth in search of fugitives, how many of you would obey?" A voice from the crowd shouted, "None!"[63]

"We march to crush out Treason, and if Slavery does not take care of itself, the fault is not mine," Lane stated. "It can never be made my duty to defend it for the benefit of Traitors. If they do not want to lose their slaves, let the Traitors lay down their arms, and our troops will be glad to leave their borders." As long as secessionists continued to fight, he would wage a hard war: "A rebellious province or State must be visited by the severe chastisement of war; Traitors must suffer the loss of property, and desolation must overwhelm them before they will acknowledge the Government against which they have revolted."[64]

As the war continued, Lane's hostility to slavery increased. "My creed is—*Let slavery take care of itself.* If it can survive the shock of war, let it live," Lane told an Indiana regiment camped in Springfield, Missouri, in November. "I do not propose to make war upon slavery, but upon rebels, and in the mean time to let slaves and slavery take care of themselves." These words echoed a position he had held for months. Yet as he warmed to his audience that November day, Lane gradually moved to a more radical position. "War, at best, is a terrible calamity to a nation," he said. "Justice, humanity and mercy, require that the conflict should be terminated as soon as possible, and with the least practicable shedding of blood."[65]

How would one achieve victory with the least amount of death? For Lane, the answer was simple: turn against slavery, the most important element to the South. Strike against slavery, he argued, and the Confederacy would crumble. "Astonishing as it may seem to you, gentlemen of Indiana," he exclaimed, "yet the fact we have repeatedly demonstrated that a heavier blow is dealt out of the realm of Secessia in the abduction or freedom of a slave, than in the killing of a soldier in arms." That was the Confederacy's weak point, its Achilles' heel. He continued, "If, then, by allowing the slave to fall into the wake of the army, and find the priceless boon of freedom, we void bloodshed, save property from destruction, and strike death dealing blows upon the head and front of this rebellion, does not every consideration that is just and good, require that this policy be adopted[?]"[66]

These words marked an evolution in Lane's approach to the war and slavery. While he assured conservative Unionists that he had no intention of carrying out an abolitionist war, the conclusion that slavery would not survive a Union victory clearly emerged from his November 1861 speech. "Gentlemen, my logic teaches me that we cannot defend and make war upon the same foe at the same time, and if it is the purpose of the Government to crush the rebels, and prevent their slaves from stampeding, two armies should be sent into the field," he stated. "The advance force might be called the Treason-crushing Army, and should be armed with offensive weapons. The other might be called the Slavery-Restoring Army, and should move about ten miles in the rear." Such an effort would cost the government an exorbitant amount of money, he continued, and would cripple the Union effort by making soldiers the servants of slaveholding interests. To applause Lane announced, "Since the rebels have failed to nationalize slavery, their battle cry is, 'Down with the Union—let slavery lift up its crest in the air,' and here I solemnly vow, that if Jim Lane is compelled to add a note to such an infernal chorus, he breaks his sword and quits the field."[67]

Lane urged a new policy. "It should be the business of Congress at its coming session to pass a law directing the President of the United States by proclamation to order the rebel States, within thirty or sixty days, to lay down their arms and return to their allegiance, or in default thereof, declare all men free throughout their domains," Lane announced. This was radical talk from a man who not more than six months before had voted for the Crittenden-Johnson Resolution and its decree of a limited war. Yet he was joining a group of radicals in pushing for true policy change. President Lincoln would eventually come to see this step as necessary for Union victory and would put forth a proclamation outlining this very policy. But that was nearly a year in the future. Unlike Lincoln, who advanced new policies with reservations and held little animosity toward the Confederates, Lane shared with his audience a desire for vengeance. "I hope the Almighty will so direct the hearts of the rebels," he bellowed, "that like Pharaoh they will persist in their crime and then will we invade them and strike the shackles from every limb."[68]

Throughout the fall of 1861 hundreds of Missouri slaves escaped into Kansas, through their own efforts or with help of federal soldiers. The fugitives included men, women, and children. A slave boy called George, about twelve years old, rode into the camp of the Third Kansas Volunteers and explained his story. According to the regiment's chaplain, H. H. Moore, George had overheard his master's family talk about slaves taking refuge with the Kansas soldiers. So, when instructed by his master to take a mule into the woods "that neither might fall into the hands of the army," George promptly rode fifteen miles and delivered himself and the mule to the regiment.[69] Other fugitives saw greater opportunity with the Kansas Brigade. Wilson, an escaped slave from Springfield, Missouri, found freedom at Fort Scott and secured a position there cooking and serving the soldiers. He set out with the brigade on a march into the Springfield area and visited his former owner, defiantly liberating his brother and sister, and claiming two spans of mules, a wagon, and various other belongings in the process.[70]

With the increasing number of escaped slaves joining the Kansas Brigade during an expedition east of Fort Scott in October, Lane ordered three chaplains to lead a convoy of fugitives into Kansas. Over two hundred former slaves, some in wagons, some astride horses and mules, and others walking, formed a mile-long procession during their exodus out of Missouri.[71] The refugees had no military escort. Guns were distributed among the men, but for show only— the Kansas soldiers had not supplied ammunition. They crossed miles of Missouri prairie and cautiously camped near Drywood when night fell. The following day, when the outline of Kansas's hills and bluffs emerged on the horizon, excitement grew. On crossing the border into Kansas, Chaplain Hugh Fisher brought the fugitives around and stood high on his horse. There, "under the open heavens, on the sacred soil of freedom, in the name of the Constitution of the United States, the Declaration of Independence, and by the authority of General James H. Lane," Fisher declared them "forever free." Over two hundred voices cried out in celebration. "Men and women who had been sighing for liberty during many long unrequited years of toil now felt and knew they were free," Fisher later wrote. "They jumped, cried, sang and laughed for joy." As the procession arrived at Fort Scott, the newly freed people "changed their names from the old plantation names to those of Northern significancy [sic], to prevent the possibility of their being returned to slavery in case the war should be a failure."[72]

Lane carried his new call for war against slavery in speeches to Northern audiences over the following weeks. To a Boston crowd he said, "'Slavery' is written on their banners, and what is ours,—is it not substantially the same, when we war for the old Union? . . . How many soldiers' lives are you willing to give to maintain slavery?" Voices responded, "None!" Lane agreed: "I will not shed a single drop of blood to save the accursed system."[73]

His speech to the New Englanders suggested a new weapon in the war against secession. "The only way we can bring this contest to a successful issue is, by striking directly and with all our power at the foundation," he declared. "I would oppose bowie-knife to bowie-knife, Indian to Indian, nigger to nigger, and freedom to slavery." To those too faint of heart for such a war, he demanded "a substitute, equally powerful, for closing the war." Otherwise, the "present policy will cause the war to drag along for years."[74]

The war did drag along. "Why is our army inactive?" Lane asked on the Senate floor in late December. He ridiculed excuses that the Union armies lacked sufficient training, equipment, or numbers. The biggest threat was a passive army. "Inaction is the bane of the volunteer," he argued. More frustrating to Lane, however, was talk among conservatives who eschewed a hard war. "I laugh to scorn the policy of wooing back the traitors to their allegiance by seizing and holding unimportant points in those States," Lane announced. "Every invitation extended to them in kindness is an encouragement to stronger resistance. The exhausting policy is a failure." More importantly, he stated that "so long as they have four million of slaves to feed them, so long will this rebellion be sustained."[75]

Lane spoke about the value of slaves to the Confederacy. "It is claimed by the friends of slavery that the institution is a source of military strength. The slaves are made not only to feed and clothe their oppressors, but to build fortifications for their defence; and even in some cases to bear arms in their service." Regarding the latter claim, stories of black Confederate soldiers had circulated through Northern press circles for months, shared in part by men such as notable black abolitionist Frederick Douglass. While these stories were rarely validated, for Lane the point remained: the African American population in the South aided the Confederate war effort. So he challenged his colleagues. "Suppose *we* had their slaves; to what lengths would they not go in an opposite direction, in the hope to recover them?" Lane answered his question forcefully. "They would bow down in dutiful submission, even to Abraham Lincoln himself. In my opinion, obtaining possession of these slaves by the Government would be more effective in crushing out rebellion, than the seizure, if it could be made, of every ounce of ammunition they possess."[76]

Lane argued that liberating slaves would gut the Confederacy's labor machine and deny the South its most important financial and political interests. He believed that emancipation would bring the Confederacy to its knees and benefit Union armies as well. "The general who commands that army, will be received with the same acclaim as was Bonaparte," said Lane, describing the French devotion to Napoleon. "They will hail him as their liberator and friend, and by their very numbers will secure safety to his army." Lane acknowledged a tactical value to freed slaves as well: "No trouble, then, in obtaining information of the enemy's operations. Interested in our success—grateful as they will be faithful—every movement will instantly be reported, endangering their champions and protectors." Though echoing the insurrectionist ideas of abolitionist John Brown and signaling a positive step toward including blacks in the ongoing conflict, Lane's talk of military value of African Americans to the Union war effort was an afterthought, a casual benefit to military emancipation.[77]

Unsurprisingly, conservatives in the Senate were appalled at the prospect of strategic and tactical emancipation. Senator John S. Carlile, a Virginian who represented the Unionist element of his seceded state, admitted surprise "to hear from the Senator that twenty million of loyal people are unable to contend with five million in rebellion . . . without liberating the four million slaves that are in the slaveholding States." He described his frustration with increasing "slavery agitation" and reminded Lane and others that the nation's founders had established constitutional protections for the institution. Ominously, Carlile announced, "If this is to be a war for the liberation of the slaves, it will not be a constitutional struggle for the maintenance of the Union and the rights of the people and of the States under it, but it would then be a war for the overthrow of the Constitution; it would be an inhuman and an unholy crusade against American constitutional liberty."[78]

Lane was unperturbed. The biggest threat to constitutional liberty in his eyes was secession, brought about by proponents of slavery. He emerged as a strong voice among a growing number of Radical Republicans, who argued that it was far better to confiscate the property of secessionists and overturn the institution of slavery than to see the constitutional Union torn apart.

As the year 1862 opened and federal armies seemed no closer to defeating the Confederacy, Lane's anxiety escalated. Radical to many of his peers, his arguments to this point had not broken a vital barrier in regard to African American advocacy. He had not yet advocated a proactive role for black Americans. Like his conservative critics, Lane had seen black people as objects. For all of his demands for federal action against slavery, it simply meant treating the black man as a commodity to be denied from the South in order to win the war. Abolitionists and leading African Americans had argued for months that the black population was an untapped resource for Union service. In early 1862, Lane began adopting that position. As before, however, his views did not come from moral reflection. Rather, the federal government's inability to defeat the Confederacy in a limited war pushed him to adopt more radical measures. The position of African Americans in the midst of the secession crisis and the battlefield meant that, ultimately, white Americans could not leave them as passive objects on the sidelines during the bitter and prolonged conflict. As a population, they were key to the Southern war effort, and Lane saw potential for them as a presence in a war zone.

"When I think who caused this war I feel like a fiend," he raved to a crowd in Leavenworth in January. "When I think that the men who have been the Cabinet officers, the Senators, the Congressmen, the Generals, the colonels; when I think that the very men who, for twenty years, have fattened on this Government, are now raising their hands to strike it down—I feel like taking them all by the throat—like throttling and strangling them all." This heightened emotion not only revealed Lane's level of anxiety but also drew in the crowd. It imposed desperation and pleaded for action. "The only way to close this war is to fight and to fight everything that stands in the way," he stated. At this point, Lane disclosed hints of a proactive role for African Americans. He revealed it with a story. "I remember well shortly after the battle of Buena Vista," he began, recalling his days as a colonel in the Mexican War:

Report came into camp that a party of Mexican men, women and children had been butchered in the mountains. I was ordered out with a detachment of men and brought forty or fifty mutilated bodies and reported to Gen. Taylor that they were butchered by the Comanches. No one ever questioned Gen. Taylor's goodness of heart or his skill as a soldier, but he replied: "The Comanches seem to be fighting on the same side we are. We won't interfere with them."

Lane looked over the crowd, and let his story sink in. His subsequent words underscored its relevance. "I don't say I would call the Comanches but I do say that it would not pain me to see the negro handling a gun, and I believe the negro may, just as well become food for powder as my son."[79]

With raw logic Lane cracked a conservative roadblock to African American military service. The fear of black men bearing arms, especially against white men, had sent shivers through American society for generations. The image of a violent and rebelling slave represented a collapse of racial order too disturbing for many whites, even in the North, to accept. But now, in an ongoing and increasingly bloody war for the preservation of the constitutional Union, Lane observed that African Americans could just as well kill a traitor, and save the lives of young white Northerners in the process. At this point in his speech, he did not advocate military enlistment of black men. Instead, his parable of the Comanches illustrated a willingness to stand back and let slaves fight for themselves, and find freedom through violence if needed.

Though far-reaching, it was an ingenious argument to place before conservative whites, who had no interest in advancing African American rights or privileges. But Lane could claim no brilliance in crafting this message. He merely described what his own racially conservative mind had come to accept in a bloody war for national survival. These arguments appealed to him now as they began to appeal to other Northern whites precisely because of the war's cost. Each month the Confederacy existed, the Union's future seemed more grim. Each day federal armies remained in the field, more young white men died from combat or disease. "We have lost just men enough for the preservation of Slavery, have made widows enough, orphans enough," Lane cried out. "Kansas has offered up enough blood to this Moloch, and so has every other State." Now, he argued, was the time to turn the tide of war. He looked over the crowd and asked them, "Who feeds this rebellion? Four million slaves. Who clothes this rebellion? Four million slaves." Then he charged, "Take them from that side and put them on this side."[80]

What should Union armies do with newly freed slaves? Lane proposed to employ them as laborers, supporting the white fighting men of the army. "One of the Cabinet Ministers asked me the other day how many slaves I could profitably use in a column of 34,000 men," Lane told the Kansas audience. "I replied 34,000— besides the teamsters I told him I wanted to see every soldier a knight-errant and behind him his squire to do all his work, so that I may use the soldier just to shoot traitors, and send them to that home prepared for them from the beginning. I would like to have the rebels killed by a gentleman. Let the soldiers go on with their killing and the squires go on with their burying." This description reinforced the image of white supremacy over African Americans in the face of emancipation. And it touched on a romanticism of war damaged by months of military stagnation and defeat, but not yet destroyed, among many Northern whites. Most importantly, though, it stealthily presented an avenue for black military action, which Lane then presented: "If the squires get guns I don't propose to punish the negro if he kills a traitor."[81] Through an image of knights and squires, Lane advocated a partnership between Northern white and Southern black men on the battlefield, albeit in a paternalistic and imbalanced way.

As his speech in Leavenworth continued, Lane's focus on African American military service increased, taking on a stronger egalitarian tone as it progressed. "The negroes are much more intelligent than I had ever supposed," he admitted. He recalled his time in the field with the Kansas Brigade and explained that he had "seen them come into camp (occasionally) looking down as though slaves. By and by they begin to straighten themselves, throw back their shoulders, stand erect, and soon look God straight in the face. They are the most affectionate, impulsive, domestic beings in the world. No one loves mother, wife, children, more than the negro, and they are an altogether smarter people than we give them credit for." Lane said he had already observed an aptitude for black military service. He explained, "After a long day's march, after getting supper for the men, after feeding and cleaning the horses, I have seen them out, just back of the tents drilling. And they take to drill as a child takes to its mother's milk. They soon learn the step,

soon learn the position of the soldier and the manual of arms. You
even see that in the innermost recesses of their souls the 'devil is
in them.'"[82]

Less than a year after outbreak of gunfire between the Confederacy and the Union, African Americans found an indomitable
proponent for breaking the color barrier for combat with the U.S.
military—a wild, racist, unpredictable, and ambitious defender
of the Union, whose enemies outnumbered his followers: James
Henry Lane.

CHAPTER 3

1862

THE DOOR OPENS

Receiving Negroes under the late act of Congress. Is there any objection?

A t the dawn of the year 1862 the Confederacy had reason for hope. Southern armies had not only survived, they had been largely victorious against a more populated, more industrially developed, and better equipped North. Northerners reflected on the bitter disappointment of defeat after defeat. Despite the war's broad front, most attention fell on a small stretch of land between Richmond and Washington, D.C., a buffer between two capitals, the most heavily militarized territory in the Western hemisphere.

The new year promised more bloody battles and an assurance that the war would linger on much longer than most had anticipated. Yet the following twelve months would see some significant advancements for African Americans. Abolitionists and radical Republicans amplified the call for greater action against slavery and more opportunities for blacks in the war. Frederick Douglass, a former slave and one of the abolition movement's most inspirational voices, expertly identified failings and prejudices within the Northern war effort and demanded full federal commitment to defeating secession through African American participation. Douglass passionately condemned Abraham Lincoln and his administration for ignoring the black population as a key to Union victory: "Our Presidents, Governors, Generals and Secretaries are calling, with almost frantic vehemence, for men.—'Men! men! send us men!' they scream, or the cause of the Union is gone." Yet, he continued, "these very officers, representing the people and Government, steadily and persistently refuse to receive the very class of men which have a deeper interest in the defeat and humiliation of the rebels, than all others."

Because of the government's obstinacy in regard to black service, Douglass declared, "it will not deserve better fortunes than it has thus far experienced."[1]

The most crucial steps in advancing black rights during the Civil War did not come from abolitionists. Douglass, editor William Lloyd Garrison, and Massachusetts senator Charles Sumner had limited influence on federal policy in 1861 and 1862. Rather, the first steps leading to black military service came from obscure corners of the country, pushed by moderate—even racially conservative—Union officials. One such individual was Major General David Hunter.

A veteran army officer who had briefly been assigned to military forces in Kansas and Missouri, Hunter found himself in charge of the Department of the South in March 1862. On paper, his command oversaw Georgia, South Carolina, and Florida. In reality, Hunter controlled only a small strip of islands along South Carolina's coast. His instructions included the expectation that he capture Forts Pulaski and Savannah, two formidable obstacles. Before reaching his new headquarters, Hunter requested reinforcements. "I have to state that my continued reflection convinces me that for an efficient action it is indispensable that more troops be sent immediately to South Carolina," he wrote to Secretary of War Edwin Stanton. "I know as well now as I can possibly know when I shall have reached there that from 20,000 to 25,000 additional troops should be sent."[2]

Hunter was one of many army commanders pressing the War Department for more men. In early 1862, Stanton and President Lincoln faced a steady stream of requests, most notably from General George McClellan in support of his massive Army of the Potomac, then in preparation for a grand campaign against Richmond.

Hunter's plea for twenty thousand more men went ignored.[3] Geographically isolated, he could not expect help from other Union forces. His department was surrounded by Confederate territory. Hunter's only option was to look locally, and the geographical location of the Department of the South provided an answer. Since November 1861, when Union soldiers captured the Sea Islands, hundreds of freed slaves tilled their former masters' plantations, providing Northern mills with valuable Southern cotton. Northern humanitarians had arrived to provide education and medical services to the residents. Northern abolitionists saw this burgeoning community as a model of self-sufficiency among the freed slaves. Hunter saw a large pool of untapped manpower for military service.

In late 1861, General Hunter's predecessor, Thomas W. Sherman, had received permission from then secretary of war Simon Cameron to arm slaves on the Sea Islands "if special circumstances seem to require it." Sherman had decided against this option. Hunter had no such qualms. Within a few weeks of his arrival in South Carolina, he requested weapons and uniforms and undertook the Union army's first formal effort to enlist black soldiers.[4]

Had Hunter limited himself to quietly creating one or two black regiments from local volunteers of the Sea Island community, he might have succeeded. Instead he annoyed his superiors and deterred potential recruits through two disastrous actions. First, on April 13, 1862, he issued a declaration that "all persons of color lately held to involuntary service by enemies of the United States in Fort Pulaski and on Cockspur Island, Georgia, are hereby confiscated and declared free, in conformity with law, and shall hereafter receive the fruits of their own labor."[5] A month later, after ordering martial law over Georgia, South Carolina, and Florida, Hunter expanded his emancipation efforts and announced that all slaves in those three states were "declared forever free."[6] The order alarmed conservatives in the North and the border states. With less patience than when handling John C. Frémont's similar emancipation order in Missouri the previous August, President Lincoln rescinded Hunter's edict with a strongly worded proclamation: "Neither General Hunter nor any other commander or person has been authorized by the Government of the United States to make proclamations declaring slaves of any State free; and that the supposed proclamation now in question, whether genuine or false, is altogether void, so far as respects such declaration." Lincoln added that issues regarding military emancipation "are questions which under my responsibility I reserve to myself, and which I cannot feel justified in leaving to the decision of commanders in the field."[7]

Hunter overextended his authority, reaching into matters of politics and policy. His efforts to create a black regiment proved no more tactful. Instead of encouraging volunteer enlistments, he ordered conscription. On May 9, he instructed his subordinates to "send immediately to these headquarters, under a guard, all the able-bodied negroes capable of bearing arms within the limits of their several commands."[8] Officers detained dozens of black men, gathering them from fields and homes, and marched them into military camps. "Wives and children embraced the husband and father thus taken away, they knew not where, and whom, as they said, they should never see again," wrote one Northern official.[9] This impolitic beginning soured local African Americans and many white Northerners (including federal officials) on Hunter's project. Later reports presented a rosier image of the treatment and morale of the men of the First South Carolina Colored Regiment's camp. However, the controversy from Hunter's emancipation order and the stories of forcible black conscription provoked a firestorm in Washington and ultimately hindered the unit's potential for service in the field.

By early June, conservatives in Congress demanded to know whether the South Carolina black regiment had been raised with the blessing of the War Department, and whether the Lincoln administration had provided these fugitive slaves with weapons and uniforms. Hunter pointed to instructions issued by then secretary of war Simon Cameron in 1861 granting authority to organize freed slaves in the Department of the South for military service. He acknowledged that he had not received specific authority to equip the men, but added that he had assumed the responsibility and outfitted them with available supplies. Unperturbed by the hostility toward his efforts, Hunter confidently professed that by the fall of 1862 he could "present to the Government from 48,000 to 50,000 of these hardy and devoted soldiers."[10]

Hunter's letter inspired Northern abolitionists but failed to draw support from Congress or the president. By the beginning of August, Lincoln's military policy regarding African Americans had gone no further than accepting them as laborers. On August 10, General Hunter informed Secretary Stanton that since he had failed to receive authority to muster the "First Regiment of South Carolina Volunteers" into federal service, he had disbanded them. "I had hoped that not only would this regiment have been accepted," he wrote, "but that many similar ones would have been authorized to fill up the decimated ranks of the army and afford the aid of which the cause seems now so much in need." He had not received the authority, "which I expected," to put the regiment into the field as U.S. soldiers, and thus "deemed it best to discontinue the organization."[11] Still, General Hunter was the first Union commander with the facilities and willingness to enlist black soldiers.

One thousand miles to the west the military leaders in Kansas faced problems similar to Hunter's command on the Sea Islands. As the North's southwestern anchor, Kansas lay far from Washington and the battlefields of Virginia, necessitating reliance on state and local authorities for wartime matters. And unlike other Northern states in the west, Kansas was in a vulnerable location, bordering two military theaters—Missouri to its east, and Indian Territory to its south. Bands of secessionist guerrillas and large Confederate armies operated near the Kansas plains, occasionally crossing the border. A handful of forts and a few thousand men were all that protected Kansas's two-hundred-mile boundary with Missouri. Yet victory required offensive operations into secessionist territory. All of this heightened anxieties in Kansas, leading to calls for more troops to defend the state, put down the rebellion, and punish secessionists.

While Kansans feared invasion by Confederate armies, an entirely different type of Southerner most often crossed the state's borders. Thousands of fugitive slaves, fresh from the fields of Missouri, Arkansas, and Indian Territory, taking advantage of the chaos from military campaigns, or simply inspired by images of antislavery Yankees, fled into Kansas seeking refuge in a state seen as a beacon of freedom. In 1860, the African American population of Kansas numbered a paltry 627.[12] In May 1862, after a year of war, Kansas senator James H. Lane told his colleagues in the Senate that Kansas had "at least four thousand fugitive slaves from Missouri and Arkansas."[13] By July 1862, Lane stated that over six thousand fugitive slaves were in Kansas.[14] While some historians and critics of Lane question the accuracy of his claims, the state clearly had become a destination for thousands of fugitive slaves. By 1865 the African American population in Kansas had reached twelve thousand.[15]

This massive influx of black refugees dramatically shifted the demographics of Kansas. Though the "black law"—or exclusion of all African Americans—had long since been abandoned by Kansans, few observers would have expected the state's white population to welcome African American emigrants with open arms. Much had happened in the state's first two years. Sectional politics and secession had pushed many moderate and conservative free-state Kansans, such as Lane, into a stronger opposition to slavery. Just as significantly, a combination of war and weather eased the introduction of black refugees into Kansas society.

In the summer of 1863, newspaper correspondent and military officer Richard Hinton informed a federal commission that the emigration of African Americans transpired during some of the best farming weather the region had experienced since white settlement there. Bountiful crops and a war that drew many able-bodied white men far away from Kansas farms created a need for laborers. Newly freed blacks stepped into this role as paid farmhands. "Kansas can sustain and make efficient a colored laboring population of 25,000," Hinton reported.[16] Daniel R. Anthony, the mayor of Leavenworth, upped that estimate: "I am of the opinion that one hundred thousand sound healthy negro men and women migrating to this state or even more would prove a vast benefit to our state. The past year the fugitive slaves from Missouri have raised a larger crop of corn in Kansas (also grain of all kinds) than Kansas has raised in the past eight years."[17]

The wartime African American migration into Kansas created a welcome pool of workers in a labor-starved community; in addition, to military leaders the emigrants presented a reservoir of potential military recruits. Chief among these leaders was Lane. As his wartime speeches evolved in their opposition to slavery and acceptance of black military service, the number of able-bodied black men in Kansas increased. By late spring 1862, the overall readiness for black military service was as high in Kansas as anywhere else in the nation, North or South. All that was needed for a black regiment was a leader with the willingness and, most importantly, the authority to put it through. In the summer of 1862, fate—with an assist from shameless self-promotion—smiled on James Lane. The War Department appointed him the "commissioner of recruiting in the Department of Kansas" and requested that he "proceed forthwith to raise and organize one or more brigades of volunteer infantry."[18] With this appointment in his pocket, Lane raced back to Kansas.

By the first week of August, Lane had opened a recruitment office in Leavenworth. To help drive enlistments, he held a mass public meeting there, warning Kansans of their vulnerable and isolated position alongside Missouri. Brigadier General James Blunt, the new commander of the Department of Kansas (a position he owed to Lane's influence), followed the senator with his own dire predictions of Confederate invasion. Some Kansans believed these warnings were exaggerated and threatened stability by alarming Unionists on the other side of the border.[19] More significantly, Lane's role as commissioner of recruiting chafed Governor Charles Robinson, long a critic of Lane's rhetoric and actions. Generally, state governments handled recruiting duties during the war. Lane's influence in Washington, D.C., had allowed him to usurp that authority. Shortly after returning to Kansas, he informed his recruiting agents, "No application to the Governor of the State, for commissions in the new regiments, will be tolerated."[20] Unsurprisingly, Robinson objected and announced that he would disregard Lane's selections and only appoint officers of his own choosing.[21] Revealing the bond between Lane and the Lincoln administration, Secretary of War Edwin Stanton stated that should the governor refuse to accept the officers selected by Lane and his men, "the President will issue commissions."[22]

Lane began recruiting with abandon. On August 5, he telegraphed Stanton that enlistment efforts in Kansas seemed promising enough for four white regiments and two black regiments.[23] His appointment as recruiting commissioner had been vague, instructing him to "raise and organize one or more brigades of volunteer infantry" for three years of service.[24] He had received no written instructions to recruit black men, so the next day he sent Stanton a telegraph clarifying that he was "receiving Negroes under the late act of Congress," a reference to the Act of July 17, 1862, also known as the Second Confiscation Act. He added a modicum of deference, asking, "Is there any objection?"[25]

That Lane opened his recruiting efforts to African Americans should not have come as a surprise to officials in Washington. In mid-July, on the eve of the passage of the Second Confiscation Act, he had told his Senate colleagues that, in regard to fugitive slaves, "We propose to use them in fighting." He added, "We have in Kansas, as reported to me, six thousand four hundred slaves. Out of this number we expect to get two regiments of infantry."[26] Lane only needed permission. He found it in the Second Confiscation Act, which authorized the president to "receive into the service of the United States, for the purpose of constructing intrenchments, or [performing] camp service, or any other labor, or any military or naval service for which they may be found competent, persons of African descent."[27] That Lincoln had not formally approved African American enlistments did not deter Lane. Years later, John Speer, editor of the *Lawrence Republican* newspaper, wrote that in the summer of 1862 Lane told him that "he had just received authority to organize three regiments of white and two of colored soldiers in Kansas." When Speer asked, in amazement, to see the order, Lane replied "that it was a VERBAL promise from the President that he would see that they were clothed and subsisted until such time as they could be brought into the line and equipped for battle."[28] The validity of Lane's claim, or even Speer's account, may never be known. But what could not be questioned was Lane's determination to recruit black men for military service.

Secretary Stanton did not immediately reply to Lane's telegraph regarding black enlistments. Lincoln's secretaries John Hay and John Nicolay later surmised that Stanton, "remembering that the inquiry came from a region of Border Ruffian memories and methods, left Lane to his own devices and responsibilities."[29] In fact, the War Department did raise an objection once a copy of Lane's General Order Number 2, which outlined his authority to receive black recruits, landed on the desk of the recently appointed commanding general of the Union army, Henry Halleck. On August 18, General Halleck wrote Secretary Stanton that the "law of July 17, 1862, authorizes the President only to receive into the military service of the United States persons of African descent. As the President has not authorized recruiting officers to receive into the service of the United States such persons for general military purposes, the inclosed order of General Lane is without the authority of the law."[30] Stanton sent a belated response to Lane, on August 23, acknowledging that while he was pleased to receive positive news of recruiting, on the matter of "that portion of your communication which contemplates the raising of two regiments of persons of African descent, you are informed that regiments of persons of African descent can only be raised upon express and special authority of the President." Stanton added that Lincoln "has not given authority to raise such troops in Kansas, and it is not comprehended in the authority issued to you." He concluded that Kansas's black regiments "cannot be accepted into the service."[31]

As with General Hunter's experiment in South Carolina, the Lincoln administration withheld its support from Lane's endeavor. Lane's thoughts about Secretary Stanton's letter remain a mystery. There is no record that he informed Stanton of any agreement, verbal or otherwise, with the president to raise a black unit. Even if Lincoln had given an informal nod to Lane, federal support through clothing, equipment, and pay would come through War Department channels. Stanton's declaration that the federal government would not accept a black regiment from Kansas essentially crushed any hope of official supply.

Lane looked for an opening and believed he found it in the passively aggressive tone of Stanton's response. The letter did not order

Lane to cease enlisting African Americans, nor did it instruct him to release those men who may have already volunteered. Though most military officers would interpret Stanton's letter as instructions to stop, Lane continued recruiting as if nothing had changed. He may have been confident that Lincoln would ultimately accept black soldiers, or that he could eventually push through Congress or other federal channels means to legitimize his black regiment. If so, such prospects were long-term matters. In the meantime, new soldiers needed tents, weapons, uniforms, and pay. For these material necessities, Lane relied on his force of personality and patronage within the Kansas military system.

The creation of a black regiment drew the attention of ambitious white men in Kansas. Enterprising civilians and open-minded soldiers saw opportunity to strike a blow for freedom, prove the humanity of black Americans, or find a new avenue for military promotion. It also meant that Lane had little trouble finding young and eager leaders for the regiment. His bigger problem was selecting the most suitable individuals to lead a controversial military organization.

New England native Ethan Earle had set to work recruiting fugitive slaves in Kansas before Lane's appointment as recruiting commissioner. Dedicated to abolitionist principles, he had approached General James Blunt in July about enlisting black soldiers. When Blunt declared that he "would as willingly have them as any other troops," Earle clarified that the men he wished to recruit would be used as soldiers, not simply as laborers. "Yes," Blunt replied, "and I will fight with them Side by Side of my white troops."[32] Happy with this assurance, Earle had awaited Lane's arrival in Leavenworth to join him in establishing the regiment. When the senator arrived by boat on a Saturday morning, Earle was waiting at the dock. Managing to speak to Lane only briefly, Earle raised the matter of black military service. He spoke of his association with a free black businessman, William Matthews, who was a leader in the local black population, and expressed their desire to begin recruiting immediately. They would not, and could not, start such an operation around Leavenworth without official backing and needed Lane to arrange the necessary orders for a military camp. Lane listened to Earle's pleas and asked him to come back on Monday to work out the details, citing other pressing matters that required his attention. Frustrated with the delay in obtaining written sanction, Earle was nonetheless encouraged when the senator urge him to "go right to work and get your men together."[33]

Politicians and "office lackeys" flooded Lane's office, preventing Earle from seeing him that Monday. The following day, as he waited for his chance to grab the senator from the throngs of people, Earle learned that arrangements for a black regiment had already gotten under way without him or Matthews. Frustrated, he forced his way into Lane's office and demanded an explanation. Getting the regiment up and going "was damned expedient," Lane responded. Though Earle had come to see the project as his own, Lane understood the need to incorporate a broad recruiting campaign and had authorized officers to begin enlisting black men at various points across the state. He offered Earle a recruiting commission and said he could raise his own company. Earle felt insulted, thinking he himself deserved overall command of the regiment. Nonetheless, the offer meant a legitimate role within a black unit. Then Earle asked whether his black colleague, Matthews, would receive a commission. Lane responded that Matthews would not because no black man would hold a command in the regiment. That was too much for Earle. He threatened to quit the project if Matthews could not have an office, declaring that his influence among the local black population was invaluable.[34]

Lane was already violating War Department instructions by enlisting black soldiers. Commissioning a black officer exceeded even Lane's bloated interpretation of his authority and likely violated his still-conservative social views. Yet in the face of Earle's threats to abandon the plan and turn the Leavenworth black population against it, Lane offered a conciliatory position. Matthews could have an office in the commissary or quartermaster departments. In that way, a black man might hold a commission but not have command in the field. Earle rejected the offer. He again threatened to leave if Matthews was not given authority to raise a company and serve over it. Realizing the sincerity of Earle's threats, Lane acquiesced. He wrote an order giving Matthews "permission to raise one company of free Colored men for the 1st Kansas Colored Volunteers to be officered by men of Colour." The order clarified that "all Commanders of Companies and Battalions in said Regiment will regard the same as regularly officered and will issue rations and Equipments accordingly."[35]

Earle later claimed that the regiment's formation was hindered by Lane's resistance to commission black officers. Writing in 1873, he declared that Lane's "hesitation created such distrust among the colored men that it took nine months to complete the Regiment, and then only by pressing men in, where as had it been permitted to have gone along as first started by Mr. Mat[t]hews and myself it could, without any doubt, have been completed within Sixty days."[36] Though perhaps correct in part, Earle's criticism was also simplistic and self-serving. Problems that hampered the organization dealt with matters largely beyond Lane's or anyone else's control.

Shortly after Earle's meeting with Lane, Matthews and a small group of prominent free black men from Leavenworth approached the senator for more information about the regiment. They asked about the terms of service for black volunteers. Lane explained that for their service, all black soldiers and their families would be guaranteed freedom by the U.S. government. However, according to Congress, black soldiers would be paid ten dollars per month—three dollars less than white soldiers. On hearing this news, most of the men refused to back the effort. Only Matthews and a man named Patrick H. Minor expressed a willingness to join the regiment.[37]

The amount of pay was not Lane's decision. The Militia Act set the rate, which remained the standard for all black Union soldiers until the last year of the war. Black regiments and their white officers across the North protested; some even boycotted all payment until the federal government equalized pay rates.[38] But that matter was truly out of Lane's hands.

Earle was only one of the ambitious men eyeing command of the black regiment. As news spread of Lane's effort to recruit blacks, a number of prominent individuals voiced their hope, even expectation, of leading the regiment. James Montgomery, a militant abolitionist made infamous through his campaigns against proslavery Kansans during the territorial conflict, appealed to Governor Charles Robinson for command: "Your Excellency is aware that a regiment of Col[ore]d men is being formed at Mound City. These men are nearly or quite unanimous in their preference for me as their Colonel."[39] Montgomery was particularly suspicious of another notable figure— Charles Jennison. Also a radical abolitionist, Jennison had supported John Brown's ruthless war against slavery and had helped lynch a proslavery man accused in Kansas of returning fugitive slaves to Missouri. His fame had grown as a lieutenant colonel in the Seventh Kansas Cavalry, the regiment that epitomized the term "jayhawker." Jennison's zeal to punish slaveholding interests often took the form of plunder and destruction, and many, even in Kansas, saw him as little more than a criminal. By spring 1862, Jennison had temporarily retired from military service. The formation of the black regiment caught his eye, and he toured the state pushing the formation of the regiment while beating the war drum generally.[40]

"Now, Governor," Montgomery warned Robinson, "allow me to say, that with my *personal* knowledge of Jennison, I cannot imagine any greater calamity that could befall the blacks than the appointment of Jennison to command them." Vainly, he declared himself to be the favorite among those who "wish to see the Negro elevated instead of being made a thief and a pest to society." Montgomery assured the governor that "there is, perhaps, no person, living, who could inspire the blacks with the same amount of courage and confidence, as I can; or who can so easily mould them to honor or dishonor."[41]

George H. Hoyt, another member of the Seventh Kansas Cavalry, also believed he was in line for an office in the regiment. Writing to prominent antislavery man George L. Stearns on August 13, Hoyt explained that the "First Regiment of Colored Kansans" was nearly organized, with arms and equipment. He expressed his confidence that Jennison would command a black brigade, while he expected to fill the lieutenant colonel position.[42] Hoyt, along with Jennison, held meetings at Osawatomie and Mound City promoting the recruitment and application of black soldiers.[43]

In the midst of this posturing, Lane chose two other officers to lead the young regiment. Captains James M. Williams and Henry C. Seaman had both served in the Fifth Kansas Cavalry, a regiment that had played an important role in the Kansas Brigade and its ventures into Missouri. Both men were recognized abolitionists concerned with the plight of slaves. And both appear to have eschewed the political posturing of the other aspiring officers. Lane ordered the two captains to take charge of the regiment's recruitment and organization. Williams traveled to Leavenworth to recruit black volunteers in the state north of the Kansas River. Seaman oversaw recruitment in the southern portion of the state, centered at Mound City. In turn, they selected recruiting officers, who were appointed second lieutenants, to fan across the various counties and communities to draw in volunteers.[44]

Recruiters began advertising. The *Leavenworth Daily Conservative* ran side-by-side, apparently competing, announcements.

Ethan Earle sponsored one advertisement, which notified able-bodied black men between eighteen and forty-five years of age that they "can now have an opportunity of voluntarily enrolling their names in this regiment." Captain Williams's posting called for one thousand black volunteers to help put down the "Slaveholder's Rebellion." Each enlisted man would receive the legal wage of ten dollars per month along with their uniforms and sustenance. Williams's publication emphasized that recruits would be accepted as regular federal soldiers and promised certificates of freedom for themselves and their families.[45]

The promise of freedom came from Lane's interpretation of Congress's amendment to the 1795 Militia Act. In his General Orders Number 3, Lane included an awkwardly worded excerpt from the militia act amendment which declared that

> when any man or boy of African descent, who by the laws of any State shall owe service or labor to any person who during the present rebellion has levied war or has borne arms against the United States, or adhered to their enemies by giving them aid and comfort shall render any such service as is provided for in this act, he, his mother, and his wife and children, shall forever thereafter be free, any law, usage or custom whatsoever to the contrary, notwithstanding: *Provided,* That the mother, wife and children of such man or boy of African descent shall not be made free by the operation of this act except where such mother, wife or children, owe service or labor to some person, who during the present rebellion, has borne arms against the United States, or adhered to their enemies by giving them aid and comfort.[46]

In short, slaves of Rebel masters could secure their freedom and that of their immediate families through service to the U.S. government.

The promise of freedom was a powerful incentive. The move struck a blow against the rebellion by weakening the labor force of the Confederacy and strengthening that of the Union. It was a win-win situation for pragmatic Unionists like Lane and furthered, in part, the aims of even the most radical abolitionists.

CHAPTER 4

RECRUITMENT

The contraband regiment is filling up finely.

W ith capable officers, and at least the appearance of federal approval, recruitment began in earnest. The *Leavenworth Daily Conservative* reported on August 6, 1862, that fifty men from that city had enlisted the first day.[1] Another fifty recruits were organized around Fort Scott.[2] Some white Kansans observed the enthusiastic recruits with curiosity. When a group of black refugees passed into Leavenworth to enlist, the *Daily Times* described them as "looking as though each had just been presented with a new watch. . . . Real plantation hands they were, and 'mighty glad to get out o' de wilderness.'"[3]

Most recruits were drawn from the large population of fugitive slaves seeking refuge near Kansas border towns. Captain Henry Seaman put together one company near Mound City in little more than a week. "A second company is well on the way," a correspondent wrote to the *Leavenworth Daily Conservative*, "and a third will probably be filled this week by those brought in from the stations at Fort Scott, Osawatomie, Paola and Garnett." The writer displayed total confidence in the recruits, noting that "the men here organized, for muscle, endurance and all that go to make efficient soldiers, are not excelled by the white soldiers of any Kansas regiment."[4]

A white Kansas soldier wrote to the *Fort Scott Bulletin* of how "scores of grinning contrabands may be seen on every upward bound train." Word of the Confiscation Act spread throughout areas occupied by Union forces, and, the writer continued, "the panting fugitives steal their way to the nearest military post, and inquire for the man that gives 'passes,' and then fly as fast as steam can carry them, to perform the labor necessarily abandoned by the brave men of the North who have enlisted to fight for the old flag."[5] The refugees performed mostly manual labor and farming duties within northern

Kansas communities. But with the recruitment for the First Kansas Colored Infantry, some runaway slaves saw an opportunity to fight for freedom in the Union army.

Most of the recruits had been born into a life of perpetual servitude. Some were the property of a single master. Patsy, for example, was the slave of Philip Dowell. Her son George Duvall, from birth until his service in Company K of the First Kansas Colored Infantry, was the legal property of Dowell.[6] Other recruits had changed owners through marriage, inheritance, and, of course, sale. In Mason County, Kentucky, in 1842, Samuel Pepper purchased a slave from his grandfather's estate, "the negro being only a child about four years old." Two years later, Pepper moved to Platte County, Missouri, bringing along the young Johnson Cooper. On August 8, 1862, the six-foot-tall, twenty-five-year-old farmhand was in Kansas and a new member of Company D.[7]

Eight First Kansas Colored Infantry soldiers carried the name George Washington. One of them was born in 1840, the property of Daniel Jones of Virginia. As a young boy Washington was given to Margaret A. Jones, his master's daughter, as a wedding present. Jones, her new husband, and their slaves moved to Platte County, Missouri, to begin a farming operation near the frontier. When Jones's husband died in 1848, she remarried and Washington became the property of Jesse Miller. Sometime in early 1862 Washington sneaked away from the homestead, risking his life to reach freedom. Evading slave patrols and suffering through the unforgiving prairie weather, Washington traveled through Parkville, Missouri, across the Missouri River, and into Quindaro, Kansas. Within weeks he learned that black men were enlisting in Leavenworth and he joined Company B.[8] Dozens of men like Washington appeared before recruiting officers of the First Kansas Colored Infantry. Born into bondage and without education, rights, or hope of freedom before the war, they volunteered for military service in Kansas to secure liberty for themselves and their family, to earn wages and respect as soldiers, and to demand a role in changing America.

William Gordon, a farmhand from Marshall, Missouri, failed in his first attempt to escape his master, Joseph F. Fields, with brutal consequences. "A short time before I came over here to enlist I ran away and was caught at Boonville, Mo., placed in jail and my master came after me," Gordon recalled after the war. "He took me back home and his half brother (Miles B. Robinson) had me stripped and whipped until my back bled. Then he had my own brother wash my back with salt and water." The torturous punishment failed to quell Gordon's desire for freedom. Once recovered, he risked his life again to reach Kansas. This next escape attempt succeeded. Gordon joined Company E and served through the rest of the war.[9]

Since 1855, Joseph Bowers and Dock Williams were slaves to related masters who lived a mile apart near Lexington, Missouri. In the wake of Union commander Colonel James Mulligan's defeat by Major General Sterling Price at Lexington in September 1861, Bowers and Williams decided to escape into Kansas. Traveling alone Bowers fled to Leavenworth, Williams to Lawrence. In April 1862 they rejoined at Lawrence, and in August they enrolled together in the black Kansas unit.[10]

Other men escaped separately and were reunited with friends after entering the regiment. Henry Davis had been born a slave in Tennessee, then was sold and separated from his family and carried west into Missouri "when I was still a child—too young to remember anything about it." He passed into the hands of another owner before being sold to Dr. Magnus Tate, near Lexington, Missouri. Davis came to know Harrison Miller, a slave on a nearby farm. "The people who owned us lived close neighbors," Miller recalled years later, "and we were together a great deal for six years before the war." The two young men escaped separately, but had the same destination. Miller explained that he and Davis "enlisted in the same company. I three weeks before he came." Once in camp, Davis encountered Phillip Porter, whom he had also known in Lexington, and learned that at least three other men in the company were from the same area in Missouri.[11] White units during the Civil War often came from single communities, with close relatives, neighbors, and friends fighting side by side. The First Kansas Colored Infantry, on the other hand, saw little prewar connection among its troops. Except for a few sets of brothers—such as Company E's David and Joseph Sanders, escaped slaves from a half-Cherokee owner in Indian Territory—and coincidental meetings among slaves from neighboring masters, the recruits were largely strangers in camp.[12]

Usually those who escaped to Kansas took great care to conceal their plans to run away. Rare were men like Spencer Payne from Howard County, Missouri, who took a chance to say goodbye to a master before going on the run. "I often heard my husband speak of 'Old Lady Reynolds,'" Ester Payne recalled of Spencer, whom she

married after the war. "I remember he told me that he was washing this day, and the old lady was quilting. When he got through
with the wash he ran up the porch and looked in the window, and
said in a whisper, 'Good bye Miss, I am through.' He then ran off
to Kansas—Leavenworth I think—and joined the army."[13] Payne
served in Company D.

These men who risked so much for freedom often had little
when they appeared before the recruiters. Slavery had denied them
wages, property, and sometimes even a surname. Lacking a family
name, slaves generally took that of their master. Friends of Private
Nelson Ross, Company E, told a pension official after the war that
"Nelson was called Nelson Ross because he belonged to Lewis Ross
and it was the custom of the colored people to call themselves by
the name of the family to which they belonged."[14] Jeremiah Fielding
of Company A had been owned by Sanford Fielding.[15] Private Allen
Minor of Company H had been born a slave to the family of J. H.
Minor in Buchanan County, Missouri.[16] And when a young fugitive slave with the first name of Jackson appeared before George J.
Martin's company of recruits in Atchison in mid-August, he looked
back to Missouri for his identity. "I intended to take the name of my
master Donnell but when I gave it at enlistment they seemed to get
it written Donald," he recalled, "hence have since during my army
service answered to the name Donald."[17] Private Jackson Donald
served in Company B throughout the war.

For those former slaves who knew their family lineage, enlist-
ment offered a chance to control their identity. Corporal Henry
Crittenden of Company F, who had been the slave of Dr. Benjamin
Long in Platte County, Missouri, later explained, "I was called Harry
Long before I enlisted but my right name was Henry Crittenden.
That is, my father's name was Crittenden but slaves were always
called by their master's name. I enlisted under my right name and
after the war I took my right name, my father's name."[18]

Some enlistees adopted a new name to conceal their where-
abouts, lest their former masters attempt to reclaim them. Freeling
Lawson, born into slavery in Kentucky, had traveled to Kansas
Territory with his master around 1855, making him one of the few
First Kansas Colored Infantry veterans with prewar Kansas ties.
Sold to a new owner in St. Joseph, Missouri, a year later, Lawson
escaped bondage after the start of the Civil War by crossing the fro-
zen Missouri River back into Kansas. "I took the name of Henry

Lawson when I ran away from Mr. Craig," he later explained, "and I hired out to George Martin at Atchison under that name and he only knew me by that name." Indeed, when George Martin took command as a company officer in the First Kansas Colored Infantry, Lawson followed and, as he later explained, "gave them the name of my father when I enlisted as I had run away."[19]

Silas Hughes of Company B was in fact named James W. Wells. "My father, George Wells, was then living in Buchanan County, Missouri," he later explained to a pension officer.

> Just prior to my enlistment I was living in Atchison County, Kansas. I wanted to enter the army but found that if I did so under my true name, James W. Wells, my father might hear of my enlistment and take steps to take me out of the army. So in order that my father might not hear that I had enlisted, I decided upon the plan of concealing the fact of my enlistment from him by assuming the name of Silas Hughes. I had known a man by that name in my boyhood and happened to think of him when deciding upon a name which I would enlist.[20]

The fact that George Wells had the ability, and desire, to travel from Missouri and interfere with his enlistment suggests that Private Hughes's father was white.

Many recruits did not know their date of birth. Regimental officers recorded a best guess of a soldier's age based on appearance, or from the recruit's estimation. Sometimes these former slaves gave clues to officials by describing earliest memories or reckoning their age during key events. Private John Brown of Company D recalled that he saw "Mexican Soldiers as they came from the Mexican War after being discharged," and that he was sixteen years old when a famous namesake, abolitionist John Brown in Kansas, "was having his troubles with the Border Ruffians," around 1856. Private Brown also related that "his parents many times told him that he was born in the same year that William Henry Harrison was elected to the Presidency which was in 1840."[21] A few men relied on comments from their previous owners, like Willis Yaunt, who recalled, "My Master told me in Feb 1851 that I was Sixteen Years old."[22]

Only a few men from the First Kansas Colored Infantry had formally recorded births. Corporal William Smith's June 1839 birth had been inscribed in a family Bible.[23] Private Jordan Wood's birth date had also been recorded in a Bible, copied by his master's daughter from a plantation recordbook. Wood did not have the information when he joined the regiment. "I didn't know my age when I went in the army," he later explained. He learned his true age only after the war, and directly from his former master's daughter, as the Bible she had used to record the information had been destroyed.[24]

The men came into recruitment camps in varying states of condition and appearance. One tall, well-dressed black man walked into Ethan Earle's office in Leavenworth to volunteer. He introduced himself as Clement Johnson, a forty-seven-year-old Methodist preacher and slave from Missouri. Seemingly well established given his status as a slave, he nonetheless fled to Kansas, risking the dangerous journey for the love of his family. Johnson told Earle that his wife and daughter were slaves in Tennessee. By joining the First Kansas Colored Volunteers, he hoped to free them. Earle eagerly accepted his service. Preachers were highly regarded leaders in slave culture. Johnson could neither read nor write, but, Earle recalled, "his language in his religious service was as good as most educated men, particularly at the burial of the dead." Such a commanding voice and presence made him more than qualified for the role of a noncommissioned officer. Earle offered him the highest enlisted position in the company and promised that if the regiment "should go down as far as Tennessee, if that State was occupied by our troops," he would do what he could to find Johnson's family. With that, Johnson enlisted, and soon he wore the rank of first sergeant.[25]

Some enlistees were aggressively recruited from Missouri. These actions sparked an outrage in Washington. One Unionist Missourian wrote to Abraham Lincoln, complaining that "about 15 days ago some 15 persons from the State of Kansas . . . came into the county of Clay . . . to 'recruit negroes for General Lane's negro brigade.'" The men raided local Missouri farms, where "they took forcible possession of some 25 negro men and about 40 horses from persons indiscriminately, and started to cross the Missouri River with them over into Kansas." A detachment of the Missouri State Militia set off in pursuit, intending to use deadly force if necessary to reclaim the stolen property. The Missourians captured eight of the Kansans and returned all of the slaves and horses to their owners.[26] Other recruiters tried more surreptitious means of drawing men from Missouri. "I purchased a boat, went down the Missouri River fifteen or twenty miles," Earle recalled after the war. "I spent several days and nights in communicating with the colored men of M[iss]o[uri], and finding a

Safe and convenient place for crossing such as wished to come across to Kansas." He was aided by a black preacher who "was supposed by the Slave holders to be sufficiently loyal to them." Like countless slaves in the South, during the Civil War and before, this brave black man presented a facade of obedience and happiness to lull slave owners into a false sense of security.[27] Granted extended liberty by his trusting owner to travel around the county and visit local markets, including one in Leavenworth, the preacher proved a valuable link between Earle and Missouri slaves. "Every Sunday he had a large congregation and communicated to his confidential ones the plans of escape from Missouri, and place of crossing the River, and kept them informed of any changes made." He and Earle devised a code to aid in the exodus. Refugee slaves were given small slips of paper with the letter "F"—a seemingly nondescript item that held no meaning to the uninformed. In fact, Earle claimed, "F" represented the letter of his company, and men who carried the code during the trek across the border into Kansas were led to Earle's unit.[28] This operation was so successful that after less than a month of recruiting, one newspaper editor proclaimed that "Jackson and Platte counties must be pretty well cleaned out [of slaves] by this time."[29]

Recruiters looked to whites for help as well. The *White Cloud Kansas Chief* printed a small news item that "W. H. Jones, of Hiawatha, is recruiting for the contraband regiment, and requests us to announce that he is paying two dollars per head for buck niggers— that is, for every negro man brought over from Missouri, he will pay two dollars to the person bringing him across."[30]

Though Kansas had a growing African American population, not all able-bodied black men were ready to enlist. When recruitment slowed, some officials may have been persuaded to take more aggressive means. Having successfully introduced the idea of black soldiers to an unsure white population, Senator James Lane tried a new approach in early August. Prefacing his words with an obligatory, yet no doubt sincere, nod to white supremacy—"Well I have always believed that a decent white man was as good as any nigger"—Lane told a Leavenworth audience that "the negroes are mistaken if they think white men can fight for them while they stay at home." This was an ingenious tactic for pandering to stubborn white critics. It thrust military service on the shoulders of the black man, placing a radical measure under the guise of conservatism. Lane was not lying. This position revealed part of his true interest in black military

service: it was a tool to protect Kansas and the Union, not a humanitarian measure. Nonetheless, Lane had spent months preparing
white Americans for this point. He announced to the Leavenworth
crowd, in a gesture to black Americans, "We have opened the path-
way. We don't [want] to threaten, but we have been saying that you
would fight, and if you won't fight we will make you."[31]
Apparently some men were willing to make good on that threat.
The *White Cloud Kansas Chief* reported:

> We are told that every negro in the State is being forced into the
> service. Able-bodied white man have about all gone to the war, and
> farmers were compelled to employ negro laborers. But these men
> are being forced away to enter the service. A farmer informs us that
> a recruiting officer solicited a negro whom he had employed, to
> volunteer, but the negro replied that he did not want to. The officer
> told him he would make him do so, and the next day sent two men,
> who forcibly took the negro away to Leavenworth.[32]

Ethan Earle accused Captain James M. Williams of paying a
man to hustle slaves across the Missouri River to his camp. "Many
slaves came into camp who had brought property, horses, mules,
teams, carriages, &c.," Earle claimed. "Those were taken from them
and then put into some company, whether they wished to enlist or
not." Not surprisingly, he continued, "men thus located and forced
into the Regiment would desert the first chance they had." Earle
rejected such recruiting tactics and promised his recruits "good
treatment, good food and rations and clothing and freedom for themselves and families, when the war ended, and pay for their services
and further, that I would never Command, or request them to go
any further than I would lead them and enlisted under these promises to their honor." He declared that he "made no promises that I
did not intend to fulfill," and bragged that "I can say, that not one
ever deserted me." (In fact, Company F did experience desertions.
At least thirty men from Company F recruited between August and
October 1862 were no longer with the regiment by January 1863,
and six men deserted in the spring of 1863.)[33]
Recruitment efforts for the black Kansas regiment extended
even beyond Missouri. Some enterprising agents may have traveled as far as Pennsylvania. "Persons calling themselves recruiting
officers for Genl James Lanes Colored Regiments are putting out
hand bills and calling meetings of colored men offering the same

inducements to enlist as are granted White soldiers," Richard Dodge
of Harrisburg informed federal officials. "This is producing the worst
effect on Enlistment of Whites; cannot it be stopped at once?"[34]
Regardless, these efforts paid off to some degree, for John Rutherford
and Jeremiah Hall, both privates in Company D, listed Pennsylvania
as their residence on company rolls. At least six enlisted men came
from other Northern states. George Smith and Dabney Snyder of
Company A and Madison Craton of Company D claimed Illinois residency. Henry Locherman, a nineteen-year-old enlistee in Company
A, had been a mason in Cleveland, Ohio. And two Company B men,
James Campbell and William Generals, were from Indiana. Campbell
was among the most distinctive volunteers—at four feet three inches
tall, he had been a racehorse jockey.[35]

According to available records, nearly 40 percent of the men
who joined the regiment from August to the end of 1862 listed
Missouri as their place of residence.[36] They were from Independence,
Lexington, Lafayette, Pleasantville, St. Louis, and other cities. They
came from farms in Clay, Howard, Buchanan, Randolph, Platte,
Morgan, Henry, and other counties. After Missouri, most recruits
that fall claimed Kentucky as their home state. It is not known how
many traveled directly from Kentucky to Kansas on their own or
had been brought to Missouri by their owners. According to available records, 34 percent of the men who joined the regiment in 1862
identified with Kentucky. At least thirty men claimed Virginia residency, while six were natives of Tennessee. Surprisingly, regimental
records of recruits in 1862 show only sixteen volunteers from Indian
Territory to the south of Kansas and two from Arkansas. Those
numbers would change drastically in the months and years to come,
as the regiment replenished its ranks in the field. In the meantime,
a significant portion of the South was represented within the ranks
of the First Kansas Colored—Virginia, Tennessee, Arkansas, North
Carolina, South Carolina, Alabama, and Mississippi. By the end of
1862 the regiment consisted of recruits from at least fifteen different
states and Indian Territory.[37]

An overwhelming majority of recruits had been slaves at the
beginning of the war. Only Company B's records provide a somewhat complete account of whether its men were slave or free before
enlistment. Of the forty-one soldiers whose preservice status is written on the company roll, only two were listed as free. Most other
companies recorded this information haphazardly or not at all.[38]

As for occupation, most men declared themselves farmers or laborers. A popular image of antebellum Southern slavery includes large plantations with dozens, even hundreds, of black field hands gathering cotton under the watchful eyes of a whip-carrying white overseer. This plantation slave system existed primarily in the Deep South. In the Upper South, which included the Border States, most slaves lived and worked on small farms. In Missouri in 1860, around one in eight adult white males owned slaves. Seventy-five percent of those slave owners had fewer than five slaves. At least 540 Missouri slave owners held twenty or more, while only thirty-eight qualified as wealthy planters with fifty or more slaves.[39]

White Kansans voiced a variety of opinions about Lane's plans for black military service. Abolitionists rejoiced at the thought of breaking the chains of bondage. "But for our successful struggle in Kansas the nation would never have been in the throes of deliverance from the monster slavery, as she is today, instead of at the chains would have been riveted for another century at least, not only upon the blacks of the South but upon the whites of the North," Lawrence resident E. B. Whitman wrote to George Stearns. He declared that he and his fellow countrymen "may furnish in the agony but better so than the living death that was being prepared for us. But I do not so expect, when Pharaoh shall let my people go, as 'Thus Saith the Lord.'—then the day of deliverance will begin to dawn." He believed it fitting that Kansas was the first to let black men strike a blow: "The experiment of using the escaped slaves, at last, not only at the spade but with the musket will I am confident be tried *here in Kansas* under some form or other. Already we have organized or nearly so, ten companies of 'Contrabands' and it is expected that two entire regiments will soon be in the field."[40]

Sol Miller, the editor of the *White Cloud Kansas Chief*, supported Lane's war against secessionists and saw the conflict as a moralistic cleansing of the nation: "The Lord has determined that Negro Slavery shall cease to exist in America; and the sooner that is wiped out, the sooner the war will end." Miller celebrated the prospect of black soldiers making conservative whites and secessionist sympathizers uncomfortable. He noted the adoption of "a practice at Leavenworth, which will set hard on the Negrophobists. Every traitor and traitor sympathizer who is now arrested, is taken to the camp of the colored regiment, near that city, and placed under a guard of negroes."[41]

Many whites adopted Lane's practical approach to black military service. "I cannot understand why negro volunteers are refused while whites are to be drafted," admitted Kansas settler Samuel Reader to his brother that August. "I consider myself a philanthropist in regard to African Slaves, still I do not carry this so far as to wish to see men of my own Race dragged from home and business which urgently requires their presence, when these same slaves ought & are willing to fight for their freedom. I wish to see this, the last resort as it is considered, adopted immediately." Reader professed his frustration with federal officials who resisted the effort: "Old Abe seems opposed to this policy and it don't make me feel very friendly towards him."[42]

Still, some Kansans cared little how black men were used in the war. "The contraband population are very much exercised at the measures taken to render them of use," the *Leavenworth Daily Times* read in late August. "Every able bodied white man has to do military duty, and like Jim Lane, our regard for that class is not sufficiently high to urge their exemption. The militia companies on duty at the Fort are each entitled to fifteen for servants and cooks."[43]

"We confess we have never been a personal admirer of Gen. Lane or his policy of arming negroes," declared Kansas City's *Daily Journal of Commerce.* The paper's editors had opposed his previous raids into Missouri, noting that "we have heretofore stood for the right of Missourians against what we conceived to be the unjust policy of Lane & Co. towards them." But, the editors continued, the prolonged conflict and unwillingness of Missourians to take care of Confederates within their own borders had changed minds. "We now go for employing everybody that will destroy bushwhackers and those who favor them, even Negroes, Indians, and Jim Lane."[44]

Naturally, black recruitment drew criticism from conservative whites across Kansas. "Gen. Lane is still going on with the work of organizing two Colored Regiments, notwithstanding the refusal of the President to accept black soldiers," complained the editor of the *Fort Scott Bulletin.* "Last Tuesday, about fifty recruits were raised here.—They have been taken to Mound City. We are heartily glad to be rid of them."[45] Some criticism centered on a distrust of Lane rather than a sincere objection to the military's use of black men. In August the *Manhattan Express* had mocked President Lincoln for holding a "Kentucky"—or conservative—position on the race question during the war: "A particular shade of cuticular [sic] deposit is a prime qualification, in the estimation of our critically discriminating Government, to fight the traitorous hounds of Jeff. Davis. It is perfectly legitimate to kill the Rebels, but it must be done according to the fine discriminating sensitive taste which prejudice, and caste, and Kentucky may prescribe."[46] A month later, the newspaper turned against Lane for his stated intentions to raise black soldiers. The editors reported finding "a letter from the War Department in Washington to Gov. Robinson, while in Topeka which throws a little light on the extent of Lane's authority, besides demonstrating very forcibly his veracity as a public man." The editor found that "Lane has received no authority to raise Negro regiments, and that none would be received by the Department. That officers appointed to command Negro regiments would not be commissioned, or receive a dollar of pay,—That Gen. Lane had no authority to commission any officer of the new regiments; and that he was not authorized to take command of the new levies now being raised, and possessed no authority beyond simply recruiting for the United States service." The editors asked rhetorically why Lane would make such claims. The answer, they reported, could be found in a certain event: "It is very significant that these statements were made throughout the State, just on the eve of a general State election! It might possibly have been of importance, in view of the pending elections, to create an impression that the 'Grim Chieftain' had abundant military patronage to bestow on the obedient ones."[47]

Grumblings about Lane concerned some of the regiment's supporters. "These are times when men should avoid mingling in partizan [sic] discussions to the detriment of the government, and whether Gen. Lane or some other person has authority to organize regiments makes little difference so far as principle is involved," pleaded a letter writer under the moniker "Union" to the Lawrence Republican. All those in favor of the Union wanted victory over secession, the author continued, "and if that can be more effectually accomplished under the charge of Gen. Lane than any other Kansas man we are unable to see any valid reason why the War Department has not acted wisely by vesting him with the requisite authority."[48]

Some opposition was more problematic. Officials in Leavenworth undermined the formation of the regiment. A provost marshal played on disquiet in the ranks by telling black recruits that they were not soldiers and granting passes to travel home for an unlimited period of time. When that failed to dissolve the unit, the provost marshal and twenty men physically entered the camp and tried to break it up. Around the same time, the conflict over command erupted into open hostility. Charles Jennison and George Hoyt found that their efforts to promote black service failed to result in senior commissions. They abandoned the project and, according to Adjutant Richard Hinton, "at least indirectly exerted themselves to destroy its efficiency."[49]

Captain Williams later identified four types of resistance to the formation of the black regiment in Kansas. The first came from Southern sympathizers. The second arose from "an intolerant prejudice against the colored race which would deny them the honorable position in society to which every soldier is entitled even though he gained that position at the risk of his head in the cause of the nation which at that time could ill afford to refuse genuine sympathy and support from any quarter." The third group Williams described consisted of "genuine loyalists" who believed the War Department would ultimately reject Lane's unauthorized endeavor and thus saw the operation as a waste of federal energy and funds, as well as a disservice to the black recruits. Lastly, Williams found a "large class who believed that the negro race did not possess necessary qualifications to make efficient soldiers, and consequently [believed] the experiment would result in defeat and disaster."[50]

Kansas cavalryman John Stearns echoed Williams's observations, noting that some resistance to the regiment "came as to be expected from those whose sympathies were with the South," and "some from those whose prejudices were so strong against the Negroes that they were unwilling that they should be utilized in any way in the work of putting down the Rebellion and some from those who feared and believed that it would be impossible to make effective soldiers of them." Stearns saw this prejudice firsthand when white federal soldiers encountered Seaman's recruits outside Fort Scott. Congregating at a hotel, "the officers in charge of the regulars were very violent in their denunciations of the blacks declaring that it would be a disgrace to wear the uniform of an American soldier if the Government was going to put it on the backs of a lot of 'niggers.'" The officers placed a military guard around a well to prevent Seaman's recruits from drawing their drinking water. "This was a little more than Capt. Seaman was willing to quietly submit to," Stearns explained, "so he ordered a cordon of guards to be placed around his camp which he made to include four or [fi]ve blocks on

Main street and adjoining thereto with orders not to let any of the regulars pass in or out without a pass." Unsurprisingly, tensions mounted, especially when black soldiers arrested a number of the white soldiers trying to run past them into town. Seaman and his black soldiers stood their ground. Eventually the two sides agreed to remove their guard posts. The episode did little to endear the First Kansas Colored Infantry to its white counterparts, although the stubbornness and discipline of the black troops earned some respect among observers.[51]

If some white Kansans eyed Lane's black soldiers warily, white Missourians frantically objected. Concerned Missouri citizens along the border pressed their Unionist governor, Hamilton Gamble, for help in defending against invasion by their former slaves. According to Richard Hinton, residents near Kansas City requested muskets for their local militia for this purpose. "It must be remembered that the request of these *loyal* gentlemen was intended for the use of a county (Jackson) where, at least six-tenths of the inhabitants are rebels or sympathizers," Hinton told the *New York Times*, "where certainly not more than two-tenths are unconditional Union, and the loyalty of the remainder very dubious." Hinton reported that the governor initially assured his citizens that there was no danger from Lane's black regiment, but repeated pressure, including that from influential state officials, finally prompted Gamble to give in to some of their demands. "Should these Springfield guns find their way to Jackson County," Hinton grimly concluded, "no one need doubt that it will not be long before they are in the hands of the active enemies of the Union."[52]

Apparently Gamble took the threat seriously. The governor wrote to President Lincoln "that organizations of negroes are forming in Kansas armed and equipped as soldiers of the United States, for the purpose of entering this state and committing depredations here." He believed this to be an illegal move designed by Lane and Jennison to carry out their "own ideas of *supporting the Union*"— a veiled reference to plunder and vengeance against Missourians. If the black regiment marched into Missouri, Gamble warned, "it will be with the deepest regret that I shall find myself obliged to give to the people of Kansas a taste of the evils of war in their own territory." He had intelligence that Confederate forces from Arkansas, Texas, and Louisiana planned an invasion of Missouri in the near future. The military response to an incursion by an illegal band of black recruits would only weaken Missouri's ability to meet this impending threat. "I appeal to you to save me from the necessity of diverting a portion of my force from this necessary object to the slaying of negro invaders and their associates."[53]

No great battle between Kansas black soldiers and Missouri Unionists occurred. Instead of raiding a neighboring state, the unit's officers struggled to create a respectable military organization among the scattered companies of recruits during the months of August and September 1862. Even basic concerns such as procuring clothing and equipment proved difficult. Military uniforms served a variety of roles for a new regiment. They established the homogeneity necessary to mid-nineteenth-century European-style warfare, which treated the individual fighting man as a peg in a tightly packed, linear machine. Officers worried about the health and well-being of the men. Soldiers needed durable clothing and shoes. The variety and lack of clothing articles among escaped slaves and black refugees streaming into Kansas were especially problematic. Standardized military clothing would go far to give credibility and legitimacy to this neophyte unit.

With minimal federal backing, Williams, Seaman, and the other officers obtained what supplies they could from old and surplus warehouses. Gray wool uniforms were drawn from stores in Leavenworth, sitting unused following General Henry Halleck's directive that soldiers be outfitted in blue.[54] Some of the men, mostly those recruited in the northern part of the state, procured the standard blue jacket and forage caps.[55] The jackets were made from coarse wool designed more for ruggedness than comfort. Those outfitted in gray yearned for the official blue coats worn by the federal armies. Yet soldiers who wore the blue found it a mixed blessing. The deep, dark hue was attractive, but under the prairie sun's rays it was impractical, the color absorbing heat rather than reflecting it. Perhaps the color's single redeeming factor was its ability to hide much of the dirt and sweat soldiers rapidly accumulated during long road marches.

The headgear resembled the kepi—a French-designed military hat similar to a modern baseball cap—except that its flat crown extended much farther forward, to the point that it rested on the small brim above the eyes. The forage cap was not useful outdoor wear. It offered little protection from the elements; sunlight, rain, and snow fell unimpeded onto a man's shoulders. Only the top of the head was guarded. The cap was dark blue and on warm, sunny days trapped heat, exacerbating the discomfort of already overworked soldiers. Nonetheless, both blue articles were standard issue for U.S. military forces in 1862, and presented those black soldiers fortunate to receive them with an aura of legitimacy. "The contraband regiment is filling up finely," the *Leavenworth Daily Times* informed its readers on August 16. "The 'Zouaves' really look well in their blue jackets and regulation caps, and will make as good soldiers here as they do in British colonial garrisons."[56]

The men were issued cumbersome Austrian-made muskets.[57] These weapons were among the thousands imported by a federal government desperate to equip the growing army in the early months of the Civil War. By fall 1862, the guns had been cast aside by white regiments that had since received new Springfield rifles and other modern weapons. Like most infantry muskets of the day, the Austrian guns were muzzleloaders. A soldier loaded each shot by pouring powder and then ramming a musket ball down the barrel from the muzzle. Once the bullet was seated, a cocking hammer was rotated back and a small brass cap containing a combustible agent was placed over a small hollow cone leading to the gunpowder. The soldier then pulled the hammer back to full cock, aimed, and squeezed the trigger. The hammer fell on the cap, causing a shower of sparks to travel into the black powder in the barrel. The resulting explosion projected the bullet out the barrel. This process had been the primary means of loading and firing a shoulder weapon for centuries. Newer technology, including breech-loading and cartridge-firing weaponry, was in the field by late 1862, but not nearly in quantities necessary to outfit the majority of Union soldiers, let alone an unpopular band of free blacks and runaway slaves on the edge of the frontier.

The standard Austrian import was the Lorenz rifle-musket, a generally well-made and satisfactory infantry firearm. Union and Confederate forces imported Lorenz rifles by the tens of thousands. Yet numerous imported Austrian muskets were poorly constructed copies of the Lorenz by local European gunmakers. Others had been high-quality weapons at one point in time, but arrived in the hands of the black volunteers as worn-down vestiges of long-past European conflicts. The reputation of Austrian-made weapons took a further blow with the influx of Consol (or tube-lock) muskets, a weapon much inferior to the Lorenz. Thus Civil War soldiers across the North and South had radically different reviews of the Austrian arms—from great admiration to utter disdain, depending largely on what happened to fall into their hands.

By all accounts, the men of the First Kansas Colored Infantry found themselves holding virtually worthless weapons. They likely carried some of the twenty-five thousand Consol muskets purchased by Major General John C. Frémont in 1861, during his tenure as commander of the Western Department. "On trial of the rifles, not one in five could be discharged without several attempts," remembered Ethan Earle.[58] Adjutant Richard Hinton complained that the Austrian muskets suffered "from constant liability to get out of order."[59] Even when the weapons fired correctly, the shooter found the experience unpleasant. John Stearns, of the Fifth Kansas Cavalry, observed Seaman's battalion during those early weeks and recalled that the weapon was "a short gun with a caliber which made up in width what the gun lacked in length, and in kicking proclivities they were as energetic as the most vicious army mule."[60] An inspection officer summed up the armament situation with the simple comment "Not good."[61]

White Civil War soldiers also suffered from supply problems, particularly in the early months of the conflict. What most white enlistees did not face, though, especially by the summer of 1862, was a denial of combat status. Newly enlisted black soldiers feared they would be used solely for manual labor. Black men and women had served Union armies in noncombat positions since Fort Sumter. These Kansas volunteers wanted action, and they joined on white officers' promises that they would indeed strike a blow for freedom on the field of battle. Their fears were not misplaced, as the man most important to the regiment's creation—James Lane—had advocated issuing a black servant to every white combat soldier.[62] In this way, even shoddy weapons and secondhand clothing initially served an important psychological role. Observers noted the difference in attitude among those black soldiers in uniform. "The camp of colored recruits presents an animated appearance," wrote a correspondent to the *Leavenworth Daily Conservative* about one of the new companies near Mound City. "These boys do not look so gay as the men in Camp Lane, who have the advantage of being uniformed and armed."[63]

When the men in Leavenworth found their Austrian muskets to be virtually worthless, they suspected it was a ploy. Earle remembered

that Williams, in order to keep his men in the ranks, "made a flam-
ing speech saying that they should, when the Regiment was completed and went south, have 'new U.S. Muskets.'"[64] Apparently this
promise allayed the fears well enough to maintain the overall integrity of the companies.

The officers pushed forward, creating a capable and disciplined
army unit. They implemented strict drill schedules to turn the
raw recruits into competent warriors, taught their men the command structure, appointed noncommissioned officers among those
enlisted men showing leadership skills and competence, and generally labored to meet standards of military readiness and decorum.
Many of the officers had had experience in white units before joining this endeavor. Captains Williams and Seaman had served as officers in the Fifth Kansas Cavalry. First Lieutenant Benjamin Jones of
Company A began the war in 1861 as a private in the Sixth Kansas
Volunteers.[65] Daniel McFarland, a lieutenant in Company D, was
a hardened veteran of the Battle of Wilson's Creek. As a private in
the Second Kansas Infantry at that battle in Missouri in September
1861, McFarland suffered a nasty wound. A Confederate bullet
ripped through the muscles, nerves, and tendons of his upper left
arm. The wound crippled him and had forced him out of the service by 1862. Yet he found he could handle the duties of an officer,
and thus brought his experience to the eager black recruits.[66] Many
of the officers were veterans of Bleeding Kansas fighting, including
Joseph Gardner. The abolitionist who battled slave-catchers at his
home in Lawrence to protect runaway slave Napoleon Simpson now
served as a lieutenant in Company F.

Other officers learned military drill alongside their men, receiving instruction from more experienced leaders and through printed
manuals. In this as in other ways, both officers and enlisted men
of the First Kansas Colored Infantry mirrored the majority of their
white regiment counterparts, Union and Confederate. The four
years of Civil War combat saw a peacetime U.S. army in 1860 of
roughly sixteen thousand soldiers—scattered across the continent—
divide along sectional loyalties and balloon into two great militaries
totaling three million men.[67] Such rapid expansion of citizens (and
ex-slaves) into soldiers required countless hours of instruction and
practice all along the military chain of command.

Carefully watched by critical whites, the black soldiers worked
hard during the weeks after recruitment. A correspondent to the

Leavenworth Daily Conservative reported that the camp of black recruits in Mound City "is kept remarkably clean, and good order prevails.—The black boys are doing regular guard duty, superintended by their own noncommissioned officers." The writer explained that "Lieut. Thrasher is in command here, and he together with his assistants are making finely drilled soldiers of the black boys."[68]

Eager to complete the organization of the regiment and to unite his command in the field, Lane ordered the various companies—totaling some four hundred men—to consolidate under a single command at Fort Lincoln in early October. The fort was a small military outpost some twelve miles north of Fort Scott. Constructed under Lane's direction the year before, it was initially intended to be a more secure defensive location should Confederate forces attack and occupy Fort Scott. The move cheered the men. It marked a hopeful beginning to service in the field.

CHAPTER 5

ISLAND MOUND

. . . an answer to the often mooted question of "will they fight."

F amed newspaper editor Horace Greeley wrote to Abraham Lincoln in August 1862, chastising the president for not pursuing a more radical policy against slavery. In his popularly printed letter entitled "The Prayer of Twenty Millions," Greeley told Lincoln that "what an immense majority of the Loyal Millions of your countrymen require of you is a frank, declared, unqualified, ungrudging execution of the laws of the land, more especially of the Confiscation Act."[1] The Second Confiscation Act, passed in July 1862, not only authorized the seizure of slaves from Confederate masters but also declared them "forever free of their servitude."[2] "That Act gives freedom to the slaves of Rebels coming within our lines, or whom those lines may at any time inclose [*sic*]—we ask you to render it due obedience by publicly requiring all your subordinates to recognize and obey it."[3]

Greeley echoed the complaints of James Lane and many other Kansans. "We cannot conquer Ten Millions of People united in solid phalanx against us, powerfully aided by the Northern sympathizers and European allies," the editor wrote Lincoln. "We must have scouts, guides, spies, cooks, teamsters, diggers and choppers from the Blacks of the South, whether we allow them to fight for us or not, or we shall be baffled and repelled."[4]

Within days Lincoln responded with his own open letter to Greeley, also published in Northern newspapers. Characteristically beginning with humility and deference, he called Greeley "an old friend, whose heart I have always supposed to be right." He then laid out, very plainly, his administration's objectives. "I would save the Union," he stated. "I would save it the shortest way under the Constitution." He continued:

> If there be those who would not save the Union, unless they could at the same time save slavery, I do not agree with them. If there be

those who would not save the Union unless they could at the same time destroy slavery, I do not agree with them. My paramount object in this struggle is to save the Union, and is not either to save or to destroy slavery. If I could save the Union without freeing any slave I would do it, and if I could save it by freeing all slaves I would do it; and if I could save it by freeing some and leaving others alone I would also do that. What I do about slavery and the colored race, I do because I believe it helps to save this Union; and what I forbear, I forbear because I do not believe it would help to save the Union. I shall do less whenever I shall believe what I am doing hurts the cause, and I shall do more whenever I shall believe doing more will help the cause. I shall try to correct errors when shown to be errors; and I shall adopt new views so fast as they shall appear to be true views.[5]

"He could not have said anything more satisfactory to the country in general," wrote Henry J. Raymond of the *New York Times*.[6] Raymond wrote in another column the same day, "We have never hitherto seen reason to believe that a decree of emancipation would strengthen the Union army or essentially weaken the rebels; and therefore we have not urged it." But if such a step should become necessary, "we believe the President will take it, and we do not believe he will be coerced into taking it a single day sooner than his own judgment tells him it can be taken with effect, and be made instrumental in preserving the Union."[7]

Some Kansas newspapers expressed frustration with Lincoln. J. W. Roberts, editor of *The Independent*, asked, "Will the President assume the responsibility of prolonging the war to save Slavery, and thereby *needlessly augment the number of the slain?*"[8] *Freedom's Champion* further questioned Lincoln's judgment: "Does the President wish to wait till he is driven from Washington, and till half of the cities of the North are in possession of the enemy, before declaring universal emancipation?" They asked, "What motive can there be for delay?"[9]

His motive for delay was a Union military victory. Before his response to Greeley's letter, Lincoln had concluded that emancipation was necessary to preserve the Union. In late July, during a private meeting with his cabinet, he read his handwritten plan for a proclamation of emancipation and asked for their feedback. He made it clear that he did not wish to debate the merits of an emancipation policy. "I said to the Cabinet that I had resolved upon this step," Lincoln later told Francis Carpenter, a painter who memorialized Lincoln and his cabinet, "but to lay the subject-matter of a proclamation before them."[10] They could offer suggestions, but he had chosen this path.

The cabinet members found nothing particularly novel about the first few paragraphs of the proclamation. One of the passages put teeth behind the Second Confiscation Act—exactly what Greeley had argued for—by officially ordering federal armies to enforce confiscation of Rebel property, including slaves. The following section announced further efforts to implement a gradual emancipation policy. This was not revolutionary, as Lincoln had personally met with representatives from the Border States on the topic.[11]

Then came the most important language in the document, a passage that surprised the cabinet members:

> And, as a fit and necessary military measure for effecting this object, I, as Commander-in-Chief of the Army and Navy of the United States, do order and declare that on the first day of January in the year of Our Lord one thousand, eight hundred and sixty three, all persons held as slaves within any state or states, wherein the constitutional authority of the United States shall not then be practically recognized, submitted to, and maintained, shall then, thenceforward, and forever, be free.[12]

With these few lines Lincoln set in motion an irreversible policy that would eventually overturn a two-hundred-year-old American institution and free four million people. The dry syntax of these lines had none of Lincoln's artistic resonance. The passage seemed stiff and unemotional: it was penned not by Lincoln the poet but by Lincoln the legal scholar. As he wrote to Greeley, what he did in regard to slavery directly reflected what he believed necessary to save the Union. Lincoln knew that this act more than any other from his administration would draw scrutiny, condemnation, and analysis from critics.

The cabinet members sat in silence. Slowly they began to respond, some expressing approval, others caution. Secretary of the Treasury Salmon P. Chase questioned its legality, but was more worried about the Southern black response. In his journal, Chase wrote that he told the president that while he would support the proclamation, he "thought that the measure of Emancipation could be much better and more quietly accomplished by allowing Generals to organize and arm the slaves (thus avoiding depredation and massacre on the one hand, and support to the insurrection on the other) and by directing the Commanders of Departments to proclaim emancipation within their Districts as soon as practicable."[13] Chase expounded on his views to General Benjamin Butler a week later, fearing that slaves would turn against masters and drive the conflict to new and more terrible heights, ultimately drawing sympathy and foreign support for the Confederacy.[14]

Lincoln listened to Chase and the others, but nothing, he later remarked, "was offered that I had not already fully anticipated and settled in my own mind, until Secretary Seward spoke."[15] Secretary of State William H. Seward expressed his approval of the proclamation, but advised the president to withhold it, at least for the time being. "The depression of the public mind, consequent upon our repeated reverses, is so great that I fear the effect of so important a step," he told Lincoln. "It may be viewed as the last measure of an exhausted government, a cry for help," he said; "it would be considered our last *shriek*, on the retreat." Seward recommended that the president wait "until you can give it to the country supported by military success, instead of issuing it, as would be the case now, upon the greatest disasters of the war!" Lincoln agreed to delay the announcement of emancipation, "waiting for a victory."[16]

For weeks his emancipation plan remained secret. Then, in mid-September, word arrived in the capital that Union forces under George McClellan had met and defeated Robert E. Lee's Army of Northern Virginia near Sharpsburg, Maryland. The Battle of Antietam was a limited strategic success for the Union; tactically, it was a draw. Nonetheless, following Lee's stunning successes against McClellan earlier in the year at the gates of Richmond, and his thrashing of John Pope's army at the Battle of Second Manassas in August, Northerners were happy to declare victory by stopping Lee's advance in Maryland. Of all the thirty-five-year-old McClellan's skills, self-promotion surely ranked among his best. "Our victory was complete," he informed his superiors in Washington.[17] To his wife he wrote, "Those in whose judgment I rely tell me that I fought the battle splendidly & that it was a masterpiece of art."[18]

Seizing the moment, on September 22, 1862, Lincoln announced his Preliminary Emancipation Proclamation. It declared that, should the states of the Confederacy continue to rebel, on January 1, 1863, "all persons held as slaves within any state, or designated part of a state, the people whereof shall then be in rebellion against the United States shall be then, thenceforward, and forever free."[19] With these words the president changed the purpose of the war from one limited to preservation of the Union, as Lincoln later explained, to a "new birth of freedom."[20]

"IT HAS COME!" ran a headline in the *Smoky Hill and Republican Union* newspaper in Junction (now Junction City), Kansas. "The death knell to Treason and Slavery has made its appearance in a *pronunciamento* of Freedom by the President," the story continued. "What a brilliant page in history!" Ignoring the restriction of Lincoln's emancipation to areas under Confederate control, the editors claimed that "despotism is at an end—and the traffic in human flesh is henceforth forever dispensed with."[21] Other radicals were more reserved in their praise of the proclamation, due to its dry technicality and endorsement of compensated emancipation. "This declaration of intention is most excellent," wrote the editors of *Freedom's Champion*, "although deferred too long by six months and made operative at too distant a period." They added, "Yet it shows that the President is moving in the right direction, even if but slowly."[22]

The black recruits of the First Kansas Colored Infantry now had evidence that the Lincoln administration was working for their interests. The men who had been drilling for weeks without knowing whether their service would be accepted by the federal government soon received orders from James Lane to report to Fort Lincoln. "So soon as I can see Gen. Blunt I will get an order to Muster in your Officers, Captain enter in the discharge of your duties at once and prove to the country that you are soldiers," Lane instructed Williams.[23]

"Yesterday afternoon in company with several officers of the Post I rode over to 'Fort Lincoln' to inspect the *negroe Regts*," Colonel N. P. Chipman, chief of staff of the Department of the Missouri, wrote to his commander, Samuel Curtis. Noting that the new regiment was to be called the "1st Kansas Infantry," Chipman added that Captain Williams was "the commander & to be Col provided these recruits 'of African descent' are mustered as U.S. soldiers." Chipman was pleased with his inspection. "Laying aside the question as to the policy or propriety of making soldiers of the Negroe and viewing them as machines of war," he wrote, "I must say that the inspection was highly satisfactory—They exhibit a proficiency in the manual and in company evolutions truly surprising and the best company is the one officered by black men. The white officers are enthusiasts and think they would rather drill & discipline black men than white. I know I have seen very many Regts longer in the service than these which would appear badly beside them."[24]

During his inspection Chipman learned that the sharp military drill covered frustration and conflict. Lane ordered that, once organized and mustered into federal service, the First Kansas Colored Infantry should "move to the front" at Baxter's Springs and report to Major General James Blunt for service. Yet Blunt wanted officials at Fort Scott to use the black soldiers to construct a telegraph line to Leavenworth. Lane balked at this request. According to Chipman, Lane argued that he "has not yet turned them over to Govt & the probability is that the Regt will go to Baxter's Springs unless they become disgusted at being ordered around without any recognition from Govt and disband." This brought Chipman to the most important part of his letter to Curtis, a plea from Captain Williams and the regiment:

> These men have been recruited with the promise that they were to fight, not work as common laborers, that they were to be treated in every way as soldiers, with like immunities &c & that they would have an opportunity to strike a blow for the freedom of their brothers. Many of them are intelligent free negroes—some have a good business at home, others leaving their families without any support; they have been kept together without pay & under but a quasi organization. They are now two months in camp and no one can tell what is to be done with them.[25]

"They ask me. I am noncommittal," Chipman told Curtis. "They ask Lane—he evades—but urges them on by adroit tactics for which he is notable." Williams spoke plainly with Chipman, telling him that unless the troops were mustered soon, the unit would disband. Chipman believed the men would be willing to provide manual labor for the department, including raising the telegraph line, temporarily if they were mustered in, "in the hope that a time would come when they might fight." But no mustering officer in Kansas would step forward without direct orders from the department. Chipman told Curtis, "You see, therefore, the question is likely to be decided by you—The scheme is one of Lane's & with him is a hobby." Chipman admitted that he believed Lane could "perhaps . . . screw the Pres[iden]t up to the point of assuming all necessary responsibility."[26] In the meantime, the fate of the regiment was unclear.

Fortunately for the First Kansas Colored Infantry, the commanding officer at Fort Scott, Major Benjamin S. Henning, proved willing to put black soldiers in the field. Whether sympathetic to their cause, or from a practical need for a few hundred uniformed soldiers, Major Henning issued orders on October 26, 1862, for a detachment to march into Missouri and scatter Confederate guerrillas operating in Bates County. The officers and men responded immediately to this first chance for combat. Captain Henry C. Seaman and 64 men from the southern battalion joined nearly 170 soldiers and officers under Captain Richard G. Ward. The two detachments included men pulled from each company. Aided by a handful of white scouts of the Fifth Kansas Cavalry, the 240-man expedition pushed toward Missouri that same day.[27]

At 2 P.M. on October 27, the group tramped up the eastern bank of the Marais des Cygnes River at Dickie's Ford, near modern-day Butler, Missouri, and made their way through the heavy timber and tall grass to the open prairie.[28] Several men on horseback watched the procession from a rise of mounds a mile to the southeast. When a small party of Kansas scouts galloped forward to investigate, the mysterious riders wheeled their horses and rode away. It was an ominous sign, a reminder that though Missouri was nominally a loyal state, Union soldiers from Kansas were unwelcome.[29]

Ward and Seaman searched for a defensive location. They found the property of Enoch Toothman, a known secessionist. Enoch's son, John Toothman, was a prisoner at Fort Lincoln. Enoch himself had departed sometime before the black soldiers arrived, leaving his wife and two daughters alone at home. Confiscating the "large double log farm house" for their own use, the Kansas soldiers tore down rail fences to erect a barricade for their camp. The men posted a U.S. flag and christened their new position "Fort Africa."[30]

Settling down in their new "fort," the officers questioned local residents, including the Toothman women, for information about guerrilla activity. The news they received confirmed the gravity of their situation. As many as eight hundred Confederates under Jeremiah V. Cockerell, Bill Turman, and other local secessionists were congregating on Hog Island (or Osage Island) a few miles to the south. The "island" was actually an irregularly shaped finger of heavily wooded land, running three miles long, surrounded by the Marais des Cygnes River and wet, marshy ground.[31] The sight of the guerrilla scouts confirmed the legitimacy of the reports. In the meantime, a few Confederates tested the Union position at Fort Africa with long-range musket shots, putting the black Kansans under enemy fire—even if ineffective—for the first time. Some of the Kansas men replied in kind. The exchange continued for a short time, "we trying to draw them off the island and the enemy trying to draw us to the bushes," Captain Ward later reported.[32] But neither group moved from the safety of their defensive positions. Thus ended their first full day in Missouri, a tense prologue to the coming fight.

On the morning of October 28, the Kansas soldiers awakened ready for action. Ward and Seaman ordered pickets to maintain a vigilant watch for guerrilla attacks and sent small patrols out of Fort Africa to investigate the area, but within sight of the main body. Periodically the patrols spotted mounted guerrillas on distant knolls and let loose a few musket shots in their direction. The strong prairie winds hampered their accuracy, especially since the enemy had taken care "to keep a respectful distance."[33] The day passed with short bursts of activity—"desultory skirmishes," as Captain Ward called them—but not the decisive engagement the soldiers wanted.

As the black infantrymen watched darkness fall upon them a second time at Fort Africa, Ward and Seaman met to discuss the situation. Rightfully concerned that 250 foot soldiers could not capture or chase away 700 horsemen, the two officers sent three runners back to Kansas for reinforcements.[34] If they could hold their position and keep the guerrillas in place through constant skirmishing until more federal soldiers arrived, they hoped to crush the county's prosecessionist movement in one swoop. It would require a combination of care and luck.

Wednesday morning, October 29, 1862, opened with nicer weather, but a new problem plagued the men—lack of food. The farms nearby boasted livestock and grain for the picking. Obtaining those provisions was the problem. Foraging left men in a particularly vulnerable position. It required spreading out, directing their attention away from possible threats, and laying down or slinging muskets to free their hands. Men carrying pigs, chickens, or bags of food were usually not able to respond to sudden attack. Thus Ward and Seaman devised a plan. They ordered Captains Andrew

Armstrong and Andrew Crew from Ward's command to march sixty
men out of Fort Africa south toward the suspected guerrilla hideout.
This force would distract Confederate forces while a foraging party
of fifty men commanded by Captains Luther Thrasher and Elkannah
Huddleston from Seaman's section scrounged as much grain and
supplies as could be found in a short time.[35]

Eager for a scrap, the diversion force traveled about two miles
from camp before spotting a group of mounted men. Armstrong
ordered Orderly Sergeant Jordan Smithers to advance on the enemy
with a detachment of skirmishers.[36] Skirmish fighting meant
spreading the men out and advancing in loose formation. This tactic allowed a commander to test out an enemy position without
committing the whole force in mass. The sergeant and his skirmishers marched toward the guerrillas, peppering them with musket balls. The horsemen fell back, fired their pistols, then fell back
a bit more.[37]

"Come on, you damned niggers!" some cried out. The Kansas
men did continue forward, "politely requesting [the guerrillas] to
wait for them, as they were not mounted," Captain Ward later wrote
of the fighting. Other Missourians saved their curses for the white
officers, calling them "damned nigger-stealers," and sent a number
of bullets in their direction. "The balls from long range rifles came
unpleasantly near," recalled one officer.[38]

The roving fight continued in this fashion for nearly four miles.
The guerrillas fell back and fired; the black soldiers advanced and
fired. The Missourians may have been trying to cut off Armstrong's
men, but they had another reason to fall back—the Kansas guns were
taking a toll. Shortly after the contest began, a black soldier's musket ball dropped a guerrilla from his horse. Minutes later another
one grabbed his side and fell. The Kansans on the right swung their
line up a ravine and caught the guerrillas on their exposed left flank.
A short burst of musketry sent "several riderless horses" galloping
across the Missouri landscape. Some of the horsemen scrambled
to help their fallen comrades and retreated. As the black soldiers
continued their advance, they passed over bloodstains in the grass,
attesting to their accuracy.[39]

By the time the officers reigned in the men, the Kansas soldiers had taken down seven guerrillas, while not one of them had
been touched by return fire.[40] Though often ignored because of later
events, this initial skirmish between Armstrong's detachment and

a small group of Missouri guerrillas may be credited as the first fire-fight by a black unit for the Union cause. And it was a success. Thrasher, Huddleston, and the foragers gathered supplies without incident. Armstrong's men returned to Fort Africa "highly elated" at having bested the enemy in an open fight and striking a small but exciting blow for freedom.[41]

The black soldiers did not have long to celebrate the victory. Only a few short hours later, at two o'clock, while many of the Kansas soldiers ate lunch, thick gray smoke billowed from the fields in the distance. Sporadic musket shots punctuated the air, and pickets came streaming in with reports of a Confederate attack. The guerrillas had set the grass on fire, presumably to cover their advance. The prairie wind blew straight into Fort Africa, the smoke stinging the men's eyes. A few soldiers started a counterfire around the fort to prevent the advancing flames and smoke from overwhelming the camp. Officers shouted out a call to arms. Soldiers scrambled for their muskets and cartridge boxes. Anxious for information, Captain Seaman organized a scouting party of eight men under the command of John Six-Killer, an enlisted Cherokee from Indian Territory. Seaman ordered them to get clear of the smoke and watch for enemy movement. He cautioned them to stay in sight of the camp, fearing that the guerrillas intended to separate small sections of the infantry force and destroy them in detail.[42]

Six-Killer and his small group charged out of the camp searching for the enemy. On emerging from the smoke, the men could see the Confederate guerrillas waiting in the distance. The sight of the enemy proved too tempting, and, one officer recalled, "their eagerness for the prey soon led to a disobedience of orders." Six-Killer and his seven companions rushed toward the enemy and out of view from camp. Seaman called for Lieutenant Joseph Gardner and sixteen men to bring Six-Killer back. However, the "Cherokees being somewhat unmanageable except by their own officers," Captain Henry Pierson fell in with the group "to aid this purpose."[43]

Within a few minutes soldiers at Fort Africa could hear the sound of musketry. The action remained hidden from view by terrain and thick smoke, increasing the tension among the main body of troops. Ward ordered Captain Armstrong to ready his men for battle. The sound of firing increased. Rather than pull Six-Killer and his men back to camp, Gardner's relief force had joined the skirmish. Order broke down as two officers, Captain Crew and Lieutenant

Huddleston, grabbed muskets and raced out of the camp toward the sound of fighting.[44]

Captain Seaman, still in overall command of the Union force, faced a crisis. As infantry soldiers, his men were trained to fight in tight formation. Serving in organized ranks, whether shoulder to shoulder or as skirmishers, the Kansans remained relatively secure. Guerrilla soldiers could do little more than harass a well-disciplined and solid force of infantry. If that infantry formation fell apart, however, individuals or small groups of men on foot would fall easy prey to mounted adversaries armed with revolvers and shotguns.

Rushing south to Gardner's position, Huddleston and Crew helped push a band of guerrillas back from high ground into a low patch of woods near a small log cabin. Gardner and the officers reorganized the men and prepared to return to camp. They did not know that in a distant cottonwood tree a guerrilla scout carefully watched the skirmish. The Confederates that Gardner's group had chased to the south were a diversionary force, tasked with drawing the Union men away from the safety of their camp. With twenty-five soldiers in blue alone and at least a half-mile away from reinforcements, the guerrilla scout in the tree signaled for an attack.[45] From a distant wood line to the east came riding 130 guerrillas "with evident intentions to cut us off from a main force," Huddleston explained. Only then did the black soldiers and their white officers realize the gravity of the situation. They were outnumbered and nearly a mile from camp with a series of rises and a high mound in the way. The officers came together for a quick assessment. Gardner, still in official command of the party, ordered the men to head back to camp. If they would be overtaken, he explained, they should seek cover in a ditch or depression, at least to protect them from the force of a cavalry charge.[46]

The remaining officers and soldiers at Fort Africa grew impatient. Unable to wait, Ward ordered Armstrong's detachment of fifty men to follow him to the fight. Marching out of the camp, he halted them behind a rise and walked forward to observe the situation. To his south he saw a group of Confederates on a ridge. To the west was Pierson and a few men from Gardner's detachment. They had separated from the rest of Gardner's men shortly after the engagement began and found high ground on a rise to maintain visual contact with both Gardner and the camp.[47] Ward ordered his adjutant, Richard Hinton, to ride to them and investigate. Hinton joined

Pierson to see Gardner's group some eight hundred yards away near the small cabin. Hinton saw the body of horsemen moving to cut them off. Thinking that Gardner's party would hold in a defensive position, he watched in shock as Gardner's men began their rush back for camp. "In place of returning to the log-cabin, where a successful resistance could be made till reinforced," he later told the *New York Times*, "our detachment headed steadily for the mound."[48]

Hinton hurried back to Ward warning of the detachment's imminent destruction. Ward ordered Armstrong to march to the northern base of the large mound and sent a messenger with a plea for help to Seaman back in camp. Within minutes two groups of reinforcements poured out of Fort Africa, one led by Lieutenant Luther Thrasher, the other commanded by Lieutenants Patrick Minor, who soon would be the first black officer to see combat in the Civil War, and Luther Dickerson.[49]

To the south Gardner's group hustled north toward safety. To the east, the large body of guerrillas rode methodically on a collision course. During the flight, Huddleston noticed the wind blowing into the charging enemy soldiers and sparked two separate fires in the heavy, dry grass in a weak attempt to blind or disorient them. The horsemen continued their steady approach to within four hundred yards, letting loose a loud yell, spurring their horses across the grassy plains toward the scrambling foot soldiers. The guerrillas held their fire, waiting for the last crucial moment to blast the Union men with pistols, shotguns, and carbines.[50]

Running up the slope, Gardner's men struggled to find a ravine on the other side. They did not make it. The Missourians came pouring over the mound on top of them. At the last moment the Union soldiers turned on their attackers and fired their muskets at point-blank range. A few horsemen went down, but the rest crashed into the little Union detachment, blasting their pistols and swinging their sabers. The infantrymen were hit from all sides. A bullet struck the front left shoulder of Private Edward Curtis, passing through his body and lodging under flesh near the shoulder blade. Moments later another bullet hit him in the lower back. A third bullet smashed into the left side of his mouth and cheek, destroying teeth and ripping part of his tongue, before exiting near his right ear.[51] Private Shelby Bannon fell from a flurry of wounds. A bullet ripped through his belly and exited at the backside of his hip, while another glanced off a rib. A Confederate sword sliced open his lower

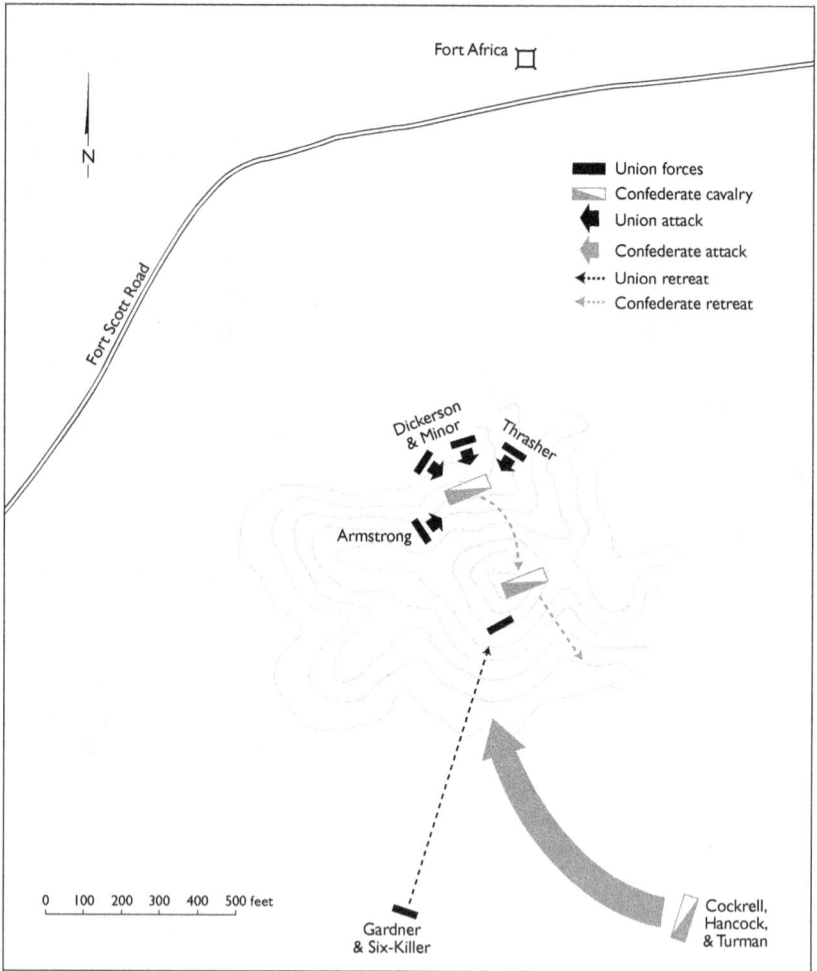

Map 2. Island Mound. Map by Bill Nelson. Copyright © 2014 by the University of Oklahoma Press.

back and he received a smashing blow to the head.[52] Amazingly, despite these gruesome wounds, both Curtis and Bannon survived.

One guerrilla used his horse as a weapon, charging directly over a black soldier and sending him tumbling to the ground. The soldier raised his head to regain his composure only to see Lieutenant Gardner fall a few yards away. The forty-two-year-old Gardner, a "large and heavy man," had received a pistol ball and a shotgun blast to his hips and legs and plunged face first into the prairie grass. A guerrilla sprung out of his saddle and pounced on the incapacitated officer. Like an executioner the Missourian pointed a pistol at the back of Gardner's head, growled, "There, God damn you, take that," and pulled the trigger. His grisly work accomplished, the Confederate turned to remount his horse but fell from a musket ball fired by the black soldier recovering from his collision with the horse.[53]

Other Confederates dismounted to finish off wounded black soldiers. Private Anderson Riley fell from a gunshot wound to the left shoulder. The bullet passed through his body and lodged next to the shoulder blade. A Confederate horseman grabbed the fallen soldier's musket and turned it on its previous owner, spearing Riley with its bayonet. "The bayonet went in just to the left of the pit of his stomach," a comrade later recalled.[54]

Their formation shattered, the black soldiers fought alone for survival. Lieutenant Huddleston found himself separated from the group and sprinted off the mound, firing his revolver and dodging incoming bullets. He escaped unscathed.[55] Infantrymen in the thick of the fight had little time to reload their cumbersome weapons. Instead, they swung their muskets as clubs or stabbed at the enemy with their long sword bayonets—"a fearful weapon," according to Hinton, that "did terrible execution in the hands of the muscular blacks."[56] When a Missourian cried out, "Surrender, you black devil!" the soldier screamed "Nevah!" and with a thrust from his bayonet "made a hole big enough to let out a dozen lives."[57]

John Six-Killer fought with ruthless efficiency. He shot two Confederates, bayoneted a third, and smashed a fourth with the butt of his gun before he fell, the victim of six bullet wounds. A short distance away, three guerrillas charged on Sergeant Edward Lowry as he fired his musket at a passing horseman. One of the attackers lowered his shotgun and blasted the sergeant with a charge of buckshot. Stunned but not dead, Lowry staggered. In his left hand he held his empty musket; in his right he grasped the long saber bayonet and desperately tried to fix it to the end of the barrel. One of the guerrillas reined his horse directly over the badly wounded soldier and called for him to surrender. Lowry swung his musket. Ten pounds of wood and metal smashed into the surprised Confederate, tumbling him off his horse. Lowry finished the man with another crushing blow to the head. He turned to see the second guerrilla charging and firing his weapon. Aiming at the largest target in reach, Lowry speared the horse with his bayonet, putting both animal and rider out of action. The final assailant also fell to a well-aimed swing of the heavy musket. Sergeant Lowry sustained three gunshot wounds in the fray but survived and carried himself from the field.[58]

A few minutes into the fight, Captain Crew was the only officer still standing inside the melee. He tried to rally the remaining enlisted men and lead them off the mound, firing his pistol as he backed his way toward the Union camp. A bullet slammed into his groin and crumpled him. Slowly he rose and continued to withdraw, only to find a handful of mounted guerrillas converge on him. They called out for him to surrender, warning that they would fire if he did not. "Never!" he screamed, adding, "Shoot and be damned!" As he yelled for his men to fight to the death, bullets cut into his stomach and heart, killing him. A guerrilla hopped from his horse and rifled through the captain's pockets, removing a gold watch and a revolver as trophies. He did not have long to enjoy them. A badly wounded soldier who had watched Crew's death "summoned all the strength in his power," rose from the ground, and charged the guerrilla as he mounted a horse. The black Kansan speared the Missourian with his bayonet and threw the body to the ground. He grabbed the captain's pocket watch from the dead guerrilla's hands, and took a trophy for himself—the now riderless horse. Weak from his wounds, the soldier collapsed on the field. But he would survive, and Crew's watch would be sent home to his family as a memento of a Union martyr.[59]

Flames and smoke from Huddleston's grass fires crept up the mound. The advancing fire threatened wounded men lying in the grass, including Lieutenant Gardner. He had survived the point-blank pistol shot to the head. Miraculously, the bullet glanced off the bone, leaving only a painful cut across his scalp. Nonetheless, the shock of that wound, and the two preceding wounds to his legs, frustrated any chance to outrun the fire. So Gardner waited until he found a slight gap in the flames and rolled onto a patch of burned ground. He remained there until carried off the field after the engagement.[60]

Captain Ward, watching the fight unfold from a mound to the north, recalled, "I have witnessed some hard fights, but I never saw a braver sight than that handful of brave men fighting 117 men who were all around and in amongst them. Not one surrendered or gave up a weapon."[61] The captain then turned to see another impressive sight. "At this juncture Armstrong came into the [fight] like a lion, yelling to his men to follow him, and cursing them for not going faster when they were already on the keen jump." Armstrong halted his men when they closed to within 150 yards of the melee. He ordered them to raise their muskets and fire at the mounted Confederates still attacking the remnants of Gardner's group. Seeing the new threat down the northern slope of the mound, the guerrillas turned to meet Armstrong's detachment, only to be surprised by another volley on their flank. It came from Lieutenant Thrasher's men, of Seaman's battalion, positioned perfectly to deliver a stunning blow to the advancing Confederates.[62]

Still determined to sweep the infantry to their front, the guerrillas charged to take Armstrong's detachment by the flank. Captain Ward, observing the enemy's maneuver from a distance, ordered his last reserves under lieutenants Minor and Dickerson to plug the gap. On seeing infantry on three sides, the Confederates swung their horses back around and retreated up the hill. The horses galloped into the smoke, now obscuring much of the mound. As they passed along the crest Armstrong's men hurtled through the prairie flames to fire a parting volley. With that, the guerrillas fled to the south, leaving the field in the hands of the black warriors.[63]

Some Union soldiers saw a large band of horsemen arrive in the distance. They were reinforcements for the guerrillas, estimated to be three or four hundred strong. Yet they did not attack. Captain Ward reasoned, "They had tested the niggers and had received an answer to the often mooted question of 'will they fight.'"[64] The survivors hurriedly gathered the wounded and dead scattered across the prairie mound. Along with Six-Killer and Crew, Corporal Joseph Talbot and Privates Samuel Davis, Thomas Lane, Marion Barber, Allen Rhodes, and Henry Gash lay dead. Gardner remained on his patch of burned ground, badly wounded but alive. Ten other men came off the field with wounds, including Sergeant Lowry and one of the youngest enlistees of the regiment, Manual Dobson. The fourteen-year-old soldier had wounds to both arms, but was more concerned with his performance in battle. He told an officer that he "couldn't kill but one of 'em," but proudly added, "I brought my gun back."[65] All of the wounds were severe: one man carried a bullet in his head, had had part of his hand shot off, and sustained a ghastly bayonet or sword wound through the lungs. An officer observed that when the soldier breathed, "the blood would spurt from the wound."[66] Amazingly, all of the wounded men taken off the field survived.

Confederate casualties were harder to determine. A Union officer noted that "their killed and wounded had been removed as fast as they fell. They could be seen to dismount as fast as one fell and, putting the body on a horse, remove it from the field."[67] Union reports estimated that eighteen guerrillas were killed and around twenty-five wounded.[68]

The Union men did not tarry on the field for long. With Confederate riders still watching in the distance, the officers hurried the men back to Fort Africa and prepared for further action. Seaman ordered cavalryman John Stearns, one of the mounted scouts, to ride to Fort Scott with all possible speed for reinforcements. He dodged guerrilla pickets along the way and reported to Major Henning that same evening, only to learn that the post had few men to spare. Henning instructed Stearns to gather up 150 black recruits at Fort Lincoln—currently performing guard duty—and lead them to the Toothman farm. He also promised to send a force of Ohio cavalry and some artillery. These reinforcements would double the original size of Seaman's expedition.[69]

Stearns and the black reinforcements took to the road the morning of October 30. The men kept a grueling pace, arriving at Fort Africa that same afternoon, completing the march from Fort Lincoln in half the time Seaman's force had originally taken. They found that all had been quiet at the Toothman farm during the previous twenty-four hours. The guerrillas had not pressed another attack. With his force nearly doubled, and the promise of cavalry and artillery support on the way, Seaman decided to take the offensive. On the morning of October 31, the combined black detachments marched toward the guerrilla headquarters on Hog Island. They were "expecting every minute to hear the boom of the Ohioan's guns," Stearns recalled. As they came upon the island, no guerrillas could be found. The Missourians had fled in haste. The Union men walked into a deserted camp, finding a few meandering horses—some of which bore wounds from the action two days before. The soldiers also discovered a herd of cattle, an important source of food for the guerrillas, and claimed it as contraband of war.[70]

Seaman's scouts found a trail and followed it for ten miles but never spotted the guerrillas. Notified that morning of Ohio cavalry coming from Fort Scott, the Missourians had abandoned the island long before the Kansans approached. For two more days the Union troops scouted the area but found no trace of their enemy. The black soldiers had fought well against a dangerous enemy deep in guerrilla territory and they had achieved their objective—to disperse the guerrillas from Bates County.[71]

The importance of the skirmish at Island Mound, as it became known, had very little to do with the specific operation. By October 1862, Union and Confederate armies had fought such bloody battles as Shiloh, where 23,746 men fell killed and wounded over two days, and Antietam, with its single-day casualty record of 22,719.[72] Two dozen dead and wounded on a farm in western Missouri hardly warranted mention beyond the local communities. Nonetheless, the small battle on this nondescript hill in the fall of 1862 marked an important milestone. It was there that a unit of black soldiers saw combat in the American Civil War for the first time. And they won.

CHAPTER 6

THE BATTLE WITHIN

. . . a conspiracy to break up and disband the 1st Regiment of
Colored Kansas Volunteers.

In the wake of the victory at Island Mound, the First Kansas
Colored Infantry's adjutant, Richard Hinton, sent dramatic
accounts of the action to the *Leavenworth Daily Conservative* and
the *New York Times.*[1] "It is useless to talk any more of negro courage," he proclaimed. "The men fought like tigers, each and every one
of them, and the main difficulty was to hold them well in hand."[2]
Despite these accolades, and moral triumph for African Americans,
once back in camp near Fort Scott, the officers and enlisted men
found that little had changed. The regiment was not yet full, had
not been mustered into federal service, and continued to face bitter white resistance. Discipline waned. Throughout the fall, desertions drained the organization of vital manpower. In isolated cases,
enlisted soldiers lashed out against military command.

One of the most tragic acts of insubordination occurred shortly
before Island Mound. Around October 5, while a few companies
remained encamped near Wyandotte, Kansas, awaiting orders to
move south to join the rest of the regiment, Sergeant Sampson
Wharfield stood watch as sergeant of the guard, responsible for mon-
itoring and approving passage in and out of camp. He confronted a
private who had received written permission from his captain and
the regiment's major, John Bowles, to leave the camp. Wharfield
refused him passage, snatching the pass from the private's hands.
Captain George Martin of Company B intervened and informed
Wharfield that the private indeed had permission to leave. When
the sergeant objected, Captain Martin reminded him "that he would
get himself into trouble by refusing to obey the orders of his superior
officers." Ordered to return the pass, Sergeant Wharfield felt around
his pocket, claimed he could not find it, and announced, "By God
the man shouldn't pass no how." When Captain Martin instructed

the private to leave camp, Sergeant Wharfield followed the soldier and grabbed him by the arm. Martin shouted for Wharfield to stand down. The sergeant paused but turned, "and he and the man commenced abusing one another."[3]

Captain Andrew J. Armstrong of Company D arrived on horseback and ordered Sergeant Wharfield to return to camp. "By God, Who are you?" Wharfield demanded. Armstrong announced that he was acting officer of the day and that if the sergeant "didn't go into Camp and behave himself he would show him who he was."[4] Wharfield stepped back and allowed the enlisted man to board a wagon and leave camp. Captain Armstrong turned his horse, pausing to tell Captain Martin to make sure the sergeant behaved and authorized him to send Wharfield to the guardhouse should problems continue.[5]

Problems continued. When Martin ordered Wharfield back to camp, the sergeant declared that he would not go until he was ready. Warned again of the dangers of disobeying orders, Wharfield said "he didn't care a God damn for his officers & that he would do as he God damn pleased." Martin had had enough. He called for a guard, and an enlisted man arrived with a musket. "When the Guard came I told him to put his bayonet to Sampson's back and force him along," Martin later testified. That set the sergeant off into a deadly fit. Noncommissioned officers carried slender swords, primarily for ceremonial purposes and to provide sergeants with a useful tool to arrange men in formation. Normally they offered little value in combat. But they still could prove deadly. Sergeant Wharfield drew his saber from its sheath and attacked the captain. Twice he cut at Captain Martin, and then lunged, intending to thrust the three-foot-long blade into the officer's body. Martin dodged the blows and jumped back. Wharfield turned on the guard, who raised his musket and pulled the trigger at point-blank range. With a loud "snap" the gun's hammer fell onto the brass cap, but the musket failed to fire. Startled, Wharfield paused, sheathed his sword, and began walking to camp.[6]

Captain Martin and the guard followed behind, leaving some distance. That proved wise, for within moments Sergeant Wharfield stopped, said that he would kill the captain anyway, and attacked with his sword again. With the guard's musket inoperable, and with no weapon of his own, Captain Martin tried to defuse the situation with words. "I asked him if he didn't know it was wrong to cut at an officer and an unarmed man with his sabre," Martin recounted calmly to officials later. Wharfield hesitated, then turned away from the captain.[7]

On reaching a fence near the camp, the sergeant again suc-cumbed to rage. With sword in hand, shouting curses and insults, Wharfield lashed out at Captain Martin, backing the unarmed officer to a fence. Arriving back on the scene, Captain Armstrong charged his horse between the two men and called on the sergeant to halt. Wharfield snarled that he was not "afraid at this God damned Cavalry." Armstrong pulled his pistol and ordered Wharfield to stop or be shot. Wharfield grabbed the horse by the bridle with his left hand and swung his sword at the mounted officer with his right. Armstrong jerked the reins to the side. The horse turned and the sword missed. Wharfield pressed his attack, prompting Armstrong to lower his pistol and fire a single shot into the sergeant's body.[8]

Wharfield paused but did not fall. "There By God, you've put one ball through me anyhow," he said. He then sheathed his sword and walked back into camp, finally ending the violent episode. Wharfield succumbed to the wound two days later. Captain Armstrong faced a court-martial for the shooting the following spring but was acquit-ted on all charges on the grounds of self-defense.[9]

Sergeant Wharfield's confrontation with officers was highly unusual but caught the attention of the regiment's critics. "A NIGGER KILLED," read the headline for a small entry in the *Liberty Tribune*. "We learn from the Leavenworth papers that a negro, one of the con-traband regiment, was shot at Wyandott[e] night before last, for resis-tance to the orders of his superiors."[10] The regiment's officers could expect such criticism from Missouri observers. The greater problem was decreasing morale within the ranks and the subsequent break-down of discipline. In early November the regiment's commander, Captain James M. Williams, learned that some white residents of Leavenworth were determined to break up the regiment, encourag-ing the new black volunteers to desert through "falsified stories and good promises."[11] These efforts hurt the unit's ability to fill the ranks and lowered morale and discipline in camp. On Saturday, November 15, Williams, Company D's black commander Captain William D. Matthews, and a contingent of the regiment went to Leavenworth to round up deserters. When the detachment entered the store of R. C. Brant, the owner called on local authorities. Leavenworth police arrived on the scene, promptly placed Williams and Matthews under arrest, and presented them to Mayor H. B. Denman, ostensibly for disturbing the peace. Denman argued the officers had no right to detain deserters in Leavenworth, for the black men were not actual soldiers. They had not been properly enlisted, the mayor contended, and the entire regiment was illegitimate.[12] Williams rejected Denman's argument. The men were clothed, armed, fed, and indeed recognized by the government, and "civil authorities had no right in time of war to interpose and prevent the arrest of offenders against the military law."[13] Unperturbed, the mayor announced his intention to prosecute the two military officers under civil law.

The confrontation was not simply a dispute over local authority. City officials actively attempted to sabotage the regiment's formation. Damning proof of the mayor's true intentions emerged when Denman pulled Matthews aside for a private conversation. The mayor assured the black officer that "he would fix my security so that I should not be bothered," but asked Matthews to leave the regiment and to encourage enlisted men to desert. Matthews reported that Denman admitted his desire to see the regiment disband before the next congressional session because he knew that "if we could be kept—together until Congress that Lane would have us recognized and paid." It was clear to Matthews that the mayor wished to "break up the whole concern" through direct interference.[14]

Williams and Matthews were released after agreeing to post five-hundred-dollar and two-hundred-dollar bonds, respectively, and to appear in court the following day.[15] The editor of the *Leavenworth Daily Conservative*, a cautious supporter of the regiment, published a short description of the confrontation the following morning and added, "We hope this affair will end beneficially to all concerned, and matters seem to have that appearance at present."[16]

Captains Williams and Matthews returned to camp to confer with their superiors. After consulting with Major T. J. Weed at Fort Leavenworth, Williams "decided to refuse to give bail, and let them arrest me if they could." More than that, Williams resolved to finish his mission of collecting deserters in Leavenworth. "Knowing that they intended to forcibly release what deserters I had already arrested," Williams later reported to a superior officer, "I applied for and got an additional guard from the Fort and started them to camp with orders to force themselves through all opposition."[17]

In the face of this force, the city police watched cautiously, not daring to challenge the resolute officer a second time. However, the police managed to separate one black soldier from the detachment. They arrested him and "put him in the Calaboose for carrying arms." "This they did for the purpose of bothering me in getting out of town," Williams reported.[18]

The following day, Captain Williams led a detachment of fourteen men to the Leavenworth jail to free the black soldier.[19] Williams recounted that he "went to the jail and told the jailer to release him which he did."[20] The *Leavenworth Daily Conservative* noted, however, that in reality the military squad "called on Policeman Gillon, acting jailor, and with drawn revolvers demanded the release of the negro."[21] Leading an armed jailbreak in one's own state was risky and threatened to further harm the regiment's public image. Still, Williams believed the use of force was necessary to solve the dispute between the Leavenworth police and his command. "I did this because I knew that [the jailor] was merely to hinder me in the discharge of my duty," he later explained to General James Blunt, "and if I did not do this it would delay the whole command for 2 or 3 days at least when I had positive orders from Major Weed to proceed immediately to Camp with my men and deserters."[22] With the enlisted man free, the First Kansas Colored Infantry detachment marched back into military lines, waiting for the mayor's next move.

Mayor Denman responded by demanding that local military officials present Captain Williams to city authorities. "I am informed that Captain James M. Williams is now at the Fort, under its protection," the mayor wrote to the commanding officer at Fort Leavenworth. "I therefore sent Mr. Dennings the City Marshall to you, for the purpose of demanding the body of the said Captain Williams in order that the orders of this court may be carried out, and the Civil Law sustained."[23] According to the *Leavenworth Daily Conservative*, Denman's primary claim was the outstanding issue of Williams's arrest and unpaid bond. "The principal point in the controversy is the Mayor's statement that Col. W. agreed to procure bondsmen, and Williams' denial of it," the newspaper reported. "Col. Williams says he agreed to go back the next morning (Sunday,) and say what he would do."[24]

Williams sent off his own demands to Major Weed, the adjutant at Fort Leavenworth. He ignored the bond issue—having already determined with Weed's approval to disregard the city's demand for bail—and launched into an accusation of conspiracy against Mayor Denman: "I am credibly informed and believe the Mayor

THE BATTLE WITHIN 103

and policemen of the City of Leavenworth Kansas have entered into a conspiracy to break up and disband the 1st Regiment of Colored Kansas Volunteers now under my command." Williams further asked that "the parties to this conspiracy be arrested and the charge investigated."[25]

Major Weed, caught in an escalating battle between military and civil authority, responded by deferring to his superiors. To Denman he wrote, "I have to say, that the right and authority of Captain Williams to arrest deserters from his camp, having been clearly and emphatically recognized by the General commanding this district, and that as the present conflict with the civil authorities has arisen while in the discharge of duties thus recognized I can see no other way to proceeding than to refer the whole matter to Brigadier General Blunt, for his decision." Weed's deferment to higher authority complied with standard military protocol; yet it also gave Williams and the black soldiers an edge. General Blunt was a friend to James Lane and a supporter of the regiment. Even though Major Weed assured Denman that "in the meantime, Capt. Williams as an officer in the service of the United States, will be held strictly amenable to the pending decision, and will be promptly delivered up to the civil authorities should it be so ordered," Mayor Denman hardly could have been appeased.[26]

The *Leavenworth Daily Conservative*, which generally had been favorable to the black unit during the preceding months, questioned Captain Williams's actions. "Upon whose authority Col. Williams acted in rescuing the negro, we are not informed," the editor wrote. "We have only stated the case in accordance with the best information we could get. If the act was authorized by the commander at the Fort, it may lead to important results in regard to the negro soldier scheme."[27] Other Kansans watched with indifference. After noting the "difficulty" between Captain Williams and Mayor Denman, the editor of the Oskaloosa *Independent* concluded that the matter was a "big muss on small capital."[28]

Public disdain compounded the regiment's problems as winter arrived in late 1862. The success at Island Mound soon faded into memory as the regiment remained idle in camp, suffering the drudgery of military life with little assurance of recognition. "The 'nigger' regiment is quietly encamped in the bottom near the city, drilling a little and eating a great deal of Uncle Samuel's hard bread and bacon," a correspondent at Fort Scott reported to the *Leavenworth*

Daily Times in December. "Officers and privates are tired of their inactivity, and anxiously awaiting the order that will give them an opportunity to show their fighting qualities." The correspondent, however, was unsympathetic to their cause. "I understand the regiment is designated as laborers, and the officers as 'superintendents,'" he continued. "If such is the case, why are they not put to work? There is enough for them to do, and in their present position they are worse than useless. But they are the special pets of the Grim Chieftain [James Lane], and of course must be taken care of even if the country suffers."[29]

Stuck in limbo, the fledgling First Kansas Colored Infantry struggled for survival. Illness swept through camp, killing some men, leading to the medical discharge of others, and contributing to malaise. On top of the hardships, the men, both enlisted and officers, had received no pay. The regiment still was not a federal organization, remaining a quasi-official state regiment, kept alive by the brashness and influence of Senator Lane. Unsurprisingly, desertions mounted, even without encouragement from white outsiders. "The Regt has lost by desertion some three hundred men or more," wrote Captain John Graton of Company C to his wife in early January, "almost enough to make us a full Regiment."[30] While enlistment and other unit records from this crucial period of the unit's existence are sparse, the First Kansas Colored Infantry lost at least 230 recruits to desertion, discharge, or death from August 1862 to January 1863.[31] Due to this high turnover, the regiment maintained recruiting camps in some communities, such as Wyandotte, to replenish the ranks.

Disciplinary problems emerged as some soldiers vented their frustration in camp. Private Henry Aggleston of Company F received a sentence of twenty days of hard labor "for mutinous conduct and contentious language to a superior officer, and insubordination and unsoldierlike conduct in camp."[32] Private Henry Bowles of Company H received a stiffer punishment—sixty days of imprisonment and hard labor—for "Mutiny and Riotous conduct."[33] A month later, Private Harrison Miller of Company C faced a court-martial for unruliness directed at his officers. When stopped after leaving camp without a pass by the regiment's adjutant, Richard Hinton, Private Miller "used abusive and threatening language" in his refusal to return. Hinton reported at Miller's court-martial that the disgruntled enlisted man proclaimed "that he did not need a pass; that he would be God damned to Hell if he would go back. That it was none of his (the Adjt's) damned business; that he (the adj't) was a damned nigger driver and secessionist a Son of a Bitch and similar language of equally abusive character." When Private Miller began striking Hinton during the confrontation, Captain Richard Ward intervened and was likewise met with a flurry of curses and blows.[34]

These incidents reveal the level of discontent within the ranks during the winter of 1862–63. Privates Aggleston, Bowles, and Miller were otherwise dedicated soldiers. Following these troubles, Bowles and Miller served the rest of the war without problems and mustered out honorably with the regiment in 1865. Private Aggleston rejoined the ranks and was killed almost two years later in battle. The hardships and low morale during the regiment's first winter culled the less dedicated men through desertion and tested even the more fervent soldiers. But the early weeks of 1863 offered new hope as President Abraham Lincoln's administration formally opened the door for black military service. As long as the regiment maintained its physical and moral integrity, it would survive. The great question was, how would it be used?

CHAPTER 7

1863

EMANCIPATION AND MUSTER

By this act you are henceforth and forever free.

Abraham Lincoln's Emancipation Proclamation went into effect on the first day of 1863. It read in part, "I do order and declare that all persons held as slaves within said designated States, and parts of States, are, and henceforward shall be free."[1] The act was a military measure, limited for political and legal reasons. It did not end slavery in loyal or federally controlled areas. Despite these limitations, it was, as a strike against slavery, important not only for black Americans but for their white allies as well. Freedom was the new watchword.

With this emancipation effort, Lincoln spoke directly to the slaves: "I hereby enjoin upon the people so declared to be free to abstain from all violence, unless in necessary self-defence."[2] Few Confederate slaves would actually hear those words, and the statement was as much a message to opponents of emancipation who decried the act as an attempt to incite insurrection. Insurrection was not necessary for the success of the Emancipation Proclamation. By walking into Union lines, Southern slaves would deny the Confederacy vital logistic and infrastructure support.

Finally, through the Emancipation Proclamation, Lincoln formally authorized what the men of the First Kansas Colored Infantry had been providing: black military service. "And I further declare and make known," Lincoln wrote, "that such persons of suitable condition, will be received into the armed service of the United States to garrison forts, positions, stations, and other places, and to man vessels of all sorts in said service."[3] The proclamation limited its call for black military service to garrison duties; but once black men were received into uniform, nothing could stop their deployment on the battlefield. The unpredictability and necessities of war, not to mention the assertive nature of some Union officers, would put them face to face with Confederate soldiers.

Lincoln's words could not eliminate the opposition of white Northerners to black soldiers, of course. Weeks after the Emancipation Proclamation went into effect, some senators debated the prudence of placing African Americans in military ranks. "We can make them work to raise corn, pork, and beef, to feed our soldiers," Senator William Richardson of Illinois said on the Senate floor on March 2, 1863. "That is the only sensible use we can put them to. I am opposed now, as I have been always heretofore, to putting this inferior race in the Army for the purpose of fighting. You will lose every battle in which you use them." James Lane countered this slight by describing the exploits of the First Kansas Colored Infantry. He told his Senate colleagues,

> There is a regiment of this class of troops in my State, with white officers appointed by the President. They have recently moved to Fort Scott, and a gentleman from that vicinity who is now here— a man of intelligence and character—tells me that when that regiment first made its appearance at Fort Scott there was the same prejudice against it that is now entertained by the Senator from Illinois; but seeing their manly bearing and their perfection in drill and discipline, that prejudice has been entirely removed.[4]

"Were they ever under fire?" Senator Anthony Kennedy of Maryland asked.[5] "They have been under fire," Lane answered, referring to the skirmish at Island Mound. "Sixteen of them were surrounded by two hundred rebels. They fought until eight of them were killed, and the other eight were down desperately wounded; and when relieved, they had thirty black-hearted traitors lying upon the prairie by the blows they inflicted upon them. In that encounter they showed as much pluck, as much steadiness, as much skill in the use of their weapons as any troops that ever fought."[6] Lane, known for extreme rhetoric, may have erred some in the details, but he did not exaggerate the unit's success in battle. By demonstrating its ability to defeat the enemy as capably as a white regiment, the First Kansas Colored Infantry helped shape policy in Washington, D.C.

The exchange between Lane and Richardson also exposed an underlying reason for resistance to black military service. Richardson said, "I accept what the Senator from Kansas says as true—I know nothing about it—that the negro regiment in his State may have learned to walk well and to dress by the colors well." But he was rather dismissive about any real military success, remarking that African Americans can "imitate exceedingly well" and that "they dance very well, and learn that quickly." In fact, it was not military aptitude that concerned Richardson. "I hope the day is not far distant when this rebellion will be over," he said. "When it is over, those who have contributed to bring about the final result will have much to do in the management of our affairs." He admitted, "I am not prepared, I am not willing to approach the question that this rebellion is to be put down by an inferior race, and that they are to control our destinies after it is over. Sir, it is a fearful question for you and me to contemplate."[7] Richardson's belief that black military service would lead to civic participation was justified. He recognized that one of the central reasons that black men served in the military was to earn recognition as legitimate partners in American government and culture. Richardson publicly acknowledged what many whites privately feared. Like other claims of black inferiority, his argument that African Americans lacked the necessary intellect for military duty covered a deeper fear that military service would lead to social equality. As a result, neither military skill nor battlefield bravery would assure the acceptance of black soldiers.

Nonetheless, battlefield success was vital for black advancement. The victory at Island Mound weakened Richardson's claim that blacks could not be combat soldiers. Lane's description of the fight put Richardson on the defense. It made him appeal to deep-seated ideas of white supremacy rather than vague criticisms of black ability. It meant that black military service could, and would, crack previously unquestioned assumptions of black incompetency.

As these debates raged in Washington, the response to the Emancipation Proclamation in Kansas was mixed. Many cheered the news. "How do you like old Abe's proc: for freeing the slaves in the Reb. states?" Kansan Samuel Reader asked a friend in the Union army. "For my part I think it the best move that has been made during the war. You doubtless know I am a dyed in the wool Ab[olitionist] of the most ultra kind and I consider it a grand step made in behalf of humanity as well as a good war measure."[8] Sol Miller, editor of the *White Cloud Kansas Chief*, also praised Lincoln, writing, "It is one of the greatest events in the history of the world, and its influence will be felt throughout the civilization."[9]

The regiment's adjutant, Richard Hinton, reported to the *New York Times* that "it need hardly be said that the people of Kansas with great unanimity sustain the President's Proclamation."[10] Hinton exaggerated, for other Kansans offered a colder response. "When the President proclaimed that his purpose was to preserve the Constitution and the Union, the people rushed to arms," a writer for the *Leavenworth Weekly Inquirer* explained. "Is it any wonder, therefore, that their ardor should correspondingly abate, and their zeal largely cool down, since they have discovered that, instead of fighting for the Constitution and the Union, they are only fighting to free the negroes, and to convert four millions of negro servants from profitable laborers into paupers?" According to this Leavenworth paper, Lincoln had fooled loyal Americans, and "no man likes to be made a dupe." The newspaper reported that an increasing number of Union supporters were turning against Lincoln's emancipation order and that any effort to force this policy on conservative citizens would fail, "as water when obstructed in its course, only accumulates a weight and volume, that will ultimately sweep all obstacles before its own irresistible tide."[11]

The *Leavenworth Weekly Inquirer* railed against the federal government's recruitment of black soldiers. "The effort now being made in Congress, to raise one hundred and fifty thousand negro soldiers, is designed, perhaps, to supply a force which shall be perfectly subservient to the Presidential will," the story read. Far from accepting it as a necessary tool in the fight against secession, the author saw black soldiers as a pawn for a power-hungry president. Lincoln's objectives would be better achieved by an army of black man, the article explained, "because the negro acts from a feeling of subservience to superior authority, while the white soldier reasons." The author was confident that this too would fail.[12]

Despite grumblings from critics, the dedicated officers and men in the First Kansas Colored Infantry demonstrated their professionalism. On January 8, Brigadier General James Blunt reviewed the regiment and was pleased with what he saw. Adjutant Richard Hinton recalled that Blunt "congratulated them upon the President's Proclamation, declared his gladness at their soldierly appearance, trusted they would endeavor to be worthy the new hope wherewith they were dowered, and declared his wish that when next he went South, the regiment should form part of the army he commanded."[13] It was a strong endorsement from an important field commander, and no doubt reassured the men that they would soon see action. They would, in fact, serve as the backbone for Blunt's operations in upcoming campaigns. But that was in the future.

In the meantime, the regiment followed Blunt's speech with a march around Fort Scott's public square. Though stationed near Fort Scott for months, the First Kansas Colored Infantry had not previously been given the opportunity to drill or hold a dress parade within the fort or town. They proudly performed their maneuvers around the square, "which I presume was very galling to the feelings of many of the inhabitants, and also some of the Regulars," Captain John Graton of Company C wrote his wife. During their maneuvers on the square, "one of the regular soldiers made some disrespectful remark." The enlisted men kept their composure while officers handled the matter. "I have heard since that the soldier was put in the guard house and [punished] for the offense by Maj. Henning," Graton happily reported, "so you see that the niggers are ahead now."[14]

Word soon arrived that General Samuel Curtis, commander of the Department of Missouri, had authorized the regiment's muster into federal service.[15] Finally the black men would be recognized as soldiers of the U.S. government, though not as officers. Lieutenant Patrick H. Minor and Captain William D. Matthews, the sole black officers of the regiment, were informed that they would not be given commissions for federal service. Little is known about Lieutenant Minor's response, but Matthews, desperate to keep his position as captain, wrote to James Lane.[16] "According to your promise in last August you gave me permission in the presence of Col J M Williams[,] Col Delahay and others to raise one Company of Colored Soldiers to be officered by Colored officers." To refresh the senator's memory, Matthews attached Lane's order, dated August 18, 1862, which authorized him "to raise one company of free Colored men for the 1st Kansas Colored Volunteers to be officered by men of Colour." It also declared that "all Commanders of Companies and Battalions in said Regiment will regard the same as regularly officered and will issue rations and Equipments accordingly." Matthews conclude by writing that "as we three did agree to officer this Company with Colored officers, So we three must agree to keep our *Sacred word*."[17]

The mustering agent, Major T. J. Weed, offered a concession. Conservatively interpreting Lane's order, he agreed to muster Matthews in as a recruiting officer. That would not do, Matthews told Lane.

"I want to be mustered as Captain of my Company as there is no captain mustered for my Company yet and the vacancy still exists." He begged the senator to reply in haste, pleading not only for himself but for the interests of his men. "I am under great obligation to these men of my Company for keeping them here as long as I have." His removal, he warned, might lead to desertions or mutiny, "for they think I am about to sell them out and it may Cause some of them to be Shot which would be a great disgrace to the Regiment." Matthews put his faith in Lane. "It is now with you Genl," he wrote, "to fulfill the promise you gave me as it was under that promise that I got the men here. Therefore I but ask for Justice regardless of my Colour— as we are all fighting for the same great and glorious Cause of Union and Liberty." Matthews closed his letter by appealing to a shared fellowship: "I am Yours as Companion and Royal Arch Mason."[18]

The regiment's white officers stood behind Matthews. "Every officer (white) signed a request of his muster, but it was not recognized," Richard Hinton wrote a fellow officer. "We are making exertions at Washington for in his behalf, believing that principle for which we struggled is now embodied in this figure."[19]

The protests did not sway the mustering officials. On January 13, when Weed and a lieutenant from the regular army mustered six companies of the regiment into federal service, no African Americans were accepted as officers. First Lieutenant Ethan Earle, Matthews's friend and associate, was placed in command of the company.[20]

The First Kansas Colored Infantry had already made history as the first black unit to see combat. It now became the first black regiment mustered into federal service in a Northern state.[21] In a sad twist, Matthews should be known today as one of the first regularly commissioned black officers of the Civil War. On January 28, 1863, responding to the letters, pleas, and petitions from Matthews, the War Department in Washington, D.C., telegraphed the mus-tering office in Leavenworth that "Major Weed is authorized by Sec[retar]y of War to muster William D. Mathews a Colored man as an officer in a Colored regiment."[22] This notification was the offi-cial approval needed for Matthews to take command of his com-pany. But for reasons unknown, nothing happened. It is unclear whether Matthews or any officer in the regiment knew of the tele-gram. Either by an accident or by interference, the approval to appoint a black man as a regularly mustered officer in the Union army in January 1863 did not reach the regiment.

For the rest of the First Kansas Colored Infantry, the muster marked a significant occasion. On swearing the enlisted men into federal service, Major Weed addressed the regiment: "It is with the sincerest feelings of pleasure that I congratulate you upon the event just concluded, your muster as soldiers into the service of the United States. By this act you are henceforth and forever free." The gravity of the moment was not lost on the former slaves. The military, led by President Lincoln, had confirmed their perpetual freedom. "I look upon this battalion mustered here to-day, as the germ of a new organization," Weed declared, "the first regiment of your color ever formed in a free State. It will grow in strength, until the new policy thus introduced shall revolutionize the war, giving Liberty to the bond, and restoring the Union to greater than its pristine glory."[23]

It would not be an easy road, Weed admitted. "You have borne the jeers and sneers of open enemies and false friends." Kansas's black soldiers would continue to endure prejudice from home as well as from their enemies. "In submitting to much," Weed said, "your triumph is greater. Go on as you have so well commenced, and you will be, as I hope and desire to see you, the model military organization of the war, in drill, discipline and efficiency." These men would endure the prejudice and work beyond it, for they now had uniforms, muskets, and the support of the government. "You are now recognized as soldiers in the army of Freedom."[24]

It was a rousing speech and a moment of great pride, but there were no parades, no thronging well-wishers. There was no immediate change for the men of the First Kansas Colored Infantry. As Major Weed concluded his remarks on the outskirts of Fort Scott, the men turned, marched in formation to their company streets, and went back to garrison duty.

Critics vented their frustration. "This regiment, which was organized without authority of law, and against orders from the War Department, and whose ranks were filled by the forcible and illegal seizure of negroes in different parts of the State, has at last been regularly mustered into the service and parties were in our city a few days since, arresting those who left the regiment, as did a large number," read one Kansas newspaper.[25] "We should like some matters connected with this regiment thoroughly ventilated. We should like to know who was the prime mover of the plan of seizing and forcing negroes into the service." Whether the writer was genuinely concerned with the well-being of the black soldiers or, like Mayor

Denman in Leavenworth, feigning concern to undermine the creation of the regiment is unclear. "How the officers have procured money, and how the regiment has been subsisted?" the writer asked. "Why it was not disbanded accord[ing] to orders from the Secretary of War?" Such questions went beyond criticizing the impressment or rough treatment of some soldiers and struck at the very heart of the operation.[26]

For those who supported the use of black soldiers, the first few weeks of 1863 were historic. "Glory Hallelujah," began Richard Hinton's account for the *Leavenworth Daily Conservative*, "this regiment is mustered into the service of the United States, as soldiers; mark that, all you who think that negroes are fit for naught but slaves. To-day they stand the best drilled six companies of Infantry ever raised in Kansas." A regiment was supposed to have ten companies of one hundred men each. After nearly two years of war, the *Conservative*'s readers knew this. Enlistments continued as officers signed up new volunteers to fill out the regiment. Slow enlistments could not be blamed for the thin ranks of men ready for muster. Hinton explained that "owing to the large number of absentees, and the imperative character of the orders relative to muster, we were able to muster only six companies of 80 men each, all sound and fit for duty. We thus have present 480 men." The term "absentees" sounded better than "deserters." Nonetheless, Hinton confidently claimed that "within three weeks from date of this muster, at least 400 absentees will be in camp, and the 1st Kansas Colored will have ten companies of full ranks."[27]

Gathering up deserters across eastern Kansas was an unsavory task, but necessary for the integrity of the unit. It became such a concern that Major General James Blunt got involved. Explaining that he had learned "at these Headquarters that men of African decent enlisting in the Colored Regiment have been deserting, and that they have not only been encouraged, but harbored," he issued an order on January 18 for "all deserters as above to immediately return to their respective companies and regiment, or they will be dealt with according to law and regulations."[28] The penalty for desertion during the Civil War could include capital punishment. Such harsh treatment, though, was not always prudent, particularly when leaders were trying to induce other deserters to voluntarily return. Nonetheless, at least some of the regiment's deserters faced stiff penalties. Two deserters from Company C were sentenced to sixty days imprisonment in the Post Guard House, with hard labor eight hours per day. They also forfeited their pay from their enlistment to the end of their sentence.[29]

Lieutenant Colonel James Williams, now enjoying a promotion and official recognition as the commander of the First Kansas Colored Infantry, detailed officers to round up deserters in various parts of the state.[30] He ordered Captain Luther A. Thrasher to "Neosho South West Mission" to investigate reports of deserters, and noted the delicate public relations role the detachment needed to play: "You are aware that great prejudice exists among some military men, toward the officers and men of this and similar organizations; Hence you are expected to so conduct the business entrusted to you as to give the least offense possible to any loyal citizens or soldiers of the union." Thrasher carried out his orders, even in the face of resistance from other units. Serving in a black regiment at this point in the war meant earning respect from Union army peers through careful yet firm dedication to duty.[31]

Some Kansans did entice black soldiers to desert—and they were not always the usual suspects. Captain George Martin led a detail of soldiers to track down deserters in Leavenworth. Having secured a few, he split up his command, personally taking some soldiers to Atchison while leaving the rest to guard the captured deserters in Leavenworth under the observation of former officer William Matthews. Since he had been denied a commission, Matthews had no official role with the regiment. According to some enlisted men, the embittered Matthews used this opportunity to encourage the men to desert. "Captain Mathews [sic] could not get mustered in as captain and he told us that none of his men had any right to serve if he could not get mustered and nobody could trust them," Corporal John McCarter later testified. McCarter said that "Mathews wrote out papers for some of the men."[32] Private George True, originally recruited by Matthews and now part of the detail assigned to track down deserters, took the advice and became a deserter himself. A year later military officials arrested him in Denver and returned him to the regiment. Back in his unit, he explained to a fellow soldier that "Captain Mathews told him if he wanted to leave and would stay out of the way it would be all right."[33]

Desertion was a double-edged sword to the regiment. The delay in mustering the remaining companies postponed the regiment's engagement in active field operations, forcing the men to remain in garrison and sapping morale. Lieutenant Colonel Williams set a strict schedule to keep the men occupied while stationed around Fort Scott. Their day started at sunrise and ended at sundown. Williams ordered the regiment to hold a dress parade every day of the week, at one o'clock in the afternoon. Immediately following the parade, on the weekdays, was battalion drill, a more combat-oriented exercise that focused on the line of battle and the movement of companies. These scheduled drills did not include the regular drilling of recruits in the morning and designated company drill at least three times a week. When not drilling, the men rotated through police and fatigue duty, carried out personal washing and cleaning tasks, and underwent further inspections.[34]

Soon officers at Fort Scott tasked black soldiers to aid in construction of fortifications, initially without Williams's knowledge. "Upon my return to Camp, I found that Co. D of my Regt had been ordered by Major Henning to Fort Lincoln where they now are doing Garrison duty at that post," Williams notified Lieutenant Colonel Thomas Moonlight of General Blunt's staff in late January. "As my Regt had not been ordered for duty, I wish to enquire by what authority this was done." He clarified that he did not wish to keep his unit from legitimate duty, but that "as my regt was but just organized I prefer to have the whole Regiment together for necessary discipline and drill." He requested that "orders come through their regular channels."[35]

Williams had reason to jealously guard the use of his troops. Extended physical labor broke men's bodies and spirits. Private Doc McWilliams, who had joined the regiment in February, watched his friend Private Joseph Bowers deteriorate under the stress of fatigue duty and poor living conditions. "Our camp was surrounded by malarious influences and the nights were chilly and cold from the frequent rain storms that prevail generally in that climate during the winter and spring months," McWilliams later said. Bowers, a vigorous and healthy man, experienced swelling in his ankles and lower legs. The symptoms followed him late into life and became grounds for a disability pension after the war. "It was no doubt the combined influences of the daily manual labour performed by claimant together with the damp chilly nights sleeping in tents upon the ground in a locality full of malaria that causes said acute pains in his ankles and legs," McWilliams testified for his friend.[36] Having just mustered into federal service, many men were breaking down physically.

The Emancipation Proclamation had outlined only support roles for black soldiers, authorizing them "to garrison forts, positions, stations, and other places."[37] The officers and men feared that the regiment would be relegated to manual labor, particularly by officers of other units eager to relieve their own men from backbreaking work. In early March, to help boost morale, Williams ordered that men working on fortifications receive a ration of whiskey, a special treat coveted by soldiers during the Civil War.[38] It did not help. At least twenty-two men deserted in March.[39]

The most wrenching blow to morale was the complete lack of pay. For months the enlisted men had endured drill and the rigors of military life with trust in the promise made by state officials and white officers that they would be recognized as federal soldiers. While their pay was to be less than that of white soldiers, they still expected to receive something. Lane ordered the company to submit their payroll forms, which were completed and approved by the district headquarters. They were forwarded to the department headquarters in St. Louis and passed into bureaucratic oblivion. Adjutant Hinton wrote in desperation to Colonel N. P. Chipman, chief of staff of the Department of Missouri, in February. "My object in writing is to ask of your kindness some definite information upon the subject," he wrote. "We can learn nothing further, and . . . it is a matter of importance both to men and officers." Hinton hoped that Chipman would see Major General Samuel Curtis for a resolution to the problem. He added that the regiment hoped to receive pay for service between enlistment and formal muster. "The am[oun]t of pay from the time of organizing (Augt 4th) to date of muster, Jan 13th is certainly a valuable consideration, being a period of over 4 months." Hinton emphasized the point: "We need the pay, men's families are suffering and something definite should be done."[40] For reasons beyond control of the regiment, nothing happened.

Frustration reached a fever pitch in April 1863. Williams warned superiors at the Department of Kansas headquarters of a potential mutiny. "In view of the fact that my Command is to receive no pay from the paymaster now paying off troops in this vicinity, and that we have for the Ten months that we have been in service, as yet not received one cent, and further that out of all this there seems to be a growing restlessness and insubordination, which are the natural results of these long trials and sufferings," he wrote, he saw no alternative than to suspend regular work operations around the camp.

Fearing that military officials would object to what might appear as submitting to the will of the rank and file, Williams stressed the explosive nature of the situation. "I feel that this Step though irregular and unauthorised nevertheless is absolutely necessary to restrain the mutinous and insubordinate Spirit which has all along manifested itself in a Small degree in the Command (Growing out of the treatment from the Government in regard to pay) from Culminating in open anarchy and perhaps mutiny."[41] Desertions continued to plague the organization. Eight men deserted in April, and thirty-two deserted in May.[42] Williams asked for the regiment's transfer away from Fort Scott, to limit the "outside influence" spurring men to leave the ranks.[43] Despite these entreaties, the men would not receive pay until July. The regiment would relocate within three weeks of Williams's letter, but not for the reasons he requested. Instead, the regiment's future was dictated by the needs of the army.

Low morale and growing discontent may have contributed to more sinister acts by a few individuals during this period. "When we were at Ft. Lincoln which is 12 miles north of Ft. Scott, three soldiers went out and ravished a white woman and her daughter whose husband was a prisoner and one of these men was a Serg[ean]t," Captain George Martin of Company B later recalled. "They were tried and convicted and taken to Baxter Springs where they were shot at dress parade in the presence of the whole Reg[imen]t."[44] Private Henry Lawson explained that for the execution, "men were detailed from each company to shoot them & the whole Reg[imen]t was drawn up in a line & I saw them shot right over their graves."[45] Captain Martin noted that "these men were members of Co. G."[46] The Adjutant General's Report of Kansas does not list any executions of members of Company G, but that company did appear to suffer the lowest morale of the First Kansas Colored Infantry. Of sixty-six recorded desertions between January and May 1863, twenty-two were from Company G alone.[47]

The regiment's complications in the early spring of 1863 were compounded by a new threat. Political feuding at the state and national levels nearly undercut its leadership. The new governor of Kansas, Thomas Carney, came into office in early 1863 as a "Lane man." Once in office, though, he had no intention of being a puppet of the senator. After his inauguration, he set about pushing his own interests through political patronage. In March, he attempted to replace Lieutenant Colonel James Williams with his own hand-picked man, R. C. Anderson. This move spurred the regiment's officers to act: they threatened to shoot Anderson if he tried to take command. Alarmed by Carney's actions, Lane and Major General Blunt forwarded Williams blank commission forms and ordered him to accept only individuals he personally approved.[48]

Carney appealed to Lincoln. "The Governor of Kansas is here," the president wrote in a letter to Lane, "asking that Lieut. Col. J. M. Williams, of a colored regiment there, shall be removed; and also complaining of the military interference of Gen. Blunt in the late election at Leavenworth." Lincoln admitted that he did not know whether Lane was involved in the affair, but asked for his "assistance to shape things that the Governor of Kansas may be treated with the consideration that is extended to Governors of other States." After all, the president wrote, "we are not forcing a Regimental officer upon any other governor, against his protest—Can not this matter be somehow adjusted?" Although Lincoln penned a note at the bottom, "Not sent because Gov. Carney thought it best not be," a final postscript to the letter simply read "To go by Telegraph."[49] Whether Lane received Lincoln's message or not, Williams retained command.[50]

In the face of desertions, insubordination, fear of mutiny, and a command crisis, the regiment as a whole retained its effectiveness while stationed in southeastern Kansas. "The colored regiment is camped one half mile south of town," Christian Isely of the Second Kansas Cavalry wrote from Fort Scott in April. "I went out yesterday and seen them drill at which they seem to be quite efficient. The whole regiment was out and formed into line of battle and went through all kinds of flank movements &c &c."[51] Drill, discipline, and a dedication to the cause kept most men in the ranks sharp.

In late winter and early spring new recruits and returned deserters filled the ranks. Some of the recruits were fugitive slaves inspired by the Emancipation Proclamation. Among them was Nicholas Taylor, a slave to William Thomas in Platt County, Missouri. Years before the war he had married Julia, a slave owned by Thomas's mother-in-law, Nancy Willis. The two masters had approved the marriage and held the ceremony in the Willis home, complete with a minister. By 1863, Nicholas and Julia Taylor had a son and three daughters. According to Julia Taylor's widow pension file, "soon after the proclamation was issued [her] husband . . . left her and [her] children with her mistress [and] went to Leavenworth, Kansas, promising to return for them as soon as he could." After successfully enrolling in

Company G, First Kansas Colored Infantry, Private Taylor obtained a leave of absence and rushed back to Missouri to carry his family to Kansas and freedom. He found "on his return [that] the former owners had spirited the two eldest children away," his widow later said, "and as the soldier was on leave of absence he had to return and took her and the two youngest children to Leavenworth where he provided room for them when he joined his command and soon left for the front."[52]

Many of the new recruits were fugitive slaves from Arkansas who flocked to General Blunt's army during his campaign around Cane Hill and Van Buren. "The large proportion of them came in teams, wagons, &c," reported Richard Hinton to the New York Times. "A train of 125 families was organized at Cane Hill, on the return of the Van Buren expedition, and sent North, with the Ninth Kansas and a commissary train. It consisted of about 50 wagons with four mules each, and several ox-wagons. A number of the young men entered the ranks of the First Regiment Kansas Colored Volunteers; the remainder, after a short stay at Fort Scott, left to seek employment in the neighboring counties."[53]

Major Benjamin Henning, colonel of the Third Wisconsin Cavalry and post commander of Union forces at Fort Scott, estimated that his men had dealt with as many as three thousand refugees—black, Indian, and white Unionists—over the previous months. About one thousand of those refugees were fugitive slaves. Henning praised the resourcefulness of the black emigrants, telling Hinton that few drew rations from the government. Though nearly all were "destitute on arrival," they eagerly sought work to support themselves, unlike the Indian and white Unionist refugees, "many of whom are still recipients of Government aid." "This is valuable testimony to the industrious tendencies of the negro," Hinton proudly declared, noting Henning's previous political sentiments, "all the more so that it comes from an old Democrat who, as long as consistent with his duty, fought the organization of the negro regiments in this State."[54]

Even with the enlistments of refugees, Lane and Blunt grew impatient with the delay in filling the regiment. In Leavenworth, the senator and the general ran into Benjamin Van Horn, the native Indianan who had helped hide two runaways below the floor of a kitchen table before the war, and told him of the regiment's problems. In early 1863, Van Horn was a state legislator who had been contracted to deliver beef to the Sac and Fox Agency, an Indian reservation in east central Kansas. He told them that more than one hundred starving and destitute black refugees were living with the Sac and Fox Indians. Van Horn suggested they send a recruiter to the agency to fill a company for the regiment. Lane and Blunt conversed. "See here, those men must be enlisted just as quick as possible," they told Van Horn, "and with your knowledge of the situation you can do it quicker and make cleaner work of it than any other man, and you must do it." Uninterested in seeking a commission with black soldiers, Van Horn "made all the excuses I could" to rebuff the request. Lane and Blunt persisted. Van Horn finally agreed to try.[55]

Blunt handed Van Horn a pen and paper and instructed him to list all the supplies he would need to outfit the company. Van Horn admitted his ignorance in military matters, explaining later, "I did not know anything more about what I would want than the man in the moon." "Well," Blunt replied, "I do and I will make it out and see that it is filed and I will warrant you that it will be the most complete outfit that ever a recruiting officer started out with."[56]

Van Horn soon had six new wall tents, eighty muskets, ammu-nition, cooking utensils, and other basic camp equipment for a full company. Two wagons, complete with draft animals, carried his supplies. Blunt even assigned an instructor to Van Horn to begin les-sons in drill and discipline as soon as possible. With his new lieu-tenant commission in hand, Van Horn made his way to the Sac and Fox Agency.[57]

In less than a month, Van Horn organized eighty recruits for Company I. Little information remains of these men, but they proved to be a rich cultural and ethnic mix. John Battice and Elwis Cuttica were Sac Indians; their complexion was listed as "Red."[58] Bully Connell and Scipio Gouge were slaves from the Creek Nation. And Private Cyrus Bowlegs had been born a slave to Seminole Indians in Florida. Taken to Indian Territory (modern-day Oklahoma) some-time before the outbreak of the Civil War, likely during the relo-cation of the Seminoles by the U.S. government, Bowlegs again emigrated with a Seminole group to the Sac and Fox Agency in Kansas during the bitter divisions of Native American tribes fol-lowing Southern secession. A fellow slave later said that Bowlegs's "knowledge of English is limited. . . . He was raised a slave among Indians not speaking English." On his enlistment, Bowlegs used the name of the Seminole family that had owned him.[59]

Other recruits were free blacks from Indian Territory. Isaac Alexander worked as a free man on a farm in the Chickasaw Nation when he joined. "I do not know how old I was when I enlisted," he later declared, "but I had grandchildren when I went in the army." Likely born in the 1820s, Alexander entered Company I "a sound hearty man" who "was free from all disease," just the sort of candidate the officers wanted.[60] Privates Nero and Elias Hardridge were both under eighteen years old, technically too young for regular combat duty in the Union army. Later that summer, when General Blunt learned of their ages, he ordered them to be discharged from the regiment on the grounds that they had been "illegally recruited and mustered into the service of the U.S., being minors . . . and the consent of their parents not having been obtained."[61]

Perhaps the most unusual recruit in Company I was John W. Smith. "I was born in Toronto, Canada, and was about twenty four years old when I enlisted," he told a pension official after the war. He was a free man who could read and write before entering the army. Moreover, "I am a Black Hawk Indian, and spoke the Indian language when I was in the army." He continued, "All of my comrades knew that I was an Indian," adding, "I did not wear my hair long when in the army, but my hair was perfectly straight." Private Smith enlisted in the regiment in March 1863 while in Leavenworth, but left no explanation within his pension file of how or why he traveled to Kansas from Canada. He served as a bugler for the regiment for most of his service.[62]

With nearly a full company of eager recruits, Captain Van Horn marched to Fort Scott to meet the rest of the regiment. Once there the men "got their old rags off and," he remembered, "all dressed in new uniforms and mustered in they were as proud as a little boy with a red wagon."[63] To turn these raw recruits into an effective fighting force, officers of Company I placed the men through a rigorous training regimen. The new recruits learned to march in tight formation by column and in line, to maneuver those lines crisply in response to command, and to coordinate each action as a cohesive unit. Infantry tactics of American Civil War armies eschewed individuality. The soldier was part of machine, one component of a tightly packed and controlled military piece of equipment. This practice had roots in European warfare, where armies made little attempt to conceal their position, and where soldiers were seen as pawns rather than as intelligent players in a deadly game of combat.

These traditional tactics allowed officers to more easily control men in battle. During the loud and chaotic fighting, where the roaring black powder weapons drowned out verbal commands and covered the field with smoke, physical contact between each soldier provided an important means of communication: move forward, shift left, shift right, or retreat.

Tactically, men fighting shoulder-to-shoulder proved a formidable obstacle to opposing forces. The linear fighting formation gave strength to a position and provided the only practical means of mass fire for most nineteenth-century armies. A single soldier with a muzzle-loading musket could do little on the battlefield by himself, but hundreds of soldiers firing simultaneously in one continuous line could send a devastating scythe of lead against an enemy position. Of course, by placing men in tight formation on an open field, officers could expect to suffer heavy casualties from the enemy's mass fire. That had become acceptable in European and American military practice.

Van Horn's new recruits mastered these tactics. Firing in tight formation of two lines required careful discipline. According to William J. Hardee's military drill manual, adopted in 1855 by the U.S. Army, men of the front rank fired in a right-hand stance with the right foot placed behind and perpendicular to the left. A man in the back row stepped slightly forward and to the right with the right foot, often resting his left arm on the front man's right shoulder to level the rifle past his head.[64] When the entire company readied in this fashion, a man in the front rank had a musket over each shoulder. This tight formation could prove hazardous if soldiers failed to control the muzzle of their weapon, as Private Abraham Kernell learned during Company I's training. While at target practice, he explained, "I was in the first Column and at the order, by the Lieutenant, [to] 'aim' the soldier who was my file not only took bad 'aim' but discharged his gun before it was brought to a proper position, and when the gun was only about two or three inches from my head." The explosion of flame, hot gas, and smoke staggered Kernell, who fell against the nearby lieutenant. He remained with the regiment through the duration of the war, but suffered permanent hearing loss.[65]

New recruits from the refugee population around Fort Scott provided some men while enlistments continued in Lawrence area and Wyandotte. Finally, by the first part of May, the regiment was at full strength and ready to take the field. All companies were ordered to regroup near Fort Scott for an assignment farther south.

Company H was stationed at Fort Lincoln guarding twenty-one Confederate prisoners when it received word of the regiment's impending departure. Part of the Second Kansas Cavalry arrived to relieve the black soldiers. Among them was Private Isely, who had earlier been impressed with the First Kansas Colored Infantry's drill outside of Fort Scott. "Some of the boys did not like the idea very much to relieve the *black niggers* but I went along without saying a word of discontentment," he told his brother. The tension may have been noticeable to the men of the First Kansas Colored, for prior to leaving camp, they performed a conspicuous demonstration of their military ability. Isely noted that an officer "put them (the negroes) through the different evolutions and manuals of arms, which they done to a perfection; while the drummers and fifer played Dixie in a manner that it would do a white soldier honor." It left a strong impression on the white soldiers: "This rather beat & silenced the always . . . loud predjudiced [sic] fault finders."[66] Soon the First Kansas Colored Infantry would again take those skills to the field of battle.

Fig. 1. James Henry Lane, the politician-soldier. Elected to the U.S. Senate from Kansas in 1861, Lane personally led troops in the field in Missouri later that summer. In 1862, he stretched his authority to raise soldiers by organizing the first African American regiment in a Northern state—the First Kansas Colored Infantry. *Photo courtesy of the Library of Congress.*

Fig. 2. James G. Blunt. As commander of military forces in Kansas and friend to Senator James Lane, Major General Blunt helped organize the First Kansas Colored Infantry. Blunt led them to victory with other Union troops at the Battle of Honey Springs in July 1863. *Photo courtesy of the Library of Congress.*

Fig. 3. James M. Williams. A steadfast abolitionist chosen by Senator James Lane to lead the First Kansas Colored Infantry, Williams took part in most of the regiment's battles and rose to brevet brigadier general during the war. Decades after the war, in Washington, D.C., he helped gain recognition for his black veterans. *Photo courtesy of the Kansas State Historical Society, KansasMemory.org.*

Fig. 4. William D. Matthews. A free black man in Kansas in 1862, Matthews helped raise a company of soldiers for the First Kansas Colored Infantry and became one of the regiment's two black officers. Because of his race, military authorities refused to muster Matthews as an officer into federal service in January 1863. The War Department eventually authorized his muster, which would have made Matthews the first black officer in the U.S. Army, but the order did not reach the regiment or Matthews. *Photo courtesy of the Kansas State Historical Society, KansasMemory.org.*

Fig. 5. Joseph Gardner.
As an abolitionist settler in Kansas, Gardner fought alongside fugitive slave Napoleon Simpson against Missouri slave hunters near Lawrence in 1860. In 1862, Gardner became an officer in Company F, First Kansas Colored Infantry. He was gravely wounded at the skirmish at Island Mound in 1862 and later died of disease in 1863. *Photo courtesy of the Kansas State Historical Society, KansasMemory.org.*

Fig. 6. Harrison Miller.
Postwar photograph of Harrison Miller of Company C. He lived as a slave on the farm of John Johnson near Lexington, Missouri, before escaping and joining the regiment in September 1862. Miller mustered out in 1865, moved to Leavenworth, Kansas, and passed away in 1910. *Photo courtesy of the National Archives.*

Fig. 7. William Gordon. Postwar photo of William Gordon, Company E. Badly whipped after trying to escape his master Joseph Fields in Marshall, Missouri, Gordon successfully escaped slavery on his second attempt and joined the regiment on August 19, 1862. After the war, he worked as the cemetery sexton in Paola, Kansas. *Photo courtesy of Phil Reaka and the Miami County Historical Society, Kansas.*

Fig. 8. James Whitfield Ross. After escaping slavery in Missouri, Ross joined the regiment on August 16, 1862, and rose to the rank of corporal in Company F. Ross mustered out in 1865, married in 1868, and had seven children. He passed away in 1926 in Mound City, Kansas. *Photo courtesy of the family of James W. Ross and the Museum of the Kansas National Guard Hall of Fame.*

Fig. 9. Jackson Donald, Company B. When he enlisted on August 15, 1862, he intended to take the family name of his former master, "Donnell." The officer recorded it as "Donald." Private Jackson Donald served with the First Kansas Colored Infantry through the war and mustered out in 1865. After the war, he reunited with his father and learned the family name was Gorl. He chose to keep the name Donald until he learned his inheritance depended on the name change. *Photo courtesy of the National Archives.*

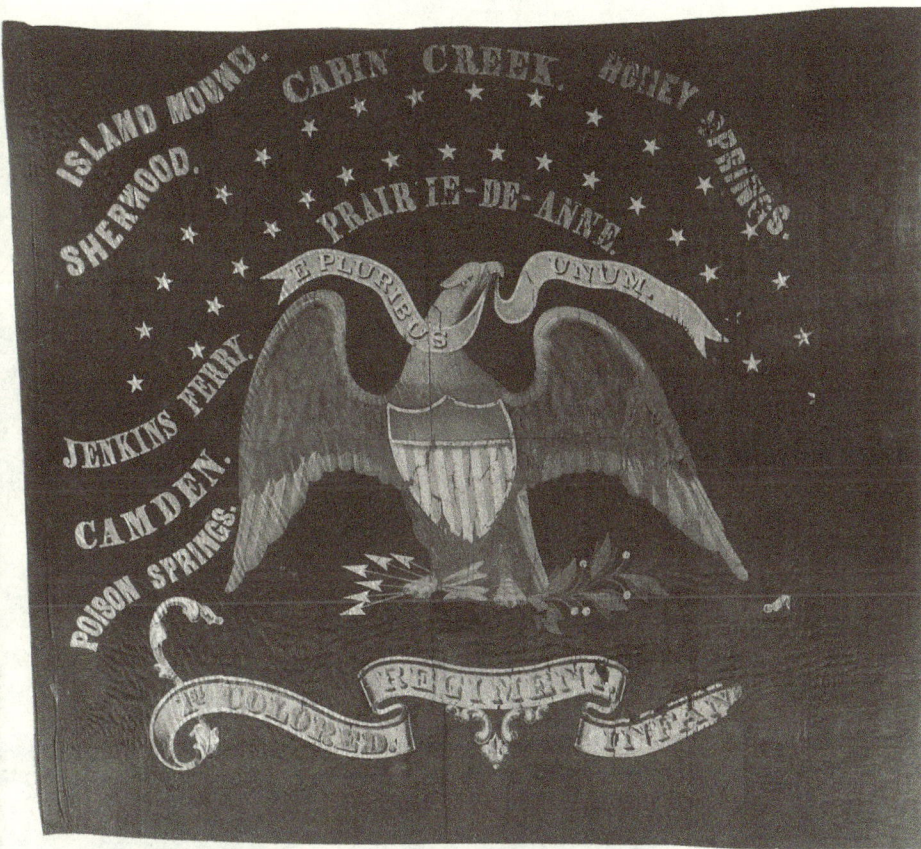

Fig. 10. First Kansas Colored Infantry Flag. The flag of the First Kansas Colored Infantry resides in the Kansas State Historical Society museum in Topeka, Kansas. Inscribed across its front are engagements at Island Mound, Sherwood, Cabin Creek, Honey Springs, Prairie-de-Anne [Prairie D'Ane], Poison Springs, Camden, and Jenkins Ferry. *Photo courtesy of the Kansas State Historical Society, KansasMemory.org.*

Fig. 11. **"A Negro Regiment in Action"** On March 14, 1863, *Harper's Weekly* published this image, titled "A Negro Regiment in Action," and a short article about the First Kansas Colored Infantry at the Battle of Island Mound. *Image courtesy of the Library of Congress.*

CHAPTER 8

SHERWOOD

It is pretty hard, but war is a serious business.

On May 4, 1863, the regiment left Fort Scott for Baxter Springs, a key military point sixty miles south, in the southeastern corner of Kansas. It was the last stop in friendly Union territory for wagon trains and combat-bound units on their way into Indian Territory. The new assignment meant patrols and scouting expeditions in southwestern Missouri.

On May 5, M. M. Ehle and sixty men of the Second Kansas Cavalry caught up with Colonel James M. Williams and the regiment on the trail to the new camp. Ehle had investigated reports of a rebel gathering near Sherwood, Missouri, a dozen miles away. He found 250 guerrillas—far too big of a force for the cavalry detachment to attack alone. Ehle appealed for help. Williams ordered two of his companies and one gun from the Second Kansas Battery to assist the cavalrymen and disperse the camp.

At daybreak, the combined force attacked, "carrying the camp in gallant style and dispersing the rebels in every direction." A second camp was found closer to the town of Sherwood, and the Kansans easily routed its defenders too. Three prisoners were rounded up, as were horses, mules, and a large store of supplies. "This has been a most successful scout, and a very profitable capture to the Government," bragged Charles Blair, the Second Kansas Cavalry's colonel. Not a Union man was lost.[1]

The successful attack on a guerrilla camp was worth celebrating. Pinning down irregular soldiers was difficult. In reality, the First Kansas Colored Infantry was not the ideal force for hunting and dispatching Missouri guerrillas. The Missourians rarely congregated in one place for any amount of time, usually only long enough to strike a vulnerable target. By the time an infantry unit traveled the many miles necessary to investigate a report of activity, the Rebels usually slipped away to a new staging area or simply disbanded and melted into the Missouri landscape. Typical was the fifty-man scouting patrol to the falls of Sholes Creek and Sherwood led by Major Richard Ward on May 9. The detachment returned after an uneventful fifteen-mile march.[2] The Kansas-Missouri border region was simply too large for foot soldiers to cover effectively. Suited for the task or not, Union commanders in Missouri needed soldiers to chase down guerrillas. The regiment owed its existence to this mission and approached the job without complaint.

Sitting at Baxter Springs and trying to guard Union supply trains from unpredictable Confederate attacks frustrated Colonel Williams. Playing on Southern ideas of honor, he attempted to prod his opponents into open battle. In a terse note to local guerrillas on May 11, Williams declared his desire "to follow as far as practicable all the rules applicable to Civilized warfare." Sneaking around, laying ambushes, and avoiding a pitched battle would not do. Williams wrote, "I therefore propose that you collect all the enemies of the United States in your vicinity and Come to some point and attack me, or give me notice where I can find your force and I will fight you on your own ground." He could not have expected the challenge to provoke a battle; rather, his intent was to justify a more brutal use of force. He declared, "If you persist in the system of Guerrilla warfare heretofore followed by you and refuse to fight openly like soldiers fighting for a cause I shall feel bound to treat you as thieves and robbers who lurk in secret places fighting only defenceless people and wholly unworthy the fate due to chivalrous soldiers engaged in honourable warfare." If the guerrillas continued their irregular and criminal activity, Williams argued, he would "take any means within my power to rid the Country of your murderous gang."[3] The Missouri guerrillas did not respond. They waited and watched for targets of opportunity. Soon they got their chance to strike a severe blow to the First Kansas Colored Infantry.

On May 18, about twenty-five enlisted men and officers from the regiment set out to forage for corn near Sherwood, Missouri. Significantly, Williams had no access to a cavalry escort. Mounted soldiers were the eyes and ears of an infantry force on the move and were particularly vital during an expedition far from camp. "There was at this time among the white soldiers a decided feeling against serving with colored troops," former Kansas cavalryman Wiley Britton wrote after the war, "and this was perhaps the reason [Williams] had no cavalry attached to his command."[4] Racial prejudice among white Union soldiers was no doubt a factor, though not the sole reason the cavalry was not at Baxter Springs. The regiment had successfully worked with Captain Ehle's detachment from the Second Kansas Cavalry only a week before, at the request of the white soldiers. Military officials in Kansas simply had no cavalry units to spare. "I am greatly embarrassed for want of troops," admitted Major General James Blunt in an assessment of the military situation along the Kansas border that month, "yet everything must be done that is possible to maintain our present lines until troops can be procured."[5] Williams had no choice but to assign a contingent of fifteen mounted white soldiers of the Second Kansas Battery. Although not cavalrymen, these artillerymen could offer some support.[6]

Confederate scouts watched the Union detachment and hurried back to their leader, Tom Livingston. Since learning that black Union soldiers were in the Baxter Springs area, Missouri guerrillas anticipated an opportunity to catch the infantrymen out of their well-defended encampment. Their anger at the sight of black men in uniform circulated back to Union lines. "The guerrilla leaders in that section declare that they will not take the colored soldiers nor the officers under whom they are serving, as prisoners of war," wrote Kansas cavalryman Wiley Britton.[7] The small foraging party was a perfect target for Livingston. The thirty-nine-year-old bachelor, clean-shaven except for a moustache, was well respected in southeastern Missouri. His broad shoulders, solid stature, and reputation as a fist-fighter helped his status as a leader in the wild and dangerous Trans-Mississippi theater. He seemed fearless in war, even sporting a distinctive, broad-brimmed white hat in battle.[8] As Confederate guerrillas, Livingston and his men dressed and equipped themselves according to individual whims or scrounging abilities. While standard Union cavalry weapons included a pistol, a sword, and a carbine, Livingston's men carried three or four revolvers, supplemented by shotguns, carbines, and any other weapon they could carry.

Guerrillas were not averse to wearing captured federal coats and hats to mislead Union soldiers. Organized armies considered this behavior criminal, akin to piracy on the sea. Yet many warriors on the Kansas-Missouri border had long since abandoned the formalities of European-style warfare. Ambush, executions, and other behavior deemed criminal by military authorities were common here. For many Missourians, the sight of armed black soldiers wearing blue uniforms was disturbing and deserving of punishment.

Learning of the approaching detachment, Livingston ordered sixty-seven of his best riders into the saddle. They soon found the unlucky band of Kansas black troops at the Rader household, the home of one of Livingston's men.[9] Mrs. Rader had been forced from the house while soldiers stacked muskets in the yard and searched the building. Some of them found a cache of corn in an upstairs room and were busily throwing the cobs into some of the five mule-drawn wagons below a window.[10] The Confederates attacked, achieving complete surprise. The Union soldiers could offer little resistance, especially the twenty black infantrymen whose muskets stood out of reach. The attack was carried out just as Livingston intended. Cohesion among the Union party evaporated. "The Artillery boys and our officers being mounted were able to get out of [the] way," Capt. John Graton of Company C wrote his wife, "but the black boys being on foot had to take it and most of them were killed."[11]

The mounted officers and artillery soldiers rode for their lives, pursued by guerrillas on excellent horses. At least two of the artillerymen were killed, presumably when their horses gave out. Livingston's men chased the rest some eight miles before reining in their mounts. The attack so overwhelmed the Union detachment that survivors estimated Livingston's force to number as high as two hundred men—nearly three times as many as he reported taking into battle.[12]

When the exhausted survivors reached Baxter Springs the alarm sounded through camp. Colonel Williams readied five companies and secured a small force of Union cavalry to respond. The odds that Livingston's men would be at the scene of the attack by the time the Kansans could get there were slim; Sherwood was ten miles away. But that did not deter Williams. Leaving at dusk, his force marched all night, stopping only two hours to rest.[13]

Evidence of the previous afternoon's carnage met the soldiers along the way. Four miles from Sherwood one of the Second Kansas Battery's men lay sprawled on the roadway, killed during the flight from the guerrillas, stripped to his underclothes. The early morning sun exposed an even more gruesome sight as the Union force arrived at the Rader house. It was here for the first time, Williams later wrote, that he beheld "the horrible evidence of the demoniacal spirits of these rebel fiends in the treatment of our dead and wounded."

Thirteen bodies lay scattered around the Rader house "with their brains beaten out with clubs, the bloody weapon being left beside them, and their bodies horribly mutilated."[14]

The house was abandoned. Expecting a swift Union response, Mrs. Rader fled from her home during the night, taking as much personal property as she could. The Union cavalrymen scouted the area for signs of the enemy while the infantrymen attended to the heart-wrenching task of gathering their dead. No shovels could be found, so the Rader house was turned into a funeral pyre.[15]

The cavalry scouts brought a prisoner to Williams, a local Missourian named John Bishop. A Union soldier identified him as a Confederate "bushwhacker," recently paroled from the prison at Fort Lincoln.[16] Parole procedures dictated that a released prisoner swear an oath not to take up arms until an opposing prisoner was released in turn. Despite the risks associated with releasing enemy combatants solely on written promises, military authorities occasionally turned to the practice when unable to accommodate large numbers of prisoners. No better example can be found than General Ulysses S. Grant's parole of tens of thousands of Confederate soldiers following the capture of Vicksburg, Mississippi, in July 1863. Furthermore, the system was based on the still strong sense of honor in nineteenth-century American culture. Many parolees took their oaths seriously, committed to maintaining their standing as honorable soldiers. Greater incentive was the threat of punishment. Persons guilty of violating parole—of taking arms before their parole terms had been met—faced execution if captured.

The Union men found blood on Bishop's clothing and federal shoes on his feet, evidence to them that he had violated his parole by participating in the attack on the black soldiers. The Kansans marched the condemned man to the house, shot him, and threw his body inside. Soon the Rader house was an inferno, consuming the bodies of Bishop and the fallen First Kansas Colored soldiers.[17]

Incensed at the treatment of his men and convinced that "the force attacking this party consisted partially of the citizens of the neighborhood, who, while enjoying the protection of our arms, had collected together to assist the rebel force in this attack," Williams ordered his force to spread destruction five miles in every direction. The Kansans destroyed the town of Sherwood and raided a dozen nearby homesteads. Residents were given a few minutes to gather as much as they could carry before the torch was set to their homes and property. Williams recalled at the end of the war, "It is my opinion that this prevented any like occurrence in this neighborhood subsequently." "It is pretty hard," Captain Graton resolved, "but war is a serious business."[18]

When Williams and his detachment returned to Baxter Springs they found survivors from the previous day's attack filtering back into camp. During the melee, several black soldiers had escaped into the thick brush. Fearful of being discovered by roving guerrilla patrols, most had remained hidden near the Rader house during the night.[19]

Livingston claimed his men killed twenty-three black soldiers and seven white soldiers. A regimental tally recorded thirteen black soldiers killed, two missing, and the loss of thirty mules and five wagons.[20] Two days after the attack a message from Livingston arrived in the Kansans' camp. "I have five of your soldiers prisoners," he wrote. "Three white and two black men." The guerrilla leader proposed a prisoner exchange, offering the white soldiers for any three Confederates held in federal captivity. "As for the Negroes," Livingston declared, "I cannot recognize them as soldiers and in consequence I will have to hold them as contrabands of war."[21]

Livingston also questioned Williams about the fate of Bishop. "If that is your mode of warfare to arrest civil citizens who are living at home and trying to raise a crop for their families let me know and I will try to play to your hand." Livingston peremptorily denied that Bishop was guilty of anything, arguing that although "Mr. Bishop was once arrested [and] taken to Fort Scott," he had been "examined and released." Turning to the matter of Bishop's execution and cremation in the Rader home, Livingston wrote that he was "satisfied that you are too high toned a gentleman to stoop or condicend [sic] to such Brutal deeds of Barbarity."[22]

Williams replied the following day. He explained that only two white soldiers from the Rader house attack were unaccounted for, and agreed to exchange two Confederate prisoners for their release. If Livingston had a third white Union soldier in custody, Williams advised him to contact higher authorities at Fort Scott for an exchange. As for the future of the black prisoners, "I have this to say, that it rests with you to treat them as prisoners of war or not but be assured that I shall keep a like number of your men as prisoners until these colored men are accounted for, and you can safely trust that I shall visit a retributive justice upon them for any injury done them at the hands of the confederate forces." Williams set a deadline of twenty days for their exchange, at which point he would "conclude that they have been murdered by your soldiers or shared a worse fate by being sent in chains to the slave pens of the South, and they will be presumed to be dead." At that point in time, Williams assured Livingston, two Confederate prisoners would share the same fate.[23]

"In regard to Bishop," Williams continued, "I have to say that he was known as a paroled prisoner of war, he was taken in arms against our forces, and was convicted of having shot a wounded prisoner, disarmed and at his mercy, he was shot and shared the fate of other soldiers for whom spades could not be found to dig their graves." How Williams obtained evidence that Bishop shot a wounded prisoner is unknown. And his declaration that the executed man had been "convicted" was a bit of a stretch, as his trial had been nothing more than a summary execution by angry Kansas soldiers. Williams added, "If this be 'brutal barbarity' compare it to the fiendish treatment [Bishop] himself visited upon one of my men and of the bodies of club bruised, and brain bespattered corpses of my men left on the prairie by your men and leave it to a candid world who profits by comparison." These black soldiers were in the service of the U.S. government, Williams argued, "and I doubt not the Government I have the honor to serve will take the necessary steps to punish her enemies ample for any such gross violations of all rules of civilized and honorable warfare." If Livingston objected to Williams's actions, "you are at liberty to 'play to my hand' as best suits your please or convenience," with the expectation that the Kansans would respond in kind.[24] Williams's threats had little effect. Livingston wrote back two days later with a threat to kill three Union men for each Confederate killed while captive.[25]

Despite these challenges, the exchange of the white soldiers progressed smoothly. Though the fate of the black prisoners hung in the balance, Williams "did not desire that white troops should be made to suffer injury on account of connection with colored troops," and thus agreed to the partial exchange. The two Second Kansas Battery men were safely released for the freedom of two Confederates.[26] At this point, Williams learned that one of the black prisoners had been murdered. The colonel fired off a message to Livingston demanding "the body of the man who committed the dastardly act." He warned that if the Missourians failed to comply, "and do not within forty eight hours, deliver to me this assassin, I shall hang one of the men who are now prisoners in my camp."[27]

Williams also used this correspondence to further justify the burning of Sherwood and the surrounding houses. "You must understand that when I burn a dwelling in a rebel country," he explained, "it is a notice to the occupants thereof to remove beyond the Federal lines, and failing to do which they will be summarily dealt with, and if afterwards found quartered upon any Union man's premises they will be treated as thieves and marauders and neither age nor sex shall shield them from the full measure of punishment due to such criminals." His real purpose was explained at the end of his letter: "I repeat to you that I am not going to lie here hunting a rebel force, who have as specific character or purpose and who are supported by persons living within our lines. Tell them from me to put their house in order, for if I cannot find the force and have a fair stand up fight, I will destroy them by taking from them the means whereby they live." This was a threat to wage war on the local civilian population.[28]

In a brief postscript, Williams tried to thwart Livingston from shifting blame for the black soldier's murder. "If you are fit to command you can control your men, and I shall act from the belief that the murder was committed by your consent and will receive no excuse therefore."[29] Livingston did shift the blame. The offender "is not a member of any company over which I have any control," he wrote in response, "but was casually at my camp." This person "became suddenly enraged and an altercation took place between him and deceased which resulted in a way I very much regret." Since the offender had left camp and his whereabouts were unknown, the guerrilla leader concluded that nothing could be done. His apathy toward a crime committed in his camp is notable. Outsiders stealing horses or destroying property in a military camp were not easily dismissed by a commanding officer, even one commanding irregular soldiers, if for no other reason than to maintain control. The fact that Livingston professed an inability to police the behavior of men within his camp to explain away the murder showed contempt for black soldiers and their officers. He simply did not care to be accountable for the lives of two black men held in arms against Southerners.[30] Finally, Livingston noted that if Williams planned to retaliate by murdering a prisoner, none of his men were in Union hands. "Consequently the innocent will have to suffer for the guilty," he remarked.[31]

Unhappy with Livingston's reply, Colonel Williams ordered the execution of a Confederate prisoner. Within thirty minutes, the order had been carried out, and Williams reportedly notified Livingston of the act. After the war Williams claimed, "Suffice it to say that this ended the barbarous practice of murdering prisoners of war, so far as Livingston's command was concerned."[32] The truth of his claim, however, is doubtful. While the fate of the remaining black prisoner in Livingston's hands does not appear in unit documents, rosters of the First Kansas Colored Infantry compiled by the state's adjutant general after the war list fifteen men killed at Sherwood—a number consistent with the thirteen killed initially and the deaths of both captured men.[33]

Vengeance killings occurred randomly during this period. At the Baxter Springs camp, a First Kansas Colored Infantry sergeant walked behind two Confederate prisoners "being marched along in the parade ground with a ball and chain."[34] Private Henry Lawson of Company B watched as the sergeant raised his musket to the back of one of the prisoners. "It was noon," Lawson remembered, "the prisoner had a ball & chain and the non-commissioned officer was walking behind & shot him dead. The officer said his prisoner started to run & shot him."[35] Years later when recalling the event, Lawson maintained that the noncommissioned officer was court-martialed for the killing. If so, the records of the court were not filed with others of the regiment.

The First Kansas Colored Infantry spent the last part of May patrolling portions of southeastern Missouri, looking for Livingston's men or any other guerrillas they could round up. Occasionally they caught sight of the enemy, such as on May 26, when a twenty-five-soldier detachment skirmished with one hundred guerrillas near Brush Creek. The Kansans emerged from the fight unscathed.[36] Generally, though, scouting operations were uneventful. Keeping away from Union combat patrols, Livingston and his men selected softer targets—what Livingston called "a sure thing"— such as supply trains, foraging parties, and, on June 8, a small group of Kansas artillery horses grazing near the federal camp at Baxter Springs. The First Kansas Colored and most of the Second Kansas Battery were in the field when Livingston struck. Of the small Union guard at camp, one soldier was killed and two captured.[37]

"I visited your lonely camp on yesterday," the Confederate leader tauntingly wrote Williams. Along with two white Union soldiers, a federal beef contractor named David Harland fell into Confederate hands. "I am not disposed to treat him even he being your beef contractor, as you had an unoffensive neighbor of mine treated, that is killed and burned," Livingston wrote, referring to Bishop. He preferred to trade Harland posthaste for a prisoner in Union custody, he said, then added an ominous warning: "I would love for the business to be hastened as much as possible, lest Harlan should imitate the example of Powers when in your hands and meet the same unfortunate fate as a penalty for attempting to escape."[38] Presumably Powers had been one of the Confederate prisoners killed under Williams's watch, perhaps the man shot by the sergeant.

Williams replied that the two artillerymen could be exchanged as requested. Harland, however, was a different matter. The beef contractor "does not in any way belong to the service," Williams wrote, and he was barely considered a contractor. Williams believed Harland was better described as "a citizen of the Cherokee nation who has in no way done service for the United States"; in fact, Harland had been arrested and paroled. Williams contended that "if you injure him you will do as great an injury to your service as to ours."[39]

Before the issue with Harland played out, events in Indian Territory drew the regiment's attention away from the ongoing feud with Livingston. Some weeks earlier, in April, Colonel William A. Phillips and roughly three thousand Union soldiers, mostly Indian recruits, had marched into the territory to challenge Confederate operations and bring support to beleaguered pro-Union Native Americans there. His campaign went smoothly at first. The federals captured an old military outpost called Fort Gibson in the northeastern portion of the territory, and on April 12 Phillips triumphantly wrote to Major General James Blunt, "We have swept this side of the Arkansas River clean." Phillips renamed the post Fort Blunt in honor of the Kansas general. Now, two months later, the situation at Fort Blunt had become desperate. After persistent Confederate pressure, and attacks on Union wagon trains, Phillips's men badly needed reinforcement and supplies.[40] The Union's hold on the northeastern portion of Indian Territory was tenuous.

Around June 8, Blunt issued orders for the First Kansas Colored Infantry to reinforce Phillips at Fort Blunt immediately. He also ordered the Second Colorado Infantry and the Second Kansas Battery to join the next wagon train to the fort.[41] Williams, harassed by Livingston's guerrillas almost daily, struggled to secure federal supplies at Baxter Springs before marching the regiment into Indian Territory. He called on military forces at Fort Scott to provide transportation for the supplies. Nothing arrived, so the regiment waited.[42] A week later Blunt sent a note to Williams. "If by any means you have failed to move your command and reinforce Col. Philips as directed per Special Orders from Hd. Qrs. Dist. of Ks., before the command of Lieut. Col. Dodd, 2nd Colorado reaches you," the order read, "your forces will not be united for the purpose of escorting the train and you assume command as the ranking officer, but comply with previous orders issued you, reporting in person to Col. Philips with your command."[43]

Colonel Williams either failed to receive the order or disobeyed it. He kept his black soldiers at Baxter Springs to wait for cavalry support and wagons from Fort Scott. In the meantime, the situation around Fort Blunt grew more perilous. Confederates tested the fort's defenses, but Phillips's Indian soldiers marched out and pushed them back. Phillips could see smoke from Confederate camps a few miles away and feared the enemy was consolidating its forces. The Grand and Arkansas Rivers converged near Fort Blunt, and the two waterways stood between the opposing forces. Recent high water levels had prevented military maneuvers in the region, but as the water level dropped, Fort Blunt might find itself confronted by an imposing Confederate army. "I have had no mail, dispatch, or communication for two weeks," Colonel Phillips wrote Blunt on June 20. "I have sent messengers to the colored regiment, but cannot hear of it. I have heard nothing of my train." In desperation, Phillips sent a large detachment of his Indian battalion under Major John A. Foreman to clear a path for the expected wagon train and escort it to Fort Blunt.[44]

Blunt worried about the physical ability of Phillips's Indian soldiers to withstand a Confederate attack, as well as the state of their morale. "The Indian troops have of late become quite discouraged, in consequence of not being supported by white troops, as has been promised them," Blunt wrote Major General John Schofield on June 26. "They have manifested a true devotion to the cause, and have made almost superhuman efforts to hold their country, in hopes every day of obtaining succor, but I have had none to send them until now."[45]

On June 24, the disparate Union relief forces finally converged at Baxter Springs. Major Foreman and his battalion of Indians arrived from Fort Blunt; the wagon train arrived from Fort Scott; and Colonel Williams and the First Kansas Colored Infantry had the reinforcements and transportation needed to move out of camp and into Indian territory.[46] "After a long, and to me a tiresome delay," Williams wrote to Blunt that day, "occasioned wholly by the persistent refusal of the Depot Q. M. at Fort Scott to furnish me with the transportation absolutely necessary for me to move my supplies with, I am happy to announce to you that my Regiment will move at 4 A.M. tomorrow for Fort Blunt there reporting to Col. Phillips in accordance with your orders." He justified his regiment's delay at Baxter Springs, arguing that "I could not have moved sooner time without first destroying a large amount of supplies which I had on hand." Venting still more, Williams declared, "I cannot close this communication without saying to you that I do not think that it was necessary to keep me here waiting so long for this supply of transportation and that a little more promptness on the part of those officers whose duties it is to furnish these wants would be desireable upon them, to comply with their orders with more promptness."[47]

Whatever the cause for delay, the relief expedition to Fort Blunt finally set off on June 25, prepared and willing to break through Confederate opposition and secure federal control of northeastern Indian Territory. Significantly, this important campaign offered the First Kansas Colored Infantry a key combat role. It was now the backbone of Major General Blunt's army.

CHAPTER 9

CABIN CREEK

... with as much ease and little confusion as if upon parade.

The route from Baxter Springs to Fort Blunt was an old and well-traveled path known as the Texas Road. Its origins dated back decades, but it was not until the Mexican War that the buffalo trail and Native American footpath emerged as a major thoroughfare. White immigrants to Texas traveled south through Missouri into Indian Territory and on to Texas. The road had two branches to Fort Blunt: one from Baxter Springs and another from southwestern Missouri. Settlers and enterprising businessmen had constructed six stations between Baxter Springs and Fort Blunt, for food, water, lodging, and other necessities.[1] By 1863, the Texas Road served as the primary supply line for military forces operating in northeastern Indian Territory.

In late June 1863, the Union wagon train moved south along the road, determined to push through to Fort Blunt. Its military escort consisted of nine cavalry companies from various regiments, six companies of the Second Colorado Infantry, a contingent of 450 men from the Indian Home Guard, and the First Kansas Colored Infantry Regiment. Captain John R. Graton of Company C remarked that the caravan "must have reached nearly as quite five miles, it resembled very much a huge snake stretched over hill and vale."[2] The Union force pulled along several artillery pieces as well, including two iron twelve-pound howitzers—named for the size of the shot it fired—manned by Company D of the First Kansas Colored. The Second Kansas Battery had recently secured two new bronze twelve-pound howitzers. Instead of dragging the old iron cannons back to Union lines, Lieutenant E. A. Smith turned them over to the First Kansas Colored.[3] Company D's acquisition was a temporary measure for the march to Fort Blunt, where they would be turned over for the site's defense.

The Union force moved along without incident until June 30, when Major John A. Foreman's Indian scouts picked up a suspicious trail. Without delay he detached twenty Cherokee soldiers under the command of Lieutenant Luke F. Parsons to investigate. Parsons's squad followed the tracks for four miles before coming upon a party of thirty Indians. Recognizing them as an advance picket from the Confederate command, Parsons attacked. Though outnumbered, the soldiers of the Third Indian Home Guard routed the enemy, claiming four Confederate dead and three prisoners.[4] While a small victory, the clash left no doubt of impending battle. The surviving Confederate scouts retreated to the main body. Each side was now aware of the other's presence.

A full engagement was not long in coming. The following day, July 1, the Union wagon train arrived at a ford at Cabin Creek. Pulling up to the steep northern banks at noon, the Union advance troops found Confederate soldiers manning hastily dug fortifications on the opposite bank. General Stand Watie, himself a Cherokee, and his Confederate force of sixteen hundred Indians and Texans were determined to block the Union wagon train.[5] At sixty yards wide, the ford offered advantages to the Confederates.[6] Although hills, thickets, and other natural obstructions dotted the prairies of Kansas, Missouri, and northern Indian Territory, armies could maneuver around them. Waterways presented a different challenge. Military units relied on bridges or fords to cross rivers and streams winding across the American landscape during the Civil War, and crossings left soldiers vulnerable. Even if a stream was shallow enough to ford and provided suitable sloping banks, transporting hundreds of men, animals, artillery pieces, and wagons was a daunting task under the best conditions. Bridges, when available, were preferable, but acted as a bottleneck, providing an inviting target for enemy soldiers. Either way, defending a water crossing provided a prime opportunity to resist an opponent on the move.

Watie's men masked their positions within the heavy timber and brush on the southern side of the creek. Captain Ethan Earle of Company F, First Kansas Colored Infantry, later recalled that "so thick was the brush that not a man could be seen."[7] Colonel James M. Williams of the First Kansas Colored and Major Foreman corralled the wagon train over a mile to the rear of the Union position and pushed forward elements of the First, Second, and Third Indian Regiments.[8] Foreman personally led the assaulting force.

As he arranged his battle line, the mountain howitzer was placed behind the Union center. Colonel Williams called on one of the twelve-pound howitzers fielded by men of the First Kansas Colored Infantry's Company D. Once in position, the twelve-pounder and the mountain howitzer let loose a barrage of shell and canister.[9] Civil War artillery shells were hollow iron projectiles filled with gunpowder and generally detonated by a time fuse. Gunners cut the length of fuse according to calculations designed to explode the projectile above a target. Fragments, from tiny metal slivers to large chunks of jagged iron, rained down on infantry. Canister fire offered a simpler method of destruction on the battlefield. The canister was nothing more than a thin metal can packed with twenty-seven one-inch iron balls. When fired, the fragile metal container disintegrated as it exited the muzzle, spraying the balls in a deadly swath. Canister turned a cannon into a giant shotgun, able to tear gaping holes through infantry ranks up to two hundred yards away.

The two Union guns wreaked havoc on the Confederate infantry in the thickets on the opposite bank—although most of the damage was psychological. The thick vegetation provided protection. "It hardly look[ed] like twenty men could stand there under fire as we did," Texan John Thomas Howard recalled, "but every one had a tree and if it had not been for that we could not have lived, for the artillery was not over a hundred yards from us."[10] Some Confederates contorted themselves into awkward positions behind trees to avoid the lethal shower of lead and iron. Howard shared the cover of one tree with fellow Texan John Tutley. During the fight, Tutley "lay flat on the ground behind a tree and I stood up astride him and we gave them the best we had," Howard later wrote.[11]

The Union Indian soldiers pushed forward under the artillery fire and peppered Watie's men with musket balls. For half an hour the firefight continued, taking a toll on the Confederate defenders. Howard saw three of his friends hit, including a man named Jim Hendrix, whose thigh was shattered during the artillery bombardment. "While the hardest of the fight was going on and while the grape and canister were flying thick," Howard later recalled, "Hendrix begged so pitifully to be taken out that some others and I carried him out."[12] Other Southerners fell back, and Union soldiers perceived that the Confederate defense was weakening. Major Foreman seized this opportunity to force a crossing and ordered his Indian soldiers forward. The men moved into the creek but found the water too high for the wagon train to cross.[13]

Frustrated, the Union soldiers withdrew for the evening and set up camp. Williams met with Lieutenant Colonel Theodore H. Dodd, commander of the Second Colorado Infantry, and Major Foreman to discuss the prospects for a crossing in the morning after, hopefully, the water level dropped.[14] They expected the Confederate soldiers to again resist the Union crossing. The officers agreed that a larger Union force was needed to break through the Confederate line. Only a small detachment would remain to guard the trains. All other soldiers, including most of the cavalry on hand, would press the attack.[15]

That evening the three officers scouted the ford, enabling Williams to formulate the battle plan. The Second Kansas Battery would position two six-pound cannons on the Union's extreme left flank. Major Foreman's mountain howitzer and one twelve-pound howitzer would be positioned within two hundred yards of the Confederate center, and the other twelve-pound howitzer would be sent to the Union right. Like a boxer's jab, the five artillery pieces would disrupt the Confederate line for the main assault. Williams ordered Major Foreman to prepare a company of his Indian soldiers to lead the attack as skirmishers, testing the enemy position ahead of the main infantry body, consisting of the entire First Kansas Colored and the Colorado infantry. The remaining force—including sections of the Ninth Kansas, Fourteenth Kansas, and Third Wisconsin cavalry regiments, and the rest of the Indian infantry battalion—would guard the flanks. In all, the Union force at Cabin Creek included white, black, and Indian units from two states and two territories.[16]

Overnight, Confederate reinforcements approached. Brigadier General D. H. Cooper led his Southern troops north from his camp near Fort Blunt while Confederate general William L. Cabell marched from Arkansas to reinforce Watie with another fifteen hundred men and three artillery pieces. These forces would double the Southern presence at Cabin Creek. But the high water that had delayed the Union crossing held Cabell up at Grand River a few miles away. Without that artillery support, and now without the element of surprise, Watie hoped to hold on until help arrived. He received word in the morning that neither Cooper nor Cabell could be on the scene until the afternoon.[17]

By eight o'clock in the morning on July 2, the Union soldiers were in position. Scouts reported that the creek had receded enough for the wagons to cross. The attack was on. Four Union cannons broke the morning stillness with a barrage against the southern bank of Cabin Creek. For forty minutes shell fragments and canister balls showered the Confederate line. Union infantry waited out of musket range. If all went well, the Confederates might abandon their defenses, and early reports gave strength to this hope. Scouts informed Williams that the enemy was in disorder and pulling back. Calling off the artillery, the colonel ordered his column forward. The Union soldiers headed to the creek, led by Major Foreman and a company of Indian soldiers. They marched unopposed to the northern bank and then down the slope into the creek. The path did appear open. Suddenly, though, a line of fire and smoke erupted from the trees and undergrowth on the opposite side. Confederate soldiers hiding behind piles of logs and dirt fired at the Indian soldiers wading through the muddy water. The volley stunned the Union troops. Two musket balls struck Major Foreman in quick succession; five more slammed into his horse. With their leader down and finding themselves vulnerable, the Indian soldiers scrambled back up the northern bank in retreat.[18]

As the advance guard fell back, the bulk of the Union infantry approached the water's edge. Williams halted the column and moved three companies into a firing position on the Union right. The Union infantry and artillery unleashed a furious barrage on the Confederates. For twenty minutes Union forces pounded the southern bank of Cabin Creek with iron cannon shell and lead musket balls. Return fire from the Confederates found a few targets. Luther Dickerson, a red-headed and full-bearded first lieutenant in Company B, First Kansas Colored Infantry, watched as one of his soldiers, "while in the act of loading his gun, was struck by a bullet which passed between the gun and his hand tearing the flesh from the inside of his fingers." Though partially disabled, the private determined to stay in the fight. Dickerson recalled, "Standing close beside him at the time he turned to me and asked me to load his gun for him, which I proceeded to do." As the lieutenant raised his left arm to draw the ramrod, a bullet struck his upper arm and embedded in the muscle near the shoulder. Dickerson carried the ball in his arm throughout the war.[19]

The Indian soldiers, having fallen back from the creek, formed up in the rear of the Union column.[20] With the three infantry companies on the right and the Union artillery still firing on the Confederates, the main Union force charged into the ford. Though the water level

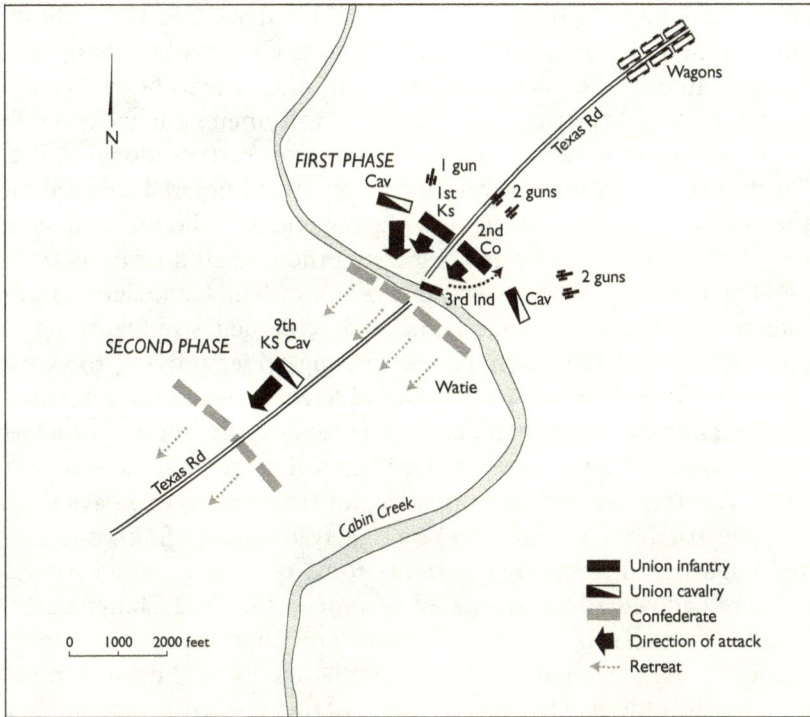

Map 3. Cabin Creek. Map by Bill Nelson.

had dropped during the night, the men of the First Kansas Colored and their fellow foot soldiers found themselves waist deep in the muddy creek. General Watie's remaining soldiers along the southern bank fired sporadically as the Union men slowly moved toward them. One bullet struck Captain Earle's haversack. The ball slowed as it passed through packages of bread and beef before striking a set of keys in his front pocket. The obstructions prevented the bullet from entering his groin, but the blow stunned him. He counted himself lucky, later remarking, "All but for my dinner and Keys, it would have been a fatal shot."[21] The irregular Confederate fire could not stop the federal force. The Union soldiers clambered up the opposite bank, chased off the Confederate stragglers, and formed up for battle.[22]

As the Texans and Confederate Indians fell back, Watie charged his horse among their ranks, calling on them to hold the line.[23] His men responded by regrouping a quarter mile from the crossing. But their line was weak. Williams directed two cavalry companies to cover the Union right flank and ordered Lieutenant R. C. Philbrick and his men of Company C, Ninth Kansas Cavalry, "to charge the advance line of the enemy, penetrate it, and, if possible, ascertain his strength and position." Philbrick's cavalrymen punched through the Confederate advance line, sending most of Watie's men running. "Seeing this," Williams wrote in his report, "I ordered forward all the cavalry in pursuit of the now fleeing enemy, who were pursued for 5 miles, killing many and dispersing them in all directions."[24]

The battle lasted only a couple of hours. The Confederate reinforcements Watie desperately needed remained stranded on the opposite side of Grand River, its rushing water proving too dangerous to force a crossing. The Grand River claimed some retreating Texans and Indians who attempted to cross during their escape from charging Kansas cavalry. Union soldiers downstream at Fort Blunt reported seeing bodies floating for the next several days.[25]

The battle at Cabin Creek was a resounding Union success. Williams proudly reported that his force of nine hundred federal soldiers had routed an estimated seventeen hundred Confederates. While estimates of enemy numbers are notoriously inaccurate, accounts seem to agree that Stand Watie's force did outnumber the Union soldiers. Union casualties totaled one killed and twenty wounded.[26] Some men also sustained injuries unrelated to combat. Second Lieutenant Ezekial Coleman, of Company A, First Kansas Colored Infantry, stumbled and fell as his company marched at double time into the battle, tearing a hole in his groin that caused a scrotal hernia. Though he stayed with his men during the fight, the injury ultimately ended his military career.[27] Confederate casualties were estimated to be about one hundred. Williams's only frustration had been the inherent limitations of his assignment. "Had there been no train to guard, so that the whole force could have been employed against the enemy," he wrote to Colonel William A. Phillips at Fort Blunt, "I don't know but I should have been able to capture the whole force." He celebrated the efficiency and bravery of all his soldiers that day: "I cannot close this communication without referring to the chivalrous and soldierly conduct of the entire command during the engagement; the whole command crossing this difficult ford, and forming in the face of the enemy, with as much ease and little confusion as if upon parade."[28]

The wagon train's arrival at Fort Blunt with supplies and reinforcements marked a significant achievement for the First Kansas

Colored Infantry. The regiment had served as the major element of an infantry column in a key battle. Treated as professional combat soldiers in a multiunit formation, the black troops had helped inflict on the Confederacy a stunning blow in the northeastern part of Indian Territory. Gone, at least for now, were fears of a service relegated to manual labor.

Shortly after arriving, the soldiers of the First Kansas Colored also received welcome news that their long-overdue pay had been delivered to their new station. Colonel Williams issued an order with advice to the men about the importance of being prudent with the money. Many of them were former slaves "just relieved from a vile bondage" and "had but few opportunities for learning the importance of saving carefully the proceeds of your toil." Williams squarely blamed the institution of slavery and white slave owners for robbing them of their earnings. "Heretofore, that has all gone to an unscrupulous Master who has used it [to fasten] still more thoroughly the chains with which he held you: every dollar gained by your labor was but another link in the iron chain." However, he declared, "the whole condition of your existence is changed." He added, "This boon which is so freely given must not be allowed to prove your ruin. You have been brought up to habits of industry and frugality, and if you depart in the least from either of these habits, it sooner or later will have the effect to destroy your whole prosperity as individuals and measurably effect [sic] your condition as a people." Williams concluded by stating, "I therefore urgently advise you to carefully save the money which is about being paid you, for the support of your families; and, as a foundation upon which to build a home for wives & children, your families and friends. To this end, I advise you, to make a deposit of such funds as you do not need, in some safe hands for transmission to your families, as safe keeping for yourselves."[29]

While they were a distinct minority within the regiment, several soldiers had been free men before the war and responsible for their own financial security. Moreover, some slaves in the American South had opportunities to earn and save money, though rarely from their owners paying wages. Instead, slaves were occasionally allowed to keep money they earned while hired out by their masters. In the South it was common practice for many non-slave-owning whites, unable to afford the cost and living expenses of slave ownership, to hire or rent laborers from local slaveholders, usually for short periods of time. This was especially true for slaves with skilled training, such as blacksmiths or masons, whose labor was highly valued in the community. Historians have estimated that between 5 and 30 percent of slaves were hired out annually in the United States.[30] The money went to the owner, but some owners allowed slaves to keep some of the earnings.

Still, there is little doubt that paternalism lay behind Williams's advice. In a time of white supremacist attitudes, patronizing comments about African Americans crept into statements of even radical abolitionists. However, as commander of the regiment Williams had genuine concern for the well-being of his soldiers. And he understood that whites watched the behavior of his men for evidence of how slaves would handle the transition to freedom. Indeed, many white Americans in both Northern and Southern states erroneously believed that blacks could not handle social and financial independence. Like other perceptions of black inferiority, these beliefs ignored seemingly obvious evidence to the contrary, such as the success of thousands of free blacks living in the United States. Decades of institutionalized racism and the determined Southern defense of slavery on the grounds that it controlled an inferior race remained deeply entrenched in the overall American psyche.

Most of the men were responsible with their money. "Several of your men have of their own free choice deposited money with my clerk to be delivered to their friends and deposited in the Bank at Leavenworth City," Daniel Adams wrote to Williams on July 15. "These funds are all deposited in my safe and will be delivered faithfully for which I consider my honor pledged." Problems arose, however, when rumors spread that the Leavenworth bank was stealing the money. Adams grew alarmed over this news and reported the development, which he believed to be an intentional fraud, to Williams: "Some *interested villain* has been telling the boys that they will never see their money again, will lose it, &c &c and one has been down to get his money, which was immediately given him. After recovering it he told me why he came for it, and after explanation he again left it. I thought I would notify you of these facts as they require correction."[31]

Though an important step, the pay the First Kansas Colored Infantry soldiers received in July only compensated for time served since official muster in January 1863. Payment did not include service prior to that period. Hundreds of men who enlisted in the summer and fall of 1862 were left uncompensated for those months. Even more troubling, the men did not receive the full Union military rate of thirteen dollars per month for enlisted soldiers because the Militia Act of July 17, 1862, declared that "persons of African descent, who under this law shall be employed, shall receive ten dollars per month and one ration, three dollars of which monthly pay may be in clothing."[32] The First Kansas Colored Infantry soldiers received only seven dollars per month in cash.[33]

Black soldiers and their white officers across the Union protested the inequality in pay.[34] In the meantime, the men of the First Kansas Colored accepted their pay and continued their service. More immediate concerns drew their attention. Confederate armies still menaced Fort Blunt. Very soon the regiment would again be tested in battle.

CHAPTER 10

HONEY SPRINGS

They fought like veterans.

R elocation to Indian Territory was a mixed blessing for the First
Kansas Colored Infantry. At Fort Blunt, the soldiers could
expect further action. The black soldiers had a key role in a combat command. They had enlisted to fight and would see their share
of combat as long as they remained a vital part of Union operations
south of Kansas. Unfortunately, Indian Territory was among the
most ignored theaters along the contiguous front.[1] The campaigns in
northern Virginia, Tennessee, and Mississippi drew most of the federal government's attention and resources. In July 1863, as the First
Kansas Colored Infantry marched into the remote western outpost,
the most famous battle of the war had just occurred in Gettysburg,
Pennsylvania, and Ulysses S. Grant had just secured the Mississippi
River with the capture of Vicksburg, Mississippi. Thus the First
Kansas Colored's new assignment at Fort Blunt hardly gathered the
attention of the Northern public or of most Union officials.

Political feuds further troubled the Union military effort in
Indian Territory. Having spent the past month worrying over
the future of Colonel William A. Phillips's Indian brigade, Major
General James Blunt also faced a command crisis back in Kansas.
Governor Thomas Carney and Major General John M. Schofield,
commander of the Department of Missouri, threatened his military
position in the region. Blunt's command had been sliced in half that
June. Schofield divided the District of Kansas into two parts—the
District of the Frontier remained under Blunt, while the District
of the Border fell under the command of Brigadier General Thomas
Ewing.[2] Senator James Lane supported Blunt, and together they
waged a bitter political campaign against Schofield and Carney that
would last through the summer and ultimately involve President
Lincoln. Blunt needed a victory, and Lane said as much to their
mutual friend Sidney Clarke. "Let Blunt know that I am watching

everything but that I deem a victory as indispensable to enable us to succeed," he wrote. "If I were him, I would not lose a moment in getting to the head of his forces & whipping somebody."[3]

Blunt needed no prodding. Beyond political expediency, he feared that Confederate forces would soon overwhelm the Union garrison at Fort Blunt. Pulling together 350 men of the Sixth Kansas Cavalry, a detachment of the Third Wisconsin Cavalry, and Captain E. A. Smith's Second Kansas Battery with its two new bronze howitzers, Blunt set out for Fort Blunt on July 5.[4] This move, combined with the First Kansas Colored's earlier march south, stripped southern Kansas of most of its Union garrison. But the general wanted a fight and accepted the risk.

In the meantime, pressure around Fort Blunt mounted. Confederate forces congregated a few miles south and set up a heavy picket guard, supplemented with rifle pits, at key river crossings. High water prevented both sides from sending across harassing patrols, and Union artillery shells kept the enemy further at bay. Colonel Phillips kept abreast of Confederate operations through a pair of valuable spies, one a woman in General Douglas Cooper's camp who smuggled dispatches in her bonnet. From these reports he learned disturbing news: Cooper was receiving reinforcements from Arkansas and Texas.[5] Nothing could be done until Blunt arrived.

The general's journey to Fort Blunt took six days. His force suffered under the unforgiving midsummer prairie sun for nearly 175 miles, but arrived safely on July 11. Phillips's Indian brigade celebrated their arrival with a large reception that night. Blunt gave a rousing speech describing the federal victory over the seemingly invincible Robert E. Lee at Gettysburg and Grant's capture of the formidable city of Vicksburg. Flush with success from Cabin Creek, men of the First Kansas Colored and their fellow soldiers found much to celebrate in July 1863. Blunt told the men that they would soon go on the attack.[6]

After the war Blunt said that he found the military situation at Fort Blunt appalling. "The administration of military affairs had been very badly conducted," he wrote, and Confederate soldiers not only crossed Arkansas River at pleasure but also placed spies "inside of the garrison in the full confidence of the commanding officer, and acting as his military advisers."[7] Blunt's postwar accusations of Phillips's apparent incompetence may have been exaggerated, as his reminiscences are highly critical of other officers and blatantly self-serving. Still, the situation at the fort was serious. Far from friendly forces in Kansas or Union-occupied portions of Arkansas, the federal garrison at Fort Blunt could not expect support if Confederates attacked.

Blunt wanted to take the field. Because Confederate pickets guarded all of the water crossings around the fort, he could not hope to make any secret move across the river—that is, if he tried to ford it. The point was moot anyway, since all of the rivers and streams were swollen with recent rains. Unperturbed, the general considered an amphibious assault. He ordered work crews to construct flatboats to ferry his army across the river.[8]

By July 15, Union spies had reported that Brigadier General William L. Cabell and three thousand Confederate soldiers from Arkansas would link up with General Douglas Cooper's six thousand men at Honey Springs within two days. Honey Springs, located twenty miles south of Fort Blunt, was a good source of fresh water along the Texas Road and had become a regular assembling station for Confederates. Blunt received the news while suffering in his quarters from a spiking fever, with symptoms similar to malaria.[9] He believed that once Cooper received reinforcements the Confederate army, nine thousand strong, would march on the Union garrison. He had only three thousand men on hand to resist.

Climbing out of bed after midnight on the morning of July 16, Blunt organized four companies of the Sixth Kansas Cavalry and four artillery pieces to carry out a surprise attack on Confederate pickets. The group marched to a ford thirteen miles up the Arkansas River, arriving near daylight. Around one hundred Confederate cavalry guarded the ford and appeared ready to defend the crossing when the Union soldiers appeared. They changed their minds when the Union artillery pieces swung into position on the riverbank. The Confederates retreated, allowing the Union contingent to cross unmolested.[10] Still trying to keep his advance a secret, Blunt and his cavalry speedily marched along the southern side of the waterway, "expecting to get in the rear of [the Confederate] pickets at the mouth of Grand River, opposite this post, and capture them."[11] If successful, the Union soldiers might be able to keep Cooper unaware of their advance. Despite these hopes, Blunt's troopers found the ford abandoned. The enemy's pickets had fallen back, likely alerted by word of the federal crossing farther up the river, and were on their way to alert Cooper.

Blunt surveyed the Grand River and found that while the water level had dropped over the previous days, it remained dangerous to ford. He called for the flatboats, and throughout the day the small crafts ferried men, horses, artillery, and supplies to the Confederate side of the river.[12] By ten o'clock that night, the crossing was complete, but not without losses: three soldiers from the Second Indian Home Guard had drowned after either jumping or falling into the river.[13]

To defeat Cooper, Blunt pulled as many men into the field as he could spare. A nominal force remained to guard the fort, giving him less than three thousand combat soldiers to face an expected six thousand Confederates at Honey Springs. If Cabell's force arrived, Blunt feared his federals would be outnumbered three to one. In fact, Cooper probably had a little more than three thousand soldiers at Honey Springs—not the six thousand Blunt believed, but slightly more than the Union attackers. Nonetheless, Blunt had confidence, and so did his men. He divided his army into two brigades. Colonel William R. Judson of the Sixth Kansas Cavalry commanded the First Brigade, consisting of the Second Indian Home Guards, companies from his own Sixth Kansas Cavalry, parts of the Third Wisconsin Cavalry, four guns of the Second Kansas Battery, and the First Kansas Colored Infantry. The black soldiers made up the backbone of this brigade. Colonel Phillips commanded the Second Brigade, which included the First Indian Home Guards, the Second Colorado Infantry, and Captain Henry Hopkins's four cannons of the Third Kansas Battery.[14]

The lengthy water crossing placed the Union men in a difficult position. They were outnumbered and on the enemy's side of the river, and they had lost the element of surprise. Confederate pickets had plenty of time to warn Cooper of an enemy advance. Further, it was night, and the Union force had twenty miles to march to meet the enemy. As far as Blunt knew, Cabell and his Confederate reinforcements could make it to Honey Springs within the next twenty-four hours. His soldiers would march all night to attack a rested, vigilant, and numerically superior Confederate force, possibly manning defensive positions.

The Confederates knew the Union men were coming. From spy reports, General Cooper suspected that Blunt would launch an attack before Cabell's reinforcements arrived. Picket reports on July 16 of Union soldiers crossing the Grand River confirmed his suspicions. But he was still unsure of the size of the federal incursion. "Up to this time," Cooper later wrote, "I had been unable to determine whether the force which crossed at the Creek Agency was merely a heavy scout or the advance of the main body of the enemy." As a precaution, he ordered Colonel Tandy Walker and his First Choctaw and Chickasaw Regiment and Captain L. E. Gillett, with his squadron of Texas cavalry, to guard a key road crossing a few miles north of Honey Springs. Any Union approach could be detected early enough to ready the entire Confederate body for battle.[15]

The Union soldiers trudged along in the darkness for a couple of hours before Blunt called for a rest. The general himself was physically exhausted, having spent nearly twenty-four hours in his saddle despite his fever. Catching a few hours of needed sleep, the Union men stirred from their temporary camp around four o'clock in the morning. A rainstorm added to their misery.

For four hours the column pushed south along the Texas Road until musket fire surprised a company of Sixth Kansas cavalrymen acting as the Union advance. The Kansans moved into skirmish formation, but a line of Confederate soldiers came charging out of the brush and threw them back. The Union advance had clashed with Walker's and Gillett's soldiers. Union officers back in the column heard the gunfire and sent the rest of the Sixth Kansas Cavalry. Lieutenant Colonel William T. Campbell led his troopers "forward at a gallop to the support of the advance." For a brief time, musket and carbine fire rippled across the prairie, and at least four Kansans went down—one killed and three wounded.[16] As the fighting continued, an increasing number of snaps split the air along the Confederate line, the sounds of misfires. Musket hammers fell on small brass percussion caps with a sharp crack, but the resulting sparks failed to ignite the black powder inside the barrels. The Texans and Indians found that the low-grade black powder ammunition they were issued had absorbed moisture from the damp morning air, decreasing its reliability. A passing rain shower during the skirmish rendered their rifles "wholly useless" except as clubs. Unable to continue a steady rate of fire, the Confederates fell back to Elk Creek, a meandering stream about three miles north of Honey Springs.[17]

The early morning engagement confirmed that Union soldiers were approaching Honey Springs, and word spread quickly. Near the Confederate camp, a young slave girl named Lucinda Davis tended a child in her master's front yard when she saw an Indian warrior race down the road. "When he see de house he begin to give de war whoop, 'Eya-a-a-a-he-ha!'" she remembered seventy years later. "When he git close to de house he holler to git out de way 'cause dey gwine be a big fight." Lucinda's owner, an elderly Creek man, yelled at the slaves to pack up a wagon and supplies. As they did, a long line of mounted Confederate Indians passed them, headed to the impending battle. "Dey had a flag, and it was all red and had a big criss-cross on it dat look lak a saw horse," she recalled. "De man carry it and rear back on it when de win whip it, but it flap all 'round de horse's head and de horse pitch and rear lak he know something going happen, sho!"[18]

To the north, troopers of the Sixth Kansas Cavalry advanced cautiously until they approached thick timber and brush just north of Elk Creek. Confederate musket fire halted the cavalrymen. Though Cooper's men were well hidden in the brush, the Kansans determined that they had found the main Confederate force. It straddled the Texas Road in a mile-long formation along the woods on the northern side of Elk Creek. Blunt and his chief of staff, Lieutenant Colonel Thomas Moonlight, watched as the Kansas cavalrymen tested the Confederate line with carbine fire. Cooper's men did not move. Both officers believed the Confederates intended to ambush the Union force when it entered the woods. Moonlight was sure that Cooper underestimated the Union force in front of him and that the Confederate general "never for a moment supposed that we were anything more than the cavalry and artillery force which had driven him from his entrenchments on the river the day before."[19] Rather than form on the south side of Elk Creek to use the waterway as a natural obstacle against Union attackers (as Stand Watie had done at Cabin Creek two weeks earlier), the main Confederate force formed on the north side, with the creek at its back. Thus the creek offered the Confederates no defensive advantage. In fact, it posed a considerable hazard in case of a withdrawal, forcing them to either clamber down the steep creek banks and wade or swim across, possibly under fire, or push their way across a solitary bridge over Elk Creek at the middle of the Confederate line. Cooper's decision to post his line north of Elk Creek suggests that he was thinking offensively. Without the creek between his line and the Union men, his Confederate soldiers could throw their entire weight against a smaller attacker and possibly envelop them. Cooper took a gamble.

While the Sixth Kansas Cavalry skirmished with Confederates, Blunt concluded that the enemy intended to remain "concealed under cover of the brush awaiting my attack." He was more concerned with the Confederate artillery, which remained hidden. Cannon fire could tear apart his advancing lines. Blunt's own artillery prepared to fire on the Confederate cannons; but until Cooper's guns revealed their location, the federal artillery had no target. Cooper's batteries withheld their fire for that very reason. As Blunt scanned the front lines for enemy cannons, incoming musket balls struck a Union soldier nearby, prompting the general and his staff to fall back.[20]

Convinced the Confederates would not leave the safety of the trees, Blunt halted his column to rest behind a slight ridge a half mile from the enemy line. It was eight o'clock in the morning, July 17. The men of the First Kansas Colored Infantry and their fellow soldiers were exhausted, having been on the move for almost twenty-four hours with barely four hours of sleep. They broke ranks and, as the rain dissipated and skies cleared, rested their feet. Hours of marching had left them hungry. They expected supply wagons to bring food, but the unpredictability of wartime operations had dealt a cruel blow: the wagons had been lost during the river crossing the evening before, leaving the men to enjoy only the meager rations they had on them. The rations included hardtack—a barely nutritious and notoriously tough cracker, or biscuit, as appetizing as its name suggests. Hardtack was a staple for Civil War soldiers due to its ease of production and durability. Men in the field often needed to soak hardtack in coffee or water just to chew it.[21]

The strain of the march caught up with the ailing Blunt. Shortly after ordering his column to break ranks, the general collapsed. His staff helped him to a fence corner, where he rested. His chief of staff, Thomas Moonlight, climbed atop a nearby farmhouse and observed the Confederate line with a spyglass. He studied the topography and happily found that Union soldiers could march unseen until the last hundred yards. This offered a twofold advantage. First, and most obviously, it protected the advancing Union men from musket and cannon fire until they were within striking distance. Second, since the Union command believed Cooper underestimated the size of their force, they could mask their true strength until they were right upon the Confederates and before the opposing general could redeploy.[22]

Moonlight briefed Blunt on the terrain. Pleased with what he heard, Blunt set about coordinating the assault. Colonel James Williams and the First Kansas Colored Infantry received word of the impending advance. According to the historian and former cavalryman Wiley Britton, Williams rode to the front of his regiment and, with cannon fire booming in the background, declared "in a clear, ringing voice":

> This is the day we have been patiently waiting for; the enemy at Cabin Creek did not wait to give you an opportunity of showing them what men can do fighting for their natural rights and for their recently acquired freedom and the freedom of their children and their children's children. I am proud of your soldierly appearance; and it is especially gratifying to know that it has been by my strenuous efforts in drilling you, in handling you, and providing for you the past months, that I find you in such splendid condition, physically and in morale. We are going to engage the enemy in a few moments and I am going to lead you. We are engaged in a holy war; in the history of the world, soldiers never fought for a holier cause than the cause for which the Union soldiers are fighting, the preservation of the Union and the equal rights and freedom of all men. You know what the soldiers of the Southern armies are fighting for; you know that they are fighting for the continued existence and extension of slavery on this continent, and if they are successful, to take you and your wives and children back into slavery. You know it is common report that the Confederate troops boast that they will not give quarters to colored troops and their officers, and you know that they did not give any quarters to your comrades in the fight with the forage detachment near Sherwood last May. Show the enemy this day that you are not asking for quarter, and that you know how and are eager to fight for your freedom and finally, keep cool and do not fire until you receive the order, and then aim deliberately below the waist belt. The people of the whole country will read the reports of your conduct in this engagement; let it be that of brave, disciplined men.[23]

With the brigades ready, Blunt ordered his men forward. The Union soldiers marched toward the Confederate line in two large columns, one on each side of the Texas Road. "The infantry was in column by companies," Blunt reported after the battle, "the cavalry by platoons and artillery by sections, and all closed in mass so as to deceive the enemy in regard to the strength of my force."[24] Marching in columns also allowed the Union units to move swiftly toward their target. When they closed to within four hundred yards, the two columns rapidly deployed into a long line of battle, shifting nearly three thousand men from a vertical procession into a single horizontal front, while maintaining discipline and organization. The maneuver required great coordination, especially in the face of the enemy. By all accounts, the men of the First Kansas Colored Infantry and the rest of the Union force accomplished it magnificently. Blunt proudly reported that "in less than five minutes my whole force was in line of battle, covering the enemy's entire front."[25]

The Union line extended several hundred yards, with the First Kansas Colored at its center. To the regiment's right marched the Second Indian Home Guards, with the Third Wisconsin Cavalry protecting the right flank. Soldiers of the Second Colorado Volunteer Infantry were on the black soldiers' immediate left, flanked by the First Indian Home Guards. The Sixth Kansas Cavalry covered the left end of the Union line. Skirmishers advanced in front of the main line to test the Confederate positions and prevent an ambush.[26]

Although Moonlight and Blunt hoped the terrain would mask the Union movements, Confederates hiding along Elk Creek saw much of the advance. Colonel Phillips, commanding the second brigade, ordered Captain Henry Hopkins and his Third Kansas Battery to advance and shell the Confederate line. The artillery teams rode to within three hundred yards of the wood line and opened fire. Suddenly, shell and canister fire rained down on the Kansas artillerymen. The Texas Light Battery, which had withheld its fire until within sight of the Union cannons, unleashed the barrage. One Kansas private died instantly, while a piece of jagged iron tore off a sergeant's leg at the thigh. His wound proved fatal. Eight horses were downed, four killed and four disabled. The Kansans spotted a Confederate gun posted in an opening in the woods and turned two of their cannons against it. "By the explosion of one of our shells," Captain Hopkins later wrote, "the cannoneers belonging to that piece and all their horses were killed or wounded."[27]

Colonel Campbell of the Sixth Kansas Cavalry noticed movement in the timber along the Union's left flank. He dismounted three of his companies and sent them into the woods to neutralize the threat. For thirty minutes the cavalrymen fought in open formation, taking advantage of the trees and undergrowth, and succeeded in pushing back the First and Second Cherokee Mounted Rifle Regiments.[28]

Cooper learned of the trouble on his right flank and sent detachments from the Twentieth Texas Cavalry and the First Choctaw and Chickasaw Regiment to help. Not content with the security of

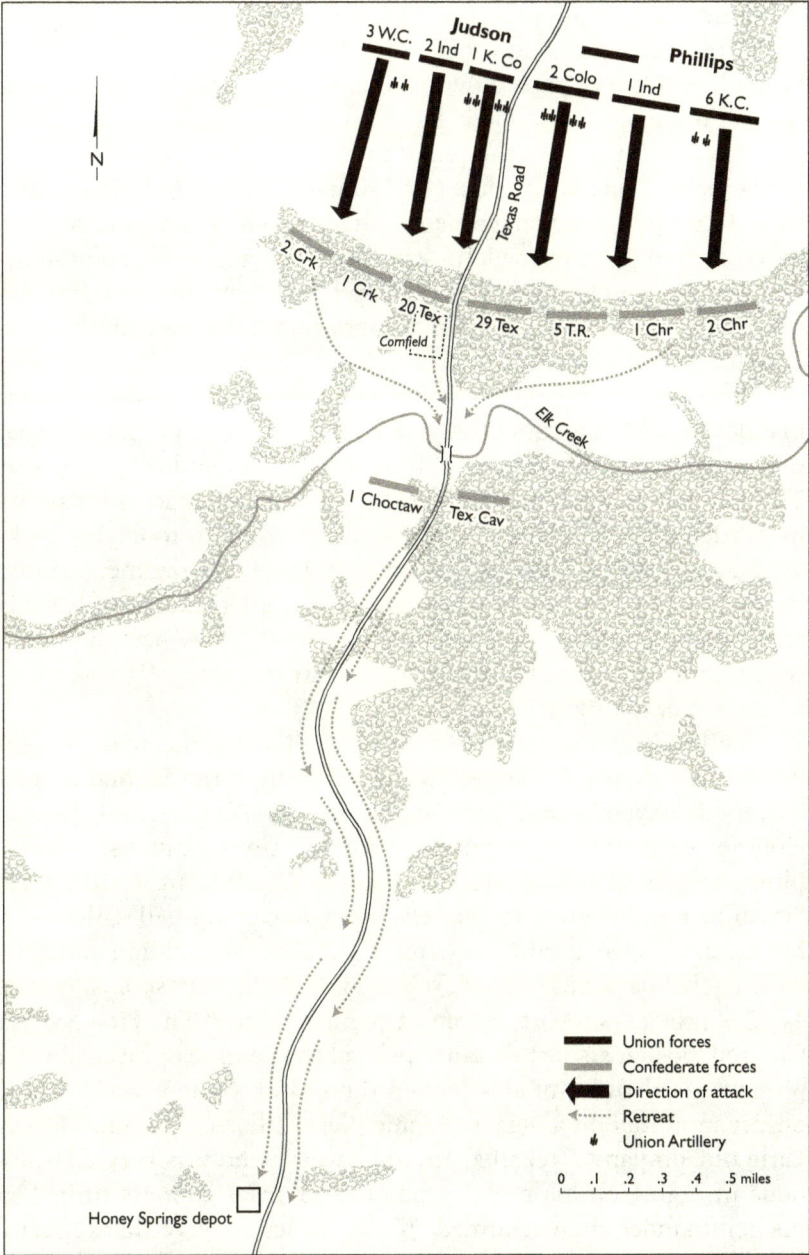

Map 4. Honey Springs. Map by Bill Nelson. Copyright © 2014 by the University of Oklahoma Press.

his flank, the general personally positioned a section of the Second Cherokee as further reinforcements. As he rode back to the center of his line, Cooper passed over a slight rise on the prairie and saw the full force of his opponent for the first time. He was surprised to find "their force larger than reported" by his subordinates, he wrote in his report, "and larger than I had supposed they would bring from [Fort] Gibson."[29] He also noticed what appeared to be Union soldiers moving off to his extreme left—a particularly vulnerable point in his line. Cooper sent a message to his Creek regiments on the left flank, ordering them to fix their lines firmly against the Twentieth Texas Cavalry near the center.[30]

With both of his flanks under pressure, the Confederate commander rode back across Elk Creek to call up the remaining companies of the First Choctaw and Chickasaw Regiment held in reserve. The Choctaws were nowhere to be found. Earlier in the day, he had ordered the regiment's colonel, Tandy Walker, to deploy pickets east of Honey Springs while the bulk of the regiment rested in reserve. Walker had misunderstood the orders and marched his entire force to the east—away from the battle. Cooper frantically sent a messenger to call Walker back, but the regiment was effectively out of the fight.[31]

While Cooper tried to shore up his flanks, the main Union line came forward. Captain Edward A. Smith of the Second Kansas Battery deployed his four guns on the right side of the Texas Road as Hopkins's battery exchanged fire with the Texas cannons. General Blunt ordered Smith to help silence the Confederate artillery. As Smith swung his guns to the left, a single cannon ball sailed over his head. "I opened with spherical-case shot, shell, and solid shot on the rebel batteries," Smith reported, "which were soon silenced, as rebel prisoners report, by my 12-pounder guns." The First Kansas Colored, posted a short distance behind the cannons, watched with pleasure as their comrades proved their skill. "There was a Rebel officer mounted on a very large and elegant horse," Captain Ethan Earle of Company F recalled after the war, "who was very conspicuous in urging on his men." One of the Kansas gunners turned to his commander and exclaimed, "Captain, let me give that officer a shot." The captain approved. The gunner yanked the lanyard, sending a cannonball at the unsuspecting Confederate. The Union men watched as "the ball entered the horse's breast, went the entire length of his body, [and] passed out directly under his tail."[32]

With the Confederate artillery suppressed for the time being, Blunt ordered Smith to move his guns to within three hundred yards of the enemy position and open fire. The general then rode to the First Kansas Colored Infantry and told Colonel Williams, "I wish you to move your regiment to the front and support this battery." Motioning to the Texas cannons, he ordered the colonel "to keep an eye to those guns of the enemy, and take them at the point of the bayonet, if an opportunity offers." Williams addressed the regiment briefly about the work ahead and cried out the order "Fix bayonet." That command, perhaps more than any in Civil War military parlance, conveyed a grim resolution. The men brought their muskets to the front and rested the buttstocks on the ground between their feet. With a smooth and practiced motion, each man moved his right hand down across his body to unsheath the bayonet from the leather scabbard hanging on the left hip—a movement akin to drawing a sword. Swinging the bayonet tips upward, the men locked the long metal spikes onto the end of their muskets and returned to the ready.[33]

Smith's cannons moved through the Colorado infantry ranks and were posted one hundred yards in front. The black soldiers followed closely behind. The Third Kansas Battery guns "fired 3 or 4 rounds of canister and 10 or 12 of shell at the rebel position on the hill," with good effect. In the face of this fire, some of the Confederates fell back toward a small cornfield. As the artillerymen adjusted the guns, orders came to cease fire for the infantry to advance. The First Kansas Colored Infantry, five hundred men strong, finally moved forward to meet the enemy.[34]

The long line of Union infantry steadily marched under a barrage of shot and shell from Confederate artillery. The Second Colorado, on the left, fired as they moved forward. To the right, the Second Indian Home Guard advanced in skirmish formation, peppering the Confederate tree line with musket balls. The First Kansas Colored, however, held their fire. "I moved my regiment at a shouldered arms, loaded and bayonets fixed under a sharp fire of the enemy . . . without firing a shot," Williams later reported.[35] The Union men did not have a good view of the enemy. "The whole space in front of us was covered with small bushes," a Confederate officer facing the black soldiers explained, "which concealed our position, and almost masked the approach of the enemy."[36] Furthermore, many of the soldiers in the First Kansas Colored carried smoothbore muskets

loaded with "buck and ball," a combination of one large round musket ball and three small buckshot.[37] Though of limited accuracy over
distances, "buck and ball" was particularly effective at close range.

Showing discipline, the black soldiers marched to within fifty
yards of the Confederate line before stopping to aim their weapons.[38]
Their ability to carry out such a bold advance was aided in part by
the Confederate soldiers' poor armament. Taking cover in the trees
were men of the Twentieth and the Twenty-Ninth Texas Cavalry
Regiments, who carried antiquated muskets and shotguns. "We was
ordered to lay down and not to fire till the enemy came in forty
yards," Private Robert McDermott of the Twentieth Texas wrote
shortly after the battle. The Texas officers waited for the Union soldiers to come into range.[39]

As the black soldiers stood shoulder to shoulder in the open prairie, Colonel Williams cried out "Ready!" A string of "clicks" rang out
as the men pulled back the hammers on their muskets. Then came
the command "Aim!" Soldiers in the front rank raised their muskets.
Each man in the rear rank shifted slightly to the right, rested his left
forearm on the upper back of the man in front of him, and leveled
his weapon over his comrade's right shoulder. For a second or two,
the opposing sides silently looked down gun barrels at each other.
Then Williams screamed, "Fire!" A long line of flame and smoke
erupted from the Union front, blasting the trees, underbrush, and
men only fifty yards away with "buck and ball." At the same instant,
the Texans unleashed their volley, "as if mistaking the command as
intended for themselves, or as a demonstration of their willingness
to meet us promptly," reported Lieutenant Colonel John Bowles, the
First Kansas Colored Infantry's second in command.[40]

A number of Texans went down in the exchange, including the
Twenty-Ninth Texas's Colonel Charles DeMorse, as a musket ball
tore through his hand. DeMorse tried to ignore the wound, but when
subordinates noticed blood streaming from his fingers, they convinced him to retire. Colonel Williams also fell. "My intention was
after delivering this volley to charge their line and take the battery,"
Williams later wrote, "which the effects of my volley had placed
completely at my disposal."[41] But the colonel was a prime target on
his horse, and Confederate bullets smashed into his face, hands, and
chest. As he reeled in the saddle, his mount stumbled to the ground
with wounds of its own. Lieutenant Colonel John Bowles, oversee-
ing the right end of the First Kansas Colored Infantry, was "ignorant

of the fact that Colonel Williams had fallen." The Confederate volley temporarily left the black soldiers without a commanding officer. Within a few minutes Bowles learned that Williams was down,
but by then, he later lamented, "it was too late to give the command 'charge bayonet,' for which every man seemed so anxiously
awaiting."[42] Instead, Bowles apparently ordered the men to lie down
and continue firing.[43] For the next fifteen minutes, the Kansans held
their place and exchanged shots with the Texans and Indians.

Hundreds of men, separated by less than half the distance of a
modern football field, loaded, fired, and loaded again. Surprisingly
few First Kansas Colored soldiers were hit. Less than three dozen out
of nearly five hundred black soldiers on the field sustained wounds.
Lying prone undoubtedly saved many, as Confederate bullets flew
overhead. However, this position left head and shoulders most
exposed to enemy bullets. At least fourteen men, almost one-half
of the regiment's casualties, were hit in the face or head. Another
seven sustained bullet wounds to the hands or arms. Six more were
shot in the chest or side. Only eight of the regiment's casualties suffered wounds to the legs.[44]

The Second Indian Home Guard on the right advanced into the
Kansans' line of fire. Bowles shouted at them to fall back and form on
the regiment's right. The Twenty-Ninth Texas heard Bowles's voice
and mistook it as a command for a general retreat. The Confederates
rose, advanced from the tree line, Bowles later recounted, "and, like
true soldiers, commenced to press, as they supposed, a retreating
foe."[45] However, the First Kansas Colored Infantry was not on the
retreat. At a distance of twenty-five yards, the black soldiers fired.
The line of Confederate soldiers shattered. The Texas flag bearer
went down; another man quickly raised the colors but fell moments
later from Union fire. A regiment's flag was a cherished object. To
lose it in battle was considered a great shame. A third Texan grabbed
the flag to save it from capture, but Bowles ordered his men to fire
on the soldier, and a hail of bullets cut him down. The rest of the
Texans fled back into the woods, leaving the flag on the prairie as a
trophy for the First Kansas Colored Infantry.[46]

With much of the Twenty-Ninth Texas stopped by the volley,
the Confederate line cracked. Private McDermott in the Twentieth
Texas wrote of the exchange, "Our officers and men behaved bravely
as long as it was prudent to stay and then we run [sic] like hell."[47]
Some First Kansas Colored soldiers tried to give chase, but Bowles,

concerned that the rough terrain would disrupt the regiment's advance, called in the companies on the right to reform along the original battle line. While the black soldiers reformed their line, an orderly of the Second Indian Home Guard rode up to Bowles and notified him that the Indian soldiers would be passing to their front in pursuit of the Confederates. As they crossed in front of the black soldiers, the Union Indians picked up the Twenty-Ninth Texas flag and claimed it for themselves. On seeing this, men of the First Kansas Colored exploded with rage. "Some of my officers and men shouted out in remonstrance, and asked permission to break ranks to get them," Bowles wrote after the battle. Concerned with keeping the regiment formed and ready to advance—and likely wanting to avoid a physical confrontation between the black and the Indian soldiers— Bowles "refused permission, and told them the matter could be righted here-after."[48] Records of the First Kansas Colored Infantry do not describe the ultimate fate of the Twenty-Ninth Texas flag.

As the Texas regiments fell back in the face of the First Kansas Colored Infantry, the Confederate right broke under the weight of a charge by the First Indian Home Guards. General Cooper, coming from the rear after looking for the missing Choctaw regiment, "discovered our men in small parties giving way."[49] The Union assault advanced so rapidly that some Confederates holding the right flank feared they would be surrounded. Lieutenant Colonel Otis Welch of the Twenty-Ninth Texas kept the center of his regiment together in an orderly withdrawal. After falling back to a more defensible location, he ordered his men to halt with the assumption "that I was supported by the whole brigade." He sent the regiment's major to firm up the right flank, but became concerned when the officer did not return. Welch ran over to his regiment's flank only to find "that all on our right had given away, and that the enemy were passing rapidly to our rear, on the right." Recognizing the situation as hopeless, he ordered the remaining Texans to retreat. Though the Twenty-Ninth Texas was a cavalry regiment, the men had dismounted for the battle. As they fell back, they learned that their horses had been pulled back with the retreating soldiers. Cut off from the main Confederate force, Welch and his men raced up Elk Creek on foot and barely escaped as the Union battle line closed in.[50]

General Cooper tried to stem the tide, watching as the number of men falling back "increased until the retreat became general." With Elk Creek at their backs, the Confederate soldiers had to swim or wade to the other side, or push their way across the single bridge at the center of their line. Some crossed at fords near the extreme right and left flanks, and Cooper ordered the Fifth Texas Partisans to defend one of the fords before realizing the cause was lost. The entire Confederate line crumbled and fell back in confusion. The First Kansas Colored Infantry took part in this pursuit, marching some three miles in formation to push the Confederates back. The Union soldiers kept up a steady pressure, foiling a few attempts by Cooper's men to regroup, though a number of the Confederate soldiers fought stubbornly as they withdrew. Captain Earle of Company F remembered that "at every creek or piece of timber and brush" the enemy "would make a stand with an attempt to check our pursuit."[51]

The Confederate commander did manage to organize a portion of his force into a temporary line at Honey Springs. The Choctaw regiment, which had missed the battle due to a misunderstanding, arrived and charged the advancing Union line. "With their usual intrepidity the Choctaws went at the enemy until their force could be concentrated and all brought up," Cooper reported after the battle. But the counterattack fizzled. "The Choctaws, discouraged on account of the worthless ammunition, then gave way, and were ordered to fall back with the others in rear of the train," he wrote.[52]

Hiding in a cave a half mile from Honey Springs, slave girl Lucinda Davis saw Confederate soldiers flee in panic. "Dey come riding and running by whar we is, and it don't make no difference how much de head men hollers at 'em dey can't make dat bunch slow up and stop."[53] With the last semblance of resistance spent, Cooper ordered the supplies stored at Honey Springs burned rather than let them fall into Union hands. The last retreating Confederates torched piles of sugar, salt, flour, and other goods. Union soldiers rushed to salvage the goods. Captain Earle recounted that the men found "plenty of bread, hams and bacon and excellent flour," a very welcome treat for soldiers who had breakfasted on hardtack.[54]

An investigation of the Confederate supply base uncovered a cache of five hundred pairs of iron shackles. The purpose of these cold metal chains was not lost on the men of the First Kansas Colored Infantry. In battle, these black soldiers fought not only for the Union and the freedom of slaves across North America, but also for their own freedom. Yet they did not seek retribution upon their defeated enemy. According to Lieutenant Colonel Moonlight, Blunt's chief of staff, the black soldiers "grinned from ear to ear at the sight of their old companions, the shackles." With dozens of Confederate prisoners now in their hands, Moonlight proclaimed, "be it said to the memory of the 1st Kansas Colored they behaved with marked humanity and kindness to the wounded, who but a few hours before had worry to place the yoke of slavery forever on their necks if within their power."[55]

Blunt's men chased the Confederate force to the east for a couple of miles before halting. After the battle, Cooper claimed that the eastward retreat was intentional and had "deceived the enemy, and created, as I anticipated, the impression that re-enforcements from Fort Smith were close at hand, and that by a detour in rear of the mountain east of Honey Springs our forces might march upon Gibson and destroy it while General Blunt was away with almost the whole Federal force."[56] In his report of the battle, Blunt made no mention of fear that Cooper would threaten Fort Gibson. Instead, he called the pursuit off, since after twenty-four hours of marching and a half day of fighting, the "artillery horses could draw the guns no farther, and the cavalry horses and infantry were completely exhausted from fatigue."[57] The earlier rain had given way to prairie sunshine and heat, leading some men, like Private Andrew Jackson of the First Kansas Colored Infantry's Company I, to collapse. During the engagement, two of his fellow soldiers later reported, "he was over came, apparently by heat, and over exertion and was left on the field until after the battle when he was picked up." Heat-related illnesses caused serious problems, for the men found Private Jackson "suffering with an affliction of the head, causing total deafness in left ear and partial deafness in right ear."[58] Thus, nursing battle casualties and thoroughly exhausted men, and with Cabell's Confederate reinforcements coming into sight, Blunt called his men back around four o'clock.[59]

The men of the First Kansas Colored Infantry and their fellow soldiers burned the rest of the Confederate supplies and marched back to the main battle site near Elk Creek to camp. Lucinda Davis, the slave hiding nearby, saw the smoke from the burning Confederate supplies and looked over to the Texas Road. "Den long come lots of de Yankee soldiers going back to de North, and dey looks purty wore out," she remembered, "but dey is laughing and joshing and going on." The men had reason to be in good spirits—they had attacked and defeated a numerically superior force. Lucinda later learned that her uncle, a runaway slave she only described as Abe, was among the happy federal soldiers. "He was in dat same battle," she recalled seven decades later, "and after de war dey called him Abe Colonel."[60] Corporal Abraham Kernell served with Company I at Honey Springs.

Blunt and his men fully expected the reinforced Confederates to strike the next morning. Despite a low supply of ammunition, Blunt was willing to risk being attacked in order to let his men rest. They spent a quiet night on the battlefield. The morning sunlight fell on a peaceful prairie. Cabell and Cooper decided to leave the Union men victorious on the field. Cooper's army was in shambles. The wounded straggled into the Confederate camp for days after the battle. Even with Cabell's reinforcements, some in the Confederate ranks did not believe Blunt's small army could be beaten. "I believe they will whip us and whip us all the time until we are reinforced from Texas or some other point," Private McDermott wrote a few days after the battle. "They are too strong for us." In fact, the power of the Union assault fooled some of the soldiers into thinking that Blunt's force was two or three times larger than its actual size. Humbled by the defeat, McDermott admitted, "They are some seven or eight thousand and good fighters. I know it for I have tried them and they are as good as we are, better drilled and better armed."[61]

The morning calm gave the First Kansas Colored Infantry soldiers a chance to survey the previous day's battle. Captain Earle wrote that the troops "found the killed of the enemy very thick about us." He reported that Union details buried 117 Confederate soldiers. The number was likely not an exaggeration, as Cooper claimed his loss was 134 killed. He did not list the number of Confederate wounded, but Blunt estimated it at 400.[62]

In comparison, the attacking Union force lost less than twenty men killed and about sixty wounded. The First Kansas Colored Infantry, fighting near the center of the line, suffered the most casualties within Blunt's command. Yet only two men were killed and about thirty wounded—a surprisingly light casualty count.[63] Lieutenant Colonel Welch of the Twenty-Ninth Texas proclaimed that in the opening volley, his men "poured upon them a galling fire."[64] But the black soldiers were prone during much of the sustained firing. And, as Captain Earle explained, the Confederates "used double barrel shotguns, which in the timber and thick brush were not very effective."[65] Perhaps most surprising, of the regiment's fourteen soldiers shot in the face or head, only two died.

All of the Union units at Honey Springs fought bravely. Still, a number of officers and men distinctly pointed out the effectiveness of the black soldiers. General Blunt, in his official report of the battle, explained, "The First Kansas (colored) particularly distinguished itself; they fought like veterans, and preserved their line unbroken throughout the engagement. Their coolness and bravery I have never seen surpassed; they were in the hottest of the fight, and opposed to Texas troops twice their number, whom they completely routed." He claimed that "one Texas regiment (the Twentieth Cavalry) that fought against them went into the fight with 300 men and came out with only 60."[66] How Blunt came about this information is unknown, and it is likely an exaggeration. Nonetheless, no one disagreed that the Texas soldiers suffered a serious defeat at the hands of their black opponents.

Captain Earle recorded a shift in attitude among some of the white Colorado soldiers after the battle. According to Earle, at one point during the pursuit, a company of the Second Colorado advanced too far from the main battle line and found themselves nearly surrounded by enemy soldiers. Two companies from the First Kansas Colored marched to their aid. "When the Colored Regiment was at Fort Scott and on the way to the fight [the Colorado men] treated us with contempt," Earle wrote, "but after this fight and the rescue of their men they would always say, 'if we are going into a fight give us the niggers.'"[67] Through discipline and bravery in battle, the men of the First Kansas Colored commanded respect from their comrades.

CHAPTER 11

FALL 1863

. . . how the boasted affection of the owners for their negroes has suddenly turned into loathing and disgust.

The First Kansas Colored Infantry returned to Fort Blunt celebrating the triumph at Honey Springs, coming barely two weeks
after victory at Cabin Creek. Although Confederate forces were reeling in Indian Territory, Major General James G. Blunt prepared his
Union soldiers for a defense of the fort. Several companies of the
First Kansas Colored received orders to occupy satellite camps for
security and logistical purposes.[1]

Meanwhile, Confederate Brigadier General William Steele
planned to unite his forces near the Honey Springs battleground and
push the Union soldiers out of Fort Blunt. He pulled together six
thousand men and requested more reinforcements, as well as ammunition from Texas to replenish empty cartridge boxes and replace the
inferior powder that had plagued the Confederates during the previous battle. Morale among the Southern soldiers plummeted during
the tedious wait. Desertions crippled the ranks. Groups of Confederates, sometimes with officers, slipped away. Worse, Steele learned
that Union reinforcements from southern Missouri threatened Fort
Smith in Arkansas, a major Confederate military base along the
Arkansas River, just east of Indian Territory. In response, Steele sent
Brigadier General William L. Cabell and a brigade of Arkansas troops
to Fort Smith, further weakening his own lines in Honey Springs. By
mid-August, Steele had only fifteen hundred men available.[2]

Blunt longed for action. "We are all spoiling for a fight," he wrote
an associate, "especially the *first nigger.*" Though Blunt respected
the First Kansas Colored soldiers for their abilities and determination, his crude language reflects the racial dynamics of even the
most enlightened white officers at the time. Logistical limitations
and orders *"to fall back—that I am too far advanced and can have
no reinforcements"* kept him in place, he complained. Nonetheless,
he and his men were confident of victory.[3]

To strengthen his force, Blunt considered another option—one that reflected his confidence in black soldiers. He envisioned a plan to push Confederate forces out of Fort Smith and "gobble up all the buck-negroes that will make good soldiers."[4] These were prescient words, as runaway slaves from Arkansas began to replenish First Kansas Colored losses and form a second black regiment in Kansas. But at this point Blunt still had to defeat Steele. Union reinforcements from Missouri finally arrived and gave him the opportunity to strike.

On August 22, Blunt pushed forty-five hundred men, including detachments of the First Kansas Colored Infantry, against Steele sixty miles south. Notified of the Union advance, Steele fell back from the Canadian River to Perryville, near the Texas border. Blunt's cavalry reached the outskirts of the town and skirmished with some Confederate Indians. Steele, still unwilling to face the full Union force, abandoned the town during a forced night march south. Though unsuccessful in defeating the enemy in battle, Blunt had achieved a strategic victory by cutting Steele's line in two and diminishing the Confederate threat in the region. He ordered his men to burn Perryville and then turned toward the tempting and now poorly defended Fort Smith in Arkansas.[5]

The small Union army covered the one hundred miles between Perryville and Fort Smith in four days. On August 30, Confederate pickets spotted the approaching enemy a few miles from the outer defenses. Aware his force was less than half the size of Blunt's, Cabell abandoned Fort Smith. On the morning of September 1, Blunt launched an attack on the fort only to find it empty. He sent cavalry and light artillery in pursuit, and triumphantly marched into the fort.[6]

With Fort Blunt and Fort Smith, Union forces held two key military positions in the Indian Territory and northern Arkansas, boosting Union military objectives and providing hope for slaves in the region. Throughout the war slaves had sought refuge in free states or with Union armies. But with the Emancipation Proclamation, the handling of fugitive slaves went from a sideline issue to a major element of federal policy. Many in the government worried about significant black migration to Union-held areas. During the summer of 1863, the American Freedmen's Inquiry Commission, formed by Secretary of War Edwin Stanton, sent letters to state and federal officials asking about the condition and habits of newly freed slaves.

The commission's objective was to help "place the Colored People of the United States in a condition of self-support and self-defense."[7]

The commission's questionnaires reveal a genuine concern for freed slaves as well as ignorance about African Americans. "Are they good-humored and peaceable among themselves, or are they quarrelsome?" the form asked. Another question read: "Are they generally docile and inclined to obey, or do they show strong individuality and a determination to have their own way?" African Americans had lived alongside whites in North America since 1620 and made up nearly 14 percent of the total U.S. population by 1860.[8] Yet slavery had led to callousness and presuppositions about African Americans among many whites. The commission was especially curious about biracial traits. Officials were asked whether they "observe any difference between blacks and mulattoes in their bodily strength, and power of endurance," whether "blacks [are] more or less prolific than mulattoes," and even whether they "perceive any difference in the intellectual capacity of mulattoes and blacks."[9]

At least half a dozen Kansans received these requests for information, including the First Kansas Colored Infantry's commander, Colonel James M. Williams, and former adjutant Richard Hinton. Williams declined to comment on most of the questions, explaining that intelligent answers "would require a protracted residence amongst and frequent intercourse with the Colored people." Such response was puzzling from a man who had spent a year in command of a black regiment. Still, he did offer his views from a military perspective. He simply wrote that "as a soldier the negro is excellent by now, & tis in this capacity that I would employ him in the suppression of the Rebellion."[10] The statement was short and succinct, offering little substance for contemporary critics and later historians.

Colonel William A. Phillips, of the Third Indian Home Guard, responded to the commission with more details about freed slaves. "My observation leads me most emphatically to recommend the enlistment of every negro soldier who can be obtained," he wrote. "In the first place you get men of better physique than can now be easily recruited amongst whites. In the second they are more teachable and more easily drilled than whites or Indians." As long as black soldiers had mentors and commanders who were dedicated and capable, Phillips believed freed blacks would continue to be excellent recruits.[11]

Thousands of other slaves in the region yearned for freedom but did not wish to migrate to distant areas. "In my observation the negroes with very few exceptions would prefer to remain where we find them, *if it were* safe for them to do so," Colonel Phillips explained to the commission. He reported that many freed slaves would resist attempts to evacuate them from Union camps to safer locations.[12] Reasons varied. Some had family still in bondage, others were fearful of the unknown, and still others only wanted to shed the shackles of bondage and had no desire to leave the place of their birth.[13] The congregation of fugitive slaves around military camps in Indian Territory and Arkansas taxed the already strained federal supply stores. Lieutenant Colonel Frederick W. Schaurte, acting commander at Fort Blunt, grew so frustrated with the number of runaways that he directed a forced evacuation. "It is hereby ordered, that all Colored People residing within the limits of Fort Blunt, who are not Officers' Waiters, nor in the employment of the Government, shall, within the next eight days, remove outside the limits of the Post," the September 18 order read. Schaurte did not intend to completely abandon the fugitives, some of whom may have been family members of recent First Kansas Colored Infantry recruits or other African Americans serving the Union. He added that if "any of the said Colored People desire to go North, transportation will be furnished them in the next return train, by applying to the Provost Marshal." He emphasized that any person failing to obey the order would be "forcibly expelled."[14]

The order outraged black Union soldiers and laborers and drew the ire of some white servicemen. Forcing desperate African American fugitives out of the safety of Fort Blunt left them vulnerable to Confederate attack, capture, and possible reenslavement. "The above Order No 3 is hereby revoked, having been issued without proper authority, and opposed to the principles of Humanity," read a counterorder from Colonel John Ritchie, commander of the First Brigade of the Army of the Frontier. Ritchie concluded: "Military Orders must be lawful to be obeyed."[15] Overall, while most white Northerners had not gone to war for the sake of African Americans, the sheer number of fugitive slaves flocking to Union lines and their ability to provide vital labor and military service changed the nature of the conflict. They could not and would not be ignored.

By September 21 the First Kansas Colored Infantry was in place at Fort Smith, strengthening the fort's defenses and scrounging for food and supplies from outlying areas.[16] That labor combined with the previous weeks of fatigue duty and marching took a toll on the unit. During the first week in October, Colonel John V. DuBois of the Inspector General's Department reviewed the men, their equipment, and their camp. His report proved highly critical. Two officers, First Lieutenant Benjamin G. Jones and Second Lieutenant Ezekiel A. Coleman of Company A, were absent without leave, and had been so since mid-August. Second Lieutenant Albert E. Saviers of Company K was in the hands of civil authorities, dating back to May, for unspecified reasons. An equipment inspection found the weapons "half clean," and the condition of both accoutrements and clothing "bad." The camp's accommodations for the sick were atrocious, the overall sanitary condition was found to be poor, and the soldiers' personal cleanliness fell far below army standards.[17]

Disease proved more deadly to Civil War soldiers—black and white, Union and Confederate—than enemy bullets or cannon balls. Between 1861 and 1865 one in twelve white soldiers died of disease. For African American soldiers, the rate was an appalling one in five.[18] Infectious diseases spread rapidly in a Civil War camp, especially within regiments from rural communities. Young men from agricultural areas contracted common "childhood" diseases, such as chicken pox and the mumps, when placed in close quarters with men from other areas. The regiment recorded its first wave of serious illness in March 1863, when at least a dozen men died from pneumonia, typhoid, "consumption," and "inflammation of the lungs." Ten more died the following month, and another nine in May. During DuBois's inspection, smallpox had made an appearance in camp. By December, nearly twenty men had fallen ill to the disease, and four of them died. The epidemic may have been worse, for the fate of some men was recorded in regimental records simply as "Died of disease."[19]

Regarding administrative matters, DuBois stated that company and regimental morning reports were "irregularly made," official war documents were "seldom read," and the officers and men "do not wear the prescribed uniform." The frustrated inspector added that "public animals are badly treated and are used for other purposes than the service of the government."[20]

Despite the poor sanitation and condition of equipment, DuBois noted that the black soldiers maintained good military bearing, good discipline, and (despite the uniform problems) appeared soldierly.

And they had plenty of firepower. The regiment boasted 26,000 rounds of ammunition, almost evenly divided between regular lead ball cartridges and "buck and ball."[21]

Shortly after the First Kansas Colored arrived at Fort Smith, the newly raised Second Kansas Colored Infantry marched into camp. Raised in Kansas during the summer of 1863, the new unit brought welcome support and camaraderie to the state's original black regiment. However, the sight of new uniforms, new tents, and new arms sparked dissension and jealousy among the First Kansas Colored veterans. Captain Ethan Earle of Company F recalled that "on seeing this Regiment so well provided for and having done no service our men were very much dissatisfied, they had not decent clothing and many were without Shoes and no tents." First Kansas Colored Infantry officers appealed to the quartermaster for help. According to Earle, "The reply was that there was every thing in the Store which we needed, but our Colonel had never sent any application requisition for them." Officers quickly acquired the necessary supplies.[22]

The regiment replenished some of its ranks with newly freed or escaped Arkansas slaves. The standard size of a Civil War regiment was one thousand—ten companies of one hundred men. That strength was nearly impossible to maintain in the face of disease, discharges, battle casualties, and desertions. By the end of 1863, the First Kansas Colored Infantry was fortunate to put five hundred healthy men in the field at any given time. Some companies needed new enlistees more than others. From October to December 1863, the regiment enlisted seventy new men. Twelve fell in with Company B, nineteen went to Company G, and Company H took in twenty-one new recruits. The rest were divided among the other companies, although Companies C and K recorded no new enlisted men during that period.[23]

In September, Blunt left Fort Smith for Fort Scott to supervise the acquisition of supplies and reinforcements for his men in Arkansas. In late October, during his absence, the long-running feud with Major General John M. Schofield, commander of the Department of Missouri, resulted in Blunt's removal as commander of the District of the Frontier.[24] Brigadier General John McNeil took over Blunt's command and arrived at Fort Smith in early November. He found Union forces at the post in rough shape. Troops were scattered about, desperately trying to protect pro-Union territory from guerrillas and small groups of Southern cavalry. These clashes took a toll on the First Kansas Colored Infantry. Corporal Bedford Greene of Company A was killed in October.[25] The regiment lost an officer in November when Second Lieutenant Eberle Q. Macey of Company C fell at a skirmish near Timber Hills in the Cherokee Nation.[26] Private Jacob Hill fell into enemy hands during another encounter. Despite earlier threats to kill or enslave captured black soldiers, his Confederate captors "were compelled to recognize him as a soldier to some extent" and detained him as a prisoner of war at Fort Washita and then at Bonham, Texas. He escaped and returned to Fort Smith in January to report his experience.[27]

McNeil had on hand the First Kansas Colored Infantry, the First Arkansas Infantry, the Second Colorado, the Second Kansas Cavalry, the Eighteenth Iowa Infantry, a battery of artillery, and several other companies, totaling some three thousand men. Since the occupation of Fort Smith, federal soldiers relied on their foraging abilities to subsist. McNeil explained that his men had plenty of salt and sugar, "but are entirely out of hard bread, coffee, candles, and soap." He knew of a vast amount of wheat and corn near Waldron, Arkansas, but he feared that Confederate forces were moving into that area, potentially depriving Fort Smith of any sustainable food supply.[28]

Shortages of equipment plagued the Union command. "The service also requires all kinds of quartermaster's and ordnance stores," he explained to General Schofield, "including arms for the new regiments and ammunition for all arms." Union officers recruiting loyal white and black Arkansans for military service had no uniforms to clothe them or enough regular officers to formally muster them.[29] On a more positive note, McNeil had complete confidence in the First Kansas Colored. After reviewing the regiment alongside the First Arkansas Infantry and an artillery battery, he complimented only the black Kansans in his official correspondence to Schofield. "The negro regiment is a triumph of drill and discipline, and reflects great honor on Colonel Williams in command," he wrote. "Few volunteer regiments that I have seen make a better appearance. I regard them as first-rate infantry."[30]

McNeil needed trustworthy troops for ongoing supply operations, so he sent the regiment east. Its main base of operations became Roseville, Arkansas, a crop-rich farming area forty miles down the Arkansas River from Fort Smith.[31] The men gathered corn, wheat, and cotton for the garrison, providing vital supplies for the upcoming winter months. The operations lasted until the beginning of December, when reports of Confederate activity around Fort Smith prompted the regiment to return.[32] They set up camp on the east bank of the Poteau River one mile south of the fort.[33] Nothing came of the expected Southern attack, and within a week the First Kansas Colored returned to foraging operations.

Before leaving Fort Smith they greeted General Blunt arriving with a procession of wagons. Rather than travel to Fort Leavenworth following his removal, as directed by General Schofield, the feisty Blunt declared his intention of leading a wagon train to Fort Blunt and then on to Fort Smith.[34] Schofield exploded with rage, especially after he received a report that Blunt's wagons held nothing more than confiscated property to be sold for personal profit. He fired off a message to McNeil ordering him to search the wagons when they arrived at Fort Smith and arrest Blunt if the accusations proved true.[35] In fact, Blunt's wagons contained badly needed supplies. McNeil wrote to Schofield that "by General Blunt's train we received 100,000 rations, without flour and little hard bread." Fortunately, another supply train on the way would bring twenty thousand rations of bread. McNeil concluded, "The supply by each train is badly wanted."[36]

Though his desire to supply federal troops in Arkansas was legitimate, Blunt made no effort to leave Fort Smith after delivery of the goods. He learned that the War Department authorized him to organize the Eleventh United States Colored Troops among Arkansas black recruits and used this as a pretext to stay.[37] "He asked my aid in that capacity," McNeil admitted to Schofield. "Desirous to facilitate the service, and with respect to his rank, I have assigned him an office and such assistance as his duty requires."[38] The assignment was only temporary and was hardly suitable for a major general. Nonetheless, it kept Blunt at Fort Smith until January.[39]

As a gesture of goodwill, the officers at Fort Smith planned a grand review on December 7 to celebrate the anniversary of Blunt's victory at Prairie Grove. Inclement weather forced a delay of two days, but December 9 was warm, one writer noted, "more like May than December."[40] Four thousand soldiers marched in formation to a large open span of prairie. The men had brushed the dust from their uniforms and polished buttons and brass belt buckles. Special attention went to the weapons. Spectators from the community looked on the thousands of muskets "glittering gaily in the splendor of the an unclouded, noonday sun."[41]

The Eighteenth Iowa led the procession, marching across the parade ground, stopping in front of a large mansion once owned by Elias Rector, a former U.S. Superintendent of Indian Affairs who had joined the Confederacy. Next came the First Kansas Colored Infantry, keeping their cadence and maintaining tight formation, until Colonel Williams called for the companies to wheel into line. Behind them marched the Second Kansas Colored, followed by the Second Kansas Battery. Other regiments included the Thirteenth Kansas Infantry, Third Kansas Battery, Third Wisconsin Cavalry, and Fourteenth Kansas Cavalry.

As the last unit took its place, thirteen cannons fired, announcing the entry of the commanding generals. Blunt and McNeil began with an inspection of the line. The generals and their staffs rode along the front and rear of the formation, looking over the soldiers—black and white. Blunt and McNeil positioned themselves at the center front and directed the regimental commanders to begin the review. Again the air filled with the sounds of barking officers, stomping feet, and muskets snapped into position in unison. One by one the regiments filed past the generals.

A dress parade served a number of purposes. Commanding officers could observe the results of training and the condition of the soldiers and equipment. It provided motivation for line officers to have their men practiced in marching and drill. Perhaps most importantly, a dress parade was intended to boost morale. Most of a Civil War soldier's life was spent in tedium—drilling, performing physical labor, or doing nothing at all. The pageantry of a grand review instilled pride and enthusiasm for the troops, if only for an afternoon.

A correspondent of the *Fort Smith New Era* watched the Union soldiers perform with great precision. Past the generals the regiments marched, "making a fine and warlike appearance," he wrote. "The mounted part of the command then passed review the second time in 'double quick,'" he continued, "giving the uninitiated a faint idea of the shock produced by a cavalry charge."[42] Arkansas Unionists also rejoiced in the display. "It was indeed, the finest treat that could be offered to a loyal man," declared the pro-Union *New Era*, "after having seen nothing but 'greybacks' for years."[43]

During this period, other accolades for the regiment came in. Champion Vaughan, editor of the *Leavenworth Times*, wrote to Colonel Williams declaring his commitment to celebrate the unit's glory. "I am truly proud of you, your officers & your men,

& I mean that the State & the country shall know the whole truth in regard to you. Unless my hand becomes palsied no Regiment shall go upon record in the State archives with a prouder name than yours."[44]

In mid-December the First Kansas Colored Infantry left Fort Smith to continue foraging operations farther east. "I supposed you would like to know where and what kind of place we are in," Captain John Graton of Company C wrote to his wife later that month. "We are stationed in a place called Roseville, containing about a dozen houses, five of them being inhabited."[45] That winter was bitterly cold. "Snowing more today," Private Henry Strong of the Twelfth Kansas Infantry wrote for an early January journal entry. Having arrived at Fort Smith days before, he declared that "the temperature [is] more suitable for Wisconsin than this latitude." Local residents claimed that it was the coldest winter experienced there in twenty years.[46] Yet Graton reveled in how the First Kansas Colored men enjoyed a bountiful supply of food: "We fare pretty well here getting plenty of fresh pork and beef butter, some potatoes and we are making all the corn meal we want."[47]

Colonel Williams noted a vast amount of abandoned land in a letter to General McNeil. "I would respectfully invite your attention to the importance of putting the abundant farms in this vicinity into some shape that they may be made to produce supplies for the next season." With these concerns in mind, Williams claimed to "have taken great care to have no fences destroyed so that they [the fields] may be cultivated" by some of the many refugees fleeing Confederate territory. He argued that such efforts would benefit the Union military and the local population. "In my opinion not less than 5,000 acres of abandoned lands under cultivation can be found within protecting distances of this Post which can be profitably cultivated, the coming season, provided assurance of permanent occupation can be given to the tenants." He hoped for immediate action by McNeil and federal officials.[48]

In the meantime, the black soldiers busily engaged in various farming and policing operations in northern Arkansas. Graton claimed that the men gathered twenty thousand bushels of corn and added, "I think there is as much more not yet gathered, there were about five miles almost continuous corn fields the rebs had put in for their own use." These supplies were a godsend for the Union garrison at Fort Smith, which had cleared all forage from the surrounding area for forty miles. Graton told his wife, "Now they are sending here for it."[49]

"We have also been in to the cotton business somewhat having collected about 150 bales," Graton wrote. Government agents worked with the regiment and local residents to collect the crop, process it into bales, and ship it north. Unlike during their days in bondage, the former slaves of the First Kansas Colored Infantry did not pick the cotton bolls for ginning. "Our men haul the seed cotton and guard the gins and [the agent] hires citizens to do the work," Graton clarified.[50] Nonetheless, the long hours of monotonous labor wore on the men, prompting Colonel Williams to offer a popular form of compensation. "In view of the heavy fatiguing labor imposed upon the troops at this Post," he formally ordered on January 13, supply officers "will issue one ration of whisky to each man of this command this day upon requisition of Commanders of Companies."[51] Captain Ethan Earle of Company F also noted the vast cotton-processing operation. "The men or a party of them were collecting and ginning Cotton and I had in my possession about fifty-thousand dollars worth stored in a Cotton Shed and under my private guard as I had been appointed Provost Marshal for Franklin County."[52]

Officers found themselves serving as community and reconstruction officials in Union-occupied portions of Arkansas. In late December, Colonel Williams received a request from a delegate of the Masonic Fraternity of Ozark Lodge of Free Masons for permission "to meet as they have in times of peace, to transact business only pertaining to that Ancient Order." Williams responded a few days later, declaring that "it will give me great pleasure to encourage all lawful meetings, and the return of the citizens of this county to their farms, peaceful avocation, amusements and social gatherings." But, he noted, "I cannot promise protection to any person not Loyal to the Government I have the honor to serve." Thus Williams informed the Masons that "the Commanding Officer at your place is instructed to issue passes to and from the meetings of your fraternity to such persons as shall establish before him their Loyalty."[53]

During this period, December 1863, President Abraham Lincoln announced a plan for reconstruction of seceded states. The proposal came to be known as the "Ten Percent Plan," for once 10 percent of a state's 1860 voting population swore loyalty to the Union, that body could form a new state government to be recognized by the president. As part of the plan, Lincoln offered a pardon and amnesty to individuals (except high-ranking Confederate officials) who took an oath of allegiance to the United States and accepted emancipation.[54] Thousands of white Arkansas residents responded.[55] Reestablishing loyalty in Union-occupied Arkansas became a full-time job for some First Kansas Colored officers. "In January [1864]," Earle declared, "I had administered the Oath of Allegiance to nearly all the men in the county, recording each man's name and requiring him to state his whereabouts during the Rebellion, all of which was put on record." Wives and widows also swore loyalty oaths. Arkansas boasted a large Unionist population. But Earle asserted that he learned "by these records, that nearly every man in Arkansas of mind, money or murder had been in the Rebel army," though "many pretended that they were forced in." The truly loyal Arkansans, he claimed, had fled to the hills and were only slowly coming down to garner protection from federal soldiers.[56]

A strong division emerged among the increasingly active Unionist Arkansans. The largest faction, headed by William Fishback, pushed for more radical change in the state. Harboring resentment against the prewar elite of Arkansas, this faction embraced emancipation and pushed greater democratization of a postwar government. The Fort Smith *New Era*, a voice for Fishback, relished the changing landscape of Arkansas society. "Our chains are broken at last," editor Valentine Dell wrote. "We again belong to, enjoy the honors, privileges, and advantages of that country which has stood pre-eminent among all nations of the earth in freedom, happiness and power."[57] The radicals poked fun at the frustrated secessionists and conservative Unionists who found themselves in the shadow of the federal armies and emancipation. "It is curious to observe how the boasted affection of the owners for their negroes has suddenly turned into loathing and disgust," the *New Era* editor wrote. "Formerly, the universal language of the pro-slaveryists [sic] was, how tenderly affectionate the whites are to their slaves! Well, perhaps masters and mistresses did love their negroes, but was their love different in kind from that they indulged for their horses, mules, and pigs, or other property?" These same people, the columnist continued, now spoke of a pitiful future for the freed men and women in their midst. "What to do to the freed Africans?" he asked. "Why, do to them as you would have them do to you. This is the treatment which One wiser than Solomon prescribes."[58]

Shortly before the war the Arkansas legislature had passed a law to expel every free black person from the state, establishing a policy that perpetual servitude was the only acceptable role for black Americans.[59] Now, only a few years later, as Union armies liberated Arkansas slaves and helped reinstitute a new state government, a Unionist Arkansas newspaper suggested equal treatment for all residents—black and white. "If the African desires work, and you can give it, employ him, and when his work is done pay him a fair and just valuation. If he is in suffering, minister to him as you would to any other sufferer in the same necessity," the newspaper read. "If he needs instruction, withhold not. Let him have all the education he has leisure and capacity to acquire, precisely as any one else."[60]

Opposition to the radicals came from conservative Unionists. This second faction generally accepted Lincoln's Ten Percent Plan, but attempted to limit the effect of emancipation and social change. Though a minority part of the Unionist force in Arkansas, the conservatives found a strong ally in Major General Frederick Steele— the Union military commander of the Army of Arkansas. Steele, a conservative Democrat, had used his authority to hinder social and political change in Union-controlled territories of Arkansas. In September 1862, on taking command of federal forces in Helena, Steele had ended his predecessor's policy of freeing fugitive slaves and halted an effort to raise a black regiment in Arkansas.[61] Proponents of emancipation, civil rights for freedmen, and more radical reconstruction looked on Steele with contempt.

As 1863 came to a close, disputes also appeared within the First Kansas Colored Infantry officer ranks. Surviving accounts document two episodes, both involving the regiment's commander, Colonel Williams. The first began as a technical disagreement in early September 1863 between Williams and Captain Andrew J. Armstrong of Company D. The captain, per his regular duties, submitted a muster roll designating the status and duties of each man in his company. "I looked over the rolls and called his attention to the fact that he had omitted to make mention in the proper place of the manner of one Harris's employment," Williams later testified. The colonel believed that Private Robert Harris of Company D had served as an officer's servant. He ordered the captain to properly record the duty. Armstrong protested, arguing that Harris had not worked in such capacity, and refused to amend the muster roll. Williams insisted that Armstrong correct the rolls as instructed and sent him away. The following day, Armstrong returned to the colonel's tent with the muster roll unchanged. When Williams again ordered Armstrong to document Private Harris's duties as an officer's servant, Armstrong flatly refused. In the face of this rejection Williams placed Armstrong under arrest, to be tried by court-martial for disobeying a lawful command of a superior officer, "conduct to the prejudices of good order and military discipline," and conduct unbecoming an officer.[62]

Armstrong had faced court-martial before, after he shot Sergeant Sampson Wharfield during a violent altercation in 1862. The court had acquitted him with a finding of self-defense. This time he was accused of instigating insubordination. The court documents provide a detailed account of accusations and testimony.

The second and third charges leveled against Armstrong declared that he "did tolerate, permit, and allow a member of Officers and enlisted men members of said 1st Kansas Coloured Inft to congregate" at his tent and that he allowed these individuals "to indulge in riotous, obscene, and ungentlemanly language toward the commanding Officer of said 1st Ks Coloured Inft." Further accusations charged that he "kept in his quarters spirituous and intoxicating liquor and did tolerate, allow, and permit a member of enlisted men of 1st Regt Kansas Coloured Inft to . . . drink said spirituous and intoxicating liquors, and did then and there use, and allow said enlisted men to use boisterous, obscene, and riotous language, this to the great disgrace and scandal of the service." Both events, Williams believed, occurred around September 5, shortly after the disagreement over the muster roll.[63]

The court met in January 1864, four months after the disputed events. By then Captain Armstrong had been removed from command of Company D. Under examination, Colonel Williams gave specific details of Armstrong's refusal to correct the muster rolls. Williams's testimony regarding the riotous behavior and intoxication at Armstrong's tent, however, was mild. When asked if he knew "anything about the circumstance of a number of Officers and enlisted men of the 1st Ks Col'd Infantry being on or about September 5th 1863 assembled at the tent of the accused at Camp Williams C. N. and indulging in riotous, obscene, or ungentlemanly language toward the Regimental Commander," Williams answered, "I know of them congregating there but am not able to give the language used by the parties, his tent was nearly in front of men's, about twenty paces apart."[64]

When asked, "Do you know whether Capt Armstrong the accused kept or allowed to be kept in his quarters any spirituous or intoxicating liquors?" Colonel Williams admitted simply, "I can't say that I know."

"Do you know of Capt Armstrong using or allowing enlisted men in his presence to use any boisterous obscene or riotous language?" the prosecutor asked.

"I do not know," Williams said.

His passive answers to the prosecution's questions suggests that he was not wholly committed to the latter charges. First Lieutenant Daniel McFarland appeared as a witness for the prosecution. He confirmed that various people had congregated at Armstrong's tent, but named only officers. "I have seen perhaps two or three together there at a time. I saw Capt. [William] Smallwood, Major [Richard] Ward, Lieut. [Granville] Lewis, and Capt Armstrong. I have seen those assembled there frequently. I don't recollect of seeing any enlisted men there when those officers above stated were there. I never saw more than one enlisted man there at a time." McFarland also confirmed the presence of "spirituous and intoxicating liquors" at the tent, and that he saw the other officers partake, but "could not say that Capt Armstrong drank any."[65]

Lieutenant Lewis confirmed that alcohol had been in camp, but "they were not kept there long," he assured the court. "They were drank up. Several officers drank them. Would not be certain whether Captain Armstrong drank any or not." He was certain, though, that "enlisted men did not drink there."[66]

Major Ward, First Lieutenant William Gibbons, and Orderly Sergeant J. Hall also testified. Gibbons may have been behind the claim of loose lips and free-flowing alcohol at Armstrong's tent. The prosecution questioned his knowledge of riotous and obscene words directed at Colonel Williams in Company D's camp. Gibbons answered, "Can't say positively that I heard any. I did not witness any such proceeding as the question relates to. The date is so far back that I cannot now state positively any thing of that kind I may have seen or heard." Although Gibbons was the fourth witness to deny knowledge of "obscene" behavior around Armstrong's tent, prosecutors inquired: "Did you ever tell the commanding officer of your regiment, that you had listened to a conversation, wherein Capt Armstrong took part, and where words disrespectful towards said regimental commander had been uttered?" Gibbons replied, "I can't now remember that I did."

The prosecution failed to secure evidence sufficient to convict Captain Armstrong of any of the charges. The court acquitted him, stating that there "does not appear to have been any sufficient ground for the arrest and trial of Capt Armstrong." The court directed criticism at Colonel Williams: "Prosecutions induced by personal feelings cannot be too strongly condemned."[67]

Both Colonel Williams and Captain Armstrong were effective officers, committed to the success of black soldiers in combat. The unfortunate incident reflected a personal disagreement, or a clash of personalities, rather than an indictment of their dedication to the regiment.

The second dispute among the officers resulted in court action against the second-in-command. According to Captain Earle, in early January 1864, Colonel Williams hosted a dinner party among officers. "It was then expected that Lieut. Col. Bowles would immediately resign or be dismissed from the Service." According to Earle, "it was there announced that Maj. Ward was to be Lieut. Colonel and I was to have the Major's office and the new Nominees boasted."[68]

Unit records show that Lieutenant Colonel Bowles had sought to resign his commission by the fall of 1863. "Have you heard anything definite in regard to my resignation whether it is to be accepted or not?" Bowles had asked Williams in a letter written from his home in Lawrence, Kansas, on October 25. "If you have please let me know at your earliest convenience as I do not wish to make a trip down there for nothing neither do I wish to be reported absent without leave." The reason for his resignation: health problems. "I have forwarded Surgeons Certification so that I may stand right on the muster roll." In a postscript he added, "If I do not get better soon and my resignation is not accepted, I shall apply for a transfer to the Invalid Corps, though I feel very loth [sic] to take such a step as present and shall not do so only as a last resort."[69] The surgeon's report confirmed Bowles's ailment. Having carefully examined the patient, a military physician concluded that he "is laboring under Chronic Diarrhea and that in consequence thereof he is in my opinion unfit for duty."[70]

Bowles enlisted help from a prominent figure—Senator James Lane—to support his case. Appealing to Major General Samuel Curtis on Bowles's behalf, Lane asked to "introduce and commend to your favorable attention Lieut Col John Bowles. He is a worthy and reliable friend of mine and a good officer. I hope you will be able to give him some detached service, he has been a long time sick and wholly without pay for a long time. I hope you will accommodate him in his wishes."[71] Nonetheless, Bowles remained on the regiment's roster as he convalesced at home.

His continued presence on regimental pay rolls frustrated some, including Captain John Graton. "Lt. Col. Bowles lays around home yet, has gone into the Tanning business," Graton told his wife in November 1864. "Reports say that he lays around home to watch it. He is reported absent without leave, and Williams is using every exertion to get him dismissed [from] the service. Bowles has been away from the Regt. for over a year now, and draws $165.00 every month, sleeps with his wife, and some one else does his work."[72] On December 17, 1864, Lieutenant Colonel Bowles was officially court-martialed for "absence without leave, and repeated disobedience of War Department orders, directing him to join his regiment."[73] Bowles successfully reversed this finding, mustering out in June 1865 with a retroactive date of December 17, 1864.[74] Whatever the cause, Bowles's absence generated dissension among the officers and left the regiment without its official second-in-command for nearly two years.

As the personal disputes played out, the regiment as a whole continued its occupation duty at Fort Smith until the opening of spring 1864. At that point, for the first time, the First Kansas Colored Infantry prepared to take part in a major Union army offensive. It offered a new role for them. In Indian Territory, the regiment had been one of a very few full-strength regiments available to Union commanders. As such, the black soldiers had served as the backbone to Major General Blunt's small operations. The military situation in Arkansas differed greatly. Union officials planned an ambitious and complicated move against Shreveport, Louisiana, a major Confederate center of the Trans-Mississippi Theater.[75] The effort required Major General Nathaniel P. Banks and thirty thousand Union troops to strike through the Red River Valley, while Major General Frederick Steele—the conservative Democrat who had opposed emancipation efforts in Arkansas—drove fourteen thousand Union soldiers (including the First Kansas Colored Infantry) down from northern Arkansas. Once united at Shreveport, Banks would take part of his command to aid in an assault on Mobile, Alabama, while Steele would clean up remaining Confederate units in the Red River Valley and reestablish federal authority in Louisiana and Texas.[76] In this ambitious campaign, the First Kansas Colored Infantry would be a supporting regiment in a supporting army.

Steele's army consisted of two parts—his direct command of nine thousand men in Little Rock, and five thousand soldiers of the Frontier Brigade under Brigadier General John M. Thayer around Fort Smith. He planned to unite the two divisions near Arkadelphia, Arkansas, for the push to reinforce Banks. Steele's command left Little Rock on March 23, 1864.[77] Meanwhile, Thayer struggled to draw his division together. First, his men—including the First Kansas Colored—were spread out in communities around Fort Smith. Second, provisions were scarce. Though instructed by Steele to live off supplies foraged during the march, Thayer found that "the resources of the country [are] exhausted by the rebel troops." Nonetheless, he was determined to meet his military obligations and push his men through on time.[78]

The First Kansas Colored Infantry began their trek to Arkadelphia on March 25.[79] By March 27, they had united with the Eighteenth Iowa Infantry, the Twelfth Kansas Infantry, and the Second Kansas Colored Infantry. Private Henry Strong of the Twelfth Kansas noted the massing of these Union soldiers in his journal, writing, "Quite an army. The Rebels had better make themselves scarce in these parts." In fact, military-age Arkansas men did lie low as the thousands of Union soldiers pushed toward Camden. "A great many people live among these uninviting hills," Strong continued. "They are mostly women and children. Tis seldom we see an able bodied man in these. Some of them are pleased to see the Feds or appear to be so, and I don't doubt some of their sincerity, while others are afraid of us." As to Southern perceptions of Thayer's Frontier Division, Strong wrote: "Wonder what they think of the darky soldiers."[80] Unsurprisingly, the sight of black Union troops elicited rage. "Only one thing stirred my Southern blood to heat," an Arkansas woman later confessed, "was when a negro regiment passed my home going to fight our own dear men."[81] Southern men would soon express their feelings about black soldiers in much harsher ways, in what would become one of the most tragic events in the Civil War west of the Mississippi River.

CHAPTER 12

POISON SPRING

Our men is determined not to take negro prisoners.

The Frontier Division found the advance from Fort Smith to Arkadelphia in late March 1864 a difficult journey. Division commander Brigadier General John M. Thayer chose a circuitous route to meet Major General Frederick Steele to increase the chances of foraging food. To make up time, Thayer ordered the division to discard nonessential gear and equipment and rush to their destination. Private Henry A. Strong of the Twelfth Kansas Infantry, serving alongside the First Kansas Colored, recorded the command in his diary: "All of the troops ordered to destroy part of the tents and blankets and clothing. Only one blanket and one extra shirt. The rest all to be burned."[1]

Poor weather made the march more miserable. Heavy rain plagued both Union columns and turned the roads into a quagmire of red clay, "which clung to the wheels with great tenacity," an engineer in Steele's army reported.[2] Union soldiers were compelled to improve the roads by laying boards or logs across the path, known as corduroying. Rail fences were the material of choice. "We make the Rebel rails suffer," Private Strong noted.[3] Thayer and Steele did not make contact until April 5—four days after the scheduled assembly—and did not fully unite until April 9.[4]

Confederate forces raced to engage the twelve thousand Union soldiers pushing south through Arkansas. Major General Sterling Price had seven thousand men at his disposal, most of them cavalrymen. Horse soldiers enjoyed greater mobility and speed, but generally could not match infantry in extended battles. The Southern commander planned to use terrain, stealth, and surprise to challenge Steele's army.[5]

Price's first attempt to frustrate the Union advance took place at Prairie D'Ane. He tried to draw the federals into a trap near Washington, Arkansas. His men occupied roughly constructed earthworks, intending to punish Steele's attacking soldiers before conducting a strategic withdrawal to entice the federal force into pursuit. On April 10, Union soldiers assaulted the Confederate line and overran the position, with few casualties. Steele had no intention of chasing Price. He planned to regroup his forces at Camden to the east. Because the move would expose his army to attack from the rear, Steele maintained an aggressive posture in front of the Confederate force to prepare for a dash to Camden.[6]

On April 11 Steele engaged the Confederate line, with similar, inconsequential results. Each side watched the other: Price tried to entice the federals into a careless pursuit west, while Steele tried to create space for a dash east to Camden. A last federal push the following day found Price's command farther away from Prairie D'Ane, toward Washington, Arkansas, giving Steele space for his race to Camden. With Union cavalry harassing Confederate pickets to mask the withdrawal, the Union army started eastward on April 13.

Price waited that morning for the expected federal attack. After a few hours he learned of Steele's redirection. He ordered an all-out pursuit, designating one division to block the federal advance while he personally attacked the rear. Guarding the Union column's rear stood Thayer's division—including the First Kansas Colored Infantry. Confederate cavalrymen quickly caught up to the Union foot soldiers and launched an aggressive strike. The attack at first broke through a weak point in the federal line, but a stubborn defense by the Eighteenth Iowa Infantry, the First Arkansas Infantry (Union), and the First and Second Kansas Colored regiments reversed the initial Confederate success and secured Steele's rear. Union casualties were light, and the First Kansas Colored did not lose a man.[7]

Price's sporadic cavalry attacks did little but harass Union soldiers who secured Camden on April 16. There Steele's army hoped to rest and regroup for the final push to Shreveport. Unfortunately, a new danger threatened to derail the campaign. Steele's quartermaster, Captain Charles A. Henry, reported that "the difficulty of procuring forage occasioned great uneasiness, as we were without any base of supplies and with an active enemy in front." Henry's reference to "great uneasiness" was an understatement. Besides twelve thousand soldiers, Union supply officers had twelve thousand animals to feed, including cavalry mounts and beasts of burden to pull the eight hundred wagons that supplied Steele's army.

The Arkansas countryside had ample corn, but Confederate cavalry units preferred to burn it rather than see it fall into Union hands.
The situation became desperate. "The chief commissary of the army
had made requisitions on me for corn for the men of the command,
as our supplies of breadstuffs were entirely exhausted," Henry later
explained. The army would soon be starving. To keep Steele's force
moving, the supply officers concluded that it "was best to try and
procure sufficient corn to furnish half allowance of forage and one-
fourth rations of meal to the man." The quartermaster planned to
send a foraging party out the following day. One regiment of cavalry
and one of infantry would escort 170 wagons sixteen miles back up
the Washington Road to a point, Henry reported, "where I knew of
there being some 5,000 bushels of corn."[8] Traveling up the Washington Road meant retracing the route Steele's army had used to escape
Price's Confederates only the day before. Despite this risk, Thayer
not only agreed to the expedition but also reduced the size of the
military escort. A full infantry regiment would take part, but accompanied by only two hundred mounted soldiers. Two cannons were
thrown in, to provide at least the semblance of artillery support.[9]

Colonel James Williams was resting on his bunk when General
Thayer and his adjutant Captain Luther Thrasher, a former officer in
the First Kansas Colored Infantry, stepped into his quarters. Thayer
told Williams of the foraging expedition scheduled to leave shortly
after five o'clock the next morning. He had chosen the First Kansas
Colored Infantry as the centerpiece of the military escort. Williams
would command the whole operation.[10]

At 5 A.M. on Sunday morning, April 17, the column organized
in front of General Thayer's headquarters. With wagons, animals,
and soldiers in place, Williams gave the order to move forward.
The foraging party consisted of five hundred soldiers of the First
Kansas Colored Infantry, nearly two hundred troopers from three
different Kansas cavalry regiments, and two artillery crews of the
Second Indiana Battery. The number of wagons had been increased
to 198 to obtain as much corn and other supplies as possible from
the Arkansas countryside.[11]

Williams had reservations about the assignment. After the war
he wrote that "as I left Camden that morning with this large train
to go out and forage upon this road, over which Steele's army had
just marched into Camden, skirmishing with the enemy continu-
ally, when it was necessary to use a whole division as a rear guard,

it was with serious misgivings as to the result." Nonetheless, he was determined to fill the wagons before returning to the relative safety of Camden. He moved his column "as rapidly as possible, keeping mounted pickets and scouts moving in the advance and on both flanks with instruction to make prompt report of any visible movement of the enemy."[12]

The long column traveled west along the Washington Road for eighteen miles before the scouts found a suitable location along White Oak Creek to base the foraging operation. Williams ordered the wagons to venture out in various directions for supplies. The largest foraging party included a part of the First Kansas Colored and one hundred wagons. Union scouts reported to Williams that Confederate patrols had been observing the column's movements. Williams "directed the wagons, as well as the officers in charge of the different details, to work all night without unhitching if necessary, to load the train." He kept a force of 250 men in reserve at camp to respond to any attack on the scavenging parties.[13] Confederate scouts, in fact, had watched the wagon train from a distance and understood its mission. Instead of directly assaulting the Union soldiers, the Confederates destroyed twenty-five hundred bushels of corn. The destruction slowed the foraging work, but by midnight most of the wagons safely returned to camp loaded with corn.[14]

Major Richard Ward relayed to Williams warnings from local slaves of a large Confederate force moving to intercept the column.[15] Williams tried to assure the major of their security. After the war, Major Ward published his account of that day in a Kansas newspaper, noting that Williams had "thought there was no danger." Williams responded with a letter to the newspaper, admitting that he had, in fact, lied to Ward. Explaining his actions, he wrote that he had "obtained further evidence that the enemy were in force within striking distance, and this very inactivity on their part only more fully convinced me that we would not return without meeting them." Yet, Williams continued, "I stated that which I knew to be false, deeming it advisable to maintain a confident feeling in the command, still hoping that with the reinforcement which had reported to me in the night I could make my way back to Camden." The reinforcements he spoke of were 375 men of the Eighteenth Iowa Infantry, almost one hundred more Kansas cavalry troopers, and two more artillery pieces on their way to meet up with the column.[16]

Williams's postwar explanation rings hollow. Ward was a respected leader who had seen action at Island Mound, Cabin Creek, and Honey Springs. He was not a man to quake at the prospect of a fight. Williams's postwar account tried to alleviate the appearance of negligence. However poorly he anticipated an attack, Williams's actions in the field that morning can draw little criticism. In haste to return to Camden, he had the formation back on the road before sunrise on April 18. Rather than hold up the column to fill the remaining wagons, Williams ordered his men to scavenge for corn and feed during the return march. Unfortunately, limited forage slowed the procession. "There being but few wagon loads of corn to be found at any one place," Williams reported, "I was obliged to detach portions of my command in different directions to load the wagons, until nearly my whole available force was so employed."[17]

Some of the Union troops may have scavenged more than corn. Wagons were later seen with "bacon, stolen bed-quilts, women's and children's clothing, hogs, geese, and all the *et ceteras* of unscrupulous plunder."[18] Responsibility may have rested more with the Union cavalrymen escorting the train. Williams reported that during the return to Camden, "many of the cavalry had, in violation of orders, straggled from their commands."[19] White Kansas soldiers earned greater notoriety than their black comrades for raiding in Arkansas. One Arkansas woman wrote that she most feared "the Kansas jay hawkers," who "looked mean enough for any thing, & the officers, as bad as the men!" During a raid on her property, a group of white Kansas cavalrymen had taken "mules, corn, sugar, molasses, flour, every thing in the world we had to eat . . . , they even took all my soap, candles, coffee & every hen, chicken, turkey, eggs &c on the place." One trooper carried away her wedding slippers.[20] On the other hand, for all the hatred of black Kansas soldiers, few Arkansas residents voiced accusations of wanton plunder by men of the First Kansas Colored Infantry. One resident of Camden admitted, "I did not find the negro soldiers impudent to a firm white man," and noted that black soldiers had protected a physician's property from plunder by white scavengers.[21]

Four miles into the return trip, the expected reinforcements of almost five hundred Union soldiers and two artillery pieces came into view, a welcome sight. Their appearance boosted the expedition's military contingent to 875 infantrymen, 265 cavalrymen, and four cannons with their accompanying crews. But, Williams explained, "the excessive fatigue of the preceding day, coming as it did at the close of a toilsome march of twenty-four days without halting, had so worn upon the infantry that fully 100 of the First Kansas (colored) were rendered unfit for duty."[22] The reinforcements arrived at a fortuitous moment, because a large Confederate force sat in waiting a mile ahead.

The Confederates—a conglomeration of Missouri, Arkansas, Texas, and Indian soldiers—gathered on the Washington Road to block the column near Poison Spring. Their commander, Brigadier General John S. Marmaduke, a West Point graduate, brought to the field a military professionalism that had been absent from previous commanders the First Kansas Colored Infantry had faced. Marmaduke's men had watched the foraging column the previous day. Their reports exaggerated the size of the military escort, leading the general to believe that the wagon train was "guarded by one regiment of cavalry, two regiments of negro infantry, and two pieces of artillery." Marmaduke's force comprised only five hundred Missouri cavalrymen and four cannons—only a harassing force against a Union military column that size. He sent an urgent request to Brigadier General James F. Fagan for reinforcements. Fagan responded by sending two brigades of Arkansas cavalry, totaling fifteen hundred men, under the command of Brigadier General William L. Cabell. Fagan tacked on Captain W. M. Hughey's four-gun Arkansas Battery for artillery support.[23]

Reinforcements reached Marmaduke on the evening of April 17. He intended to throw this combined group against the Union column near White Oak Creek, until scouts brought him new information. "After proceeding some 2 miles I learned that the guard had been re-enforced by one regiment of cavalry, a battalion of white infantry, and two pieces of artillery," Marmaduke later wrote. "Deeming my force too small to succeed," the general halted the Missouri and Arkansas troopers and ordered them back to camp.[24] Determined to overwhelm the Union expedition, Marmaduke called on Major General Sterling Price for help. On the morning of April 18, Price ordered Brigadier General Samuel B. Maxey's cavalry division to join Marmaduke. Maxey's division included the Twenty-Ninth Texas Cavalry and the First and Second Choctaw Regiments—soldiers that had been defeated by the First Kansas Colored and the rest of General James G. Blunt's Union force at Honey Springs nine months earlier.[25]

As the Eighteenth Iowa Infantry and the cavalry reinforcements met Williams, Union cavalry scouts in advance of the column traded shots with Confederate pickets. They easily pushed the Southerners back a mile before cresting a small hill near Poison Spring. The initial contact did not alarm the Union officers, who were aware of Confederate scouts in the area. Minutes later, around 10 A.M., the Kansas cavalrymen found a line of Confederates advancing against them. Marmaduke was throwing his Arkansas troops into battle to capture the hill.[26]

Though all of Marmaduke's regiments were cavalry units, he had the men dismount and fight in a heavy skirmish line, an arrangement more open than the regular shoulder-to-shoulder formation, but solid enough to carry out basic military maneuvers. Furthermore, many of the Southern soldiers carried rifle muskets, which had greater range and power than traditional cavalry carbines or shotguns. The Union cavalry fell back, and the Confederates rushed forward on foot to form a new battle line.[27]

Maxey's division of Texans and Indians arrived on the field in time to see General Cabell and his Arkansans move into position on the hill. Maxey outranked Marmaduke and had authority to take command of the combined Confederate force. Yet when Marmaduke briefed him and asked for orders, Maxey wisely deferred command, reasoning that "as [Marmaduke] had put on foot the expedition and knew the position of affairs," he should carry out the plan of action. Marmaduke suggested that Maxey's division swing to the Confederate left and hit the Union train from the south. He would then rake the Union line with artillery fire and push his Missouri and Arkansas troops forward from the east. The Confederate line would be a large "L" converging on the front and right side of the Union column.[28]

When Williams learned of the Confederate line advancing in his front, his force was not prepared for battle. Part of the First Kansas Colored Infantry was at the front of the wagon train, while a significant portion under the command of Major Ward remained in the rear guarding the end of the column. He halted the train and ordered the Eighteenth Iowa Infantry to relieve Ward and the rear guard to bring the entire First Kansas Colored together at the front. The two cannons of the Second Indiana Battery were put into firing position, one on each side of the road. At Williams's command, the two six-pound James cannons sent a few shells toward the Confederate line.

Williams later explained that he intended this initial artillery fire "for the double purpose of ascertaining, if possible, if the enemy had any artillery in position in front, and also to draw in some foraging parties which had previously been dispatched upon either flank of the train."[29]

As the Indiana guns fired, Ward and the remaining First Kansas Colored companies reached the front of the column, having run on the double-quick nearly three-quarters of a mile. "On arriving at the head of the train," Ward explained, "we found that it was being parked as closely as the nature of the ground would admit, but still occupying nearly three-quarters of a mile of the road."[30] Williams positioned the regiment to the front, facing down the road toward Camden. The artillery fire indeed alerted some of the foraging cavalry units, who hastily returned to the train. Williams ordered them to secure the infantry flanks. A detachment of the Fourteenth Kansas Cavalry covered the left, while portions of the Second and Sixth Kansas Cavalry regiments formed on the right. Captain William M. Duncan, commanding the Eighteenth Iowa Infantry, drew his men into line on the road at the rear of the train and waited with orders from Williams to "keep a sharp lookout for a movement upon his rear and right flank."[31]

Marmaduke's men kept their cool under the probing shots of the Indiana cannons. Skirmishers peppered the Union line with carbine fire but did not press an attack. According to Marmaduke's plan, the Missourians and Arkansans would not advance until Maxey's Texans and Indians attacked the Union right flank. The heavy timber and brush along the southern part of the road helped hide this flanking movement but hindered Maxey's progress. He noted later that "the division was delayed half an hour longer from engagement than I anticipated, owing to the nature of the ground."[32] A Texan complained that as the units marched in line of battle through the timber toward the Union line, "we were somewhat retarded by the dense thickets, and undergrowth on our route, and frequent halts had to be made to reform our necessarily broken line."[33] Pushing through the brush proved even more difficult for a Texas artillery battery under the command of Captain W. Butler Krumbhaar. Having no axes, the artillerymen could move cannons only by bending and breaking trees and saplings in their way.[34]

While the thick brush obscured the size of the Confederate force moving to the south, Union officers caught glimpses of Southern soldiers through clearings. "Seeing this," Williams later explained, "I ordered forward the cavalry on my right, under Lieutenants [Barnett B.] Mitchell and [Robert] Henderson, with orders to press the enemy's line, force it if possible, and at all events to ascertain his position and strength." He feared that the "silence of the enemy in front, was but for the purpose of drawing me on into the open ground which lay in my front."[35]

Williams watched his cavalry ride off into the woods. A lone horseman rode up to his command and asked for Colonel Charles DeMorse—the colonel of the Twenty-Ninth Texas Cavalry. The Confederate messenger had become disoriented in the thick vegetation and walked into the federal line. Before he could react, Union soldiers captured him. Colonel Williams conducted a quick interrogation. "From him I learned that General Price was in command of the rebel force, and that Colonel DeMorse was in command of a force on my right." Indeed, DeMorse was leading a brigade of Texans to strike the First Kansas Colored. However, Major General Price was not present. The Confederate soldier may have lied in order to alarm his captors, for if Price was in front of them, the Union forage train could be facing an army of many thousands. Regardless, the situation grew increasingly desperate.[36]

As Williams pondered the information from the Confederate captive, gunshots rang out a few hundred yards to the south. Henderson and Mitchell, commanding portions of the Sixth and Second Kansas Cavalry Regiments respectively, had led their men into the timber south of the wagon train until coming to a clearing. They charged across the field directly into the sights of DeMorse's brigade of Texans taking cover in the brush on the other side. A surprising volley stunned the Union horsemen, knocking down a number of men, including Lieutenant Henderson, who fell with a bullet to the abdomen. The Union troopers fired their carbines and pistols for a few minutes, but beat a hasty retreat as Confederate fire increased.[37]

As the cavalry skirmished with the Confederate line, Williams redeployed the First Kansas Colored. Companies A, B, E, H and one of the Second Indiana Battery's guns were moved to the right, bending the regiment to meet the threats from the south and the east. Major Ward described it as "nearly in the form of the segment of a circle, the convex side being outward toward the enemy, Companies C and I being on the north side of the road facing toward the east, companies D and F on the south side of the road facing in the same direction, whilst on my extreme right the men were drawn up in line face due south." Companies G and K were placed behind the line in reserve.[38]

Major Ward had just arranged the battle line when the troopers of the Sixth and Second Kansas Cavalry regiments came fleeing back from their exchange to the south. He ordered the remnants of the Sixth Kansas Cavalry to form up on the First Kansas Colored Infantry's immediate right flank and posted the remaining Second Kansas Cavalry soldiers on their right. This ragged cavalry line would be the only thing closing the gap between the First Kansas Colored and the Eighteenth Iowa—a distance spanning at least two hundred yards. The men dismounted and faced south into the woods they had just come running from. Ward hoped they could help hold the line, but after the war he claimed that after the initial clash in the clearing, the cavalry "was of no further use during the day."[39]

Almost immediately artillery shot and shell rained in from the east. Captain S. S. Harris's Missouri Battery and Captain W. M. Hughey's Arkansas Battery, each with four guns and stationed one thousand yards to the east, bombarded the Union soldiers and wagon train. Within minutes, Krumbhaar's Texas Battery, having been dragged through the thick Arkansas undergrowth to a location less than half a mile south of the First Kansas Colored, joined in. It was nearly noon, and the full engagement at Poison Spring had begun.[40]

Major Ward ordered his men to lie down to reduce their exposure to the barrage. The move helped conceal the regiment's location. For several minutes the Confederate guns shot blindly toward the Union line, inflicting little damage, until a jagged piece of shell struck one unfortunate black soldier in the back. He instinctively jumped up, spun around, and flailed his arms. A Confederate artillery officer adjusted his guns on the man's position. Suddenly shot and shell rained down on the helpless First Kansas Colored Infantry. Major Ward proudly watched his men withstand the torrent of exploding shells. "Although this was much the severest artillery fire that any of the men had ever before been subjected to, and many of the men were thus under fire for the first time," he told his superior after the battle, "they were as cool as veterans and patiently awaited the onset of the enemy's infantry."[41]

At 12:30, the Confederate artillery fire tapered off; DeMorse's Texans were on the attack. The officers and men of the First Kansas Colored Infantry readied their weapons. They could hear the

N

McMurtrey's BN

14th MO Cav BN

2nd AR Cav (Siemons')

Wright's Regiment

Poe's AR BN

Crawford's Regiment

Skirmishers
14th KS Cav

1st Kansas Col

Wagon Train

Skirmishers
6th KS Cav Det

18th Iowa

Skirmishers
2nd KS Cav

Gunter's BN   31st TX

1st Choctaw
2nd Choctaw
WALKER

29th TX Cav
30th TX Cav
Welch's Company
DEMORSE

3rd MO Cav
4th MO Cav
8th MO Cav
GREENE

1st ARK Cav
2nd ARK Cav (Morgan's)
4th ARK Cav
7th ARK Cav
Trader's Regiment
CABELL

Upper Washington Road

Union forces
Confederate forces
Direction of attack
Retreat
Union Artillery
Confederate Artillery

0   500   1000 feet

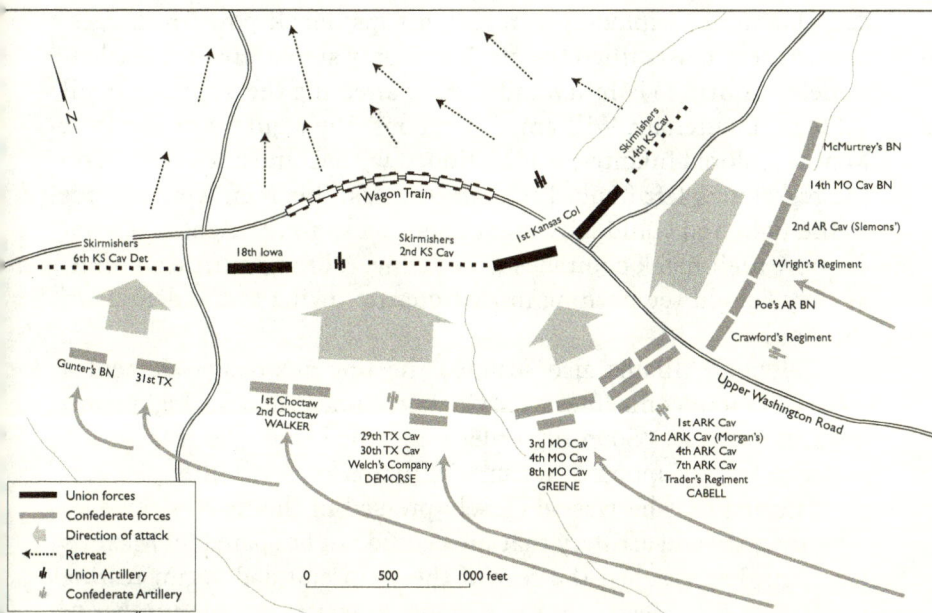

Map 5. Poison Spring. Map by Bill Nelson. Copyright © 2014 by the University of Oklahoma Press.

breaking of branches and crunching of leaves and twigs in the dis-tance as the Confederates pushed through the timber. "From the position of the ground it was useless to deliver fire until the enemy were within 100 yards," Major Ward declared. The Confederates marched slowly through the rough terrain and finally came into view. When they did, the world seemed to explode. "Raising the well known Texas yell, we dashed at them," one Texan later wrote, "and met with a warm reception."[42] Ward screamed the order to fire. A sheet of flame and smoke erupted from the right half of the black regiment, sending forth devastating "buck and ball" projec-tiles at the Confederates. Fortunately for the advancing Texans, the terrain mitigated the Kansas musket fire. The Confederates were on a slight downslope, advancing uphill toward the wagon train. This variation caused many of the black soldiers to fire high. "My field and staff officers were fortunately all dismounted," Colonel DeMorse recalled. "A horse in the rear of the line could not have escaped five minutes."[43]

The Texans pressed the attack. For fifteen minutes the two sides loaded and fired, creating a cacophony of ear-splitting cracks and deep booms as exploding percussion caps, black powder charges, and artillery blasts filled the air. Thick gray smoke covered the battlefield, limiting visibility and further affecting the accuracy of all soldiers. Lieutenant William C. Gibbons, the adjutant of the First Kansas Colored Infantry, was stationed with Companies C and I on the regiment's left flank. Facing to the east, his men were not yet in the fight and could only crane their necks to the right and wonder how their black comrades were faring. It brought little comfort, as they "could see nothing in that quarter owing to the density of the smoke."[44]

Colonel Williams also scanned the line anxiously. He sent a request for four companies from Captain Duncan and the Eighteenth Iowa in the rear. "Soon my orderly returned from the rear with a message from Captain Duncan," Williams reported after the battle, "stating that he was so closely pressed in the rear by the enemy's infantry and artillery that men could not be spared."[45] Maxey's left flank had reached the rear of the train and had begun testing the Union right. Based on the prisoner's report and the number of Confederate artillery pieces firing on his position, Williams suspected that the enemy outnumbered his command. The assault confirmed those fears. "From the force of the enemy, now for the first time made visible," he explained, "I saw that I could not hope to defeat him." But he did not abandon the train. General Steele and the Union army camp were only ten miles away. Infantry reinforcements could be on the scene in two hours—maybe sooner—and cavalry reinforcements could come more quickly. The din of the artillery surely could be heard by Steele and his men, Williams believed. The sound of the guns would be their message for help. With this in mind, Williams "resolved to defend the train to the last, hoping that re-enforcements would come from Camden."[46]

"Heard heavy cannonading this morning out on the Washington road," Private Henry A. Strong of the Twelfth Kansas Infantry wrote in his diary, "the very one Col. Williams['s] foraging command went out."[47] General Thayer ordered his cavalry to mount up and be ready to move out as soon as General Steele approved. But Steele did nothing. Some twelve thousand Union soldiers sat in Camden, listening to the distant battle.[48]

Meanwhile, the initial assault on the First Kansas Colored Infantry began to crumble. "My men went in with spirit, shouting and fighting undauntedly," Colonel DeMorse said of his Texans;

"but in a little while it became evident that we were outnumbered and that the fire upon us was heavier than we could bear."[49] In fact, the Texans were not outnumbered. DeMorse's Texas brigade alone included the Twenty-Ninth, Thirtieth, and Thirty-First Texas Cavalry regiments, and Captain William Welch's Independent Cavalry Company. Though the Texas units were all undersized at the battle, their combined force amounted to over six hundred men.[50] Even with every fourth man acting as a horse-holder so that the other cavalrymen could fight dismounted, DeMorse had 450 soldiers in the fight. That matched the number of men in the First Kansas Colored ranks that day, but at least one-third of the black soldiers were posted on the left facing east or were standing in reserve.[51] The calm demeanor and disciplined fire of First Kansas Colored companies facing south overwhelmed the Texans and sent them reeling.

Before retreating the Texas soldiers thinned the black regiment's ranks. Among the fallen was Second Lieutenant John Topping of Company B, killed during the brief but spirited exchange.[52] DeMorse's men also leveled a destructive fusillade on the Second Indiana Battery gun, stationed behind the black soldiers on the right. Half of its gunners went down. The initial Confederate assault proved too heavy for the thin line of Kansas cavalry skirmishers standing between the First Kansas Colored and the Eighteenth Iowa. Black soldiers on the regiment's right looked to the west to see a vast expanse, their flank unsupported.[53]

Colonel DeMorse watched as the left half of his brigade broke for the woods. He rushed to the men and called for them to rally. As he did, Captain Krumbhaar's Texas battery, posted only three hundred yards from the Union line, went into action. Krumbhaar had standing orders from DeMorse to "fire whenever he could see anything to fire at." With the Texas brigade fleeing, Krumbhaar had an open view of the Union line. He ordered his men to fire. DeMorse watched as his artillery commander calculated the range and "dropped his shells most effectively in the very midst of the enemy and near their artillery." The Missouri and Arkansas batteries on the Confederate right joined in, and DeMorse's retreating Texans stopped and turned to see the devastation. "The effect was immediately discernible," DeMorse proclaimed. "Our men above gave a loud shout." Rejuvenated, the Texans rallied to attack again.[54]

During the first clash between the First Kansas Colored and DeMorse's Texas brigade, Captain Duncan and his Eighteenth

Iowa traded shots with Colonel Tandy Walker's two regiments of Confederate Choctaws on the extreme Union right. The fighting there was, for the time being, comparatively light. Walker had delayed his attack against the Eighteenth Iowa because of reports that Union cavalrymen were on his left. They were members of the Sixth Kansas Cavalry, posted as skirmishers. The cavalrymen guarded the Union extreme right flank but posed no serious threat to the advancing Confederate force. The sound of his Texas comrades firing far to the right had snapped Walker into action and he pushed his men forth. Yet the Confederate Indian soldiers approached the Iowans cautiously. The two sides exchanged shots, but neither gained a clear advantage for the time being.[55]

Back near the Union center, undergoing the fierce bombardment, Major Ward spied the Texans regrouping for another assault. He notified Williams and asked for more troops to strengthen the line. Williams sent forward Companies G and K from their reserve position. Ward ordered Company K to form on the extreme right, where the cavalrymen had been. He moved Company G directly into the line to help plug a gap. This new, bolstered line of black soldiers had just fallen into formation when DeMorse's Texans struck again, "this time in two columns, yelling like fiends," Ward remembered.[56]

As the second Confederate assault launched, Williams arrived on the scene. He noted that the Texans advanced "with colors flying and continuous cheering, so loud as to drown even the roar of the musketry." The men of Companies G and K, now thrown into the line, unleashed a volley. The blast stunned Private George Washington of Company K too. He felt an explosion of white-hot sparks pepper his face. "I had a double load in my gun," he later learned. "Another comrade had loaded my gun and I did not know it, so when I started into battle I put another load in." For muzzle-loading weapons, the mistake was all too common. Fortunately for Washington, the double-charged musket did not rupture. Instead, he explained, "When I fired the gun the powder blew out of the cap tube into my eyes." In pain, he "stayed right in ranks and fought on," helping hold the line against the advancing Texans.[57]

Krumbhaar's battery continued to fire into the First Kansas Colored by elevating its guns to clear the heads of the Texans. The men of the Twenty-Ninth Texas recognized the black soldiers as their old nemeses from Honey Springs. Flushed with rage over the previous loss to the First Kansas Colored, the Texas soldiers cried out as they pushed forward, "You First Kansas Niggers now buck to the Twenty-ninth Texas!"[58] The musketry increased, and Williams watched a Confederate flag fall to the ground twice under the intense fire from his black soldiers; but it was raised immediately both times.

The intensity of the fight surpassed anything the black Kansas soldiers had experienced before. Men on both sides fell, some killed instantly; others writhed in pain as heavy lead slugs tore muscle and crushed bone. First Lieutenant Charles Coleman, standing among his men in Company H, fell during an assault that Williams declared "was the loudest and most terrific it has ever been my lot to listen."[59]

Lieutenant Haines of the Second Indiana Battery rode up to Williams, and the two officers called on Ward for a situation report. Ward pointed to the single Indiana cannon behind them and shouted that only two of the crew members were still in action. Realizing that the undermanned gun was a liability, Williams ordered the Indiana artillerymen to pull back to the rear of the wagon train. They had just begun to limber the piece when a large body of Texans charged in their direction, intending to capture the cannon at its most vulnerable moment. Unperturbed, one of the remaining Indiana gunners, Private Alonzo Hinshaw, grabbed two loads of canister, rammed them down the barrel, and primed the cannon. He aimed the gun at the advancing Texans, yanked the lanyard, and "poured into the advancing column a parting salute at the distance of about 300 yards." Hinshaw's actions stunned the Confederate column and electrified the First Kansas Colored. "The effect was terrific," Ward wrote in his report after the battle, identifying Private Hinshaw by name to give him credit for such a brave feat. The blast of double canister at close range crushed the momentum of the second Confederate assault fifteen minutes after it had begun. The First Kansas Colored continued to pour a destructive stream of "buck and ball" as the Texans retreated.[60]

The black soldiers had held the line again, but at a frightful cost. Williams scanned the regiment to see that "fully one-half of my infantry engaged were either killed or wounded." A number of officers were out of action. Despite the decimation, Williams observed, the "line of battle was as perfect as when first formed, the live men standing between the bodies of their gallant comrades." As he passed, soldiers held muskets tightly—bayonets fixed—and shouted,

"Colonel, let us charge 'em!" Williams wrote more than twenty years later that their acts of valor "should be placed on record as indicative of the soldierly qualities of those brave men who so manfully held their line that day. It will never be forgotten by me." The men did not charge. Their enthusiasm notwithstanding, those still standing were in no position to attack. Many of them dug through the cartridge boxes of the dead and wounded for ammunition.[61] Ammunition problems also plagued the Union artillery. Williams learned that the Second Indiana Battery's other cannon, stationed on the left, had fired all of its ammunition but solid shot. He ordered Lieutenant Haines to take the entire battery to the rear of the train.[62]

General Maxey, frustrated by the stubborn Union defense, ordered one of Marmaduke's brigades to join the next attack on the federal line. This brigade of Missourians led by Colonel Colton Greene had been held in reserve and were anxious to join the fray. They aimed for the center of the First Kansas Colored Infantry, where the line bowed. Williams saw the larger Confederate force preparing for a third attack, knowing his men could take little more. He ordered Major Ward to hold the line long enough for him to personally arrange for the Eighteenth Iowa to support a tactical withdrawal. A bullet struck his horse just as Williams turned to ride down the line. Major Ward offered the colonel his own horse. Williams mounted the animal and resumed his ride to the Eighteenth Iowa.[63]

DeMorse's Texans then advanced. Major Ward and the black soldiers on the right end of the line leveled their muskets at the Confederates. Unlike the previous two assaults, the third attack was a coordinated effort along the whole Southern line. Greene proudly watched as his Missourians "advanced at the double-quick with loud cheers, passed the line, delivered several well-directed volleys, and charged the enemy through burning woods and a dense smoke."[64] The black companies near the bend in the Union line took the brunt of the Missourians' fire. They held for the time being. The Eighteenth Iowa, on the extreme Union right, faced an attack by Confederate Choctaws. General Maxey observed the long assault and noted that "one continued shout was heard, and an unfaltering advance of all that part of the line."[65]

On the Union's left flank, Captain John Graton, Lieutenant Gibbons, and Companies C and I had been lightly engaged, taking some artillery fire, but they had seen little of the enemy. Suddenly around one hundred blue-clad soldiers, some on foot, some mounted, moved across their front. Gibbons conferred with Graton, and the two men agreed that the soldiers were likely Union cavalry skirmishers falling back. However, Gibbons was "soon undeceived by the appearance of a large body of infantry dressed in gray, following directly after, and the appearance of 400 or 500 rebel cavalry crossing the road farther off on the right of their infantry." It was Cabell's Arkansas troops, ordered forward by Maxey to crush the Union left. Gibbons hurriedly readied his men and ordered them to fire. The musket balls stalled the Arkansas soldiers, but could not hold them back long. Gibbons saw a large group of Confederate cavalry swing to his left. His men would soon be flanked. He ordered them to fall back about sixty yards and reform their battle line. "Again our men poured a deadly volley among the enemy," Gibbons explained, "but it was impossible to hold the ground."[66]

When he saw portions of the line crumble, Gibbons called out for his men to fall back as orderly as possible. As they did, Gibbons made an unintentional, and ungraceful, exit. Grabbing the pommel of his saddle, he attempted to mount but tripped over his sword, losing his balance. His horse took off, dragging him along the ground. He managed to free himself after a short distance and regain his mount, but not before all of his men had run past him. He turned to see "the enemy were bearing down on us with a yell." After the battle, he explained, "I need not say I mounted quick and rode away quicker."[67]

The remnants of Companies C and I formed up near the train, but their retreat exposed the rest of the regiment to Cabell's men. Seeing the threat, Ward ordered the rest of the regiment to fall back slowly. He positioned the exposed companies on the left to cover their vulnerable side. Under intense fire, the black soldiers executed the move brilliantly. "We here made a stand of about ten minutes," Ward reported after the battle, "when I perceived that the enemy had succeeded in flanking my extreme right, and that I was placed in a position to receive a cross-fire from their two lines." Company G took the brunt of the crossfire during these tense few minutes.[68]

Though ordered to hold the line until Williams returned, Ward realized the regiment faced utter destruction. Even the highly disciplined men of the First Kansas Colored Infantry could not stop a combined attack of three Confederate brigades. He ordered a retreat, wishing, he later reported, "to save even a fragment of the gallant regiment which for nearly two hours had, unaided, sustained itself against Price's whole army."[69] Union soldiers did not face Price's entire army that day, but Ward's exaggeration may not have been intentional. His black soldiers were outnumbered as much as five to one during the latter part of the battle. When Ward ordered the retreat, the black soldiers fell back along the wagon train. Some ran for their lives, but most continued to load and fire as they withdrew. Lieutenant Gibbons saw the rest of the regiment break for the rear and realized that flanking Confederate cavalry threatened his own retreat. Dispensing with formalities, he ordered the survivors of Companies I and G to scatter and head for the Eighteenth Iowa. There, he hoped, they could regroup for a better defense.[70]

The Confederates kept up the pressure, cutting the Kansas soldiers down as they moved past the wagons. It was a gratifying victory for the Southern soldiers. The hatred many Confederates held for these black troops was manifested by their acts of vengeance as they passed over the battlefield. "If the negro was wounded," one Confederate soldier declared, "our men would shoot him dead as they were passed."[71] Some of the wounded Kansans continued to resist, including one prostrate black soldier who gnashed his teeth into the calf of a standing Southerner. He held on until a gun butt smashed open his skull. Some of the uninjured saw the fate of wounded comrades and dropped their muskets and gear to help carry their friends from the field. Many others held on to their weapons while aiding their comrades, determined to save both equipment and men from Confederate hands.[72]

When the surviving black Kansas soldiers made it to the rear of the train, Williams and Ward formed a battle line behind the Eighteenth Iowa. The Confederates pressed the attack, and Williams pushed his men forward to aid the Iowans. The black and white Union soldiers stood together to unleash a volume of fire, but it was not enough to stop the converging Confederate brigades. "The Eighteenth Iowa maintained their line manfully, and stoutly contested the ground until nearly surrounded," Williams declared, "when they retired, and, forming again, checked the advancing foe, and still held their ground until again nearly surrounded."[73] By this time the wagon train was lost. The Union men had no hope of regaining their forage and supplies. Yet they made repeated stands during the retreat to protect their own lines from disintegrating and to save their four cannons. The Second Indiana Battery's Lieutenant Haines desperately tried to lead his two horse-drawn guns from the field.

But the heavy brush hindered the escape. The Sixth Kansas Cavalry's artillery crews faced a similar problem.[74]

As they pursued the Union soldiers, Confederates passed through the abandoned wagons. Some officers worried that the men would break ranks to scour the captured supply train for food. Tandy Walker, commander of the Choctaw regiments, admitted that he "feared here that the train and its contents would prove a temptation too strong for these hungry, half-clothed Choctaws." But he claimed he "had no trouble in pressing them forward, for there was that in front and to the left more inviting to them than food or clothing—the blood of their despised enemy."[75]

The fighting retreat continued onto a plantation. The Union soldiers formed a temporary battle line near slave cabins. Greene's Missourians shouted, "Here's your mule!" and cheered their home state as they slammed into the Union position.[76] The federals fell back again, only to form another battle line. This process continued until the Union men withdrew to a large ravine. The artillery crews reined in their exhausted horses to overcome this nearly impassable barrier.

As Confederate cavalry closed upon them, Williams ordered Haines to spike the guns—a command to render the cannons inoperable, often done by obstructing the primer hole or muzzle—before the enemy captured them. It was heart-wrenching act for an artilleryman. The loss of even one cannon was seen as dishonorable. Facing a hopeless situation, Haines obeyed the order and commanded his men to cut the horses loose and disable the guns. In a final expression of grief, the young officer jumped atop one of the gun tubes and swore never to leave his cannon. With little time to spare, Williams shouted that the cannons were a lost cause and that the officer's new priority was to save his men to fight another day. His point was clear: battlefield honors and etiquette were no longer in play—this was a matter of survival. Haines wisely heeded the colonel's advice, jumped down from the cannon, and set about helping his artillerymen escape.[77]

Minutes later, Private Dickson Wallace of the First Choctaw Regiment ran up to one of the abandoned Union guns, jumped atop its metal tube, and "gave a whoop," his commander Walker observed. This was followed "by such a succession of whoops from his comrades as made the woods reverberate for miles around."[78] The Union survivors crossed the ravine under the echoes of the exultant Confederates. Williams formed his remaining cavalry to

cover the infantry as it escaped into a swamp. General Maxey, taking command from Marmaduke, happily watched his men crush the
Union resistance. "Not a false step had been made," he reported;
"not a position attacked but was taken."[79]

By the time the federals reached the swamp, the pursuit had
spanned two miles. The retreat turned into a flight for life—every man
for himself. Exhausted, Private William Gordon of Company E, First
Kansas Colored Infantry, sought relief and concealment. "I remember during our retreat while over heated I jumped into a lake and hid
along the shore," he recalled, "lots of our men did the same thing."[80]

With Union resistance shattered, Maxey called off his men and
ordered them back to the train. The Confederate troops may have
continued their attack and killed and captured more Union soldiers,
but their commander had a larger concern. It had taken nearly four
hours from first contact to capture the wagon train. If Steele had
sent Union reinforcements from Camden, they could arrive at any
time and reclaim the wagons. Thus Maxey decided to organize his
force and secure the spoils.[81] The Confederates found the wagon train
in almost perfect condition. Thirty of the wagons were too badly
damaged to move or were missing their teams. But Maxey proudly
reported that "about 170, with teams and everything complete, were
saved." The Confederates also carted off the four Union cannons.[82]

In complete control of the battlefield, with dozens of wounded
and dying federal soldiers around them, Confederate forces then
partook in one of the Civil War's most notable atrocities. A group
of Texans roamed the field, shooting and bayonetting wounded
black men, while chanting a vengeful banter. "Where is the First
Nigger now?" some cried out. Their comrades answered, "All cut to
pieces and gone to hell by bad management."[83] Members of Cabell's
Arkansas brigade challenged each other to a morbid competition as
they led the captured wagons off the field: each driver counted the
number of "nigger heads" he could crush under his wheels.[84]

The Confederate Choctaw soldiers roamed the battlefield muti-
lating and scalping the dead and dying black men. Even some white
Confederates were taken aback by the carnage. "The havoc among
the negroes had been tremendous," a Texas lieutenant wrote that
evening; "over a small portion of the field we saw at least 40 dead
bodies lying in all conceivable attitudes, some scalped & nearly all
stripped by the bloodthirsty Choctaws."[85] An Arkansas cavalryman
echoed those thoughts: "You ought to see the Indians fight Negroes,

kill and scalp them. Let me tell you, I never expected to see as many dead Negroes again. They were so thick you could walk on them."[86] One group of Indian soldiers dug a grave for a (presumably white) Union soldier, but used the bodies of two black soldiers for a macabre adornment. "For a headstone they put up a stiff negro buried to the waist," recorded the pro-Confederate *Washington Telegraph*. "For a footstone another negro reversed out from the waist to the heels." The newspaper headlined the account as "CHOCTAW HUMOR."[87] Eventually some officers halted the barbaric frenzy. Colonel Sim Folsom used the flat of his sword to push his men back into line, Choctaw veterans recalled, "thus saving many nappy heads from being scalped." After his death thirty-six years later, his obituary in the *Confederate Veteran* declared, "His faithful followers regretfully say that this was the only time that 'Col. Sim' ever 'went wrong.'"[88]

The execution of black soldiers at Poison Spring was not an impulsive outburst of vengeance. As historian Gregory Urwin writes, the killings were "part of an ongoing program of racial intimidation that took its cues from the basic values of antebellum Southern society."[89] Since receiving word of Abraham Lincoln's Emancipation Proclamation and the use of black soldiers in Union armies, Arkansas secessionists had advocated a fierce response. John Eakin of the *Washington Telegraph* told Confederate readers, "It follows irresistibly that we *cannot* treat negroes taken in arms as prisoners of war, without a destruction of the social system for which we contend. We *must* claim the full control of all negroes who may fall into our hands, to punish with death, or any other penalty, or remand to their owners. If the enemy retaliate, we must do likewise; and if the *black flag* follows, the blood be upon their heads."[90] Confederate soldiers at Poison Spring shared the sentiment. "I have seen enough myself to know it is correct our men is determined not to take negro prisoners, and if all the negroes could have seen what occurred that day, they would stay at home," one Confederate wrote home. Some in the First Kansas Colored Infantry ranks were runaways from local slave owners, and this soldier recognized a few among the dead. "Among the killed was Dr. Rowland's Clabe and Kyle's Berry and old man Edwards' boy was captured. I have told how they were disposed of." In his letter, the unknown Confederate touched on a key reason for the violent retribution against black soldiers—to deter slaves and other African Americans from taking up arms. "What I have seen reminds me of the talk I gave Henry and

John," he mused. "They may have been there as I have had no information as yet from home. If so, they are convinced by this time."[91]

Though Maxey feared that Union reinforcements approached
from Camden, General Steele did not send aid to Williams. His inaction puzzled Union officers in Arkansas and brought an avalanche of
criticism. The *Fort Smith New Era* reported that "firing was heard
at Camden but Gen. Steele would not reinforce Col. W[illiams]
although he had 12,000 men at his command. After the fight an officer rode to Gen. Steele's headquarters and said, 'Great God! Why
didn't you send us reinforcements?'"[92] Another writer for that paper
declared that "Thayer had his cavalry saddled and ready to go but
Steele did not or would not order it out," and added that there "is
great blame attached to Steele, and I feel almost certain he is not
the right man."[93] Criticism of Steele spread as far as the *New York
Times.* "Great complaint is made by the Kansas officers of the indifference manifested by Gen. Steele as to the fate of this command," a
correspondent wrote. "The reports of the guns were plainly heard at
Camden. Gen. Thayer, Col. Cloud, Col. Crawford and others begged
to be allowed to reinforce, but all requests were denied."[94]

The survivors of the battle straggled back toward Camden. The
more fortunate casualties had slight wounds to arms or hands—the
"walking wounded." Others suffered serious injuries but managed to
drag themselves to safety with help from comrades or through sheer
determination. Jesse Brown of Company E was shot in the back just
left of his spinal column. The ball pierced his left lung and remained
lodged in his chest. He managed to reach Camden, and afterward
surgeons removed the ball through an incision by his left nipple, the
ball thus completing its passage through his body.[95] Private Frank
Grayson of Company I sustained a severe wound to the hip during
the battle and was left behind during the retreat. Confederate soldiers
captured the suffering Grayson, "but thinking him so badly wounded
[they] did not guard him." He later escaped "by dragging myself
away" nearly three miles before white soldiers from the Eighteenth
Iowa Infantry found him and carried him to safety.[96]

Company E's Private Amos Adair was among at least nine black
survivors with two gunshot wounds. He suffered wounds to his knee
and to his midsection near the right kidney.[97] Not all of the wounds
came from bullets or cannon shot. Samuel Jefferson of Company K
nursed a battered right leg, struck by a tree limb, presumably felled
by the intense Confederate musket and artillery fire.[98]

Williams and a small group of men struggled to escape through the marshy Arkansas backwoods throughout the afternoon. After eight exhausting miles, they believed they were out of immediate danger from the victorious Confederate army. Still, roaming Confederate patrols could easily sweep them up if they dared to venture onto an open road. They had to stay out of sight on their way back to Camden and Union lines. Finding Camden presented another problem. Williams spied a clearing and cautiously rode his horse to the edge of the brush, while the rest of his party remained hidden. He found a cotton field being tended by about thirty slaves, with no white overseer in sight. Williams called out to them. Startled, the men and women in the field looked about "in utter astonishment." An elderly slave who, Williams remembered, "seemed to 'take in the situation'" directed his fellow laborers to continue their work and keep their heads down, not wanting to attract attention from any overseer. Immediately the slaves "commenced hoeing again with renewed vigor." On seeing the colonel's blue uniform, a look of shock passed across the old man's face. "Golly, massa, what you doing here?" Pointing to a road that passed the plantation house forty yards to the east, he said, "You better look a little out, dese woods is full of confeds; one whole army just go down dat road!" Williams asked for directions to Camden. The elderly slave described the route and provided an excellent briefing of recent Confederate activity in the area. The survivors safely found their way back to Camden by eleven o'clock that night. Williams kept the rest of his party hidden, and the old man never realized that his directions helped save black federal soldiers.[99]

Throughout the evening and into the next day survivors trickled into Camden. Union musicians beat a steady drum rhythm during the night to help guide soldiers in. The battle-weary men recounted the struggle and great carnage left on the field. Williams told his superiors that "many wounded men belonging to the First Kansas Colored Volunteers fell into the hands of the enemy, and I have the most positive assurances from eye-witnesses that they were murdered on the spot."[100] Word of atrocities spread among the garrison. "Report is that the Rebels killed all the darkies that fell into their hands, wounded too," Private Strong recorded in his diary. "Also the officers over the darkies."[101]

Attempts to recover the dead generated more controversy. "The Rebels refuse to let our men go out with flag of truce to bury our dead," Strong wrote the day after the battle. "Report is that the reason they will not grant it is because their loss is so much greater than ours they do not want to let it be known how many they have killed."[102] A writer to the *Fort Smith New Era* believed that Confederates refused to allow Union burial parties on the battlefield because of their antipathy toward the black soldiers. "No flag of truce went out for three days and not till the rebels sent in and told him to send out and bury his dead niggers, and to send white men, as they would allow no negroes in their lines." When federal soldiers were finally allowed to visit the battlefield under a truce, it was too late for some of the stranded casualties who had avoided the execution squads. "Wounded officers and men suffered and died for three days without attention," the *New Era* correspondent reported. Showing his frustration with the Union command, the writer admitted, "I do not know how true it is, but I more than suspect that Steele is to blame." The burial parties confirmed the earlier reports "that many had been murdered after capture."[103]

As is common with traumatic events, some unreliable—even ridiculous—rumors spread following the battle. A correspondent to the *New York Times*, praising the discipline of the black soldiers, wrote that "it is reported that early in the fight, one of the negroes, attempting to run, was instantly shot dead by Col. Williams. Our entire line broke out into a wild cheer and the fight proceeded vigorously."[104] No other source has surfaced to corroborate this fanciful account. It was likely invented to portray the First Kansas Colored as a solid fighting force. But the regiment did not need myths to prove their bravery.

In the days following the battle, as the last of the survivors found their way back to Camden, the companies reformed and the officers made an accounting of their losses. They were staggering. Company A recorded 20 men killed and wounded. Company B lost a total of 19. Casualties for the other companies were: Company C, 20; Company D, 12; Company E, 16; Company F, 15; Company G, 27; Company H, 13; Company I, 17; and Company K, 23. The total came to 182—out of an original 463. The regiment suffered 39 percent casualties. Nearly 2 out of 5 black soldiers at Poison Spring were killed, wounded, or missing.[105]

According to a major study of Civil War casualties, the overall ratio of wounded to killed in action during the war was 4.8 to 1.[106] At Shiloh, around 1,750 of 10,000 Union men hit by enemy fire were killed. Just over 3,000 of the more than 17,500 Union casualties at

Gettysburg were killed in action.[107] Based on these numbers, 15 to 18 percent of the men struck down at those two battles were killed or mortally wounded. The carnage on the fields west of Camden, Arkansas, in April 1864 far surpassed that statistic. Of the First Kansas Colored Infantry's 182 casualties at Poison Spring, at least 110 were killed or mortally wounded in the action—60 percent.[108] Rarely did a Civil War regiment suffer such an extreme number of deaths in a single engagement. According to William F. Fox's *Regimental Losses*, only eight Union organizations lost more men killed in one battle—six of them heavy artillery regiments during Grant's push to Richmond in 1864. The two infantry regiments were the Fifth New York at Second Manassas (117 killed) and Fifteenth New Jersey at Spotsylvania (116 killed). The First Kansas Colored Infantry losses at Poison Spring should rank ninth, but for unknown reasons Fox did not include the black Kansas regiment in his report of highest battle losses.[109]

Losses among the white regiments fighting alongside the First Kansas Colored cannot be ignored. The combined number of killed, wounded, or missing reported among the federal units at Poison Spring was 301.[110] At least 80 of those men belonged to the Eighteenth Iowa.[111] Most of the casualties among the white units, though, were men captured. General Maxey reported that his Confederate force took 100 prisoners off the field of battle. Only a few were First Kansas Colored men. "We turned over 62 prisoners yesterday morning to Genl Price," wrote Lieutenant William Murphy Cravens, an officer in Tandy Walker's Confederate Choctaw brigade, "among them a negro Capt and three negros." Cravens continued, "The Captain who was a white man and the three negros are said to have disappeared from among the prisoners. They have gone to join their companions lying at Poison Springs."[112] Cravens himself had captured a young black soldier during the battle. "We fought one African Regiment," he wrote his wife the next day, "and I got me a likely boy about 15 years-old." Cravens's intentions for the prisoner are unclear. His short, hastily written letter suggests that he considered enslaving the young man—either for himself or for another soldier. "I gave him to a Choctaw man to keep when the fight was over," he explained. When Cravens found the Choctaw soldier after the battle, the prisoner was gone. "He told me that boy was dead: 'White man shoot him up,'" Cravens wrote.[113]

Some officers and men of the First Kansas Colored were captured and kept alive. Captain Andrew J. Armstrong of Company D and First

Lieutenant Bethuel Hitchcock of Company G, both assumed killed in action, were captured during the battle and detained unharmed. The Confederates held at least three black enlisted men who had been wounded. None of this was known by the men in the regiment until a white officer from the Second Kansas Colored Infantry, captured at a later battle, escaped and reported the news that summer.[114]

The treatment of the few black prisoners is uncertain. However, bits of information have come to light regarding a couple of men. Major Ward recorded many years after the war that one badly wounded enlisted soldier was found by the Confederates and used as a medical test case. "His arm had been shattered by a fragment of shell," Ward wrote in 1886, "and the rebel surgeons wished to try the experiment of unjointing it at the shoulder, and he thereby escaped the fate of the rest of the wounded who fell into their hands."[115] Another enlisted man, Private Thomas Payne of Company C, was also kept alive after capture. Like the others, he was assumed dead. In fact, Confederates sent him to Marshall, Texas, where he was "held as a slave." He remained there for over a year before finally escaping in late July 1865—after the end of the war—and reporting to federal authorities in Shreveport, Louisiana. He rejoined the regiment for the last months of service. In Payne's case, at least, Confederates were serious in their threats to enslave captured black Union soldiers.[116]

Despite the ferocity of the battle, and the devastating effect of the First Kansas Colored musket fire, the Confederates lost fewer men than their opponents. Maxey believed his force suffered no more than 145 casualties, while Marmaduke estimated that total Confederate losses were barely above 80 men.[117] Colonel DeMorse, commanding the brigade of Texans that was pushed back twice by the First Kansas Colored, claimed he only lost 3 men killed and 28 wounded.[118]

Though it suffered a painful loss at Poison Spring, the First Kansas Colored Infantry proved a formidable fighting force. Virtually every Confederate officer reported the Union presence at the wagon train to be substantially larger than it was, due in large part to the stubborn defense by the black soldiers. DeMorse believed his Texas brigade was outnumbered during its first assault against only a handful of companies of the First Kansas Colored. He agreed with both Maxey and Marmaduke that the entire Union force was at least twenty-five hundred men—an estimate more than double the military escort's actual size.[119] Even two decades after the war, Marmaduke claimed that his men had faced four infantry regiments and one cavalry regiment.[120]

CHAPTER 13

THE END OF THE CAMDEN CAMPAIGN

. . . a disastrous one barely saved from being a perfect rout.

Surviving Union soldiers from the Poison Spring battle straggled into Camden over the next two days, exhausted and demoralized. Many needed medical attention. Two Union surgeons examined Private Amos Adair's wounds. Buckshot was embedded in his knee, and a bullet had struck near his right kidney, lodging in the small of his back. Amazingly, doctors found the injury to be little more than a painful flesh wound, and they removed the ball with few complications. Adair survived, but his wounds took him out of frontline service for the remainder of the war.[1]

A lead ball had mangled the right arm of Green Washington from Company G. Slivers of bone from his shattered humerus were suspended in muscle and sinew. An inch below the bullet's entry wound doctors found a deep gash from a Confederate bayonet. Washington could count himself fortunate. He had engaged in hand-to-hand combat at Poison Spring and survived.[2]

White soldiers delivered Private Giles Green to a hospital tent in Camden. During the heat of battle, a Confederate bullet struck Green on the right side of his neck. He had managed to stay on his feet until the Union line broke, then passed out. Retreating white soldiers saved his life, literally carrying the black soldier to Camden. While recovering there, he learned that doctors planned to evacuate the wounded to better medical facilities in northern Arkansas. Unwilling to leave the regiment, Green walked out of the hospital and to the first black soldiers he could find—the Second Kansas Colored Infantry. He marched in their ranks for the next few days before finally reuniting with his own command.[3]

The disaster at Poison Spring left Major General Frederick Steele's army even shorter on provisions. Private A. F. Sperry of the

Thirty-Third Iowa Infantry recalled that "meat could be obtained, but hard-tack grew more rare and valuable, with each succeeding day."[4] After reporting the loss of the supply wagons at Poison Spring, the army's quartermaster, Captain Charles A. Henry, determined that Steele's soldiers had "only half forage for the animals of this command for one day." In desperation, he requested that "all the worthless animals attached to this command be collected and turned out to graze . . . under charge of a suitable guard." He explained there were "over 10,000 animals attached to this command for which it will be impossible to provide forage after the next two or three days."[5]

A wagon train of supplies from Pine Bluff brought some relief on April 20, two days after Poison Spring, but Steele's men had to risk more foraging expeditions to keep themselves fed.[6] The Twelfth Kansas Infantry guarded one expedition and barely escaped a Confederate attack, but managed to haul a supply of meat and potatoes into Camden on April 21.[7] These efforts kept the army alive but hardly in condition to advance on Shreveport. Events farther south soon proved such an advance unnecessary. Reports filtered to Camden that Major General Nathaniel Banks, leading the main thrust against Shreveport along the Red River, had been defeated. Couriers confirmed the news on April 18 and 22. Banks was in full retreat. More bad news arrived when Steele learned that Confederate general Edmund Kirby Smith was approaching Camden with eight thousand infantrymen.[8]

Although the federal situation at Camden was tenuous, Steele was not ready to abandon the town. With ten thousand soldiers at his command he reported that their location "is a strong place," since "the rebels have fortified it for us."[9] He hoped that supplies could come from Union boats on the Arkansas River. "It is useless to talk of obtaining supplies in this country for my command," he told his superiors. "The country is well-nigh exhausted, and the people are threatened with starvation."[10] After the war, Captain Ethan Earle of Company F remembered the opposite, claiming that "it seemed like our boyhood days of give away" as "provisions and forage were abundant." Why the Union command failed to secure these resources was something "that officers and men in the line could not comprehend," Earle explained, noting that "when teams were sent out for [provisions], their owners all had protection papers from our General and the teams would come back empty."[11] These

accounts convinced many Union soldiers that Steele was too sympathetic to the Southern—and secessionist—population. In any case,
Steele's army was in real trouble. Unable to secure supplies locally
or from federal ships, the general sent the large wagon train from
Pine Bluff back for more supplies. On April 25, the train and its military escort were attacked at Mark's Mill. Like Poison Spring, it was
a total loss for the Union.[12]

On April 26, Steele called an end to the campaign. He quietly
marched his army out of Camden toward Little Rock. Captain
Earle recalled that on leaving Camden, "orders were given to burn
and destroy everything that the officers mandated; the men were
allowed nothing but their muskets, cartridge box and ammunition."[13] "The whole road over which we travelled afforded unequiv-
ocal signs of perturbation on the part of the Yankees," Confederate
surgeon William McPheeters recorded in his diary on April 28.
"The whole road was strewn with old boots, shoes, overcoats, blankets, pantaloons, and every other article of dress, and various other
things, besides tents, wagons, and other camp equipage were left
half-burned showing that they were anxious to get rid of all unnecessary baggage in their flight."[14] Confederate cavalry chased the
Union column and on April 30 caught it at the Saline River, at a
place called Jenkins' Ferry. Federal engineers constructed a pontoon
bridge across the swollen river while Union infantry made a desperate stand to hold off the Confederate attack.

The First Kansas Colored Infantry did not play a significant
role in this engagement, but its sister regiment, the Second Kansas
Colored, made its mark. After helping hold the line against an
Arkansas brigade earlier in the fight, the regiment saw a section of
Confederate artillery unlimber directly to its front. Colonel Samuel
Crawford, the Second Kansas Colored's commander, led his men in
an attack. Volleys from the federal soldiers raked the Confederate
unit, killed most of battery's horses, and chased off Southern infantry support.[15] Leveling their bayonets, the Second Kansas Colored
soldiers screamed "Poison Springs!" and charged, crashing into the
Confederate position, capturing the guns, and shooting and bayonet-
ing men who tried to surrender. A supporting white Union regiment
witnessed some of the slaughter. "One of our boys seen a little negro
pounding a wounded reb in the head with the but[t] of his gun and
asked him what he was doing," a private of the Twenty-Ninth Iowa
Infantry recalled. "The negro replied he is not dead yet!"[16]

The Confederate attack against the Union line at Jenkins' Ferry failed, leaving hundreds of dead and wounded Southerners on the field. General Kirby Smith pulled his regiments back to reform, allowing Steele's army to escape across the pontoon bridge. The Second Kansas Colored remained as a rear guard and helped recover Union wounded on the now quiet battlefield. Though victorious, some black soldiers sniped at the distant Confederate line. Others continued their vengeance for Poison Spring on wounded Confederates. Private John H. Lewis of the Eighteenth Texas Infantry, hiding behind a tree stump with a bullet wound to his leg, watched some of the Second Kansas Colored men roam the battlefield. "Soon I looked around and saw some black negroes cutting our wounded boys' throats, and I thought my time would come next." Lewis gained his footing and limped to safety.[17] A. J. Williams, acting sergeant major for the Thirty-Third Arkansas Infantry, was not so lucky. He was "shot through the body, had his throat cut through the windpipe and lived several days," recalled his brother David S. Williams, also serving with the Thirty-Third Arkansas. "I saw several who were treated in the same way."[18]

Jesse R. Jones of the Fourteenth Texas Infantry recovered from the shock of a hip wound to find himself alone among the dead and grievously wounded. Shortly afterward a line of black soldiers approached. "One of the negroes threw his gun on me to shoot," Jones remembered, "but I begged him out of it."[19] Nine enlisted men of the Second Kansas Colored were among the 150 Union soldiers left on the battlefield, too badly wounded to retreat to Little Rock with the rest of Steele's command. C. R. Stuckslager and William L. Nicholson, two Union surgeons, remained to care for these men. While tending to the wounded, the doctors witnessed a Confederate officer raise his pistol and shoot three of the black soldiers in the head as they lay in the field hospital. Stuckslager reported that another black soldier "had his arm pierced through by a sabre in the hands of a Confed[erate] officer."[20]

The six remaining Second Kansas Colored men died two weeks later when placed inside a small storehouse apart from captured white soldiers. Nicholson was nearby when gunshots came from the storehouse. Someone stated, "The niggers are catching," and Nicholson watched as a Confederate soldier walked from the building with revolvers in each hand. The surgeon rushed to the scene to find "all the poor negroes shot through the head."[21] Five of the

soldiers died instantly; the sixth lingered a few days before succumbing to his wound. This wanton execution troubled the
Confederate high command, and Stuckslager noted that the "per-
petrator of the atrocious crime was arrested by order of Gen[era]l
Parsons and sent to Camden."[22] Stuckslager admitted that he did
not know the outcome. However, Lieutenant John Hayes of the
Second Kansas Colored, who escaped from Confederate hands after
the battle, reported that the offending Confederate officer was
hanged for the crime.[23]

The battle at Jenkins' Ferry cost the Union army 600 casualties.
Confederate forces suffered between 800 and 1,000 killed, wounded,
and missing.[24] Tactically, it was a Union victory. The stubborn infantry action allowed Steele's army to cross the Saline River and escape
to Little Rock. Kirby Smith, the Confederate commander, failed to
crush the Union army despite its vulnerable position. But whatever
satisfaction Union soldiers gleaned from the Jenkins' Ferry encounter was muted by the utter failure of the Camden expedition. From
the beginning, the First Kansas Colored Infantry and the rest of
Steele's army had suffered from a lack of food, terrible weather, and
Confederate harassment. Private Henry A. Strong, whose Twelfth
Kansas Infantry served alongside the First Kansas Colored in the
Frontier Division's Second Brigade, recorded frequent rain showers
in his diary throughout the march, complaining that the Arkansas
countryside was "either swamps or pine flats, and there's not much
difference in them in this wet weather." The early fascination with
Arkansas's natural wonders had worn off for Strong and his fellow soldiers due to the tiresome marches and the rain. "We see no
more clear, pretty streams," he confided to his journal, "all sluggish
streams, fit only for alligators to live in."[25]

The campaign pushed the men to their physical limits. From
their initial rush to meet Steele at Arkadelphia through their scram-
ble to the safety of Camden and then Little Rock, soldiers of the
Frontier Division destroyed excess baggage and nonessential articles
on at least three different occasions, and individuals continued to
shed isolated articles throughout the march.[26] Men who discarded
their wool blankets or extra socks and shirts during the heat and
humidity of the day endured wet clothing and cool temperatures
at night. Worse than the forced road marches were the too-frequent
halts. Officers, anxious to keep the column moving and hesitant to
release the men to sit down lest units ahead suddenly surge forward,

left the men in limbo, standing uncomfortably in formation for various lengths of time. "Roads are so rough and muddy that the teams can scarcely get along," Private Strong explained of one day's march. "Stop every five minutes."[27] A. F. Sperry of the Thirty-Third Iowa Infantry explained, "One of the most wearisome and vexatious things in the world is compulsory delay." And during the retreat to Little Rock, Sperry wrote, "We had it under the most disagreeable circumstances."[28]

Much of the delay and frustration for the infantrymen came from wagons and artillery pieces stranded in the mud. During the retreat after Jenkins' Ferry, men of the First Kansas Colored helped corduroy four miles of road for cannons to roll over.[29] This construction required chopping trees and laying them side by side, a disagreeable physical task on top of their normal marching. Fear of Confederate attack accompanied physical hardship on the entire march to Little Rock. Steele pushed his force onward, prompting Captain John Graton of Company C to sum up the inglorious end of the campaign as simply "a very severe march of seven days."[30]

Back in Little Rock on May 3, Steele's exhausted army took account of its condition. "The fatigues of our unhappy campaign seems [sic] just now to over come me. I feel sore all over, my head & whole body aches," Kansas cavalryman Christian Isely noted.[31] Private Ephraim Alston of Company G, a forty-year-old farmhand who had been with the regiment since December 1863, collapsed during one of the intense road marches. He arrived at Little Rock in an ambulance suffering from an acute pain on the left side of his chest. Alston spent most of the rest of his military service in the hospital. Until his death twenty-five years later, severe chest pain and congestion prevented Alston from lying on his back or left side.[32]

The failure of the expedition and the entire Red River Campaign shocked people across the North. "It is not too much to say that Steele's movements so far have been a complete failure—a disastrous one barely saved from being a perfect rout," a correspondent to the *New York Times* wrote.[33] Many soldiers placed sole blame on General Steele. Cavalryman Christian Isely complained to his wife of the "foul play of Gen. Steele. The whole army is very indignant about him." Isely explained that the belief that Steele "is a Conservative or Copperhead and is afraid of hurting the rebels" circulated among "nearly all" of his colleagues.[34] The *Leavenworth Daily Times* defended Steele, proclaiming, "The fault of the Government was in entrusting the expedition to a military sham; in leaving the *execution* of the plan, to Banks. It could not have failed with a competent head. The gallant fights at Pleasant Hill and Cane River—the more gallant victory of Steele at Jenkins' Ford—put this point beyond dispute."[35]

How the men of the First Kansas Colored felt about Steele is unknown. Little commentary on the army's leadership has been found from its soldiers or officers. Captain Earle pondered the lack of Union support from Camden during the battle at Poison Spring, and after the war he concluded that "the only reason I can assign for reinforcements not being sent to us was that the Rebels were in great force, North, South, East and West, on the South only six miles, and it was thought better to sacrifice our entire force than to bring on general battle out there and perhaps lose the city and possibly the Army."[36] The regiment soon learned it would return to its previous springtime duties. "Division have orders to march for Ft. Smith immediately we shall start in the morning," Captain Graton wrote to his wife three days after the regiment walked into Little Rock. "It will probably take ten or twelve days to Reach."[37] By mid-May, First Kansas Colored soldiers were back at Fort Smith.[38]

The regiment found Fort Smith in high alarm. All businesses were closed. Those soldiers left behind in garrison were manning defensive positions, and the acting commander, Colonel William R. Judson, had even impressed local men for repairing and strengthening fortifications. Messages from Union spies two days earlier reported eight thousand Confederates on the move. The arrival of the Frontier Division from Little Rock reassured Judson and the garrison, as did reports that the advancing Southern army was only a heavy scout testing the Union line. The First Kansas Colored Infantry was given the task of strengthening Fort Smith's defenses, particularly the construction of complex rifle pits large enough to hold six thousand men. Within a couple of weeks, the fortifications were imposing. "The place is impregnable," Brigadier General John Thayer reported to General Steele on May 28, "the forts are nearly completed, and a continuous line of rifle-pits, with an extensive abates from the Arkansas around to the Poteau River."[39]

The previous months had been difficult for the regiment. But its ability to maintain integrity and competency in the face of the disaster at Poison Spring and the continued rigors of garrison and scouting earned the respect of others. "We were pleased to witness the performance of this fine regiment when on parade last Monday," the *Fort Smith New Era* reported of a July 4 military event. "Organized under the most unfavorable auspices, and for months after its organization not being paid or hardly recognized as a regiment, it has proved itself worthy of all praise, and is most truly, as has been said of it, among the best regiments in the field." Recognizing the regiment's hardships, the editor declared that "no troops have done harder marching, endured more fatigue, or withstood and beaten back any more determined assaults, than the First Colored. We have noticed it when on parade, several times, and always find the same precision made in the movements, and the same ready obedience to orders given, showing not only the drill and good discipline that it has received, but the aptness with which the black man learns. Col. Williams may well be proud of his regiment."[40]

The newspaper was a defiant pro-Union publication that had long supported the First Kansas Colored and other black soldiers. Nevertheless, it reflected the influence black soldiers had in changing attitudes during the Civil War. Only six years earlier, concern over free blacks in Arkansas prompted severe action. One group of Arkansas citizens published a circular bemoaning the free African American as "worthless and so depraved an animal," and a year later the state government passed a law requiring the relocation of free blacks out of state boundaries by January 1, 1860.[41] The *New Era* editorial did not signal eradication of racial prejudice in Arkansas, but it did reveal change. By their dedication and ability under adverse circumstances, the First Kansas Colored Infantry earned the respect of many Northern and Southern whites and helped pave the way for the successful recruitment and use of other black soldiers in the region.

The soldiers also received continued support from Senator James Lane in Washington. "The negro soldier has now proved his capacity for endurance equal to the white soldier," he told his Senate colleagues in the early months of 1864. "He has shown his fighting qualities to be, if not equal to those of the white soldier, valuable to the country. So far as I am concerned, I desire to put the one upon the same footing as the other. Let us have no discrimination between the soldiers who sustain the flag of the country and who mingle their blood in the same great cause."[42] He tried to meet this proposal by advocating retroactive pay for those men of the First Kansas Colored who had served before the regiment's federal muster in January 1863.[43] Lane recognized, with remarkable clarity for a man who had previously embraced strong racial prejudice, that the unequal treatment of black soldiers by their own government undermined larger Union interests. And he seemed to accept some of that blame:

> Sir, we have lost a great deal by discriminating against the colored soldiers. In my opinion, had they been placed on the same footing at the outset with the white soldiers, the so-called confederate government would not have dared to discriminate against them in the exchange of prisoners. We invited that pretended government to discriminate against them. We made the discrimination ourselves, and said to Jeff. Davis and his accursed pretended government, in effect, You may discriminate between the black and white soldiers clothed in our uniform and shedding their blood for the same cause. We induced the pretended confederate government to discriminate against the colored soldier. In violation of all the rules that govern civilized warfare, they have dared to do it upon our invitation. It is time for our own honor that we strike down the discrimination between the soldiers of the United States. We have catered to this prejudice too long. When we put the uniform of the United States upon a person, he should be the peer of any one who wears the same uniform, without reference to complexion.[44]

Lane had come a long way in his attitudes toward African Americans. Necessity may have opened the door to military ranks for black men, but their success in that role—an experiment in the eyes of many whites—influenced public opinion.

Lane admitted his larger concern for white men in July: "I should like to see every white man in the Army of the United States returned to his family and his home, and his place filled by a negro." This signaled a major departure from the "white man's war" attitude that had thwarted black participation during the first year of the war. Three years of death and destruction had changed attitudes. "I am not so devoted to, so much the lover of the negro race that I would permit them to remain at home enjoying its luxuries while white men are called upon to defend them," he said. "I should be glad to vote for a proposition that would call out a million negro troops that the white troops may be relieved from the dangers and the fatigues of the Army; and I hope that this Government will increase its energy, and that the time will soon come when we shall be grappling with this rebellion with an army of negroes sufficient to close it out." Lane saw the use of black soldiers to defeat the Confederacy as appropriate given the root cause of the Civil War: "I do not believe myself that God will be fully satisfied unless this rebellion is closed out by the slaves, property in which caused the rebellion."[45]

CHAPTER 14

FLAT ROCK CREEK

The water was red with blood of the dead negroes.

Toward the end of summer 1864, as the First Kansas Colored Infantry again settled into occupation duty in northern Arkansas, Captain John Graton of Company C escorted a wagon train from Fort Smith to Fort Gibson (earlier known as Fort Blunt) in Indian Territory with several companies. The wagons continued on to Fort Scott under the escort of Kansas cavalry, but Captain Graton and the black soldiers stayed at Fort Gibson. The rest of the First Kansas Colored Infantry, the Fifty-Fourth United States Colored Troops (USCT), and the First Arkansas Light Artillery remained at Fort Smith under the command of Colonel James M. Williams.[1]

Soldiers at Fort Gibson joined hay-gathering operations across the prairie. Though Union forces held the fort, Confederate cavalry still posed a threat, occasionally striking isolated foraging posts. On August 24, Texas Confederates attacked the camp of the Eleventh USCT a few miles outside Fort Gibson. Surprised by the early dawn raid, the unit gained its composure and mounted a fierce defense, eventually pushing the Confederates back. Union reinforcements set out to find the Texans. Kansas infantryman Henry A. Strong was among them. "The Rebs fired all the hay that was put up," he recorded in his diary that night, "but did not damage much as twas most all hauled in to the Fort." His regiment, the Twelfth Kansas Infantry, arrived at the Eleventh USCT camp at 3 P.M., but the mounted Confederate soldiers had fallen back across the Arkansas River. "Surgeon Gen[eral] was killed and four colored soldiers," he wrote. In the federal camp the Union men found one dead Confederate—a Choctaw soldier.[2]

On September 16, First Lieutenant David M. Sutherland and thirty-seven men of Company K, First Kansas Colored Infantry, joined Captain Edgar A. Barker and ninety men of Company C, Second Kansas Cavalry, on a hay-gathering assignment for the Fort

Gibson garrison.[3] The party made camp fifteen miles west of the fort near Flat Rock Creek on the eastern plains of Indian Territory. Their work was time consuming and laborious, but the garrison needed hundreds of tons of hay to feed the many mules, horses, cows, and other domestic animals through the harsh prairie winter.[4]

The black soldiers helped provide protection for the detail. According to some sources they joined in the cutting and gathering of hay.[5] The Union work crew did not know that Confederate scouts had reported the hay-gathering efforts at Flat Rock Creek and the large Union wagon train expected from Fort Scott. Brigadier Generals Richard Gano and Stand Watie led two thousand Confederate soldiers with the intention of attacking both.[6]

A few miles from the harvesting camp the Thirtieth Texas Cavalry and the First Cherokee Regiment broke from the main force and moved to the far right, planning to swing around the Union soldiers and cut off their retreat. The remaining Southern soldiers stopped at the foot of a large mound, rested, and waited. General Gano and his staff walked to the top of the mound and quietly observed the Union work party with satisfaction. From that elevated position they "could view their camps, and with spy glasses could see them at work making hay, unaware that the rebels were watching them."[7] Colonel Charles DeMorse later wrote to the *Clarksville Standard* that "from the top of this mound, with the aid of the glass, could be seen the working party, mowing hay as if in perfect security." DeMorse was the commander of the Twenty-Ninth Texas Cavalry— the First Kansas Colored Infantry's nemesis from Honey Springs and Poison Spring. Now the Texans had the black Kansas soldiers in their sights again and eagerly awaited the chance to crush them.[8]

Gano ordered his force to move toward the camp. Within one mile he sent the Twenty-Ninth Texas and the Thirty-First Texas regiments under Lieutenant Colonel Otis Welch to the right while Stand Watie and his force swung to the left. Gano led the remaining Texas brigade down the center. "The clouds looked somber and the V-shaped procession grand as we moved forward in the work of death," he later reported. Gano saw the Thirtieth Texas Cavalry and First Cherokee arrive behind the Union camp as a blocking force. The encirclement was nearly complete.[9]

At this point Union soldiers at camp became aware of the threat. Federal scouts raced their horses to Captain Barker with news that at least two hundred mounted Confederates approached the foraging party. The captain called in both the cavalry and infantry and formed a battle line along a ravine near the rear of the camp. That location, he concluded, was the best defensive feature in the area and well positioned to protect the hay. Once the men were in place, Captain Barker led a small party of scouts to investigate. The group rode less than two miles before realizing the scope of the threat. Barker could see a thousand Confederates marching toward his camp and closing quickly. He wheeled his reconnaissance party around and galloped back to his men. A Confederate advance guard took off in pursuit, exchanging shots with the federals while trying to cut them off. Barker and his men made it to camp safely, but with little time to do more than warn the other federals.[10]

The land around Fort Gibson, like much of the Trans-Mississippi Theater, was open prairie, well suited for mounted operations. Had the entire Union force been cavalrymen, Barker might have tried to carry out a fighting withdrawal. But three dozen men of the foraging party were infantry soldiers. Barker dismounted his own men to fight at the ravine.

The Union soldiers just finished arranging their line when the massive Confederate force attacked from five different points. W. T. Sheppard, a private with the Fifth Texas Partisan Rangers, described the advance across the rough ground. "While we were making a charge on the enemy's camp on foot, we passed over some ground where beef cattle had been corralled while the ground was wet, which left it in a rough condition, but at this time was dry and full of holes." A number of the Confederates lacked proper footwear. Sheppard sustained his only injury during the war in this advance when a soldier behind him stepped on one of his homemade spurs. "I being barefooted," Sheppard recalled, the sharp metal spur "shaved off a good slice of the back part of my heel." He continued with his unit to press the attack.[11]

They marched to within two hundred yards. Accurate fire from the white and black Union soldiers checked the Confederate line. Mounted Confederates charged three times, trying to break the Union defensive position. But each time, Barker explained, they were "handsomely repulsed by the colored infantry and dismounted cavalry."[12]

For thirty minutes the firefight raged, gray smoke wafting over the battlefield. The Union line held, but in the face of such overwhelming odds, total defeat was inevitable. No reinforcements were in earshot of the action. Echoes of cannon fire might carry to Fort Gibson, but only the attacking Confederates had artillery on hand, and they had not yet used it. Even if reinforcements had been sent, they would have taken an hour or more to arrive. The Confederate force soon completed the encirclement. Rather than surrender, Captain Barker ordered those men still with horses to form up. He would lead them in a charge against a weak point in the Confederate line. It was not an offensive move, but an escape attempt. He told the black infantrymen and the dismounted cavalry troopers to do their best to escape on foot to the Grand River, a mile distant. Sixty-five Union cavalrymen spurred their horses, wielding pistols and sabers, toward a small opening in Stand Watie's line. Confederate soldiers converged and met them with a crash. Barker and fourteen of his men escaped the melee. Most of the other cavalrymen were captured.[13]

Soldiers on foot faced a desperate situation. Outnumbered twelve to one, their only hope of escape was along Flat Rock Creek. The men, black and white, only made it two hundred yards down the creek before they saw the way blocked by the Thirtieth Texas Cavalry and First Cherokee. The federals formed a rough defensive position in the trees and reeds along the creek and fired on the advancing Confederates.[14] The Texans and Indians stopped. Within a few minutes a Confederate officer appeared alongside a man in a blue uniform. They carried a white flag and slowly approached the creek. Gano had decided to offer the remaining Union soldiers the opportunity to surrender, "with the assumption that their lives would be spared," explained Colonel DeMorse.[15] He had ordered a subordinate to present the terms. To help convince the Union men, the Confederate officer took a federal lieutenant—a man captured during Barker's breakout charge. Despite the odds, the Union soldiers rejected the offer with musket balls. Black soldiers expected no mercy from the enemy. The murder of their wounded and captured comrades by some of these same Confederates at Poison Spring was a recent memory. The Confederate officer and his prisoner ducked and fell back as muskets and carbines peppered the trees and creek line.[16]

Though terribly outnumbered, the desperate survivors found cover along the creek banks. According to cavalryman Private George Duvall, the black Kansans maintained a strict discipline in their defense, firing carefully aimed volleys rather than sporadic shots as the Confederates pressed attacks. This tactic continued until most of their ammunition was spent.[17] In the meantime, frustrated by the stubbornness of the Union force, Gano's men brought up their cannons. "One shot thrown in their midst, had the desired effect: they scattered in all directions along the Creek," Colonel DeMorse recalled.[18] Confederate soldiers charged with a yell. With ammunition nearly gone and artillery fire tearing up the trees and earth, all semblance of order disintegrated. Lieutenant Sutherland shouted at his men to save themselves, and the Union soldiers ran for their lives. Some fled down the creek banks; others tried to hide among the trees and reeds. Dismounted Confederate soldiers cautiously walked into the abandoned camp and along the creek. To their dismay, few federals could be found. "The defenders disappeared among the thickets and very high weeds that covered the banks of the creek," recalled Captain George Grayson of the Second Creek Regiment, "and for a few minutes after reaching the deserted camps it did not appear that there was anything for us to do more than burning the camps and the great ricks of hay that stood about on the field."[19]

As the Texans scanned the area, Confederate Indians ran down the banks to the water. DeMorse wrote that "the vengeance of the red man was not thus to be appeased, and his natural sagacity suggested that in the creek, and under the tall grass and bushes overhanging the banks, the 'contrabands' might be found."[20] The Indian soldiers carefully searched the waterline. Within minutes they found one black Kansas soldier in the weeds and shot him. Grayson recalled that "at another point another [negro] was found and shot, and it now appearing that these were to be found hid in the weeds, the men proceeded to hunt them out much as sportsmen do quails." Thus began a furious search of the brush. On being discovered, a few of the black soldiers begged for mercy, crying out, "O! master spare me." But, Grayson noted, "the men were in no spirit to spare the wretched unfortunates and shot them down without mercy."[21]

Confederate soldiers found some of the First Kansas Colored men trying to hide in the creek itself, "with noses protruding from under the water." These unfortunate men were unceremoniously shot and dragged onto the bank by the Indian soldiers. Colonel DeMorse watched the carnage but shied away from describing the scene in detail to his Texas readers, only writing, "Call to memory the Choctaws at Poison Springs, and you have the remainder of the fight described."[22] Another Texas soldier recorded more particulars after the war. Jefferson Braze of the Thirtieth Texas recalled that "the water was red with blood of the dead negroes. The few Indians who were along with the army (called Southern Indian) dragged the dead bodies from the river and took all that was of any value from them."[23]

Captain Grayson, commanding some of the Confederate Indians, later wrote, "I confess this was sickening to me, but the men were like wild beasts and I was powerless to stop them from this unnecessary butchery." As he sat on his horse observing the murder of black Union men, one of his soldiers captured a white Kansas cavalryman. The Indian pulled his prisoner over to Grayson and asked, "Should we not kill him too?" Grayson told him no, remarking that "it was negroes that we were killing now and not white men." He instructed the man to turn the white prisoner over to the Confederate guard, already holding a few dozen Union cavalrymen. Writing of this event in his autobiography, Grayson mused, "Here was found some mother's son whom the fortunes of war had caught on the adverse side. Probably a good young man in the main, whose life hung for a moment upon a word from me while he was too frightened to talk or plead for his life. I sided with him and prolonged his life."[24] He offered no such reflection on the lives of the First Kansas Colored men dragged out of the creek and executed.

General Gano's report did not describe Union soldiers being killed after surrender. He summarized the battle's end with a poetic but chilling statement: "The sun witnessed our complete success, and its last lingering rays rested upon a field of blood."[25] On that bloody field lay two dozen First Kansas Colored Infantry soldiers. Texan W. T. Sheppard summed up his perception of the dead with the comment, "After the battle they were all 'good' negroes."[26]

After the last of the Union soldiers had been captured, killed, or chased away, Confederate soldiers turned to the federal supplies, rounding up twenty-five horses and twelve mules. They took personal effects from the dead Union men, including pistols and breech-loading carbines, but destroyed the hay machines and wagons and claimed to have burned as much as three thousand tons of hay. It was a crushing blow to Fort Gibson's supply stores.[27]

The casualty figures proved absurdly disproportional. Gano claimed that his force captured 85 prisoners and killed 73, the dead being "mostly negroes." Five other Union soldiers were mortally wounded. In contrast, he reported only 3 men wounded.[28] The Union commander, Captain Barker, reported that he lost 40 killed and 66 captured. Nearly all of the captured were Second Kansas Cavalry troopers. He claimed that only four of the original thirty-seven men from Company K survived.[29] First Kansas Colored regimental records list 29 deaths at Flat Rock Creek. This discrepancy may be found in the fact that some presumed dead were actually captured alive. Confederate Captain Grayson reported that while he watched Indians shoot down every black soldier they found, Indian soldiers "on other parts of the field had captured some six or eight."[30] From the First Kansas Colored Infantry, Lieutenant Sutherland, Sergeant James Brown, Corporal Isom Wood, and Privates Perry Clarkson, John Gains, and London Thompson were all spared summary execution at the hands of vengeful Confederate soldiers and spent the remaining months of the war as prisoners. They did not return to the regiment until October 1, 1865.[31]

A handful of Union men escaped along the creek and miraculously made it back to Fort Gibson. Among them was Private George Duvall. He remained hidden along the creek until nightfall and then stealthily crept past Confederate pickets. He returned to Fort Gibson with his musket in hand but his cartridge box empty.[32] Private Samuel Jefferson may also have returned to Union lines from this fight. According to regimental records, Jefferson died on October 25 at Fort Gibson of wounds received in action.[33] There is no other known engagement for the regiment at that time, and unless Jefferson's wounds came from an unrecorded skirmish, he may have been Company K's last casualty from the Flat Rock Creek fight.

Basking in the victory at Flat Rock Creek, Confederate officers planned their next move. Union prisoners confirmed that a large supply train from Fort Scott was expected in their camp the following day. With this information, Gano and Watie ordered their men to make camp on the battlefield and prepare to move north in the morning, to intercept the wagon train if possible.

Hours later, as a faint light pierced the early morning sky and the Confederates stirred from their beds, one Southerner noticed a pair of boots sticking out from a pile of brush in camp. Assuming they belonged to a dead Union soldier, he grabbed ahold of the perfectly good footwear only to find the owner kick his legs in response. Unable to escape during the night, the unfortunate soldier had tried to hide in the bushes until the Confederate force left. But, noted W. T. Sheppard, the federal soldier "had failed to take up the slack in his legs," thus leaving his shoes a tempting target for a foot-sore and supply-starved Confederate soldier. Instead of a free pair of boots, the Southern trooper captured a white cavalryman.[34]

With this last captive secured, Gano's and Watie's men mounted up and rode north. Major Michael Looscan and a battalion of Confederates remained as a rearguard to protect the larger force from any federal response from Fort Gibson. Indeed, a short time later a cautious Union patrol came into view. Looscan's Confederates aggressively attacked the patrol, sending them in retreat.[35] The rest of Gano's and Watie's men marched north along the Texas Road toward Fort Scott. Failing to find the wagon train before dark, the Confederate officers worried that the Union supply line might be on a road east of Grand River. They marched back a few miles to a location between the two roads and spent the night of September 17 on the prairie. Mounted scouts patrolled the countryside to gather information.

Gano and Watie learned that a Union detachment was encamped at Cabin Creek, near the site of the First Kansas Colored's battle over a year before. In the morning, still unsure of the wagon train's location, Gano led a contingent of four hundred men toward the creek while Watie and the balance of the force remained in camp. Gano's Texans advanced cautiously to the outskirts of the Union position, nearly ten miles away. Around midday, advance scouts informed Gano that hundreds of wagons were at a stockade nearby. They had found the supply train. The colonel hastily drew up an order for Watie to bring up his men. The combined force would overwhelm the enemy.

It would be hours before Watie and the Indian soldiers arrived. In the meantime, Gano's men tried to keep out of sight, lest the Union garrison learn of the impending threat. They failed. Federal patrols spotted some of Gano's men late that afternoon. With the enemy alerted, Gano planned action as soon as Watie's command arrived, which happened, finally, around midnight. Almost all Civil War engagements took place during the day. The difficulties and hazards of managing a battle in darkness prompted most commanders to suspend hostilities—or at least offensive operations—until first light. Anxious to attack the Union encampment and wagon trains at Cabin Creek, Gano did not wait for the morning sun. His soldiers moved cautiously in the darkness toward the Union camp until met by a call to halt. The voice of a Union picket demanded to know who approached. Gano identified himself and requested that the Union commander receive a flag of truce, intending to demand his surrender. The sentry asked for five minutes and walked off into the darkness. Hundreds of Confederate soldiers stood, impatiently, waiting for an order to advance. Bright moonlight allowed the Southerners to see some of the obstacles in their way, among them large earthworks. But much of what lay ahead remained a mystery.[36]

Fifteen minutes passed with no reply from the Union garrison. Suddenly came the sounds of mules and horses stomping their feet and wagon wheels creaking. Gano recognized that the federals were trying to pull their supplies closer to the main Union position, a wooden stockade. Taking this as an answer to his request for a truce, he ordered his men forward. It was almost three o'clock in the morning, September 19. Within minutes gunfire erupted. The Union soldiers inside the wooden stockade suffered little from the initial barrage. However, the wagons and teams remained in the grassy fields outside the walls. The musket shots scattered the teamsters and sent horses and mules into a frenzy. Wagons collided, flipped, and careened across the dark prairie. High bluffs, some reaching one hundred feet, ran along part of Cabin Creek. Some frightened wagon teams unwittingly charged over the edge, crashing into a jumbled mass of wood, metal, and horseflesh at the bottom.[37]

Gunfire lasted through the night. With a flare for the dramatic, Colonel DeMorse recalled that "the bright flashes of musketry along both lines, the white smoke of the bursting bombs, the whistle of the minnie [sic] ball, accompanied by the guttural sound of Howell's artillery as it belched forth its iron messengers of death, at the hour of midnight, under the brilliant lustre of the moon and stars, upon both parties engaged in the death struggle, rendered the scene sublime."[38] The sun's early rays proved that the large earthworks the Confederates had seen in the moonlight were nothing more than piles of hay ringing the Union stockade. Nonetheless, stubborn Union defenders made good use of their sturdy wooden stockade and continued to resist Confederate attacks.[39]

Gano coordinated his attacks, sweeping the stockade with artillery fire and charging the position from numerous angles. By 9 A.M., the last Union defense had crumbled, and the Confederates swept over the camp. Though nearly half of the three hundred wagons had been lost in the night across the prairie or over the high bluffs, Gano's and Watie's men rounded up over $1 million worth of Union supplies. Jubilant Confederate soldiers found new footwear, jackets, hats, pants, weapons, and other personal items to replace missing or damaged articles. They also broke into the food stores and satisfied aching stomachs, stuffing their haversacks for later meals. They carted off 130 wagons.[40]

Their mission complete, jubilant Confederates turned southward for the long march to Southern-held territory. Their three-day advance along the supply route from Fort Scott was an unmitigated success. Yet they remained in Union-controlled territory. Having gone from hunter to hunted, the Confederates and their newly captured wagon train were now vulnerable, and anxious to reach safety beyond the Arkansas River.

At midday, as the last of the salvaged wagons fell into line, the Confederate advance guard found a strongly posted Union line across their front. It was Colonel James Williams and his brigade of exhausted but ready infantrymen—including a large portion of the First Kansas Colored Infantry—from Fort Smith. Learning of the attack on the hay-gathering detail, they had pushed themselves north along the Texas Road until reaching Pryor's Creek, a dozen miles south of Cabin Creek, around 11 A.M. Williams learned—likely from Kansas cavalrymen fleeing to Fort Gibson—that the wagon train had already been captured. Realizing that it was too late to save the supplies and that further marching would only exhaust his men, Williams had called a halt to wait for the inevitable return of the Confederate force south. Soon enough the first Confederate scouts came into view.[41]

Gano claimed that his advance force pushed the Union soldiers back three miles. Perhaps he meant Union skirmishers, for neither Colonel Williams nor Captain Graton of the First Kansas Colored noted any forward or rearward movement at Pryor's Creek. On the contrary, Graton explained that although the Confederate soldiers advanced in line of battle, "when they had got to about a mile of us they halted and did not seem very anxious to attack."[42] For some time the sides faced off, skirmishers trading shots. By 4:30 P.M., the Confederates still had not pressed the attack.[43] Williams grew impatient and ordered a section of Parrott rifles to fire on the enemy line. Named for their inventor, Robert Parker Parrott, these large guns were easily distinguished by their long black cast-iron gun tubes, reinforced at the breech by a thick band of wrought iron.[44] More importantly for the federal soldiers at Pryor's Creek, the Parrott rifles could accurately fire ten-pound projectiles at their enemy across the mile-long divide.

The Union guns aimed at what appeared to be a Confederate artillery battery. "The second shot from our guns struck right in front of theirs," Graton declared. "You had better believe that there was some scampering to get away from there." The Confederate cannons blasted a few rounds in response, but the balls fell well short of the Union line. "They could not reach us, while a few shots from our guns, completely broke up their lines, and they were glad to get behind some mounds nearby," Graton happily reported.[45]

Shortly after the one-sided artillery duel, darkness descended. Skirmishing parties harassed each other, but neither Williams nor Gano chose to press an attack. The Confederate commander noted his opponents' lack of aggression and concluded that his men had held the federals in check.[46] In reality, Williams believed his command was on the verge of collapse from exhaustion, "having marched eighty-two miles in the last forty-six hours, carrying their knapsacks."[47] Graton concurred, writing to his wife that "our men being very much exhausted from hard marching without rest, and the enemy being cavalry and our force infantry, prevented us pursuing the advantage thus gained."[48] Knowing that he blocked the most direct route for the Confederate escape south, and desperate to let his men rest, Williams hastily set up camp and watched his opponents for the night.

As they gazed across the prairie, Union pickets could see tiny specks of yellow and orange lights across the horizon. The Confederate campfires confirmed that Gano's and Watie's men were bedding down for the night. Creaking wood and the familiar sound of wheels scraping rock assured the Union soldiers that the Confederates were bringing up the captured wagons for the morning breakout attempt. The Union soldiers threw themselves on the ground for an uneasy but much needed rest.[49]

As dawn broke, Union soldiers readied for battle. Rolling up packs, adjusting gear, and checking muskets, the men of the First Kansas Colored Infantry and their comrades prepared for the Confederate attack. But all that could be seen was the smoke from smoldering campfires. The Confederates were gone. The nighttime sounds of Confederate camp activity had been nothing more than a ruse. Gano reported that after dusk his force "created the impression that we had parked the train for the night by running an empty wagon over a rocky place for two hours, while our train was being moved with all possible dispatch toward the Arkansas River."[50] The creaking wood and scraping metal had been a single wagon dragged by tired mules in a circle over the roughest ground Confederates could find. Campfires along the ridge were also part of the ploy, for the Confederate soldiers had no rest that night.

On September 28, Gano's wagon train arrived safely at camp far south of Fort Gibson. The Confederates were exhausted, but thrilled by their success. Gano reported the outcome of his expedition: "We were out fourteen days, marched over 400 miles, killed 97, wounded many, captured 111 prisoners, burned 6,000 tons of hay and all the reapers or mowers—destroyed altogether from the Federals $1,500,000 of property, bringing safely into our lines nearly one-third of this amount (estimated in greenback)." For this success, his force lost nine killed and forty-five wounded.[51]

CHAPTER 15

END OF THE WAR

You have returned victorious.

The attack at Flat Rock Creek proved to be the last major engagement for the First Kansas Colored Infantry. Still, the regiment
continued to lose men. Crudely referencing his own regiment in a letter to his wife in November 1864, Captain John Graton of Company
C wrote, "The 1st Nigger is out of luck this year." On November 19,
guerillas attacked a regimental detachment at Timber Hills, Indian
Territory. Details of the event were sparse. Captain Graton knew
only that "Capts. Thrasher and Welch, Lt. Macy and four or five
others were run onto by a party of about sixty rebs and it is supposed that they are either killed or captured, it is uncertain which."
According to Graton, word of the event came from "a fellow by
the name of Jones [who] outrun and got away from there." Captain
Benjamin W. Welch and Second Lieutenant Eberle Q. Macey were
killed in the skirmish. Both men had recently returned to the field
after recuperating from wounds received at Poison Spring. Macey
had a new wife at home when he fell at Timber Hills.[1]

Despite these sporadic episodes, the First Kansas Colored soldiers spent much of their time in late 1864 in monotonous duty.
They were "very busy building winter quarters," Captain Graton
wrote from Fort Smith, adding that he sent "out all the teams I
can get hold of almost every day with 30 or 40 men and tear down
houses and bring in the roofing and floor boards to build quarters
of." Few local residents objected, since "all the country around
here is deserted and farms abandoned."[2] The semi-permanent quarters at Fort Smith offered only occasional respite, as the regiment
frequently participated in foraging expeditions and patrols around
northern Arkansas and eastern Indian Territory. Orders often came
suddenly. "I was going to finish this letter at my leisure this evening
but first at dusk I received an order to get the Regt ready to escort a
Forage Train, and to take along seven days rations," Graton wrote to

his wife. "We are to be ready to morrow morning at 8 o'clock. Forage is scarce and we have to go a long distance. If the weather is good we may have a pleasant trip but the weather is very changeable at this time of the year."[3]

The expedition was a ten-day, fifty-mile journey to Cane Hill, Arkansas. Escorting forty wagons, the detachment came across ample food and supplies. "Our boys found plenty of Apples and lived on them and pork for several days. I think we must have killed and eaten about three hundred hogs on this trip," Graton explained. Yet the soldiers were "in camp just four days, and had not hardly got straightened round when we were ordered out again and were gone . . . fifteen days." Their new assignment had been "down the river this time about seventy five miles, to get the freight of a boat which had sunk."[4]

The soldiers eagerly anticipated transferring from Fort Smith, but an "order to evacuate this place was countermanded by the President, at the hesitation of the people of Arkansas, and reached this place a few days ago," Graton noted.[5] "The troops would have all been glad to have been able to get away from here," he explained. "We have never been able to get more than half rations since coming here." As he penned the letter to his wife, he heard boat whistles. "It may be that we have a supply of rations on hand," he added, "I learn that there are four of them, just got in." These supplies were welcomed by the men, since, as Graton explained, "a fine time of the year for boating it is not, the middle of Winter."[6]

Officers suffered from the coarse diet, though usually not to the same degree as the enlisted men. Able to purchase provisions at the commissary while stationed in northern Arkansas, the regiment's commissioned officers had access to "flour, beef, coffee, rice, beans and bacon," and Captain Graton "succeed[ed] in getting five lbs of sugar, the other day." Most of the regiment subsisted on "simply bread, coffee and meat." Without a well-rounded diet, soldiers suffered from vitamin deficiencies. In one letter to his wife, Captain Graton mentioned, almost as an afterthought, that his "mouth has been getting sore for several days I think it is a touch of the scurvy, and is occasioned by a lack of fruits and vegetables. I have not had a plenty of fruit and vegetables since I have been in the army."[7] He admitted that apart from the soreness in the gums, his health was quite good. For enlisted men, whose diet may have been less diverse, scurvy was usually more severe. By the time he left the army in

April 1865, Company A's First Sergeant Joseph Carris had lost nearly all of his teeth from scurvy. A female friend later testified before a pension examiner that after Carris's discharge, "the scurvy afflicted him that I was forced to cook his victuals very soft."[8]

Constant marching and labor during winter months took a toll on the men. Even though most were in the physical prime of their lives and had been strong laborers with few health problems before enlistment, the strain weakened their immune systems. From the beginning of the regiment's formation, disease had periodically swept through camp. The most lethal period had been March through May 1863, when thirty-four died of diseases such as typhoid, pneumonia, and consumption. In 1864, disease claimed fewer lives, but many survivors never fully recovered. Regimental doctors battled an array of ailments. Diarrhea, dysentery, malarial diarrhea, ulcers, jaundice, inflamed liver, inflammation of the kidney, chronic hepatitis, syphilis, secondary syphilis, typhoid, bronchitis, scurvy, scrofula, cholic, asthma, headache, hernias, constipation, catarrh, boils, neuralgia, meningitis, anemia, dropsy, influenza, mumps, lumbago, night blindness, and sunstroke made up about *half* of the afflictions they faced. The most serious diseases were measles and smallpox. Each produced an epidemic in camp. According to existing records, physicians identified twenty-two serious cases of smallpox between late September 1863 and January 1864, and fourteen cases of measles in May and June 1864.[9]

The physical strain of lengthy marches and manual labor caused a large number of muscle and joint injuries. Men sought medical treatment for sprains to knees, wrists, and shoulders.[10] Some soldiers reported to the regimental doctor with unexplained inflammations and aches. Private Giles Gully joined the regiment in Arkansas in April 1864, and early the next year, on a march between Fort Smith and Little Rock, his right foot swelled so badly that he could not walk on it. The regimental surgeon inspected the swelling and lanced it to drain the fluid. Gully spent nearly a month recuperating but never fully recovered from the aftereffects. Years later he reported, "Every time now I walk much it swells up & am compelled to stop a day or two on acc[oun]t of it."[11]

Other injuries resulted from accidents or negligence around camp. Lacerations, punctures, burns, and careless handling of weapons disabled almost a dozen men.[12] The most troubling medical cases involved criminal activity or altercations. In separate incidents,

Joseph Corrasky of Company A and John Johnson of Company K reported to the doctor with knife wounds to a leg. Those injuries may have been accidental, but the blade that cut into Hurley O'Bannon's chest was thrust with bad intent. On October 30, 1864, O'Bannon was the unhappy guest of the regiment's guardhouse when an argument with a fellow prisoner escalated. The unidentified man pulled a knife and slashed at O'Bannon. In the medical review of the wounds, the physician found that the blade struck first "on the superior spinous process of left illium, 2d near centre of twelfth rib of left side." In short, the knife glanced off his ribs. The doctor found that both wounds were "superficial on account of the knife being arrested by the bones." A simple dressing was applied, and O'Bannon was back in the ranks by November 6.[13]

Life-changing injuries struck in surprising, nondescript ways. During one of the many marches across Arkansas in the winter months of 1864, the regiment approached a river ford. Stripping down to keep their clothes dry, the infantrymen waded through the current. "It was intensely cold and I remember that ice was floating down the river," recalled Sergeant Isaac Alexander of Company I. Shivering his way through the icy water, Alexander suddenly felt a searing pain in his left knee. "It was such a sharp pain that it caused that leg to give way and I fell in the water," he later said. "I was not more than ten feet from shore at the time and the water was not more than knee deep so I got up and hobbled along out of the water." Once dressed, the men continued their journey to Fort Smith. Alexander nursed his leg, feeling fortunate that his role as a sergeant allowed him to step out of the ranks.[14]

He did not seek medical attention from the regimental surgeon at Fort Smith. Instead, Alexander obtained a "pain killer" ointment from an unknown source and continued his regular duties with his company. Another march to Ozark followed by a long trek to Little Rock added to the stress, and his leg rapidly worsened. In Little Rock he again tried to avoid the hospital, and asked Captain Granville Lewis for permission to rest in his tent. The regimental surgeon investigated and instructed the sergeant on how to care for the leg. Medical practice of the 1860s was more art than science, and treatment occasionally produced greater problems for the patient than the original affliction did. Sergeant Alexander had such an experience. The surgeon "first told me to bathe my leg in cold water," Alexander later said, "and that seemed to make it worse." The doctor then applied a mysterious medicated substance to the sergeant's leg. Alexander thought it was a mustard poultice. Whatever it was, he never forgot the result: "it took all the skin off." Not surprisingly, none of the treatments led to a recovery. Instead Alexander found his leg tense and involuntarily retracting. "My leg was drawn up to about an angle of 90 degrees and I had to walk with a crutch," he told a pension officer years later. As he was now unfit for duty, the military discharged him in June 1865.[15]

One soldier told of being injured by lightning while standing guard during a rainstorm. Private Willis Yaunt stated that "the major's Horse was struck by this strike of lightning within one rod of where I was standing [and] the lightning struck the bayonet of my gun[,] shocking me" and partly disabling his left arm.[16] Private John Smith, convalescing at the Fort Gibson hospital, found himself and two other recuperating soldiers detailed to a saltworks on the Little Illinois River in December 1864. While tending to vats of brine, Smith stumbled and fell into the boiling mix. The brine scalded his legs, destroying the skin and inflicting permanent injuries.[17]

To replace soldiers lost from disease and injury, the First Kansas Colored Infantry added men through continued recruiting and the draft. Between December 1864 and April 1865, 128 newly enlisted men were assigned to the regiment.[18] Eighty-three of them were volunteers who had accepted payment to serve as substitutes for conscripted, and wealthy, white men.[19] The federal government fully authorized this manner of substitution and even provided a standardized form for the purpose, Form Number 40. The one signed by eighteen-year-old James Ball declared that he "HEREBY ACKNOWL-EDGED to have agreed with William Armstrong, Esq., of 16th Sub Dist Jackson Co., Kan (Northern Dist Kas) to become his SUBSTI-TUTE in the Military Service, for a sufficient consideration paid and delivered to me, on the ninth day of March, 1865." For this undisclosed amount of money, the newly enlisted James Ball agreed to serve for one year, "unless sooner discharged by proper authority." Private Ball, unable to read or write, signed his consent with the customary "X" by his printed name.[20] These 128 recruits, draftees, and substitutes were appointed to the First Kansas Colored Infantry on paper, but never received assignments to specific companies. Instead they served their military time in Northern camps, far away from the regiment in Arkansas, and in May 1865 were mustered out of service.[21]

248 SOLDIERS IN THE ARMY OF FREEDOM

The regiment experienced one notable administrative change during the last few months of the war. In December 1864, the War Department assigned a new designation to the First Kansas Colored Infantry: the Seventy-Ninth United States Colored Troops (New).[22] The "(New)" was used to distinguish the regiment from a previous Seventy-Ninth USCT organized in Louisiana, which had been incorporated into the Seventy-Fifth USCT.[23] This new naming protocol affected almost all black regiments during the war, and appeared to be random. It began in the spring of 1863 after Secretary of War Edwin Stanton ordered the creation of a new bureau of black soldiers. Among the first USCT units were regiments raised and equipped by the War Department, rather than those organized by state officials, as the First Kansas Colored Infantry had been.[24] The timing for receiving federal USCT designation, and the number assigned, had no bearing on the chronology of that regiment's creation or entrance into military service. Thus in late 1864, the first black regiment to be raised in a Northern state and the fourth black regiment to be mustered into federal service officially became the Seventy-Ninth USCT.

Events in Washington in early 1865 brought new promise to the men of the First Kansas Colored Infantry. Before he was president, Abraham Lincoln warned that "this government cannot endure, permanently half-*slave* and half-*free.*" "A house divided against itself cannot stand," he told fellow Americans, prophesying that the political battle over slavery "will not cease, until a crisis shall have been reached, and passed."[25] During the first year of the war slavery had remained largely untouched. In the second year, the black soldiers had been promised freedom by Senator James Lane. In 1863 Lincoln's Emancipation Proclamation had formalized the federal government's promise of their freedom. Yet both of those promises had limits. The former covered only black Union soldiers and their families. The latter extended only to those areas under rebellion on January 1, 1863.

Four years into the war slavery still existed, legally, in much of the United States, including Missouri, where almost half of the black Kansas soldiers were from. In early 1865, Lincoln and antislavery members of Congress worked to end slavery permanently, across the nation. They pushed passage of a new constitutional amendment.

Early efforts to abolish slavery through a new amendment in 1864 failed when Democrats in the House of Representatives prevented proponents from reaching the necessary two-thirds majority.[26] In

January 1865, Lincoln pushed again. Conservatives and some moderates in Congress still resisted. Lincoln and the amendment's supporters lobbied carefully, but tirelessly, to draw in the necessary votes. Having won reelection in November 1864, Lincoln saw abolition as the will of the majority. "Hence there is only a question of time as to when the proposed amendment will go to the states for their action," he had said in December. "And as it is to so go, at all events, may we not agree that the sooner the better?"[27] Indeed, the tide had turned at the dawn of 1865. Before Congress took a vote on the Thirteenth Amendment, Missouri took its own steps toward emancipation. On January 11, 1865, Governor Thomas C. Fletcher issued a proclamation abolishing the institution in that state.[28]

On January 31, 1865, the House of Representatives—the only federal obstacle—voted on the Thirteenth Amendment, with a final tally of 119 for, 56 against, and 8 abstentions.[29] The passage sparked "an outburst of enthusiasm" great enough for mention in the record of congressional proceedings, the *Congressional Globe*. "The members on the Republican side of the House instantly sprung to their feet," the *Globe* recorded, "and, regardless of parliamentary rules, applauded cheers and clapping of hands." People in the galleries joined in the celebration, as males ripped off their hats and women waved their handkerchiefs, "adding to the general excitement and intense interest of the scene."[30]

Ratification by the Northern states was swift. Illinois responded first, ratifying the Thirteenth Amendment on February 1. Rhode Island and Michigan followed the next day. As the tide of ratification swept across the North, officials in the federal government debated whether ratification by the South was required. Republicans like Senator Charles Sumner of Massachusetts preferred not to place the fate of the amendment on former Confederate states. Lincoln advocated ratification through a three-fourths majority of all the states. Eventually, on December 18, 1865, twenty-seven states ratified the amendment, making slavery illegal across the nation.[31]

As these events occurred, soldiers of the First Kansas Colored Infantry saw a future of victory in war and freedom. But their day-to-day tasks remained the same. Armies in Virginia and South Carolina under Generals Ulysses S. Grant and William T. Sherman slowly ground down the remnants of Robert E. Lee's and Joseph E. Johnston's armies and drew the most attention. The surrender of Lee at Appomattox Courthouse on April 9, 1865, marked a symbolic end of the Civil War, although Johnston and other Confederate forces across the South continued their resistance. "We have no other news of importance except the evacuation of Richmond and subsequent surrender of Lee's Army, which you may well imagine was [a] source of Great rejoicing," Captain Graton wrote his wife.[32] Yet the traumatic news of President Lincoln's assassination five days later sent a jubilant Northern population into shock. Captain Graton described the effect in camp:

> I had not more than got awake before I heard a heavy explosion and after a short space another, and yet another, and soon all the bells in Little Rock were [ringing]. I then remarked to some of my men who were standing around that there must be some prominent personage dead, thinking [it] might be Secretary Seward. We heard a few days since that he was very sick. But in a few minutes an orderly came around with the dreadful news that Abraham Lincoln was Dead, assassinated in the city of Washington. I was perfectly astounded. And I felt as our surgeon says that every person in the United States will feel that they have lost a Father. And I think that no man since Washington's Day has gone to his grave more universally or sincerely regretted by the people.[33]

Over the next several weeks, the remaining Confederate armies across the South surrendered to federal forces, bringing the war to a formal end. However, the men of the First Kansas Colored Infantry saw no sudden release from military service. By April 1865, the regiment had not seen combat in months. Their service had involved occupation duty, a mission even more greatly expanded for federal armies with the fall of the Confederacy.

The cessation of hostilities allowed officers and men to turn to personal matters. In March 1865, Congress had passed a law authorizing retroactive pay to black soldiers for service before 1863 and for inequalities in pay compared to white soldiers. The law referred to the black South Carolina troops raised by Major General David Hunter but did include a provision that

> in every case where it shall be made to appear to the satisfaction of the Secretary of War that any regiment of colored troops has been mustered into the service of the United States, under any assurance by the President or the Secretary of War, that the noncommission officers and privates of such regiment should be paid

the same as other troops of the same arm of the service, shall, from the date of their enlistment, receive the same pay and allowances as are allowed by law to other volunteers in the military service.[34]

Ten First Kansas Colored Infantry officers petitioned the War Department for pay due their men.[35] The officers stated that "when they entered upon their duties as recruiting officers as aforesaid, they were instructed that the persons so enlisted would receive the same pay and allowances, that were or might be paid and allowed to other volunteers in the Military service of the United States." Until May 1864, the U.S. government paid the regiment's enlisted men ten dollars per month, three dollars of which had been deducted for clothing, leaving the troops with barely half of the rate white Union soldiers received for the same work and risks. The petition concluded,

> Wherefore in view of the above facts we would respectfully request: that in accordance with Sec. 5, Act of Congress, Approved March 3th [sic] 1865, an order be issued directing the Pay Department to cause the enlisted men of said regiment, enlisted as aforesaid, to be paid the same pay and allowance paid and allowed, to other regiments in the U.S. service at and during the period, dating from the date of their original enlistment to include the 30th day of April 1864.[36]

The July 1865 petition to the War Department failed. The Bureau of Colored Troops replied that the creation of the First Kansas Colored Infantry "did not emanate from the sources specified in the Act of Congress herein cited, and the payment request cannot, therefore, under existing law, be ordered."[37] James Lane's extralegal efforts to put black men into uniform in Kansas hung like a pall over the regiment.

As summer ended, the federal government finally relieved the First Kansas Colored Infantry from duty. In Pine Bluff, Arkansas, on October 1, 1865, the War Department officially mustered out of federal service 23 officers, 97 noncommissioned officers, and 401 privates.[38] Except for one officer and three men on detached service, one private from Company I serving time in a military prison, and a few other men convalescing in hospitals, those 521 soldiers comprised all that was left of the 1,505 men who had served in the First Kansas Colored Infantry's ranks over its three years in existence, marking an attrition rate of more than 60 percent.[39] At least 232 died, deserted, or were discharged in 1862 before official muster. They are not included on the official roster of the *Adjutant General's Report of the State of Kansas*. According to the official roster, 93 enlisted men and officers were discharged for various reasons (most often illness or disability) between January 1863 and October 1865. Sixty-five men deserted, never to return. The regiment lost 172 men to disease, fatal accidents, or other non-combat-related deaths. Twenty men who had been mustered in, or enlisted late in the war, disappeared from the rolls without adequate explanation or accounting. And 174 men were killed in action or died from wounds received in action.[40]

In a war in which three out of four deaths occurred from disease, the First Kansas Colored Infantry defied the odds. According to available records, it lost more men to bullets and shell fragments than to sickness.[41] The First Kansas Colored's high rate of combat loss is clear when compared to the wartime total of black battle fatalities. Of the approximately 180,000 African American soldiers who served during the Civil War, 2,751 were killed in battle or died of wounds.[42] The First Kansas Colored Infantry soldiers made up less than 1 percent of the total number of black Union soldiers in service, but suffered 6 percent of total black combat fatalities.

For the most part, the regiment's losses were spread evenly throughout the companies. Based on statistics covering soldiers in the regiment between January 1863 and October 1865, the average company lost 17.2 men to disease or lethal accidents; the highest was Company D, with 23 men, and the lowest Company K, with 8. Except for especially high numbers in Companies G and I, each company lost an average of 4 men to desertion.[43] Company G bucked the trend, with 20 men, while Company I followed with 13 desertions. Discharges within companies ranged more widely. Company A recorded only 3 discharges, while 16 men were discharged from service early in Company F. Finally, until September 1864, the ravages of combat had culled the First Kansas Colored Infantry ranks fairly evenly. Each company lost an average of 14.1 men killed in action by summer 1864. Then the massacre of Company K at Flat Rock Creek occurred. As a result, that company ended the war having sustained 46 men killed in action—a statistic nearly double the number of Company K men who died of disease, deserted, or were discharged.[44]

Shortly after muster out, the men boarded the steamboat *Prairie Rose* for transportation to Kansas and full discharge. They arrived in Leavenworth, where three years before the city's mayor had labored to break apart their organization by arresting its members and encouraging them to desert. Now, as combat veterans, victorious in war, the men marched down the streets of Leavenworth with pride and were greeted with applause by the black residents. The procession halted at a large church, where it was greeted by local officials who heaped praise on the regiment.[45] The keynote address was delivered by John H. Morris, a prominent African American resident who had served as an officer in the Kansas Colored Militia, which helped repel General Sterling Price's Confederate threat to Kansas in 1864.[46] He had "been delegated by the colored citizens of Leavenworth to express to you their joy at your return home safe from the dangers and vicissitudes of the war, and to return to you their thanks for your long and gallant services in defence of the government." He spoke at length, proclaiming to the soldiers before him that "it has been your fortune—and it will be a lasting title of renown—to have borne an honorable and conspicuous part in the greatest civil war recorded in history."[47]

Morris summarized the great social upheaval brought by four long years of open conflict. "At the commencement of this war, few anticipated the great and momentous changes so soon to be wrought by it," he said. Indeed, at the start of the war, white men,

eager for glory and greedy for honor, disdained the proffered services of the colored man. At first they would not even allow him to drive a wagon in the train of their army. Nay, more, they would not allow him to wear the cast off clothing of their soldiers, lest the imperial blue of the republic should be desecrated and dishonored. It was under these circumstances—filled with insolence and pride—that the Northern Army, in obedience to the cry of "On to Richmond," marched to plant their standard on the walls of Richmond.

Humiliations at Bull Run and then in Virginia tempered this enthusiasm and elevated anxiety among white Northerners, he explained. Even when the bonds of white supremacy weakened and the federal government opened the door slightly for black service, "the government could not entirely emancipate itself from the hateful spirit of caste. Still awed by the traditions of the past, it had not the courage to say, 'We want you to fight in defense of the life of the nation'; but they said, 'We want you as laborers, and for your better organization and control, we will enroll you in companies, and embody you into a regiment, and for your protection we will arm you.'" Morris stated, "It was by this sneaking, back-door arrangement, that you were smuggled surreptitiously into the service of your country."[48]

Morris reviewed the First Kansas Colored Infantry's battlefield success at Island Mound, Cabin Creek, and Honey Springs. He spoke of the bravery and tragedy at Poison Spring:

> You have returned victorious—proud of dangers past, of many toils cheerfully borne, and of honorable scars bravely won. You return with your standards, but their starry fields and silken folds are no longer bright and untarnished. They are begrimed and torn; but they have been begrimed by the smoke of battle, they have been rended by the balls of the foe. You have borne those banners proudly aloft, full in the front of battle. You have encircled them with a wall of living fire. You have hedged them about with gleaming bayonets. You have carried them amid the din and wreck of battle far into the ranks of the foe, where the steel flashed brightest, and the Angel of Death reaped his harvest of men as the reaper reapeth the grass.[49]

Morris reminded his audience that "you have not been the only men of our race who have won renown in this war." Nearly 180,000 black Americans helped the Union army defeat secession. So, he asked, "what is to be their future political status? Are they to enjoy the full fruition of so many toils, of so much valor and devotion, or shall they still remain aliens in the land of their birth?"[50] Morris demanded the right to vote and equal citizenship with whites. He recognized that many white Northerners, as well as the conquered Southerners now regaining their full place within the Union, opposed racial equality. Andrew Johnson, having taken the helm as president following Abraham Lincoln's assassination, appeared increasingly soft on the former secessionists. By the late summer of 1865, many former Confederate communities instituted strong restrictions against newly freed slaves. Black Codes in states like Mississippi required African Americans to have written evidence of annual employment and mandated that blacks remain within their work contracts on punishment of loss of wages already earned and possible arrest. Vagrancy was punishable by virtual enslavement on plantations, and blacks faced restrictions on property ownership and rental.[51] With this oppression looming, Morris exclaimed, "As a reward for our services in the cause of the nation, it is proposed in re-constructing the lately rebellious States, to hand the colored people over to the tender mercies of the late rebels, to the end that they may vent their baffled rage and spite upon the poor negro. Such an arrangement would nullify the Emancipation Proclamation, and practically re-enslave the black population of those States." But he professed confidence in the Republican Party, which "sustained the war [and] will make good the pledged faith of the nation, and preserve its honor unsullied." He added, "The North needed and used the black men of the South in this war. Let them not delude themselves with the idea that they no longer need them."[52]

As a final political thought, Morris addressed the issue of colonization, or relocation of freed slaves from the United States to a colony in Africa or Central America. The idea was impractical, he argued—an impossibility. Yet, more importantly, he voiced the thoughts of millions of African Americans, including the black Kansas veterans before him: "We don't want to leave this country, and we don't intend to do it. If we had no other reason, we would not go, because our enemies want us to go. There is an old axiom that bids you not to do that which your enemies want you to do. We intend to remain here, because this is our country, though like an unkind step-mother, she would spurn us from her bosom; still she is our mother."[53]

Morris looked over his audience and instructed them: "It should be your ambition to prove that you can be as useful in peace as you have been terrible in war. You have, by your courage, branded as a lie the assertion that black men were cowards. Now, by morality, industry and economy, brand that other lie that negroes are vicious, lazy and improvident." He echoed a message of responsibility with their new freedom, care with their earnings, and dedication to their hard-fought political responsibilities. Morris predicted a glorious future ahead:

> Then, the Republic, unvexed by internal dissensions, reposing on a broad and enduring base of equal and exact justice to all men, baptized anew in the fountain of liberty, and regenerated with that life-giving principle, will go on to the completion of her noble destiny,

and live in coming ages the wonder and admiration of the world, surpassing in glory and grandeur all that is told of the past, all that we behold in the present, and all that the brightest visions of the future disclose.[54]

When the speeches were complete, the veterans of the First Kansas Colored Infantry Regiment—the first black regiment to see combat during the Civil War and the first raised in a Northern state—enjoyed a feast provided by the people of Leavenworth. As the soldiers enjoyed the celebration, they knew that within hours the regiment would forever disband, leaving each man alone to continue the struggle for freedom and equality in American society.

EPILOGUE

The veterans of the First Kansas Colored Infantry helped end slavery in the United States. Their choice to fight in war opened a new path in life. Yet their future with freedom was not free from racial discrimination. White communities in the North and South still denied many African Americans equal rights and privileges. Nonetheless, freedom from slavery offered many of these veterans the power, for the first time, to determine their destiny. Bondage had denied them property ownership, the choice of occupation, and even the right to marry. The veterans looked forward to new opportunities, but with an air of uncertainty. Would they be able to reunite with families? How would they make a living? Where could they start a new life?

Unfortunately, there are few primary sources to tell the story of First Kansas Colored Infantry soldiers' postwar lives. I have reviewed some two hundred pension files of the regiment's veterans at the National Archives. Within some pension folders, one may find priceless documents, written long after the war by the veterans, as well as by pension officers, families, friends, and even former slave owners. They offer us a glimpse of the challenges these veterans faced.

For many, the first priority was to reunite with wives and children. Regimental documents did not record marital status, but, according to pension records, a significant number of First Kansas Colored Infantry soldiers were single during their service. For the married men, the strain of wartime separation was compounded by the fear that slave owners might sell family members during the soldier's absence. In the nineteenth-century South, while white families followed patrilineal customs—where the father stood at the center of the family—slave families often centered on the mother.[1] This matrilineal custom among slaves was due not to negligence by slave fathers but to circumstance. Male slaves were often separated from their families. Southern state law did not recognize slave marriages. Consequently, when a female slave gave birth, the father had no legal rights over the child. Slave codes across the South endorsed matrilineal customs among African Americans through laws dictating that a child inherited the racial and slave status of the mother. These codes were contrary to English common law, which all American states except Louisiana had adopted.

Slave owners benefited from this system by encouraging female slaves to have children, thereby increasing the value of their slaveholdings. The matrilineal practice protected white supremacy by ensuring that offspring of female slaves and white fathers were themselves regarded as slaves. If the Southern states recognized patrilineal inheritance of race and status among slaves, such children would be free and "white." Technically, Southern communities restricted all interracial sexual relations. However, white officials often proved selective in enforcing such codes, vigorously prosecuting African American men found with white women, yet ignoring instances of their white peers engaging in voluntary or forced sex with slave women. Determining a slave child's status through the mother afforded slave owners larger profits from slave births and greater leeway from their peers in regard to sexual activity with slaves, all at the expense of African American men and women.[2]

For the veterans of the First Kansas Colored Infantry, these customs hindered the reunification with loved ones. Yet, through remarkable resiliency, many black soldiers did reunite with their family. First Sergeant Clement Johnson of Company F enlisted in 1862 after receiving Captain Ethan Earle's promise of help in finding Johnson's wife and daughter. He had last seen them in Tennessee. The regiment never reached Tennessee; it got no closer than northern Arkansas. But that was enough. According to Captain Earle:

> When our Regiment arrived at Fort Smith, about the first colored people we met were his wife and daughter of this man. They heard in Tennessee that a Colored Army was coming down from Kansas. They procured passage in a government Steamer to Fort Smith, from there he procured conveyance in a govt. train to Leavenworth where I saw them after the war, happy in the enjoyment of their freedom. Mr. Johnson remained with the Regiment to the close of the war; then joined his family in Leavenworth.[3]

Inspired by the Emancipation Proclamation in January 1863, Nicholas Taylor left his wife Julia and their four children in Missouri with the promise of returning for them after joining the army.

He fulfilled that promise shortly after enlisting in the First Kansas Colored Infantry, only to find that two of his children had been whisked away by their master. Taylor rescued his wife and remaining children and settled them in Leavenworth before rejoining the regiment. After the war, when he reunited with his wife, Taylor found the family complete. His wife had managed to locate the two enslaved children and had brought them to Kansas.[4]

Growing up a slave to Harvey Gleanes near Lexington, Missouri, Benjamin Carter met a young slave girl named Catherine a few miles down the road at Squire Walton's farm, and the two fostered their relationship as well as slaves on different plantations could manage. They married in the fall of 1861. "We were married by old Uncle Jerry, an old colored man owned by Walton," Catherine said. By September 1862, Carter was in Leavenworth, Kansas, joining the First Kansas Colored. "I had one baby by Carter and it was still a small baby when he went into the army," Catherine later said, but "the baby died during the time of the war."[5] After his discharge, Carter returned to Missouri and formally married Catherine under the new Missouri Constitution.[6]

Long before the war Jeffrey Markham of Company E had been a slave to Paul Choteau in Indian Territory and married to a fellow Choteau slave. Since slave marriages had no legal standing, their marriage ended when Choteau sold Jeffrey to Leroy Markham in 1855. At the Markham residence, Jeffrey met and married Harriett.[7] Harriett Markham followed her husband to war, serving as a cook and laundress for the regiment. Her presence may have saved his life when his health failed in 1864. "I was with my husband Jeffr[e]y Markham with the Regiment . . . in the spring of 1864," she later said, "and my said husband contracted disease of Liver in line of duty and continued to suffer with said disease while in camp at Little Rock Ark[ansa]s in the spring 1865 and in August and September while at Pine Bluff A[rkansas]." When officers ordered Markham to report to the hospital for treatment, Harriet "asked the commanding officer for the care of my husband and he gave me leave for the care of my said husband."[8] Markham survived his illness and the war.

While the families of white soldiers agonized over possibility that their fathers, brothers, and husbands would succumb to disease or fall in battle, black family members bore the added burden that their soldiers expected far worse treatment if captured. The vengeful execution of wounded men at Poison Spring made widows of women like Susan Newby, whose husband Private Silas Newby fell there. Susan had married Silas at her owner's house in 1859 and the couple had two children before his death in 1864. She filed for a pension shortly after the war. Testifying on her behalf for the pension was Hector A. Chinn, her former owner.[9]

The war ended other marriages, but not always through death. Moses Jenkins fled slavery and joined the military following the sale of his wife. He had been the property of a man named Ruby in Independence, Missouri, and married to another of Ruby's slaves, Harriet. Early in the war, according to a friend, Harriet "was disposed of to a slave trader by the name of Porter and was taken south."[10] The forty-two-year-old Jenkins walked away from his master when Union troops passed through Independence a short time later.[11] He followed them out of Missouri and traveled to Lawrence, where he found recruiters for the First Kansas Colored Infantry and a place in Company G.[12] In December 1864, while at Fort Scott for medical treatment and light duty, Private Jenkins married a woman named Annie. He was discharged for disabilities a few months later, and the couple moved to Lawrence. In 1866, Harriet traveled to Lawrence. When she learned that Jenkins had remarried and was determined to stay with his new wife, Harriet returned to Independence, Missouri, and also remarried.[13]

Green Craig of Company B had been a slave in Holden, Missouri, and married to Fannie, the slave of another master. The couple had a daughter when he escaped to fight in the war. He returned to Holden after discharge to learn that his wife and daughter had been sent to Texas by their master to keep them from Union lines and emancipation. He heard that Fannie had remarried in Texas. With nothing to hold him to Missouri, Craig moved to Kansas and eventually married a woman named Maria, whose own first marriage had ended through wartime separation. Maria had been among the thousands of slaves who fled to Kansas from Arkansas during the war. Her first husband, Jack Jenkins, had encouraged her to "come with the others and he said he would come as soon as he could, but he never came here." Wishing to stay in Kansas, and believing that Jenkins had abandoned her, Maria married Craig. When asked about her first husband's fate, she replied simply, "The last I heard of him he was still living at Van Buren, Crawford Co., Ark."[14]

Other soldiers in the First Kansas Colored Infantry simply chose not to reunite with the women they left behind. Alfred Alexander left a wife and five children when he joined Company A in August 1862. He never returned to the family, choosing instead to marry another woman in Wyandotte, Kansas, in 1866. Both women filed widow pension claims after he died.[15]

Squire Creecy lived with a slave woman named Clarinda in Greenton, Missouri, before he escaped and joined the service in Kansas in 1863.[16] Although they belonged to different masters who lived three miles apart, the two managed to maintain a steady relationship.[17] "I do not know about their marriage but suppose they were married after the fashion in slavery time," a friend and former slave stated.[18] In 1864, while serving with Company K during the regiment's time in Fort Smith, Private Creecy came across a friend, Margaret Collins. The two had been owned by the same master in Missouri and by chance had reunited in Arkansas. Margaret's first husband had fled slavery for Canada, while she had been sent to Arkansas by her master and eventually freed. Private Creecy married Margaret at Fort Smith, the service conducted by a black preacher in a formal church. Clarinda, back in Greenton, never remarried.[19]

George Shields's story followed a similar pattern, with a twist. Before the war, Shields was committed to Letty Robinson, a slave on a neighboring farm. "George W. Shields and I lived together as man and wife before the war when we were very young but our masters would not let us marry," Letty recalled. "We continued to live together as husband and wife until he went into the army." Shields served as a noncommissioned officer in Company C through the regiment's entire service. Rather than return to Letty, Shields married a woman named Henrietta White. Letty did not remarry, but she did not give up on Shields. When Henrietta died, George and Letty reunited, moved to Wyandotte, Kansas, and, finally, were formally married. They lived together until he died in 1909.[20]

Most veterans of the First Kansas Colored Infantry sought a new place to live. Many of them, especially those who enlisted in 1862, had run away from the only communities they had lived in. Some settled in distant places. Company C's First Sergeant, Henry Davis, had been sold as an infant and taken from Tennessee to Missouri. "Neither my parents nor my brothers or sisters accompanied me to Missouri," he later said, "and I have never known anything about my relations."[21] By the late 1890s he was living in Colorado, and in 1903 he died in the National Military Home in California.[22]

Daniel Campbell moved to North Dakota after a few years in Kansas. Joseph Simpson lived in California and New Mexico. Edward Clark lived in Seattle and Denver. Charles Houston settled in Colorado, and Adam Spencer chose Illinois.[23] James W. Wells, who had adopted the alias Silas Hughes in the service, lived in Atchison, Kansas, until he married in 1871. He and his new bride moved to Minnesota. In 1889, William H. Smallwood, who had served as captain of Company G, moved to Anoka and found his fellow First Kansas Colored veteran Wells serving as a doorman to the Minnesota House of Representatives. Wells spent the rest of his life in Minnesota, dying in 1920.[24]

Soldiers who joined the regiment in Indian Territory and Arkansas often returned to their prewar communities. Harriett Markham, who had nursed her soldier husband in Arkansas, applied for a widow's pension long after the war. Testifying on her behalf was the son of her former owner, who explained to a pension officer in 1891, "After the war [Harriett and Jeffrey Markham] returned here and lived together as man and wife until Jeffrey died some ten or twelve years ago."[25] Giles Gully and Samuel Miller were among a handful of men who had joined the First Kansas Colored Infantry in Camden, Arkansas, only days before the battle at Poison Spring. Both men mustered out with the regiment, and both chose to reside in Arkansas. Gully stated that after being discharged in Leavenworth, he promptly turned around and "came to Little Rock Ark. & settled 12 miles from town and remained there ever since in Ashley Township."[26]

According to available records, a significant proportion of the veterans from Missouri settled in Kansas. Harrison Miller joined the regiment after running away from Lexington, Missouri, and chose Leavenworth after the war.[27] Jeremiah Fielding had been a slave near St. Joseph, Missouri. After the war, he spent three years in Douglas County, Kansas, before settling in Wyandotte, Kansas, for the remainder of his life.[28] Philip Dudley of Company B lived in several Kansas towns—first Emporia, then Ottawa, and finally Council Grove.[29]

Private Jackson Donald was another ex-slave from Missouri who settled in Kansas after the war. He had tried to enlist under his master's family name (Donnell) because he did not know his father's last name. "My father was known as James, as a slave," Donald told a pension officer, "and as well as I remember my father was sold to a man named Walker, down near Lexington Mo, when I was not more than four years old." After his discharge, Donald lived in Leavenworth. In 1866 he attended a celebration in Quindaro, Kansas. There he met his father, nineteen years after their forcible separation. His father's name was James Gorl. "He told me that he took the name Gorl from the name of his father's master back in North Carolina, and who owned him before he came into possession of Rob[ert]t Donnell," Donald recalled. Two years later, Donald moved to Quindaro to be closer to his father. In 1908 Donald told a pension officer that his father "asked me to change my name from Donald as I had it in the army to Gorl, his name. I told him I saw no reason for so doing and would keep my name as it was." But several years later, Donald explained, he changed his mind. "I received a letter some time ago from father stating that he had made his will," he said, "and had willed nothing to Jackson Donald but had willed something to Jackson Gorl, and if I would change my name as indicated I would get what he had so willed me. Otherwise I would get nothing. Hence I took the matter up with the Pension Bureau to change my name as a pensioner from Donald to Gorl. This is the only reason I have or ever had for the change of my name as indicated."[30]

Wherever they settled, many veterans brought with them physical and emotional scars from hard service in the ranks. Disease, injury, and combat wounds wrecked men who had entered the military in excellent physical shape. Private John Bean returned to his home near Vinita in Indian Territory carrying buckshot in his lower leg. "He was a great dancer before the war," his friend Simon Lynch remembered, "and after he came home I had a party at my house & I wanted him to dance & he told me that his dancing was over on account of a wound in the ankle which was done at Poison Springs in a fight when on the Camden Raid under Gen Steele."[31] Like many of his fellow veterans, Bean had been a laborer. Now he and his comrades found themselves newly freed citizens struggling to make ends meet with broken bodies.

"I was never sick before I enlisted," William Gordon, formerly a private in Company E, stated after the war; "at any rate I don't remember that I was. I did not have any doctor treat me during the five years before I enlisted." Indeed, his physical conditioning and endurance as a young man in 1862 had been so remarkable that despite a severe whipping by his master's half-brother only weeks before his enlistment, Gordon had escaped slavery and withstood

the physical hardships of military life for months with few problems. Even though a bullet at Honey Springs destroyed two of his
teeth, Gordon remarked, "My general health was good until the
summer of 1864." He developed a mysterious soreness in his eyes
during the Camden Expedition, and by the summer of 1865 his
body was wracked with illness. He spent his last few weeks with
the regiment in a hospital gripped with pain from diarrhea and suffering through bouts of malaria-based delirium. "I wasn't able to do
any hard work when I was discharged and I have never been able
to do any hard work since then," he explained to a pension officer
years later.[32]

Joseph Bowers fled slavery and joined the regiment with his
friend Dock Williams. He described a similar decline in health from
his military service. "Up to the time of my enlistment, I never knew
what sickness was," Bowers said.[33] Williams corroborated the claim,
noting that he had heard both of their owners before the war "boast
of [Bowers's] value as a chattel on account of his physical sound-
ness."[34] Poor conditions around Fort Scott in 1863 and a shard of
Confederate artillery shell, which shattered the toes on one foot
in 1864, sent him home a crippled man. Bowers spent his first few
months after discharge cared for by friends and family. Years later,
a fellow veteran attested to a pension official, "There has not been
hardly a month or week but that I haven't seen him and his condition. He's always about the same only growing a little worse."[35]

Private John Smith's misstep into a vat of boiling brine in 1864
disabled him for years. In 1866 a pension officer reported that the
twenty-four-year-old veteran "has been a patient as a dependent
freedman in the U.S. Hospital for Refugees & Freedmen at Little
Rock Ark having been unable to fill any occupation."[36] Two years
later, his situation had not improved. A physician attested that
Smith was totally disabled, still showing "several ulcers on each
foot & leg, with large cicatricis marking the places where others
have been."[37]

The most common affliction suffered by First Kansas Colored
Infantry veterans was rheumatism, a diagnosis that covered a variety
of joint, muscle, and bone ailments during the Civil War. Symptoms
varied from sharp pains to soreness, but generally amounted to stiff-
ness and aches. Sergeant Isaac Alexander, whose trip across an ice-
filled river in Arkansas led to a serious leg injury, stated to a pension
officer in 1895, "I have suffered from rheumatism of left leg ever

since my discharge."[38] He relied on a crutch or walking sticks for the remainder of his life. The pain in Corporal Jack Costin's arm and shoulder from a bullet wound at Poison Spring was diagnosed as rheumatism.[39] Private Harrison Miller blamed rheumatism for soreness in his back.[40] And Private William Turner's rheumatism followed meteorological patterns. "Every two or three weeks when damp weather came, I would have rheumatism on up to date of discharge," he told a pension officer. "It continued about the same in service, but now the older I get, it gets worse."[41]

Hernias were common. Cyrus Bowlegs found that hard marching and strain from his cartridge box and belt irritated a previously benign bump near his waist. By late 1863, "the pain in my back and groin got so bad and the lump in my right groin got so large and painful that I went to Dr. Harrington, the Reg[imen]t[a]l Surg[eon] and he examined me and told me I was ruptured and was not fit to march or do any other duty."[42] The regiment discharged Bowlegs that December. In 1888, the injury became the basis for his pension application. Officials wanted to determine whether the injury was in fact related to his military service. His boyhood friend William Noble wrote on his behalf: "I have seen him stripped for ball playing or swimming many times more than I can recall," Noble attested. "He was a sound man in every way up to the time he enlisted and had no injury whatever or I would have known of it." Noble verified Bowlegs's injury on account of his own hernia. "I was ruptured myself during the Seminole War and have worn a truss since 1842," he declared. When Noble saw Bowlegs after his discharge,

> he complained of pains in his back and groin but I did not pay any attention to it. . . . After we refugees moved back to the Seminole Country one Sunday about 1867 he complained so much more than usual of this pain that came on him in the U.S. Service I told him that it was perhaps similar to my own case, that he should come with me and strip and I would examine him. We went a short distance from the church and stripped. I first showed him where my injury was then I felt of him carefully until I found the place and pointed it out to him telling him he was ruptured and that he must wear a truss afterwards.[43]

Though generally afforded better food and subjected to less strenuous labor in the service, some of the regiment's white officers too ended the war with permanent injuries. Captain Shebua Creps of Company F suffered a severe chest and lung ailment in the after-math of Poison Spring. The regiment's surgeon later attested that he had found Creps "sitting on a log wholy [sic] exhausted" during the retreat and had carried him on his own horse until out of danger. "The next day," the doctor continued, "I treated Creps for pain in the chest or lungs."[44] Two months later he was in the Fort Smith hospital for "disease of the lungs." Creps managed to stay with the regiment until it mustered out, but his health never fully recovered. He died in 1886 from lung and throat disease, likely related to his wartime illness.[45]

Discussions of Civil War medical treatment must include a reference to amputation. The heavy lead musket balls and jagged iron shards of Civil War cannon shell ripped and shattered legs and arms, often leaving little hope of reconstruction. Wounded flesh, infected with debris, often turned gangrenous. Amputation—cutting off the damaged area in hopes the wound would heal more cleanly—became a common practice in Civil War medicine. Union medical officers recorded almost 30,000 amputations during the Civil War. Of those, over 21,000 patients survived. Confederate amputations may have reached as high as 25,000.[46]

Following major battles, amputations created a hellish scene at field hospitals. One man at a surgical tent at Gettysburg later remarked that "the pile of arms and legs placed there like a pile of stove wood, would have filled a wagon bed."[47] Surprisingly, few First Kansas Colored Infantry soldiers underwent amputation. Of all the ailments, wounds, and injuries described in the pension records and the regiment's medical records, only one soldier appeared to have undergone a battle-related amputation. First Sergeant Randolph Morgan's left elbow was shattered by a Confederate bullet at Poison Spring. Ironically, it appears that his arm was amputated by a Confederate physician. A document in his service record states that he was captured while suffering in a hospital in Camden and includes the notation, "Wounded left elbow amp. May 25."[48]

Charles Anderson of Company F lost a finger to combat, but the removal apparently was completed by the bullet. Describing his wartime injuries to pension officials, he explained that the pinky finger on his right hand was "shot off" during the war, but he did not describe a formal amputation.[49] Private Fox Holt did undergo a medical amputation, but of toes that had already "sloughed off" from frostbite. The physicians removed small portions of the exposed bones to aid in healing.[50]

Wilbert Lindsey underwent an amputation due to a gangrenous bullet wound, but *after* the war. Lindsey had served in Company G from February 1863 to October 1865 and left the service in good health. Less than a year later, in June 1866, while working as a deck-hand aboard a steamer in Kansas City, Lindsey and friends ventured into town. The group passed by an African American–owned saloon in an alley near Main Street. They "noticed that there were a number of colored men in the saloon," Lindsey later recalled, "and as they were talking and laughing and apparently having a pleasant time we stopped in and I sat down on a chair about fifteen feet back from the door." He had just gotten comfortable when a bullet smashed through the saloon wall, striking him in the leg "about four inches below the knee passing through the leg and out through the opposite side of the building as I was informed the next morning." Lindsey, two colleagues, and the saloon owner soon found themselves the only men in the bar as everyone else fled in panic. Helped by his friends back toward the boat, Lindsey passed out after limping fifty yards. His friends dragged him back to the saloon, "where the proprietor made me a bed on the floor and I staid there that night."[51] Over the next few weeks, friends cared for Lindsey as doctors monitored the wound. He remembered that the weather "was very hot and the wound soon got bad and after a while mortification set in," leading a team of doctors to amputate the limb just below the knee.[52] Though he lost half of his leg, Wilbert Lindsey survived and became one of the longest-living First Kansas Colored veterans, dying in 1936 at well over ninety years of age.[53]

Almost all of the veterans found sufficient means of income after the war.[54] Most became farmers or laborers. "When I was first discharged I did as much work at my trade as anyone could do," stated George Washington, who had served in Company K. "I quarried rock some of the time. I consider I did as much work from the time I was discharged until about 1886 as any man could do."[55] Henry Holmes, formerly of Company K, eventually found work at Beaver Canyon, Idaho, hauling timber.[56] Edmund Prater, a large man who was described by several friends as having "a most peculiar walk" in which he "walked 'slew footed' [and] turned his feet out nearly straight," to the point where he "walked nearly on his ankles," worked in a stone quarry and brickyard around Lawrence, Kansas, following the war.[57] Men with more severe disabilities sought less strenuous occupations. "Since discharge my occupation has been that of a porter or deliveryman for grocery stores," Joseph Bowers told a pension officer.[58] A friend testified to Bowers's work ethic in the face of disabilities from wartime service: "I have seen him driving a delivery wagon when he was hardly able to get on his wagon."[59]

Other black veterans pursued more specialized work. Carr Taylor served as a Baptist preacher when he was not making money sawing wood.[60] John W. Smith, the Black Hawk Indian from Canada, also found a career as a minister (supplemented by labor activities), variously living in Missouri, Texas, and Arkansas.[61] Though in poor health, William Gordon managed to secure permanent employment in 1881 as a cemetery sexton in Paola, Kansas. "I used to do light work and since I became sexton I have not tried to do any hard work," he later said. "I nearly always hire someone to dig the graves."[62] And Moses Holt, formerly a private in Company E, became the operator of a billiard hall in Fort Scott, Kansas.[63]

Few First Kansas Colored Infantry veterans remained in military service. Pension files indicate that only one enlisted man served in the U.S. Army after the Civil War. Samuel Davis, who had been a private in Company K, reenlisted in 1866. From that period to 1880, Davis served in Company G of the Thirty-Eighth United States Infantry and Company C of the Twenty-Fourth United States Infantry, part of that time as the principal musician in the regimental band.[64] On the other hand, several white officers of the regiment continued military service after the war, including Lieutenant Colonel Richard Ward, Captain John Graton, Captain Elkannah Huddleston, and Captain Benjamin Jones.[65] The regiment's first commander, James M. Williams, had the most notable post–Civil War military service. He had risen to the rank of brevet (or honorary) brigadier general of volunteers during the Civil War. During the postwar drawdown of federal military forces, he received an appointment of captain to the Eighth U.S. Cavalry in the regular army. Williams served bravely in the West during military battles with Native Americans, receiving a brevet promotion to major in 1867 for "conspicuous gallantry displayed in engagements with Indians on the Verde, Arizona."[66]

Whatever occupation the veterans chose, and wherever they settled, a reality all had to face, in some form, was lingering beliefs in white supremacy. Almost two centuries of race-based slavery had buried perceptions of race deep into American society. Prejudice against black Americans remained prevalent across much of the United States, particularly in the former Confederacy. Andrew Jones and General Dudley, two former enlisted men, worked together on the steamboat *White Witness* on the Missouri River around 1870. According to Dudley, before one voyage "the Captain of the boat hired about three Irishmen to one colored man on that trip and I was afraid there would be a row on that trip." He warned Jones against joining the crew. Jones brushed him off and set off on the steamboat. "When the boat returned to Leavenworth Ks. from her trip to Fort Bent," Dudley later said, "I went down to the landing and met the boat, and the first thing I heard after the boat landed was that Andy Jones had been cut to pieces with a hatchet by the Irish deckhands." The fight left him with severe wounds to his arms, shoulder, and belly. Dudley remembered that "his entrails were out and had to be pushed back and the wound of [the] stomach sewed up."[67] Jones somehow survived his wounds.

The veterans who moved farther west may have sought communities with less established racism. A few veterans avoided whites by moving deep into Indian Territory. Cyrus Bowlegs, who had been raised a slave among Seminole Indians, never gained a mastery of the English language. He spent the remainder of his life among the Seminoles and their former slaves.[68] Late in his life, former Company I soldier Bully Connell lived on a remote farm around Muskogee, in the Creek Nation. A friend remarked that Connell "lived in the back woods [and] would have no transaction with white men." Later, a pension official reported that Connell's widow Mary was a very old Indian woman with limited English and who practically refused to see any white people.[69]

Most veterans managed to live, even thrive, in multiracial communities after the war. They interacted with whites and Indians, showing no animosity for previous events. Several pension applications included supporting testimony from former masters or their family members. Some veterans even testified in support of former owners who applied for compensation for the loss of slave property during the war. Congress passed laws in 1864 and 1866 that offered financial compensation to loyal citizens whose slaves served in the federal army during the Civil War. Slave owners were to receive three hundred dollars for slaves who enlisted, and one hundred for slaves who were drafted.[70] The application required that a former slave owner provide proof of loyalty during the conflict and evidence of ownership of the black soldier at the time of his enlistment. The former masters of 185 First Kansas Colored Infantry soldiers from Missouri filed paperwork for compensation in 1866 and 1867. Proof of loyalty came most often in the form of oaths and supporting testimony from established officials. Occasionally the applicant provided wartime documents attesting to loyalty. For instance, Isaac Peace, former owner of John Burton from Company B, attached a permission slip he received from Union authorities in May 1864 to carry a firearm.[71]

Several applications included a purchase receipt for the slave. "Know all men by the presents that J. J. Shelby have this day sold J. H. Peacock a negro boy named Gabe age about Twenty one years old," began the 1851 bill of sale for Gabriel Clark, who eventually served in Company K. Peacock bought Clark for nine hundred dollars.[72] When former owners could provide no receipt of slave purchase, they described the circumstances of ownership. Edward Dobson, the former owner of Manuel Dobson—who had been seriously wounded at the skirmish at Island Mound—declared that "the mother of said Manuel Dobson belonged to the claimant, and the said Manuel Dobson for whom Compensation is claimed, was born the property of said Edward M. Dobson."[73] Harrison Miller appeared before a notary public on behalf of his former owner Washington Johnson for compensation.[74] Miller and fellow veteran George Shields also supported Johnson's compensation application for former ownership of Thomas Cheek of Company C.[75] Efforts by former slave owners in Missouri to obtain federal compensation for black military service proved fruitless. In 1867, a Republican-dominated Congress ended the program before money had been allocated.[76] The compensation applications now sit unpaid in First Kansas Colored Infantry personnel files at the National Archives in Washington, D.C.

Several veterans of the First Kansas Colored Infantry had not received pay or benefits for service before the January 1863 muster. Twenty-five years after the regiment disbanded, James Williams traveled to Washington, D.C., to lobby on behalf of his former black soldiers. Through his work, on September 23, 1890, Congressman Ormsby Thomas of Wisconsin, from the Committee on War Claims, recommended to Congress the passage of bill S. 2471, which recognized the service of First Kansas Colored Infantry soldiers at the battle of Island Mound.[77] The bill requested payment to the veterans and families of men killed during the skirmish, "the sums which would have been due had their original muster been regular." The bill credited the First Kansas Colored Infantry with influencing "President Lincoln in issuing his proclamation of New Year's Day, 1863, which put in force the provisions of the act of July 17, 1862, and forecasted the freedom and citizenship of persons of African descent." It concluded with the message, "They fought to sustain the nation; the nation can not afford to withhold payment for the time they were in the ranks doing duty, whether the muster, concerning which they had neither knowledge nor control, was regular or irregular."[78] On March 3, 1891, the bill became law. It read in part, "Be it enacted by the Senate and House of Representatives of the United States of America in Congress assembled, That all officers of the First Kansas Colored Volunteers who were mustered into the service of the United States on or before the second day of May eighteen hundred and sixty-three, shall take rank and be entitled to pay from the date when they respectively held and performed the duties of their rank in said regiment." The law also named eight men killed and six men wounded at Island Mound for federal recognition and benefits.[79]

On October 7, 1890, Williams returned to Kansas from his lobbying efforts in Washington, D.C. He arrived in Leavenworth, where "a large contingent of old colored soldiers met him at the depot and escorted him proudly up to his hotel." Through the rest of the day, according to a city newspaper, "he was besieged by those anxious to again look into his honest, loving face. It was a general love feast as it were, and greatly revived the loyal feelings of old times." That evening, veterans of the First and Second Kansas Colored Infantry regiments held a reunion in Leavenworth. The festivities began with music and celebration. A band played "Marching through Georgia" to the boisterous approval of the congregated veterans. Old officers of the First Kansas Colored Infantry walked onstage, including Elkannah Huddleston, Daniel McFarland, and William Matthews.

At 8 P.M., the meeting was called to order. Matthews, the black officer denied a commission in Company F in January 1863, was unanimously elected chairman. He stood before the assembly:

> I say to you we have several here who have proved themselves gallant soldiers. We have here Col. Williams, that gallant man who was the first to lead black boys in blue in times of this country's

greatest peril. We have here a lieutenant colonel who did some
fighting, and whose gallantry the colored people have not forgotten. Colonel J. M. Williams was the hero of the First colored regiment; Col. Crawford was the colonel of the Second and Third
colored regiments.

He continued: "The men who will speak to-night will tell you
about these regiments. In referring to this matter I will simply say
before I introduce to you one whom I have not words to eulogize,
and I doubt whether there is a representative from this state who
is able to express to you the merits which belong to the gallant
Colonel Williams." Matthews told the crowd, "Colonel Williams,
in company with Colonel Anthony, two old veterans[,] made it possible that you and I are sitting here to-night."[80]

Williams took the floor. The applause from the gathering shook
the hall for "fully a minute before the audience qui[e]ted sufficiently
to listen to the speaker." Once able to speak, he recounted the prejudice the regiment faced in the same city over two decades earlier.
"I tried to do my duty, and as I say, in the organization of colored
troops in Leavenworth," he said. "We had the evil authorities all
against us and I believe to-day there are four indictments on file
against me in the court house for enlisting colored troops. I consider them papers of honor." They had tried to arrest him, Williams
declared, "but I did not fear them. I would do it again."[81]

Recounting victory in battle, Williams turned to his recent time
in Washington:

> On investigating the records of the war department I came upon
> the records of the different regiments in the United States service.
> I found that there is not on file a single regiment that begins with
> the record of the old First Kansas. The records there show that you
> lost more men in proportion to the number enlisted than any regi-
> ment in the United States service of any color. The records show
> that you lost more men in a single engagement in proportion to the
> number enlisted than any regiment in the United States service.
> The records show that your conduct, whilst it was brave in the
> field, in camp it was with respect to all. You received many com-
> pliments on your behavior and were always in the front rank. The
> records show that you had the respect of the rebel army.

Unfortunately, the records were not complete. During his visit
to Congress, Williams learned that the action at Island Mound was

not recorded at the War Department. Through his efforts, "the report of that action is now on file, and is a part of the public records of the country." Similarly, although he had submitted a full account following the battle at Poison Spring, "they had no report of it at the war department. Neither did they have on file a report of that terrible engagement at Jenkins Ferry." But, he told the veterans, "I found it out and these reports are now there and made a part of the history of our country."[82]

Williams beamed at the sight of his old command:

> I am so proud to meet so many of these men who took up their muskets in the war; and of those who started in with the old First Kansas regiment and went through with me. Some of them went through with many wounds and others by luck came out as strong as when they entered the service, and many of them now live in Kansas with free homes and are well to do and are influential men and good citizens.

He stated confidently, "From all I can hear those who were discharged have settled in Kansas and have become good citizens." He concluded his speech with the promise that "when I can favor my old soldiers I will do it cheerfully."[83]

Other notable white and black figures spoke to the crowd as well. At the end of the evening, a resolution committee presented to Williams a message of thanks. Representing "some ten different regiments, of infantry, cavalry and artillery, to-night to shake hands with one of the old vanguards of freedom and equal rights both political and civil," the assembly praised Williams, "who by inclination and position gave to the people of these United States a demonstration of the fact, new only to this generation, that soldierly courage, daring and fortitude is not wanting in those of the class of people whose only vocation for two hundred years was the hewing of wood and drawing of water."[84]

Before the presentations ended and the assembly enjoyed the feast before them, the resolution concluded with a simple but heartfelt recognition of Williams and the First Kansas Colored Infantry regiment:

> and while all men of all the various commands did well their part—to the commander, officers and men of the 1st Kansas Colored belongs the honor being in the van and of influencing the immortal Lincoln in bringing about the freedom of our race.[85]

A Note on Sources

"Surely no other chapter of modern history has been so faith-fully or so elaborately recorded by ordinary men and women," Henry Steel Commager wrote; "in the American Civil War Everyman was, indeed, his own historian."[1] Historian Randall C. Jimerson noted that, "separated from home and family, virtually every soldier wrote frequent and informative letters or recorded daily observations in private diaries."[2] Historians have enriched books and articles about the Civil War with poignant firsthand accounts of men and women who lived it. Yet there is a notable deficiency of black American voices. For many modern readers, and still some historians, the Civil War is mostly a white man's war. This is not to say that historians or readers fail to recognize that the conflict was directly tied to slavery, or misperceive the significance of the war on race relations. Rather, the absence of African American perspectives leads often unwittingly to a treatment of them as objects within historical writing, not subjects.

There are two reasons for this deficit. First, the traditional approach to history focuses on leaders, seeing politicians, generals, and wealthy businessmen as the shapers of society. African Americans and other minorities, including women, are often ignored or at least marginalized. This problem, fortunately, is largely a relic of the past. Indeed, black veterans and historians, and some white ones too, championed the African American story of the Civil War shortly after its conclusion. For instance, Joseph T. Wilson, a veteran of the Second Louisiana Native Guards and the Fifty-Fourth Massachusetts, published *The Black Phalanx*, a comprehensive review of black Civil War service, in 1890. W. E. B. DuBois, one of the leading black scholars of the late nineteenth and early twentieth centuries, challenged traditional views of African American history and, in particular, Reconstruction through his own scholarship. Unfortunately, these works were largely passed aside by leading scholars as covering a niche topic. During the mid-twentieth century, in conjunction with the civil rights movement, scholars increasingly saw African Americans, American Indians, women, other minorities, and even poor whites as important players in history—as factors who shaped cultures, economies, ideologies, and societies. The establishment of the GI Bill also helped break down traditional historical scholarship by introducing a new and wider demographic of students to historical study. An increasing number of black students entered universities, and history programs were infused with white students from laboring and middle-class families. Many of these students, including Dudley Taylor Cornish, author of the 1956 book *The Sable Arm: Black Troops in the Union Army, 1861–1865*, approached historical study "with less of an elitist-oriented methodology."[3] Historians since the 1950s have continued this trend.

The second reason for the deficiency in African American voices of the Civil War may be found in the scarcity of primary material. Historical sources dictate the telling of the story as well as the topic. A friend once asked why so many Civil War books and documentaries include statements from Mary Chesnut, the wife of a South Carolina politician during the war. "Was she important?" he asked. "Yes," I replied, "at least in that she has given historians a great deal to work with." Chesnut kept detailed diaries, filled with commentary. Her writing provides Americans 150 years later with insight to her time, her life, and her culture. We do not find this type of primary material from most black soldiers, especially among the mostly fugitive slaves west of the Mississippi River. A few eastern black regiments, like the Fifty-Fourth Massachusetts Infantry, had well-educated and active writers in their ranks. Thus the story of black Civil War soldiers tends to come from, and be about, these few regiments.

While writing *Soldiers in the Army of Freedom*, my goal was to place as much emphasis as possible on the enlisted men. Finding their voices proved challenging. The white officers of the First Kansas Colored Infantry left a great number of letters, photographs, and personal stories. I mined those sources for valuable descriptions of the regiment's common experience, while attempting to keep the officers' personal stories from dominating the narrative.

Perhaps letters and diaries are tucked away in family archives somewhere, but none of the descendants of enlisted men I talked to had such sources to share. My hopes faded even more as I found in military service files a steady stream of enlistment forms signed with a simple "X." Almost all of the enlisted soldiers were illiterate. As a result, much of the material I initially gathered gave details *about* the men, but not *from* them. Information from muster roll cards, medical cards, arrest orders, assignment orders, and casual mention in the letters and memoirs of white officers provided bits and pieces of their stories, but little to help us understand the men as individuals.

This changed some when I turned to pension records. From these dusty old files, in first-person narrative, were stories of combat, marching, slavery, friendship and marriage, pain and pleasure. Here the details of life emerged. Men who could not write sought pension officers or local officials to transcribe their verbal accounts. Widows detailed relationships and memories of husbands and children, telling of life before emancipation and of reunification after the war. Two pension files had photographs, providing a glimpse at the faces of two men among hundreds of names on the roster. The photographs were of aged veterans, not the young men who served in the war. But they were First Kansas Colored Infantry soldiers.

The pension files came with their own problems. Most of them had scant information that was useful for a historical narrative. Few soldiers provided information about their lives. In some cases the written accounts contained little more than a list of ailments blamed on the war. Moreover, these accounts were recorded long after the events in question. They do not disclose the real-time hopes and fears of soldiers in the middle of a campaign or fresh off the battlefield. They are stories of men looking back, benefited by hindsight, and generally telling only what they thought was important for receiving financial assistance.

And this leads to my greatest concern regarding the pension documents. Created and filed with the government to justify monetary compensation for wartime injuries and ailments, the pension files offer a skewed look at military service. I found myself excited at the details within the files, but realized that those particulars were most often depressing. Sickening wounds, debilitating injuries, life-changing illness—the pension files show these once proud soldiers as broken men. I worried that heavy usage of these documents would imbue the entire book with a dismal or disheartening tone.

As I considered this problem, an important thought came into view—it was war. The First Kansas Colored Infantry existed for three years during the United States' deadliest conflict. The regiment took part in several significant engagements, in some of the toughest terrain and weather in the United States, and filled their time with a great deal of manual labor and a poor diet. The pension files may be grim, but so were the soldiers' experiences. Overall, I attempted to provide balance by using the pension files to humanize the story, while not overburdening the reader with misery.

Perhaps letters, diaries, and memoirs of black Kansas soldiers will emerge from attics and closets as time passes on. If so, we may hope that families share them and offer the eager students of history new voices to hear.

Comprehensive Roster of the First Kansas Colored Infantry, 1862–1865

The following roster is a comprehensive list of individuals known to have served with the First Kansas Colored Infantry between 1862 and 1865. It was compiled through a comparison of the official roster printed in the Kansas Adjutant General's Report for the regiment and the Compiled Service Records of the Seventy-Ninth USCT (New) (formerly First Kansas Colored Infantry) at the National Archives and Records Administration, Washington, D.C.

The Kansas Adjutant General's Report roster only includes soldiers who were officially mustered into federal service. The Compiled Service Records at the National Archives include information on those soldiers as well as basic enlistment information for over 230 individuals who enrolled in the regiment but failed to muster in (often for reasons not recorded).

It is important to note that several discrepancies exist in the roster and within the compiled records due to inconsistent name spellings, incomplete records, faulty record keeping during the Civil War, and other various factors. For instance, several soldiers were transferred to different companies, particularly during the early months of the regiment's existence. As such, the Adjutant General's Report and Compiled Service Records include several duplications, often with variations in spelling. I have done my best to avoid duplications of names and to spell both personal names and place-names as they are given in the written records. The roster includes the individual's name and available information regarding age, residence or birthplace, date he enlisted or joined the regiment, and brief comments regarding his fate or when he left the regiment.

Field and Staff

Name	Joined	Remarks
Colonel James M. Williams	1/13/63	Mustered out 10/1/65
Lt. Colonel John Bowles	1/13/63	Mustered out per Special Order No. 335, dated 6/1/65
Lt. Colonel Richard G. Ward	—	Mustered out 10/1/65
Adjutant Richard J. Hinton	1/13/63	Promoted Capt., Second Kansas Colored Infantry, 10/21/63
Adjutant William C. Gibbons	1/27/64	Mustered out 5/15/65
Quartermaster Elijah Hughes	1/13/63	Mustered out 10/1/65
Surgeon J. Fulton Ensor	11/1/64	Mustered out 10/1/65
Surgeon Samuel Harrington	1/15/63	Resigned 1/26/64
Asst. Surgeon Chauncey S. Burr	4/23/65	Mustered out 10/1/65
Asst. Surgeon Elias G. Macy	1/26/63	Resigned 6/15/65
Asst. Surgeon Abijah D. Tenny	5/2/63	Resigned 7/20/64
Chaplain George W. Hutchinson	5/2/63	Resigned 6/18/64
Sgt. Maj. Stephen B. Smith	8/9/62	Mustered out 10/1/65
QM Sgt. Henry Clay	8/9/62	Mustered out 10/1/65
Commissary Sgt. Stephen Berry	1/13/63	Reduced to ranks, Co. E, 3/13/65
Commissary Sgt. Robert Cox	9/15/62	Reduced to ranks, Co. B, 8/25/65
Commissary Sgt. Orin Miller	9/7/62	Mustered out 10/1/65
Hosp. Steward Robert Gibbons	11/9/63	Discharged 6/29/65 for disability

Company A

Name, Age, Residence	Joined	Remarks
CAPTAIN		
Huddleston, Elkannah Clinton, Kans.	5/2/63	Mustered out 10/31/65
Crew, Andrew	—	KIA Island Mound, Mo., 10/29/62
FIRST LIEUTENANT		
Jones, Benjamin G. Iola, Kans.	5/2/63	Promoted to Capt., Co. B, 2/11/65
Smith, William R.	4/22/65	Mustered out with regiment 10/1/65
SECOND LIEUTENANT		
Coleman, Ezekiel A.	1/13/63	Discharged per Special Order No. 90, War Dept., 1865 (left service due to severe hernia sustained at Cabin Creek; War Dept. updated his record to honorable discharge in 1887)
Lewis, Mellen	—	No evidence of muster in
FIRST SERGEANT		
Smithering, Jordan, 24 N.C.	8/10/62	KIA Poison Spring, Ark., 4/18/64
Carras, Joseph, 24 Shelby, Ky.	8/9/62	Mustered out 10/1/65
SERGEANT		
Smith, George, 25 Ill.	8/9/62	KIA Roseville, Ark., 3/25/65
Legget, Dempsey, 25	8/9/62	Mustered out 10/1/65
Smith, William, 22 Lexington, Mo.	8/8/62	Mustered out 10/1/65
CORPORAL		
Berry, Wesley, 26 Washington, Ky.	8/7/62	Mustered out 10/1/65
Bland, Robert, 24 Monroe County, Ky.	8/7/62	Mustered out 10/1/65

Company A

Name, Age, Residence	Joined	Remarks
CORPORAL (CONT.)		
Bowles, Riley, 26 Mo.	8/13/62	KIA Poison Spring, Ark., 4/18/64
Edwards, Jacob, 22	8/7/62	KIA Poison Spring, Ark., 4/18/64
Greene, Bedford, 21 Mo.	8/15/62	KIA Baxter Springs, 10/6/63 (Co. books say killed at Poison Spring)
Gregg, John, 29	8/11/62	Died of flux, Little Rock, Ark., 6/27/65
Johnson, Elliot, 22 Lexington, Mo.	8/7/62	Mustered out 10/1/65
Lacey, Pleasant, 25 Mo.	8/10/62	KIA Poison Spring, Ark., 4/18/64
Powers, Richard, 25 Ky.	8/7/62	Mustered out 10/1/65
PRIVATE		
Alexander, Alfred, 25 Cooper County, Mo.	8/20/62	Mustered out 10/1/65
Andrews, Hugh	1/13/63	Died Ft. Scott, Kans., 1/30/63
Austin, Robert, 22 Burlington County, Va.	8/9/62	Mustered out 10/1/65
Bailey, Wesley, 19 Woodward County, Ky.	8/9/62	Mustered out 10/1/65
Bell, Walter	8/10/62	No evidence of muster in
Benton, John, 22 Mo.	8/10/62	KIA Poison Spring, Ark., 4/18/64
Blackwood, David	8/10/62	No evidence of muster in
Bolden, Peter	8/10/62	No evidence of muster in
Bowman, Williams, 22	8/8/62	Deserted Baxter Springs, C.N., 4/28/63
Bowers, Joseph, 21 Green County, Ky.	8/12/62	Mustered out 10/1/65

Company A

Name, Age, Residence	Joined	Remarks
PRIVATE (CONT.)		
Boyd, David	8/10/62	No evidence of muster in
Boyd, Parris	8/10/62	No evidence of muster in
Bright, Alfred, 24 Stanford, Ky.	8/12/62	Mustered out 10/1/65
Burton, John, 25 Mo.	8/10/62	KIA Poison Spring, Ark., 4/18/64
Butler, Richard, 30	8/6/62	Discharged 8/1/63 for consumption
Clay, Henry, 25 Lincoln County, Ky.	8/8/62	Mustered out 10/1/65
Colman, Moses	8/18/62	No evidence of muster in
Combs, James, 22 Mo.	8/12/62	Died, date unknown
Compton, Reed	8/10/62	No evidence of muster in
Davis, William, 21 Versailles, Ky.	8/8/62	Mustered out 10/1/65
Davis, Princeton	8/5/62	Died 5/16/63 of smallpox
Dodson, Solomon	8/10/62	No evidence of muster in
Donon, James	8/10/62	No evidence of muster in
Downing, James, 19 Winchester, Ky.	8/8/62	Mustered out 10/1/65
Dressing, Jerry, 25 Ky.	8/8/62	Mustered out 10/1/65
Edwards, John, 22 Mo.	1/13/63	Deserted Ft. Smith, Ark., 3/31/63
Ellis, John, 19 Winchester, Va.	8/9/62	Mustered out 10/1/65
Erving, James, 28	8/12/62	KIA Poison Spring, Ark., 4/18/64

Company A

Name, Age, Residence	Joined	Remarks
PRIVATE (CONT.)		
Erving, John, 19 Ky.	8/15/62	KIA Poison Spring, Ark., 4/18/64
Farral, Arron	8/10/62	No evidence of muster in
Fielding, Jerry, 27 Buchanan County, Mo.	8/9/62	Mustered out 10/1/65
Foster, Larkin, 20 Ky.	8/9/62	Mustered out 10/26/65
Foster, Solomon, 30	8/9/62	Mustered out 11/29/65
Fox, David, 25	1/13/63	Died Ft. Scott, Kans., 3/19/63
Freeman, Moses Jackson County, Mo.	8/14/62	Mustered out 10/1/65
Gregg, Henry, 22	1/13/63	Died Ft. Gibson, C.N., 7/22/63
Guest, Alfred, 25 Ky.	8/10/62	Died Pine Bluff, 9/22/65
Harvey, Franklin, 22	8/16/62	Died, date unknown
Henry, John, 21 Tenn.	11/8/63	KIA Poison Springs, Ark., 4/18/64
Howard, James	8/10/62	No evidence of muster in
Hurley, Thomas, 40	1/13/63	Discharged for disability Ft. Gibson, C.N., 10/13/63
Jackson, Henry, 24 Ky.	8/8/62	KIA Poison Spring, Ark., 4/18/64
Jackson, Joseph, 23	1/13/63	Died Ft. Gibson, C.N., 8/15/65
James, Sandford, 25	1/13/63	Died Ft. Scott, Kans., 3/21/63
Jenkins, Edward	10/8/62	No evidence of muster in
Jeremiah, Edward, 28 Mo.	8/20/62	KIA Poison Spring, Ark., 4/18/64

Company A

Name, Age, Residence	Joined	Remarks
PRIVATE (CONT.)		
Lasley, Aleck	4/16/64	Deserted 5/21/64, not mustered in
Lee, Giles	4/16/64	Deserted 5/21/64, not mustered in
Locherman, Henry, 19 Cleveland, Ohio	8/10/62	Mustered out 10/1/65
Mayo, William, 23 Prestonburg, Ky.	8/20/62	Mustered out 10/1/65
Merriman, Louis, 30 Richmond, Va.	8/12/62	Mustered out 10/1/65
Monan, Horace, 25 Clark County, Ky.	8/12/62	Mustered out 10/1/65
Myers, William, 28 Liberty, Mo.	8/10/62	Mustered out 10/1/65
Nelton, Isaiah, 20 Camden, Ark.	4/16/64	Killed Poison Springs, Ark.
Nolan, Henry, 37	1/13/63	Died Ft. Scott, Kans., 6/7/63
Oldham, John	8/10/62	No evidence of muster in
Parker, Nelson Shelbyville, Ky.	8/9/62	Mustered out 10/1/65
Parks, Joseph, 22 Morgan County, Mo.	8/9/62	Mustered out 10/1/65
Perry, Commodore	8/10/62	No evidence of muster in
Perry, Thomas, 25 Montgomery, Md.	8/9/62	Mustered out 10/1/65
Porter, Robert	8/10/62	No evidence of muster in
Pucket, Moses	8/10/62	No evidence of muster in
Rasmus, Jacob	8/17/62	Discharged 5/21/65 for rheumatism
Richardson, Hines	4/16/64	Deserted 5/21/64, not mustered in

Company A

Name, Age, Residence	Joined	Remarks
PRIVATE (CONT.)		
Russell, Charles	8/10/62	No evidence of muster in
Scott, Dock, 24 Leavenworth, Kans.	1/13/63	Died in Little Rock, Ark., 4/6/65, of disease
Sheldon, William, 25 Ft. Scott, Kans.	1/13/63	Died Baxter Springs, C.N., 6/3/63
Smith, Samuel, 20 Lynchburg, Va.	8/9/62	Mustered out 10/1/65
Snyder, Dabney, 22 Quincy, Ill.	8/8/62	Mustered out 10/1/65
Steele, David, 29 Warsaw, Ky.	8/19/62	Mustered out 10/1/65
Stone, Shelby, 22 Shelbyville, Ky.	8/16/62	Mustered out 10/1/65
Straws, Price	9/7/62	No evidence of muster in
Taylor, George	1/13/63	Died at Camp Henning, 1/22/63
Thomas, Henry, 22 Lexington, Mo.	8/14/62	Mustered out 10/1/65
Thornton, Joseph, 23 Henry County, Mo.	8/8/62	Mustered out 10/1/65
Walker, Henry, 23 Richmond, Va.	8/10/62	Mustered out 10/1/65
Walker, John, 26 Lexington, Mo.	12/20/62	Mustered out 10/1/65
Walker, William, 25 Layfayette County, Mo.	8/10/62	Mustered out 10/1/65
Ward, William, 19 Leavenworth, Kans.	8/14/62	Died, date unknown
Washington, Greene, 23	8/16/62	Mustered out 6/10/65

Company A

Name, Age, Residence	Joined	Remarks
PRIVATE (CONT.)		
Wasson, Allen, 22 Independence, Mo.	8/16/62	Mustered out 10/1/65
Wilkinson, Robert, 23 Mo.	8/9/62	KIA Poison Spring, Ark., 4/18/64
Woodrom, Benjamin, 20	—	Died Ft. Gibson 7/11/63
Wyatt, Richmond, 21 Mo.	1/13/63	Died Ft. Scott, Kans.
Young, Riley, 25 Ft. Scott, Kans.	1/13/63	KIA Sherwood, Mo., 5/18/63
ADDITIONAL ENLISTMENTS		
Black, Nathaniel, 19 Giles County, Tenn.	4/16/64	Mustered out 10/1/65
Blane, George Camden, Ark.	4/16/64	Died Ft. Smith, Ark., 7/12/64
Branch, Abram, 21 Lincoln County, Tenn.	11/30/63	Mustered out 10/1/65
Evans, Joseph, 23 Mo.	11/8/63	KIA Poison Spring, Ark., 4/18/64
Fields, William, 23 Platte County, Mo.	5/21/64	Died in hospital 9/7/65
Gidd, Huston, 22 Giles County, Tenn.	4/16/64	Mustered out 10/1/65
Gully, Giles, 20 Ala.	4/16/64	Mustered out 10/1/65
Gully, Isaac, 18 N.C.	4/16/64	Mustered out 10/1/65
Gully, Luke	4/16/64	Deserted 5/21/64, not mustered in
Gully, Paldo	4/16/64	Deserted 5/21/64, not mustered in
Magmar, William, 24 Jefferson County, Ark.	11/8/63	Mustered out 10/1/65
Melton, Isaiah, 20 Camden, Ark.	4/16/64	KIA Poison Spring, Ark., 4/18/64

Company A

Name, Age, Residence	Joined	Remarks
ADDITIONAL ENLISTMENTS (CONT.)		
Mitchell, George, 27 Md.	5/4/63	Mustered out 10/1/65
Newly, Joseph, 24 Portsmouth, Va.	4/22/65	Mustered out 10/1/65
Swink, Alfred	—	Died of disease, 5/64
Swink, Charles, 22 Walton County, Ga.	4/16/64	Mustered out 10/1/65
Yell, James Danville, Ark.	3/31/64	Died Ft. Smith, Ark., 10/22/64

Company B

Name, Age, Residence	Joined	Remarks
CAPTAIN		
Martin, George J. Atchison, Kans.	1/13/63	Resigned 4/10/64
Jones, Benjamin G., 27 Iola, Kans.	2/11/65	Mustered out 10/1/65
FIRST LIEUTENANT		
Dallas, Walter J., 21 Baldwin City, Kans.	7/12/65	Mustered out 10/1/65
Dickinson, Luther Atchison, Kans.	2/24/63	Resigned 9/65
Lyon, Joseph H.	—	No evidence of muster in
White, William G.	1/13/63	Resigned, Ft. Scott, Kans., 2/23/63
SECOND LIEUTENANT		
Topping, John	2/24/63	KIA Poison Spring, Ark., 4/18/64
SERGEANT MAJOR		
Smith, Stephen B., 34 Atchison, Kans.	8/9/62	Promoted to Sgt. Maj. 1/26/63

Company B

Name, Age, Residence	Joined	Remarks
FIRST SERGEANT		
Bassett, Newton, 27 Harrison County, Ky.	1/13/63	Mustered out 10/1/65
Whalon, John, 35 Liberty, Ky.	1/13/63	Mustered out 10/1/65
SERGEANT		
Cooper, Henry, 26 Shelbyville, Ky.	8/25/62	Mustered out 10/1/65
Holden, Peter	8/5/62	KIA Poison Spring, Ark., 4/18/64
Johnson, Henry, 23 Shelby County, Ky.	8/14/62	Mustered out 10/1/65
Warfield, Sampson	8/5/62	Killed during altercation with officer, 10/5/62
CORPORAL		
Brown, Hannibal, 22 Franklin, S.C.	8/14/62	Mustered out 10/1/65
Caston, Jack, 21 New Hanover, N.C.	8/11/62	Mustered out 10/1/65
Cox, Robert, 17 St. Louis, Mo.	9/15/62	Mustered out 10/1/65
Davis, Robert	1/13/63	Died Ft. Gibson, C.N., 8/3/63
Fisher, David, 23 Danville, Ky.	8/15/62	Mustered out 10/1/65
Foster, Samuel, 23 Johnson, Mo.	8/15/62	Mustered out 10/1/65
Houston, Charles, 22 Mo.	8/15/62	Mustered out 10/1/65
Parker, Albert, 21 Jackson, Ala.	8/15/62	Mustered out 10/1/65
Riggs, Benjamin, 20 Jackson County, Mo.	8/14/62	Mustered out 10/1/65
PRIVATE		
Adams, Edward Ft. Scott, Kans.	8/20/62	Died Jenkins' Ferry, Ark., 5/4/64

Company B

Name, Age, Residence	Joined	Remarks
PRIVATE (CONT.)		
Andrew, Burrill	8/5/62	No evidence of muster in
Armstrong, John	8/5/62	No evidence of muster in
Berry, John	8/10/62	No evidence of muster in
Berry, Lewis	8/10/62	No evidence of muster in
Biggerstaff, James	1/13/63	Died Ft. Gibson, C.N., 7/27/63, of disease
Blair, Emanuel	1/13/63	Died Ft. Scott, Kans., 3/27/63, of inflammation of the lungs
Bowles, Henry, 21 Cauper County, Mo.	9/1/62	Mustered out 10/1/65
Bowman, Benjamin Ft. Scott, Kans.	8/12/62	KIA Poison Spring, Ark., 4/18/64
Bradley, Squire	8/10/62	No evidence of muster in
Brown, Judd, 23 Shelby County, Ky.	8/13/62	Mustered out 10/1/65
Brown, Samuel, 26 Va.	5/5/62	Mustered out 10/1/65
Brown, William, 20	5/14/62	Died Ft. Scott, Kans., 3/6/65, of consumption
Burton, John, 23 Va.	8/17/62	Mustered out 10/1/65
Campbell, James, 21 Indianapolis, Ind.	8/9/62	Mustered out 10/1/65
Carey, Thomas, 24 Monroe County, Ky.	8/15/62	Mustered out 10/1/65
Caston, Abraham	1/13/63	Died Ft. Scott, Kans., 4/24/63, of typhoid fever
Clark, Alexander	1/13/63	Deserted Baxter Springs, C.N., 6/14/63

Company B

Name, Age, Residence	Joined	Remarks
PRIVATE (CONT.)		
Cooke, Thomas	8/10/62	No evidence of muster in
Corneal, George, 22 Fayette County, Ky.	9/15/62	Mustered out 10/1/65
Cox, Robert	9/15/62	Promoted to Cpl. 8/31/65, Regimental Command Sgt. 3/13/65
Craig, Green, 46 Lincoln, Ky.	9/15/62	Mustered out 10/1/65
Craig, Henry	1/13/63	Died Ft. Scott, Kans., 5/19/63, of disease
Debell, Henry, 19 Harrisburg, Ky.	9/15/62	Mustered out 10/1/65
Derrett, George	8/18/62	Died 3/1/63
Dickinson, Wesley	8/10/62	No evidence of muster in
Doan, Perry Ky.	8/9/62	Mustered out 6/3/65
Donald, Jackson, 19 Buchanan County, Mo.	8/15/62	Mustered out 10/1/65
Doxsay, Harrison	8/10/62	No evidence of muster in
Dudley, Philippi Lexington, Ky.	8/15/62	No evidence of muster out on file
Easly, David, 45 Halifax, Va.	8/15/62	Mustered out 10/1/65
Estus, William, 30 Clay County, Mo.	8/15/62	Mustered out 10/1/65
Fields, Henry	8/10/62	Deserted 9/62
Ford, Charles	1/13/63	Died Ft. Scott, Kans., 5/19/63, of disease
Franklin, William	1/13/63	Discharged Ft. Smith, Ark., 12/16/63, for disability

Company B

Name, Age, Residence	Joined	Remarks
PRIVATE (CONT.)		
Gains, Thomas	1/13/63	Discharged Ft. Smith, Ark., 12/16/63, for disability
Gains, William H.	8/2/62	Died Ft. Smith, Ark., 6/28/64, of dropsy
Generals, William, 24 Ind.	8/18/62	Mustered out 10/1/65
Hains [Harris], Elijah, 16 Jefferson City, Mo.	9/15/62	Mustered out 10/1/65
Hains, Harrison	1/13/63	Died Ft. Scott, Kans., 4/16/63, of suffocation of the lungs
Hamilton, Belle	8/10/62	No evidence of muster in
Hamilton, Henry	1/13/63	Died Ft. Gibson, C.N., 7/16/63, of disease
Hammond, Thomas, 20 Johnson County, Mo.	8/9/62	Mustered out 10/1/65
Hayden, Lawyer	8/10/62	No evidence of muster in
Hedgepath, Henry	8/10/62	No evidence of muster in
Howatter, Charles	8/10/62	No evidence of muster in
Hughes, Silas, 20 Shelbyville, Ky.	8/14/62	Mustered out 10/1/65
Jackson, Andrew	1/13/63	Died Ft. Scott, Kans., 3/26/63, of pneumonia
Jefferson, Benjamin	1/13/63	Discharged Ft. Smith, Ark., 12/16/63 for disability
Johnson, Louis	1/13/63	Died Ft. Gibson, C.N., 8/19/63, of disease
Johnson, Martin, 45 N.C.	5/5/62	No evidence of muster out on file

Company B

Name, Age, Residence	Joined	Remarks
PRIVATE (CONT.)		
Jones, Julius, 26 Bedford County, Va.	8/15/62	Mustered out 10/1/65
Jones, Thomas	—	Deserted 4/30/64, not mustered in
King, James, 26 Clinton, Mo.	8/5/62	Mustered out 10/1/65
Lawson, Henry, 18 Fleminsburg, Ky.	8/5/62	Mustered out 10/1/65
Lightner, Lewis	8/10/62	Died of typhoid 10/3/62
Mark, Vincent	1/13/63	Died Ft. Scott, Kans., 4/19/63, of typhoid
Matthews, Peter, 18 Shelby County, Ky.	8/15/62	Mustered out 10/1/65
Miller, Benjamin, 25 Ky.	8/16/62	No evidence of muster out on file
Miner, John, 16 Platt County, Mo.	8/27/62	Mustered out 10/1/65
McNeil, Robert, 15 Ark.	12/20/63	Mustered out Pine Bluff, Ark., 10/1/65
Murphy, John	1/13/63	Discharged Ft. Smith, Ark., 12/16/63, for disability
Nichols, Willis, 20 Ky.	8/15/62	Died Ft. Scott, Kans., of disease
Parker, Joseph	1/13/63	Discharged Ft. Smith, Ark., 12/16/63, for disability
Petty, Wesley	8/10/62	Rejected by surgeon
Price, James	8/10/62	No evidence of muster in
Prophet, Daniel S.	8/10/62	No evidence of muster in
Redman, James	8/10/62	No evidence of muster in

Company B

Name, Age, Residence	Joined	Remarks
PRIVATE (CONT.)		
Russell, Isaac, 26 Platt County, Mo.	8/15/62	Mustered out 10/1/65
Shepard, Allen H.	8/5/62	No evidence of muster in
Shepard, John A.	8/5/62	No evidence of muster in
Smart, Robert	8/10/62	No evidence of muster in
Smith, Isaac, 24 Ky.	8/18/62	Mustered out 10/1/65
Smith, Jerrett, 39 Garret County, Ky.	8/18/62	Mustered out 10/1/65
Smith, Newton	8/10/62	No evidence of muster in
Snead, George, 25 Ky.	8/9/62	No evidence of muster out on file
Stewart, Samuel	8/10/62	No evidence of muster in
Turner, Allen S., 19 Howard County, Mo.	8/15/62	Mustered out 10/1/65
Washington, George, 18 Pleasantville, Mo.	5/15/62	Mustered out 10/1/65
Washington, William, 23	—	—
Clinton County, Mo.	2/7/63	Mustered out 10/1/65
Wheeler, George, 38 Buchanan, Mo.	8/15/62	Mustered out 6/7/65
Whitaker, Charles	8/15/62	KIA Poison Spring, Ark., 4/18/64
Williams, Anthony	1/13/63	Died Ft. Scott, Kans., 4/10/63, of consumption
Williams, Dennis	8/18/63	KIA Poison Spring, Ark., 4/18/64

Company B

Name, Age, Residence	Joined	Remarks
PRIVATE (CONT.)		
Williams, Sampson	8/10/62	No evidence of muster in
Wilson, Dock, 35 Randolph, Mo.	8/15/62	Mustered out 10/1/65
Wilson, Jerry, 38 Howard County, Mo.	8/9/62	Mustered out 10/1/65
Wilson, Joseph	1/13/63	Died Ft. Scott, Kans., 3/23/63, of disease
Wines, Isaac	8/10/62	No evidence of muster in
Woods, Dee	8/10/62	No evidence of muster in
Woodson, Benjamin	8/10/62	Died of disease 7/11/63
Yount, Willis, 23 Jefferson City, Mo.	8/5/62	Mustered out 10/1/65
ADDITIONAL ENLISTMENTS		
Breedlove, Andrew Ft. Gibson, C.N.	5/27/63	Deserted Ft. Smith, Ark., 6/29/64
Campbell, Louis	10/21/63	Deserted Ft. Smith, Ark., 12/5/63
Clay, Henry, 24 Polk, Ark.	10/2/63	Discharged Little Rock, Ark., 5/24/64 for disability
Deer, August, 25 C.N.	5/27/63	Mustered out 10/1/65
Fine, Anthony, 25 Miss.	5/5/63	Discharged Little Rock, Ark., 5/24/64 for disability
Fox, Esan, 45 Fayetteville, Ark.	10/26/63	Mustered out 10/1/65
Hall, Caesar, 16 Scullyville, Choctaw N.	12/5/63	Mustered out 10/1/65
Hall, Jacob, 40 Humbo County, Ala.	5/27/63	Died Ft. Smith, Ark., 1/12/64, of pneumonia

Company B

Name, Age, Residence	Joined	Remarks
ADDITIONAL ENLISTMENTS (CONT.)		
Hall, William, 18 Scullyville, Choctaw N.	5/27/63	Mustered out 10/1/65
Jessie, Louis Ft. Smith, Ark.	10/21/63	Deserted Ft. Smith, Ark., 12/5/63
Johnson, Simeon Ft. Gibson, C.N.	6/1/63	KIA Poison Spring, Ark., 4/18/64
Lowry, Jesse Ft. Gibson, C.N.	6/1/63	Discharged Ft. Smith, Ark., 12/16/63, for disability
Martin, Jacob, 19 Ark.	10/3/63	Died Ft. Smith, Ark., 10/1/64, of disease
McGowell, James Ark.	3/1/65	Rejected Little Rock, Ark., by examining surgeon 6/2/65
McKinney, John Ft. Gibson, C.N.	5/27/63	Died Ft. Smith, Ark., of disease
McNeil, Robert	4/16/64	No evidence of muster in
Monroe, James	4/21/63	Died Ft. Smith, Ark., 11/15/63, of disease
Murray, Emmet, 19 Johnson County, Ark.	12/5/63	Mustered out 10/1/65
Rodgers, Jefferson, 27 Choctaw Nation	12/5/63	Mustered out 10/1/65
Taylor, Carr, 20 Mecklenburg, N.C.	4/23/63	Mustered out 10/1/65
Thompson, Jacob	10/21/63	Deserted Ft. Smith, Ark., 12/5/63
Walker, Samuel Pleasant Bluffs, C.N.	12/5/63	KIA Poison Spring, Ark., 4/18/64
Walker, William, 16 Pleasant Bluffs, C.N.	12/5/63	Mustered out 10/1/65
Washington, Charles	8/10/62	No evidence of muster in
Wilson, Robert, 19 Tahlequah, C.N.	5/27/63	Mustered out 10/1/65

Company C

Name, Age, Residence	Joined	Remarks
CAPTAIN		
Graton, John R., 27 Leister, Mass.	1/13/63	Mustered out 10/1/65
FIRST LIEUTENANT		
Sholes, Augustus T., 19 Green Bay, Wisc.	1/13/63	Promoted to Capt., Co. K, 7/21/65
SECOND LIEUTENANT		
Jackson, Alfred T., 20	8/18/63	Mustered out 10/1/65
Macey, Eberle Q. Harrison County, Ky.	5/6/63	KIA Timber Hills, C.N., 11/19/64
Welch, Benjamin W. Ft. Scott, Kans.	1/19/63	Promoted to Capt., Co. K, 5/2/63
FIRST SERGEANT		
Davis, Henry, 23 Tenn.	9/2/62	Mustered out 10/1/65
Dempsey, Archie, 26 Washington County, Va.	9/4/62	Deserted Ft. Scott, Kans., 5/1/63
Shields, George W., 25 Washington County, Va.	9/4/62	Mustered out 10/1/65
SERGEANT		
Bowler, James, 25 Fayette County, Ky.	9/2/62	KIA Poison Spring, Ark., 4/18/64
Strampkey, Sanford, 38 Tenn.	9/2/62	Mustered out 10/1/65
Williams, George, 24 Bedford County, Va.	9/2/62	Poison Spring, Ark., 4/18/64
CORPORAL		
Brown, Primus, 32	9/6/62	Died Ft. Scott, Kans., 4/1//63, of pneumonia
Campbell, David, 28 Wyandotte, Kans.	9/4/62	Mustered out 10/1/65
Dayton, Simon, 27 Wyandotte, Kans.	9/14/62	Died Ft. Scott, Kans., 1/27/63, of congestive fever

Company C

Name, Age, Residence	Joined	Remarks
CORPORAL (CONT.)		
Letcher, William, 24 Ft. Scott, Kans.	11/25/62	Died Baxter Springs, C.N., 6/6/63, of disease
McIntosh, Lewis, 22 Wyandotte, Kans.	9/22/62	Deserted Ft. Scott, Kans., 5/1/63
Moore, Davis, 23 Clay County, Mo.	9/14/62	Mustered out 10/1/65
Porter, Philip, 22 South Branch, Va.	9/2/62	Mustered out 10/1/65
Read, Joseph, 30 Boil County, Ky.	9/4/62	KIA Poison Spring, Ark., 4/18/64
Taylor, John, 26 Berkley County, Va.	12/28/62	KIA Poison Spring, Ark., 4/18/64
Young, John Fayette County, Ky.	9/4/62	KIA Poison Spring, Ark., 4/18/64
MUSICIAN		
Washington, Henry, 15 Cooper County, Mo.	11/25/62	Mustered out 10/1/65
PRIVATE		
Asberry, Henry, 30 Wyandotte, Kans.	9/6/62	Died Ft. Scott, Kans., 3/9/63, of consumption
Austin, Robert, 30 Ft. Scott, Kans.	12/30/62	Deserted Ft. Scott, Kans., 1/18/63
Barton, Thomas, 18 Layfayette, Mo.	11/25/62	Mustered out 10/1/65
Beal, Henry, 17 Clay County, Mo.	9/18/62	KIA Poison Spring, Ark., 4/19/64
Beal, Thomas, 16	9/14/62	Died Ft. Gibson, C.N., 8/20/63, of accidental wounds
Bradford, James, 54 Culpeper, Va.	9/6/62	Mustered out 10/1/65
Brooks, Alfred, 16 Lafayette County, Mo.	12/28/62	Mustered out 10/1/65
Burton, Thomas, 18 Lafayette County, Mo.	11/25/62	Mustered out 10/1/65

Company C

Name, Age, Residence	Joined	Remarks
PRIVATE (CONT.)		
Butler, Peter, 34 Va.	9/18/62	KIA Poison Spring, Ark., 4/18/64
Campbell, Charles, 18 Wyandotte, Kans.	10/1/62	Died Ft. Scott, Kans., 3/9/63, of pneumonia
Cheek, Thomas, 17 Layfayette County, Mo.	11/25/62	Mustered out 10/1/65
Childs, Isaac	8/7/62	No evidence of muster in
Christopher, Dennis	8/17/62	No evidence of muster in
Clay, Cassius M., 24 Jefferson County, Mo.	8/13/62	KIA Poison Spring, Ark., 4/18/64
Clemens, Hender, 20 Platt County, Mo.	10/1/62	Died Ft. Smith, Ark., 11/4/63, of pneumonia
Crenshaw, Robert, 24 Ky.	9/18/62	KIA Poison Spring, Ark., 4/18/64
Curry, David, 16 Layfayette County, Mo.	11/25/62	Mustered out 10/1/65
Curtis, Edward, 43 Mason County, Ky.	9/18/62	No evidence of muster out on file
Curtis, John, 40 Mason County, Ky.	10/1/62	No evidence of muster out on file
Duncan, Mance	8/25/62	No evidence of muster in
Edinston, Noble, 29 Marion County, Ky.	9/25/62	Mustered out 10/1/65
Edward, William, 24 Woodford County, Ky.	9/25/62	Mustered out 10/1/65
Elliott, Enos, 22 Woodford County, Ky.	9/4/62	KIA Poison Spring, Ark., 4/18/64
Fields, John, 19	9/12/62	Died Ft. Scott, Kans., 2/8/63, of pneumonia
Gilbert, William	8/11/62	No evidence of muster in

Company C

Name, Age, Residence	Joined	Remarks
PRIVATE (CONT.)		
Gilmore, Alexander	10/1/62	Died Ft. Scott, Kans., 1/9/63, of pneumonia
Gooding, Marcus, 30 Saline County, Mo.	1/7/63	Mustered out 10/1/65
Gray, Luke, 54 Chaptico, Md.	9/2/62	Mustered out 10/1/65
Green, Aaron, 19 Franklin County, Ky.	1/7/63	Mustered out 10/1/65
Green, Anthony, 35 Leavenworth, Kans.	12/28/62	Mustered out 10/1/65
Green, Brutus, 27 Pocahantas County, Va.	9/6/62	KIA Poison Spring, Ark., 4/18/64
Harrison, Peter, 20 Layfayette County, Mo.	12/28/62	Mustered out 10/1/65
Henderson, Doctor, 25 Layfayette County, Mo.	9/22/62	Mustered out 10/1/65
Henry, Patrick, 25 Otawah County, Va.	9/2/62	KIA Poison Spring, Ark., 4/18/64
Hill, Thomas	10/10/62	No evidence of muster in
Jackson, Andrew	8/9/62	No evidence of muster in
Jefferson, Thomas	8/7/62	No evidence of muster in
Johnson, William	8/6/62	No evidence of muster in
Johnston, William	8/6/62	No evidence of muster in
Jones, William H.	8/6/62	No evidence of muster in
Keen, Henry, 23 Woodford County, Ky.	12/28/62	Died Pine Bluff, Ark., 8/21/65, of remittent fever

Company C

Name, Age, Residence	Joined	Remarks
PRIVATE (CONT.)		
King, Isaiah	8/22/62	No evidence of muster in
Kinzie, Edward, 45	8/19/62	Mustered out 6/7/65
Lacey, Lewis, 23 Walden, Va.	9/22/62	Died Pine Bluff, Ark., 8/17/65, of typhoid fever
Lewis, Henry	8/18/62	No evidence of muster in
Lewis, John	8/8/62	No evidence of muster in
Long, Joseph, 17 Ft. Scott, Kans.	11/25/62	Died Ft. Gibson, C.N., 7/19/63, of wounds received in action at Honey Springs
Lovelace, George, 28 Barns County, Ky.	1/7/63	Mustered out 10/1/65
McMannus, George	8/9/62	No evidence of muster in
Merrill, James, 16 Layfayette County, Mo.	12/28/62	Mustered out 10/1/65
Miller, Harrison, 26 Madison County, Ky.	9/12/62	Mustered out 10/1/65
Moppin, Albert, 21 Ridgely County, Mo.	9/6/62	Mustered out 10/1/65
Morton, Richard, 23 Ft. Scott, Kans.	12/28/62	Died Ft. Gibson, C.N., 4/18/63, of inflammation of the stomach
Newberry, Silas, 26 Richmond, Va.	12/28/62	KIA Poison Spring, Ark., 4/18/64
O'Bannon, Hurley, 19 Shelby County, Ky.	9/2/63	Mustered out 10/1/65
Parker, Solomon, 40 Mason County, Ky.	9/12/62	Discharged Little Rock, Ark., 7/15/65 for disability
Peppins, Henry, 27	9/25/62	Drowned in Grand River, C.N., 7/17/63

Company C

Name, Age, Residence	Joined	Remarks
PRIVATE (CONT.)		
Peyton, Daniel, 23 Layfayette County, Mo.	9/2/63	Mustered out 10/1/65
Pierson, Henry, 21 Sullivan County, Mo.	12/28/62	Mustered out 10/1/65
Ramsey, Alexander	8/25/62	No evidence of muster in
Reed, Isaac, 25 Woodford, Ky.	9/25/62	Mustered out 10/1/65
Reynolds, John, 20 Platt County, Mo.	10/1/62	KIA Poison Spring, Ark., 4/18/64
Riley, George	8/9/62	No evidence of muster in
Rose, William, 17 Clay County, Mo.	9/14/62	Mustered out 10/1/65
Smith, John, 22 Sabine County, Mo.	11/25/62	No evidence of muster out on file
Speaks, John T., 15 Clay County, Mo.	9/14/62	Mustered out 10/1/65
Taylor, George, 36 Oldham County, Ky.	1/7/63	Mustered out 10/1/65
Thornton, Robert, 15 Jackson County, Mo.	9/9/62	Mustered out 10/1/65
Todd, Hazel	10/10/62	No evidence of muster in
Turner, Allen H.	8/9/62	No evidence of muster in
Van Buren, John, 21 Wyandotte, Kans.	9/9/62	Mustered out 10/1/65
Washington, George, 22 Wyandotte, Kans.	10/1/62	Died Ft. Scott, Kans., 2/15/63, of epilepsy
Watson, Joseph, 22 Richmond, Va.	11/25/62	Died Little Rock, Ark., 7/23/65, of fever
Williams, Alexander, 22 Conventown, Ky.	9/2/62	Mustered out 10/1/65

Company C

Name, Age, Residence	Joined	Remarks
PRIVATE (CONT.)		
Williams, Robert, 40 Ky.	9/25/62	Mustered out 6/7/65
Williams, Solomon, 25 Saline County, Mo.	12/28/62	Mustered out 10/1/65
Wilson, Joseph, 32	12/28/62	Deserted Ft. Scott, Kans., 1/18/63
Wood, Jordan, 24 Oldham Co., Ky.	9/2/62	Mustered out 10/1/65
Worthington [Washington], George C. Lincoln, Ky.	9/2/62	Discharged September 1865
Young, William	10/10/62	No evidence of muster in
ADDITIONAL ENLISTMENTS		
Dewly, Samuel, 21 Saline River, Ark.	4/29/64	Killed at Ivy Ford, Ark., 1/18/65
Goff, Elias, 39 Little Rock, Ark.	5/8/64	Mustered out 10/1/65
Jones, Harrison, 23 Saline River, Ark.	4/30/64	Mustered out 10/1/65
Norman, Amos, 21 Princeton, Ark.	4/28/64	Died Pine Bluff, Ark., 9/24/65, of congestive fever

Company D

Name, Age, Residence	Joined	Remarks
CAPTAIN		
Armstrong, Andrew J., 30 Emporia, Kans.	1/13/63	Mustered out 10/1/65
Matthews, William D.	8/?/62	African American officer, denied muster in
FIRST LIEUTENANT		
Copeland, H. E.	—	No evidence of muster in

Company D

Name, Age, Residence	Joined	Remarks
FIRST LIEUTENANT (CONT.)		
McFarland, Daniel D., 21 Minneola, Kans.	1/13/63	Resigned Ft. Smith, Ark., 7/20/64
McGinnis, James A., 27 Hartford, Kans.	2/20/65	Mustered out 10/1/65
SECOND LIEUTENANT		
Granville, Lewis M., 22 Elwood, Kans.	1/13/63	Promoted to Capt., Co. I, 2/11/65
Minor, Patrick H.	8/62	African American officer, denied muster in
FIRST SERGEANT		
Jones, Andrew, 26 Lafayette, Mo.	8/8/62	Mustered out 10/1/65
SERGEANT		
Benton, Thomas, 39 Ky.	8/8/62	Mustered out 10/1/65
Ridings, Henry, 24 Sabine County, Mo.	8/15/62	Mustered out 10/1/65
Strogdon, John	8/8/62	Died Roseville, Ark., 3/13/64, of disease
CORPORAL		
Carter, Robert Ft. Lincoln, Kans.	2/12/63	Died Camp Ben Butler, Kans., 5/12/63, of disease
Green, Charles, 25 Lafayette County, Mo.	9/15/62	Mustered out 10/1/65
Haden, Peter, 26 Ky.	8/8/62	Mustered out 10/1/65
King, Voltus, 23 Lafayette County, Mo.	9/15/62	Mustered out 10/1/65
Lemmons, John, 24 Buchanan County, Mo.	8/8/62	Mustered out 10/1/65
Rutherford, John, 27 Pa.	8/8/62	Mustered out 10/1/65

Company D

Name, Age, Residence	Joined	Remarks
CORPORAL (CONT.)		
Scott, Lewis	8/8/62	Died Camp Ben Butler, Kans., of diarrhea
Sinkler, William, 24 Ray County, Mo.	9/15/62	Mustered out 10/1/65
Washington, William	8/8/62	Died Roseville, Ark., of disease
Wesley, Charles Ft. Smith, Ark.	11/15/63	Died Ft. Smith, Ark., 2/21/65, of disease
MUSICIAN		
Craton, Madison, 21 Rock Island, Ill.	8/8/62	Mustered out 10/1/65
Isence, Rolla, 23 Ray County, Mo.	8/8/62	Mustered out 10/1/65
PRIVATE		
Allen, John, 23 Jackson County, Mo.	9/15/62	Mustered out 10/1/65
Allen, William, 27	8/8/62	No evidence of muster out on file
Armstrong, George M., 24 Clayton, Mo.	9/15/62	Mustered out 10/1/65
Ballow, Hankerson, 40 Madison County, Ky.	8/8/62	Died Little Rock, Ark., 1/27/65, of diarrhea
Barton, Isaac	8/17/62	No evidence of muster in
Baxter, Richard, 23	8/8/62	Mustered out 10/1/65
Briggs, Jackson, 19	9/15/62	KIA Poison Spring, Ark., 4/18/64
Brown, Isaac	8/17/62	No evidence of muster in
Brown, John, 1st, 27 Marion County, Ky.	8/8/62	Discharged Little Rock, Ark., 5/24/65, for disability
Brown, John, 2nd, 22 Platt, Mo.	8/8/62	Mustered out 10/1/65
Brown, John A., 33 Va.	9/15/62	Mustered out 10/1/65

Company D

Name, Age, Residence	Joined	Remarks
PRIVATE (CONT.)		
Brown, Rafe, 43 Logan County, Ky.	9/15/62	Discharged Little Rock, Ark., 6/21/65, for disability
Bushnell, Daniel	11/25/62	No evidence of muster in
Callaway, John W., 24	9/15/62	Died Tahlequah, C.N., of diarrhea
Carper, Martin	8/17/62	No evidence of muster in
Carter, John	8/17/62	No evidence of muster in
Cave, Joseph	8/26/62	No evidence of muster in
Clark, Elliot	8/17/62	No evidence of muster in
Clark, Squire, 25	8/8/62	KIA Poison Spring, Ark., 4/18/64
Cloud, Jeff, 26	9/15/62	KIA Poison Spring, Ark., 4/18/64
Coffey, Smith	8/17/62	No evidence of muster in
Colston, Edward	8/17/62	No evidence of muster in
Coons, Marshall	8/24/62	No evidence of muster in
Cooper, Johnson, 25 Marysville, Ky.	8/8/62	Discharged Little Rock, Ark., 6/21/65, for disability
Crittenden, John	8/24/62	No evidence of muster in
Daniels, John, 22 Lafayette County, Mo.	8/8/62	Mustered out 10/1/65
Davis, George, 20 C.N.	8/8/62	Died Ft. Smith, Ark., of diarrhea
Davis, Henry	8/24/62	No evidence of muster in

Company D

Name, Age, Residence	Joined	Remarks
PRIVATE (CONT.)		
Dean, Cale	8/17/62	No evidence of muster in
Doherty, Jerry	8/24/62	No evidence of muster in
Doherty, Vincent	8/24/62	No evidence of muster in
Emery, Adam, 22 Wamath County, Ky.	8/8/62	Mustered out 10/1/65
Farmer, Alphard	8/24/62	No evidence of muster in
Farrell, William, 23 Ray County, Mo.	8/8/62	Mustered out 10/1/65
Ferguson, Alfred	8/17/62	No evidence of muster in
Field, Willis	9/30/62	No evidence of muster in
Firstol, Perry	8/17/62	No evidence of muster in
Gibson, Joseph, 18	8/8/62	Died Ft. Lincoln, Kans., of disease
Glass, James	8/24/62	No evidence of muster in
Grant, Allen, 21 Lafayette County, Mo.	8/8/62	Mustered out 10/1/65
Grisby, William, 23	8/8/62	KIA Sherwood, Mo., 5/18/63
Hall, Isaiah, 33	8/8/62	Died Ft. Smith, Ark., 10/12/64, of disease
Hall, Jeremiah, 43 Burks County, Pa.	8/8/62	Mustered out 10/1/65
Harris, Robert H., 21 Lafayette County, Mo.	8/8/62	Mustered out 10/1/65
Hedgepath, Squire, 34	8/8/62	Died Ft. Smith, Ark., 12/6/63, of disease
Henderson, Edward	8/17/62	No evidence of muster in

Company D

Name, Age, Residence	Joined	Remarks
PRIVATE (CONT.)		
Hippie, Moses, 19	8/8/62	Died Ft. Smith, Ark., 2/21/63, of disease
Holmes, David	8/17/62	No evidence of muster in
Holton, Holt, 41	8/8/62	Died Camp Ben Butler, Kans., 5/12/63, of disease
Howard, Henry	8/20/62	No evidence of muster in
Hueston, Nathan	8/17/62	No evidence of muster in
Jackson, Emanuel, 20	8/8/62	Deserted Ft. Scott, Kans.
Johnson, James, 25	9/15/62	Deserted Ft. Scott, Kans.
Johnson, Richard, 26	8/8/62	Deserted Tahlequah, C.N.
Johnson, Thomas J., 21	9/15/62	Discharged Little Rock, Ark., 6/23/65, for disability
Johnson, William, 22	9/15/62	Died Ft. Lincoln, Kans., of disease
Kelly, James, 35	8/8/62	Discharged Little Rock, Ark., 5/24/65 for disability
Kerchibald, Alfred, 23 Buchanan, Mo.	8/8/62	Mustered out 10/1/65
Lee, Samuel, 29 Bourbon County, Ky.	8/8/62	Mustered out 10/1/65
Linn, Lewis	8/8/62	KIA Poison Spring, Ark., 4/18/64
Logan, Flem	9/30/62	No evidence of muster in
Marshall, John, 19	8/8/62	Died Ft. Lincoln, Kans., of disease
Mayo, Alexander, 19	8/8/62	Died Camp Ben Butler, Kans.

Company D

Name, Age, Residence	Joined	Remarks
PRIVATE (CONT.)		
McClure, Henry	8/17/62	No evidence of muster in
McGraw, Jesse	8/8/62	Died Camp Henning, Kans.
Merrill, Woodson	8/20/62	No evidence of muster in
Moore, Albert, 19	9/15/62	Died Ft. Gibson, C.N., of disease
Mosby, Winston	8/8/62	Died Camp Henning, Kans.
Mosby, Charles	8/24/62	No evidence of muster in
Oldham, Dock, 19	8/8/62	Died Camp Ben Butler, Kans.
Parks, Milton, 22	8/8/62	KIA Poison Spring, Ark., 4/18/64
Payne, Spencer, 22 Buchanan County, Mo.	8/8/62	Mustered out 10/1/65
Poster [Porter], Harrison, 22 Platt County, Mo.	8/8/62	Mustered out 10/1/65
Powels, Samuel	8/24/62	No evidence of muster in
Powels, William	8/24/62	No evidence of muster in
Prophet, Green	8/17/62	No evidence of muster in
Reynolds, George	8/24/62	No evidence of muster in
Rice, Daniel, 26	8/8/62	Died Ft. Lincoln, Kans., of disease
Ridings, James, 22 Indian Nation	9/15/62	Mustered out 10/1/65
Ridings, Montgomery, 20	9/15/62	Died Camden, Ark., 5/31/64, of wounds received in action at Poison Spring, Ark.

Company D

Name, Age, Residence	Joined	Remarks
PRIVATE (CONT.)		
Russell, Anderson	8/17/62	No evidence of muster in
Sanders, Henry	8/24/62	No evidence of muster in
Scantling, Junius	8/5/62	No evidence of muster in
Simpson, Calvin, 29	8/8/62	KIA Poison Spring, Ark., 4/18/64
Simpson, Jordan, 30 Va.	9/15/62	Mustered out 10/1/65
Simpson, Richard, 23	9/15/62	Died Ft. Lincoln, Kans.
Simpson, Robert, 31	9/15/62	Died Tahlequah, C.N.
Smith, Henry	8/24/62	No evidence of muster in
Stinman, Amos, 29 Jackson County, Mo.	8/8/62	Mustered out 10/1/65
Taylor, Henry, 23 Jackson County, Mo.	8/8/62	Mustered out 10/1/65
Taylor, Thomas	8/24/62	No evidence of muster in
Thrasby, Martin	8/24/62	No evidence of muster in
Thomas, Pendelton	8/17/62	Died of smallpox 12/28/63
Townsend, Austin	8/24/62	No evidence of muster in
Turner, William, 23 Platt County, Mo.	8/8/62	Mustered out 10/1/65
Van Buren, Martin	9/15/62	No evidence of muster in
Webb, George, 23	8/8/62	KIA Sherwood, Mo., 5/18/63
Wesley, John, 23 Ray County, Mo.	8/8/62	Mustered out 10/1/65
Wilder, Henry, 38 Owen County, Ky.	8/8/62	Discharged Little Rock, Ark., 6/21/65, for disability

Company D

Name, Age, Residence	Joined	Remarks
PRIVATE (CONT.)		
Wilson, Frederick	8/17/62	No evidence of muster in
Winfield, John	8/24/62	No evidence of muster in
Yocum, John, 28	8/8/62	Mustered out 10/1/65
Young, Lawson	8/10/62	Deserted, arrested 4/13/64, no discharge listed
Young, Thomas, 29	8/8/62	KIA Poison Spring, Ark., 4/18/64
ADDITIONAL ENLISTMENTS		
Bates, Dock, 38 Lawton County, Ala.	11/12/63	Mustered out 10/1/65
Davis, George C., 20 Ft. Gibson, C.N.	7/5/63	Mustered out 10/1/65
Ephraim, Daniel, 25 Washington, Ark.	4/8/64	Mustered out 10/1/65
Ephraim, Logan, 19 Tenn.	5/17/64	Mustered out 10/1/65
Ephraim, William, 27 Washington, Ark.	4/8/64	Mustered out 10/1/65
Francis, Cato, 45	9/15/62	Discharged Ft. Gibson, C.N.
Hedgepath, Willis, 29	—	Discharged Ft. Gibson, C.N., for disability
Hughes, Lewis, 29 Bourbon County, Ky.	8/8/62	Discharged Little Rock, Ark., 5/24/65, for disability
Martin, George, 20 Sebastian County, Ark.	11/29/63	Mustered out 10/1/65
McMurtry, Crayson, 18 Rome, Ark.	4/8/64	KIA Poison Spring, Ark., 4/18/64
Walker, John, 26 Bourbon County, Va.	2/10/64	Mustered out 10/1/65

Company E

Name, Age, Residence	Joined	Remarks
CAPTAIN		
Thrasher, Luther A., 26 Iola, Kans.	12/14/63	Mustered out 10/1/65
FIRST LIEUTENANT		
Bowton, Eli F., 32 Albany, Kans.	4/23/65	Mustered out 10/1/65
Gibbons, William C. Mound City, Kans.	1/13/63	Promoted to First Lt. and Adjt. 1/27/64
Overdear, John	1/13/64	Resigned 7/4/64
REGIMENTAL COMMAND SERGEANT		
Berry, Stephen, 28 Shelby County, Ky.	1/13/63	Mustered out 10/1/65
FIRST SERGEANT		
Nelson, John H. Mound City	8/9/63	Died Ft. Smith, Ark., 12/14/64, of typhoid fever
Reed, Harrison, 22 Mo.	1/24/63	Mustered out 10/1/65
SERGEANT		
Burgis, Charles, 44 Ala.	8/9/62	Mustered out 10/1/65
Carter, Moses, 27 Cherokee Nation	8/8/62	Mustered out 10/1/65
Gale, Hamlin Mo.	8/12/62	KIA Poison Spring, Ark., 4/18/64
Jackson, Isaac, 19 Mound City, Kans.	8/8/62	KIA Poison Spring, Ark., 4/18/64
Markham, Jeffrey, 23 Cherokee Nation	3/23/63	Mustered out 10/1/65
Riley, Abraham, 36 Ala.	8/28/62	Mustered out 10/1/65
CORPORAL		
Bean, George, 20 Cherokee Nation	1/19/63	Mustered out 10/1/65
Brice, Houston, 23 Mo.	8/9/62	10/1/65

Company E

Name, Age, Residence	Joined	Remarks
CORPORAL (CONT.)		
Harrison, Thomas, 20 Mo.	8/9/62	Died Ft. Smith, Ark., 11/17/64, of diarrhea
Hytower, Andrew, 26 Ky.	8/19/62	Mustered out 10/1/65
Lynch, Allen, 22 Cherokee Nation	1/24/63	Mustered out 10/1/65
Merrill, Dennis, 22 Mo.	8/28/62	Mustered out 10/1/65
Reed, Harrison Mound City, Kans.	1/24/63	Mustered out 10/1/65
Smith, Charles, 19 Mo.	8/12/62	Mustered out 10/1/65
Vann, Rufus, 41 Mo.	8/9/62	Died Little Rock, Ark., 2/21/65, of disease
Whittington, John, 41 Ky.	8/14/62	Mustered out 10/1/65
PRIVATE		
Adair, Amos, 35 Cherokee Nation	8/12/62	Mustered out 10/1/65
Adams, John	8/5/62	No evidence of muster in
Allen, Josiah	3/21/63	Deserted 5/4/63
Bean, Arthur, 19 Cherokee Nation	8/15/62	Mustered out 10/1/65
Banks, Howard, 28 Mo.	8/13/62	Mustered out 10/1/65
Berry, Rezine	8/5/62	No evidence of muster in
Brown, John, 22 Ft. Scott, Kans.	8/12/62	Mustered out 6/7/65
Bell, Moses, 18 Ft. Scott, Kans.	1/13/63	Died Ft. Scott, Kans., 4/29/63, of disease
Bannon, Shelby, 45 Lincoln County, Ky.	8/20/62	Discharged Ft. Scott, Kans., 8/11/64, for disability due to wounds received in action at Island Mound, Mo., 11/9/62

Company E

Name, Age, Residence	Joined	Remarks
PRIVATE (CONT.)		
Campbell, Manuel	8/5/62	No evidence of muster in
Carey, George, 18 N.C.	8/12/62	Mustered out 10/1/65
Carter, George	1/28/63	Rejected by surgeon 6/28/63
Clarke, Thomas	8/8/62	No evidence of muster in
Clay, Henry	8/6/62	No evidence of muster in
Cockerell, Edward, 20 Ft. Scott, Kans.	1/13/62	KIA Sherwood, Mo., 5/18/63
Craig, Jacob, 35	1/13/62	Died Ft. Gibson, C.N., 8/25/63, of disease
Davis, John, 18 Mo.	8/12/62	Mustered out detached roll, Leavenworth, Kans., 10/31/65
Dimmery, Ezekiel	8/5/62	No evidence of muster in
Duncan, Williams, 24 Harrison County, Ky.	8/15/62	Discharged Little Rock, Ark., 6/15/65, for disability due to wounds received at Poison Spring, Ark., 4/18/64
Field, Christopher	8/5/62	No evidence of muster in
Fields, Harrison	8/5/62	No evidence of muster in
Fisher, Edward, 18 Mo.	8/12/62	Mustered out 10/1/65
Fisher, John, 33 Va.	8/12/62	Mustered out 10/1/65
Fremont, Alexander	8/5/62	No evidence of muster in
Fugit, Harrison	8/6/62	No evidence of muster in

Company E

Name, Age, Residence	Joined	Remarks
PRIVATE (CONT.)		
Fulkinson, George	8/5/62	No evidence of muster in
Garth, Joseph	8/8/62	No evidence of muster in
Gordon, William, 18 Lafayette, Mo.	8/19/62	Mustered out 10/1/65
Gray, William	8/7/62	No evidence of muster in
Harris, Norman	2/2/63	Died 3/19/63
Hill, Jesse	8/6/62	No evidence of muster in
Holt, Moses, 18 Cherokee Nation	8/12/62	Mustered out 10/1/65
Homan, Thomas, 26 Shenandoah, Va.	8/20/62	Discharged Little Rock, Ark., 6/15/65, for disability
Huddleson, William	8/6/62	No evidence of muster in
Jackson, Henry, 21 Ft. Scott, Kans.	1/13/63	Died Ft. Gibson, C.N., 8/25/63, of disease
Jennison, Charles, 18 Mound City, Kans.	8/13/62	Discharged Columbus, Ohio, 8/5/65, per Special Order No. 421, War Dept.
Johnson, Henry, 20	8/12/62	Died Ft. Smith, Ark., 1/4/64, of disease
Johnson, David, 18	1/13/63	Deserted 12/10/63
Lewis, George	8/5/62	No evidence of muster in
Lyons, Dennis, 21 Ft. Scott, Kans.	1/13/63	KIA Sherwood, Mo., 5/18/63
Martin, John	—	Deserted 2/17/63
McKinzie, William, 19 Ky.	8/19/62	Mustered out 10/1/65
McNair, Ephraim, 18	1/13/63	Died Ft. Scott, Kans., 5/25/63, of disease

Company E

Name, Age, Residence	Joined	Remarks
PRIVATE (CONT.)		
Means, Franklin, 22 Mo.	8/19/62	Mustered out 10/1/65
Miller, Edward, 24 Ky.	8/20/62	Mustered out 10/1/65
Miller, Isaac	8/7/62	No evidence of muster in
Montgomery, Joseph, 18 Ft. Scott, Kans.	1/13/63	Died Ft. Gibson, C.N., 9/7/63, of disease
Musgrove, Elijah, 44 Ark.	8/12/62	Mustered out 10/1/65
Nave, George, 20 Cherokee Nation	8/28/62	Mustered out 10/1/65; died on steamer *Prairie Rose* en route from St. Louis, Mo., to Ft. Leavenworth, Kans., 10/24/65, of disease
Overton, Solomon	1/14/63	Deserted 5/4/63
Parker, William	8/5/62	No evidence of muster in
Paro, William	8/7/62	No evidence of muster in
Payton, Amos, 24 Mo.	1/24/63	Mustered out 10/1/65
Pleasant, William A.	8/8/62	No evidence of muster in
Prater, Edmond, 26 Ft. Scott, Kans.	8/12/62	Discharged Ft. Scott, Kans., 6/8/64, for disability
Riley, Adam, 18 Cherokee Nation	9/1/62	Mustered out 10/1/65
Riley, Anderson, 22 Cherokee Nation	8/18/62	Mustered out 10/1/65
Ross, Nelson, 18 Cherokee Nation	9/1/62	Mustered out 10/1/65
Ross, Thomas, 33 Cherokee Nation	9/1/62	Mustered out 10/1/65

Company E

Name, Age, Residence	Joined	Remarks
PRIVATE (CONT.)		
Rodgers, Isaac, 18 Cherokee Nation	8/1962	Mustered out 10/1/65
Sanders, Daniel, 19	8/28/62	Mustered out 10/1/65
Sanders, David, 18	8/28/62	KIA Poison Spring, Ark., 4/18/64
Sanders, Joseph, 18	11/10/62	KIA Poison Spring, Ark., 4/18/64
Smith, William, 31 Ft. Scott, Kans.	1/13/63	KIA Sherwood, Mo., 5/18/63
Solomon, Amos, 18	8/12/62	Deserted 6/27/64
Stonestreet, John	8/7/62	No evidence of muster in
Taylor, Charles, 21 Cherokee Nation	8/25/62	Mustered out 10/1/65
Thompson, Alexander, 18 Mo.	9/1/62	Mustered out 10/1/65
Vann, Jesse, 19 Ft. Scott, Kans.	1/13/63	Died Ft. Scott, Kans., 5/23/63, of disease
Vann, Wesley, 20 Cherokee Nation	8/9/62	Mustered out 10/1/65
Vinson, Clark, 23 Mo.	8/20/62	Mustered out 10/1/65
Walker, William	8/5/62	No evidence of muster in
Ware, David, 24 Mo.	8/14/62	Mustered out 10/1/65
Washington, George	4/15/64	Deserted 4/20/64
Wesley, Marcus	1/22/63	Arrested for drunkenness, deserted 5/4/63
Wesley, Richard, 18 St. Louis, Mo.	9/14/62	Discharged Little Rock, Ark., 6/15/65, for disability
White, John H., 19 Ft. Scott, Kans.	1/13/63	Died Ft. Scott, Kans., of disease
White, Peter, 21 Ft. Scott, Kans.	1/13/63	KIA Sherwood, Mo., 5/18/63

Company E

Name, Age, Residence	Joined	Remarks
PRIVATE (CONT.)		
Williams, Burgis	1/13/63	Sick in hospital, deserted 5/4/63
Wise, Phillip	8/7/62	No evidence of muster in
Woodley, Peter, 19 Ft. Scott, Kans.	1/13/63	Died Ft. Smith, Ark., 12/24/64, of disease
Woodrow, George, 24 Mo.	8/12/62	Mustered out 10/1/65
ADDITIONAL ENLISTMENTS		
Anderson, George, 23 Ft. Scott, Kans.	1/24/63	KIA Poison Spring, Ark., 4/18/64
Anderson, John, 31 Roseville, Ark.	12/1/63	KIA Poison Spring, Ark., 4/18/64
Bean, John, 19 Cherokee Nation	1/19/63	Mustered out 10/1/65
Brown, Jesse, 28 Cherokee Nation	1/22/63	Mustered out 10/1/65
Burgis, Samuel, 33 Mo.	4/1/63	Mustered out 10/1/65
Burgis, William, 44 Ft. Scott, Kans.	1/13/63	Deserted 5/4/63
Carter, Wiley, 25 Cherokee Nation	5/25/63	Died Pine Bluff, Ark., 9/26/65, of disease
Cartright, Reuben, 23 Ft. Scott, Kans.	1/28/63	Died Little Rock, Ark., 6/1/65, of dropsy
Dial, Henry, 20 Mo.	7/1/63	Mustered out 10/1/65; died on steamer *Prairie Rose* en route from St. Louis, Mo., to Ft. Leavenworth, Kans., 10/26/65, of disease
Grimmit, David, 23 Cherokee Nation	1/29/63	Mustered out 10/1/65
Grissim, Willis, 23 Mo.	1/24/63	Mustered out 10/1/65

Company E

Name, Age, Residence	Joined	Remarks
ADDITIONAL ENLISTMENTS (CONT.)		
Hall, Mead	8/7/62	No evidence of muster in
Holt, Fix, 30 Cherokee Nation	1/19/63	Died Ft. Smith, Ark., 7/2/65, of congestive fever
Landrum, Carl, 18 Cherokee Nation	2/6/63	Mustered out 10/1/65
Lynch, July, 21 Cherokee Nation	3/13/63	Died Ft. Smith, Ark., 10/10/64, of typhoid fever
Mack, Jacob, 24 Ft. Scott, Kans.	3/26/63	Died Roseville, Ark., 1/18/64, of disease
Mason, Robert, 21 Ky.	1/22/63	Mustered out 10/1/65
McCarter, George	4/13/64	Deserted 4/25/64
Merrill, Lafayette, 23 Ft. Scott, Kans.	3/16/63	KIA Poison Spring, Ark., 4/18/64
Monday, John Ft. Gibson, C.N.	7/5/63	KIA Poison Spring, Ark., 4/18/64
Monroe, James, 33 Mo.	1/14/63	Mustered out 10/1/65
Rider, James, 19 Cherokee Nation	1/14/63	Mustered out 10/1/65
Sanders, Lewis, 22 Cherokee Nation	3/16/63	Mustered out 10/1/65
Washington, Charles	—	Deserted 4/30/64
Young, George, 19 Ft. Scott, Kans.	1/24/63	KIA Poison Spring, Ark., 4/18/64

Company F

Name, Age, Residence	Joined	Remarks
CAPTAIN		
Creps, Shebua S.	8/?/63	Mustered out 10/1/65
Earle, Ethan Parkville, Mo.	1/13/63	Resigned Ft. Smith, Ark., 6/21/64

Company F

Name, Age, Residence	Joined	Remarks
FIRST LIEUTENANT		
Gardner, Joseph	1/13/63	Died Camp Davis, C.N., 8/24/64, of chronic diarrhea
Olis, John G.	—	No evidence of muster in
SECOND LIEUTENANT		
Heinman, Fred	—	Temporarily attached to regiment from Ninth Wisconsin
Reynard, Asa Leavenworth, Kans.	1/13/63	Resigned 5/2/63
REGIMENTAL COMMAND SERGEANT		
Miller, Orin, 41 Madison, Ky.	9/17/62	Promoted to Sgt. 1/13/63, Regimental Command Sgt. 8/25/65
FIRST SERGEANT		
Carter, John, 30 Geasels, Tenn.	8/16/62	Mustered out 10/1/65
Johnson, Clement, 27 Grenup, Ky.	8/27/62	Discharged Little Rock, Ark., 5/29/63, for disability
SERGEANT		
Grimes, Douglas, 46 Fayette, Ky.	9/16/62	Mustered out 10/1/65
Phillips, James, 24 St. Louis, Mo.	8/24/62	Mustered out 10/1/65
CORPORAL		
Crittenden, Henry, 30 Bourbon, Ky.	8/28/62	Mustered out 10/1/65
McCurtis, John, 26 Tenn.	9/17/62	Discharged Little Rock, Ark., 5/29/65, for disability
McNeal, Henry, 32 Baltimore, Md.	10/3/62	Died Little Rock, Ark., 2/9/65, of disease
Ross, Whitfield, 30 Topeka, Kans.	8/16/62	Mustered out 10/1/65

Company F

Name, Age, Residence	Joined	Remarks
CORPORAL (CONT.)		
Tilton, Benjamin, 24 Bolanes, Mo.	8/27/62	Mustered out 10/1/65
Washington, George, 1st, 30 Flimen, Ky.	8/27/62	Mustered out 10/1/65
Winser, Charles, 24 Johnson County, Mo.	10/20/63	Mustered out 10/1/65
PRIVATE		
Addison, Thomas	10/20/63	Deserted 12/15/63
Aggleson, Henry, 23 Leavenworth, Kans.	9/30/62	KIA Sherwood, Mo., 5/18/63
Anderson, William A., 22 Leavenworth, Kans.	9/10/62	Discharged Ft. Smith, Ark., 10/11/63, for disability
Austin, James, 24 Little Rock, Ark.	8/10/62	Killed Ft. Gibson, C.N., 9/30/64, during quarrel
Banks, John, 28 Independence, Mo.	9/17/62	Mustered out 10/1/65
Barber, David, 47 Jefferson, Ky.	8/16/62	Discharged Little Rock, Ark., 5/29/65, for disability
Barber, Marion	8/16/62	KIA Island Mound, Mo., 10/29/62
Bates, Baswood, 23 Wyandotte, Kans.	10/20/62	Died Ft. Scott, Kans., 4/28/63, of disease
Bates, John, 21 Wyandotte, Kans.	10/20/62	Died Ft. Scott, Kans., 3/5/63, of disease
Beck, Robert, 21 Lexington, Mo.	9/21/62	Mustered out 10/1/65
Berry, Alfred C., 25 Ft. Scott, Kans.	11/10/62	Discharged Ft. Smith, Ark., 10/27/63 for disability
Bird, John, 40 Leavenworth, Kans.	8/17/62	Died Ft. Smith, Ark., 7/27/64, of old age
Bledsow, Thomas, 21 Wyandotte, Kans.	8/28/62	Died Ft. Scott, Kans., 6/18/63, of disease

Company F

Name, Age, Residence	Joined	Remarks
PRIVATE (CONT.)		
Boster, James	8/12/62	No evidence of muster in
Bosworth, James, 25 Leavenworth, Kans.	8/17/62	Died Ft. Scott, Kans., 3/17/63, of disease
Broadhurst, Scott	10/4/62	No evidence of muster in
Brown, Thomas, 38 Topeka, Kans.	8/16/62	Killed Ft. Scott, Kans., 3/9/63, by a soldier of the Third Missouri
Brown, Wesley, 23 Leavenworth, Kans.	9/30/62	KIA Poison Spring, Ark., 4/18/64
Buckner, Francis, 22 Wyandotte, Kans.	8/20/62	Died Ft. Scott, Kans., 11/10/63, of disease
Carey, Ruben, 33 Ft. Scott, Kans.	1/12/63	Discharged for rheumatism 9/26/65
Carpin, Larker, 22 Leavenworth, Kans.	8/16/62	Deserted Ft. Scott, Kans., 5/4/63
Carter, Benjamin, 22 Jefferson, Va.	9/30/62	Discharged Little Rock, Ark., 7/27/65, for disability
Clark, David, 24 Clay, Mo.	8/16/62	Mustered out 10/1/65
Clark, Edward, 18 Clay, Mo.	8/16/62	Mustered out 10/1/65
Clemens, Daniel, 32 Leavenworth, Kans.	8/27/62	KIA Poison Spring, Ark., 4/18/64
Comes, Wesley, 23 Ft. Scott, Kans.	8/10/62	Discharged Ft. Smith, Ark., 12/16/63, for disability
Cragg, Samuel	8/15/62	No evidence of muster in
Davidson, James K.	8/15/62	No evidence of muster in
Davis, Samuel	8/16/62	KIA Island Mound, Mo., 10/29/62
Deane, Edward, 25 Topeka, Kans.	8/16/62	KIA Poison Spring, Ark., 4/18/64

Company F

Name, Age, Residence	Joined	Remarks
PRIVATE (CONT.)		
Dickenson, Adison, 27 Leavenworth, Kans.	8/17/62	Died Ft. Smith, Ark., 8/10/64, of intermit- tent fever
Denisan, John	8/16/62	No evidence of mus- ter in
Dennis, Isaac	8/16/62	No evidence of mus- ter in
Dobson, Manuel, 24 Mo.	8/27/62	Discharged Little Rock, Ark., 5/29/65, for disability
Dorsy, William	8/15/62	No evidence of mus- ter in
Dudley, General, 28 Platt County, Mo.	8/22/62	Mustered out 10/1/65
Edwards, Cyrus	8/15/62	No evidence of mus- ter in
Elicks, Thomas	8/15/62	No evidence of mus- ter in
Fields, Solomon	8/15/62	No evidence of mus- ter in
Gash, Henry	9/24/62	KIA Island Mound, Mo., 10/29/62
Gibson, James, 33 Cherokee Nation	8/16/62	Mustered out 10/1/65
Gray, William	8/16/62	No evidence of mus- ter in
Greer, David, 25 Leavenworth, Kans.	8/16/62	Died Ft. Smith, Ark., 12/11/63, of disease
Gregg, John	8/15/62	No evidence of mus- ter in
Grosshart, James	8/15/62	No evidence of mus- ter in
Harris, Calvin, 28 Franklin, Colo.	8/10/62	Discharged Little Rock, Ark., 6/18/65, for disability
Hathaway, Spencer, 32, Richmond, Va.	8/16/62	Mustered out 10/1/65

Company F

Name, Age, Residence	Joined	Remarks
PRIVATE (CONT.)		
Haze, Frank, 25 Wyandotte, Kans.	9/18/62	KIA Sherwood, Mo., 5/18/63
Hews, Gabriel, 23 Platt, Mo.	8/27/62	Mustered out 10/1/65
Hightower, Beardsley, 26 Morton County, Mo.	8/16/62	Died Roseville, Ark., 1/19/64, of smallpox
Hill, Adam, 22 Topeka, Kans.	8/16/62	KIA Poison Spring, Ark., 4/18/64
Hockley, James, 29 Riley, Ky.	8/16/62	Mustered out 10/1/65
Hockley, Thomas, 21 Riley, Ky.	8/16/62	Mustered out 10/1/65
Howard, Samuel, 23 Morton County, Mo.	8/16/62	Died Little Rock, Ark., 7/19/65, of intermittent fever
Hutchin, James	4/1/63	No evidence of muster in
Jackson, Andrew, 1st, 20 Leavenworth, Kans.	8/28/62	Deserted Ft. Smith, Ark., 1/4/64
Jackson, Joseph	8/15/62	No evidence of muster in
Jackson, William	8/16/62	No evidence of muster in
Johnson, Lazarus, 21 Bucklin County, Mo.	8/16/62	Mustered out 10/1/65
Johnson, Milton, 26 Leavenworth, Kans.	8/20/62	KIA Sherwood, Mo., 5/18/63
Jones, Daniel	3/20/63	Deserted 5/24/63
Knight, Thomas	8/27/62	No evidence of muster in
Knight, William, 20 Leavenworth, Kans.	8/27/62	KIA Sherwood, Mo., 5/18/63
Lane, Thomas	8/16/62	KIA Island Mound, Mo., 10/29/62

Company F

Name, Age, Residence	Joined	Remarks
PRIVATE (CONT.)		
Lee, William, 26 Leavenworth, Kans.	8/22/62	Discharged Ft. Scott, Kans., 9/26/63, for disability
Little, Milton	8/27/62	No evidence of muster in
Lowe, Woodson	8/22/62	No evidence of muster in
Mackey, Thomas	1/13/62	No further record
Mackner, John, 18 Cherokee Nation	11/26/62	KIA Poison Spring, 4/18/62
Madden, Stephen B., 33 Mermistead County, Ark.	8/16/62	Mustered out 10/1/65
Maddox, John, 24 Lexington, Ky.	8/10/62	Mustered out 10/1/65
Madison, Robert, 23 Nashville, Tenn.	8/20/62	Mustered out 10/1/65
Marrion, Thomas	8/16/62	No evidence of muster in
Martin, Charles, 39 Sumner, Tex.	8/10/62	Mustered out 10/1/65
McCarter, John, 23 Tenn.	9/10/62	Discharged for disability 5/29/65
McCordes, John	8/20/62	No evidence of muster in
Mitchell, George, 35 Lexington, Ky.	8/20/62	KIA Sherwood, Mo., 5/18/63
Mitchell, Joseph, 27 Lexington, Ky.	8/10/62	Promoted to First Sgt., Co. K, 5/2/63
Mitchell, Thomas, 24 Lexington, Ky.	8/17/62	KIA Honey Springs, C.N., 7/18/63
Mockner, John, 20 Lexington, Ky.	11/26/62	KIA Poison Spring, Ark., 4/18/64
Peale, George, 24 Benton County, Ark.	8/11/62	Mustered out 10/1/65
Perrin, Harvey, 21 Leavenworth, Kans.	8/18/62	Died Ft. Scott, Kans., 2/7/63, of disease

Company F

Name, Age, Residence	Joined	Remarks
PRIVATE (CONT.)		
Perrin, Jackson, 38 Burrell, Ky.	8/17/63	Mustered out 10/1/65
Phillips, Thomas	—	KIA Honey Springs, Indian Territory, 7/17/63
Perrin, Richardson, 24 Leavenworth, Kans.	8/12/62	Deserted Ft. Scott, Kans., 5/4/63
Phillips, William, 24 Leavenworth, Kans.	8/17/62	Died Ft. Smith, Ark., 12/15/63, of smallpox
Pitts, Andrew	8/22/62	No evidence of muster in
Pointer, Alfred, 32 Lexington, Ky.	8/20/62	KIA Poison Spring, Ark., 4/18/64
Porter, Jordan, 25 Benton, Ark.	8/27/62	Mustered out 10/1/65
Porter, Minor, 22 Leavenworth, Kans.	8/17/63	KIA Sherwood, Mo., 5/18/63
Pulham, Alexander, 26 Leavenworth, Kans.	8/16/62	Died Tahlequah, C.N., 10/26/63, of wound received in action at Cabin Creek, 7/2/63
Reed, David, 26 Wyandotte, Kans.	9/20/62	Sick in hospital; no evidence of muster out on file
Reed, Lewis, 22 Leavenworth, Kans.	8/18/62	Died Neosho River, C.N., 6/27/63, of disease
Rhodes, Allen	8/18/62	KIA Island Mound, Mo., 10/29/62
Richardson, Jackson, 27 Leavenworth, Kans.	8/16/62	Deserted Ft. Scott, Kans., 5/4/63
Richardson, William, 23 Jennis Co, Ky.	8/16/62	Mustered out 10/1/65
Robinson, Armstead	8/15/62	Deserted 4/3/63
Robinson, Joshua, 28 Leavenworth, Kans.	8/10/62	Deserted Ft. Scott, Kans., 5/4/63

Company F

Name, Age, Residence	Joined	Remarks
PRIVATE (CONT.)		
Rodgers, Jacob, 38 Leavenworth, Kans.	8/4/62	No evidence of muster out on file
Samuels, Robert, 28 Bourbon, Ky.	8/28/62	Mustered out 10/1/65
Selectman, William, 20 Bourbon, Ky.	8/16/62	Died Roseville, Ark., 1/8/64, of musket shot
Shephard, John W.	8/18/62	No evidence of muster in
Shepherd, Allen, 32 Jackson County, Mo.	2/7/63	Mustered out 10/1/65
Smith, Davis	8/22/62	No evidence of muster in
Smith, Green, 27	9/16/62	Died Ft. Scott, Kans., 4/9/63, of disease
Smith, Thomas	8/30/62	No evidence of muster in
Stevens, George, 26	8/17/62	KIA Sherwood, Mo., 5/18/63
Talbot, Joseph	8/16/62	KIA Island Mound, Mo., 10/29/62
Tall, Dudley W., 37 Clay, Mo.	8/10/62	Discharged Little Rock, Ark., 6/1/5/65, for disability
Thomas, Pendleton, 25 Leavenworth, Kans.	8/17/62	Died Roseville, Ark., 12/28/63, of smallpox
Thompson, David, 20 Topeka, Kans.	8/16/62	KIA Poison Spring, Ark., 4/18/64
True, George, 28 Mo.	8/10/62	Mustered out 10/1/65
Warren, Minor	8/15/62	No evidence of muster in
Waters, James, 26 Choctaw Nation	1/13/63	Mustered out 10/1/65
Williams, John, 25 Fluvannah, Va.	8/16/62	Mustered out 10/1/65

Company F

Name, Age, Residence	Joined	Remarks
PRIVATE (CONT.)		
Williams, Monroe, 23 Springfield, Mo.	11/20/63	Mustered out 10/1/65
Wilson, Andy, 21 Ralston, Ky.	8/10/62	Mustered out 10/1/65
ADDITIONAL ENLISTMENTS		
Anderson, Charles, 38 Ky.	10/20/63	Mustered out 10/1/65
Coleman, Robert, 30 New Orleans, La.	1/20/63	Mustered out 10/1/65
Dandridge, Scipio, 39 Sayett, Ky.	10/20/63	Discharged Little Rock, Ark., 7/15/65, for disability
English, Thomas, 24 Sebastien, Ark.	12/20/63	KIA Poison Spring, Ark., 4/18/64
Foster, William, 26 Sayett, Ky.	10/20/63	KIA Horse Head Creek, Ark., 2/17/64, in skirmish with guerrillas
Gee, Greenbury, 32 Mercer County, Ky.	2/20/65	Died 10/4/65 of congestive chill
Hall, William, 29 Alexandria, Va.	8/1/63	Mustered out 10/1/65
Henry, Joseph, 28 Benton, Mo.	3/20/63	Mustered out 10/1/65
Holley, Frank, 29 N.C.	10/20/63	Mustered out 10/1/65
Jackson, Andrew, 2nd, 20 Mo.	7/12/63	Discharged Little Rock, Ark., 5/29/65, for disability
Johnson, Dublin	10/20/63	Deserted 12/15/63
Johnson, William B.	8/16/62	No evidence of muster in
Jones, Jerry, 23 Richmond, Va.	5/10/63	Died Ft. Smith, Ark., 4/30/64, of disease
Mack, George, 28 Cherokee Nation	10/20/63	Mustered out 10/1/65

Company F

Name, Age, Residence	Joined	Remarks
ADDITIONAL ENLISTMENTS (CONT.)		
Martin, Jacob, 20	10/20/63	Deserted
Murray, George, 20 Baldwin, Mo.	8/20/64	Mustered out 10/1/65
Phillips, Thomas H., 19 Richmond, Va.	4/11/64	Mustered out 10/1/65
Spencer, Adams, 26 Washington County, Ark.	7/20/63	Mustered out 10/1/65
Star, Toby, 20 Cherokee Nation	5/20/63	Mustered out 10/1/65
Stevens, Washington, 28 Christian, Tenn.	7/13/63	Mustered out 10/1/65
Thompson, Joseph, 20 Ft. Scott, Kans.	6/1/63	KIA Poison Spring, Ark., 4/18/64
Tilton, Andrew, 26 Bedford, Tenn.	10/20/63	Mustered out 10/1/65
Turner, Lafayette, 27 Peters, Va.	10/20/63	Discharged Little Rock, Ark., 6/18/65, for disability
Underwood, Grant, 31 Richmond, Va.	8/21/64	Died Warren, Ark., 8/17/65, of intermittent fever
Wallace, Henry, 27 Nashville, Tenn.	12/6/63	Mustered out 10/1/65
Washington, George, Second, 24 Rappahannock, Va.	8/20/64	Mustered out 10/1/65
Waters, Henry	10/20/63	Deserted 12/15/63
Watson, John, 47 Bottleville, Va.	12/6/63	Mustered out 10/1/65

Company G

Name, Age, Residence	Joined	Remarks
	CAPTAIN	
Hitchcock, Bethuel Lawrence, Kans.	8/16/65	Mustered out 10/1/65
Smallwood, William H. Wathena, Kans.	3/9/63	Resigned Little Rock, Ark., 4/19/65
	SECOND LIEUTENANT	
Smith, Andrew J. Clinton, Kans.	5/2/63	Mustered out 10/1/65
Stokes, Albert J.	—	No evidence of muster in
	FIRST SERGEANT	
Morgan, Randolph, 25 Boone, Ky.	1/13/63	Mustered out 10/1/65
	SERGEANT	
Gray, Charles Ft. Scott, Kans.	1/13/63	KIA Poison Spring, Ark., 4/18/64
Henderson, Charles, 28 Washington, Ark.	1/13/63	Mustered out 10/1/65
Johnson, Andrew, 28 Lincoln, Ky.	2/7/63	Mustered out 10/1/65
Maddox, James, 36 Harrison County, Ky.	1/13/63	Mustered out 10/1/65
Sims [Simms], Milton, 25 Ky.	2/3/63	Reduced to ranks; mustered out 10/1/65
	CORPORAL	
Adams, Wiley, 24 Jackson, Mo.	2/7/63	Mustered out 10/1/65
Bell, Joseph, 23 Platte, Mo.	2/7/63	Mustered out 10/1/65
Berry, Sampson, 44 Lincoln, Ky.	2/7/63	Mustered out 10/1/65
Burns, Jefferson Ft. Scott, Kans.	1/13/63	KIA Poison Spring, Ark., 4/18/64

Company G

Name, Age, Residence	Joined	Remarks
CORPORAL (CONT.)		
Farrell, John, 33 Topeka, Kans.	2/7/63	Mustered out 10/1/65
Gregg, Andrew, 20 Jassemin, Ky.	2/7/63	Mustered out 10/1/65
Jackson, Joshua, 22 C.N.	2/7/63	Mustered out 10/1/65
Roberts, Charles, 28 Lee, Va.	2/7/63	Mustered out 10/1/65
Smith, Elijah, 26 Gerard, Ky.	2/7/63	Mustered out 10/1/65
Williams, Edmund, 24 Jackson, Mo.	2/7/63	Mustered out 10/1/65
Wilson, Franklin, 45 Jefferson, Tenn.	2/7/63	Mustered out 10/1/65
MUSICIAN		
Absalom, Dimmery, 27 Lawrence, Kans.	2/7/63	Mustered out 10/1/65
PRIVATE		
Allen, Edward	10/6/62	No evidence of muster in
Arkins, Elijah Ft. Scott, Kans.	2/7/63	Deserted Baxter Springs, C.N., 6/4/63
Barclay, Jack Ft. Scott, Kans.	1/13/63	KIA Poison Spring, Ark., 4/18/64
Brewer, James Ft. Scott, Kans.	1/13/63	KIA Poison Spring, Ark., 4/18/64
Brown, Albert	9/6/62	No evidence of muster in
Brown, Charles	9/18/62	No evidence of muster in
Buchamp, Joseph, 45 Lawrence, Kans.	2/7/63	Mustered out 10/1/65
Burnam, Lindsey Ft. Scott, Kans.	2/7/63	Died Ft. Scott, Kans., 4/21/63, of disease

Company G

Name, Age, Residence	Joined	Remarks
PRIVATE (CONT.)		
Carter, Jackson Ft. Scott, Kans.	2/7/63	Deserted Ft. Scott, Kans., 3/11/63
Carter, Joshua Ft. Scott, Kans.	2/7/63	Died Ft. Scott, Kans., 12/9/63, of disease
Clark, Edmond Lawrence, Kans.	2/7/63	KIA Poison Spring, Ark., 4/18/64
Clark, Lilburn	9/2/62	No evidence of muster in
Clay, Henry	9/2/62	No evidence of muster in
Davenport, John	9/14/62	No evidence of muster in
Davidson, Jacob, 33 Jackson, Mo.	2/7/63	Mustered out 10/1/65
Davis, Elijah Fort Scott, Kans.	2/7/63	Deserted Ft. Scott, Kans., 3/11/63
Davis, Jackson Ft. Scott, Kans.	2/7/63	Deserted Ft. Scott, Kans., 3/13/63
Davis, Joseph Ft. Scott, Kans.	2/7/63	Died Ft. Scott, Kans., 5/21/63, of congestive chills
DeShay, General	9/4/62	No evidence of muster in
Dennis, Pitman Fort Scott, Kans.	2/7/63	Deserted Ft. Scott, Kans., 3/13/63
Drisdom, Jacob, 27 Jackson County, Mo.	2/7/63	Mustered out 10/1/65
Drisdom, Leonard Ky.	2/7/63	Drowned Ivy Ford, Ark., 1/21/65
Duncan, George Fort Scott, Kans.	2/7/63	Deserted Ft. Scott, Kans., 4/25/63
Early, John Fort Scott, Kans.	2/7/63	Deserted Ft. Scott, Kans., 3/13/63
Ellis, George	9/12/62	No evidence of muster in

Company G

Name, Age, Residence	Joined	Remarks
PRIVATE (CONT.)		
Freeman, Stephen, 28 Cherokee Nation	2/7/63	Mustered out 10/1/65
Fortner, Matthew Ft. Scott, Kans.	2/7/63	Deserted Ft. Scott, Kans., 5/13/63
Giles, Green, 18 Graysowles, Tex.	2/7/63	Discharged Little Rock, Ark., 2/4/65 by order of Maj. Gen. Reynolds
Gray, James, 34 Ill.	2/7/63	Deserted Ft. Scott, Kans., 3/13/63
Gregg, Stephen, 21 Jackson County, Mo.	3/9/63	Died Little Rock, Ark., 5/20/65, of scrofula
Grosshart, Joseph Ft. Scott, Kans.	2/7/63	KIA Poison Spring, Ark., 4/18/64
Gunther, William, 23 Tahlequah, C.N.	2/7/63	Died Little Rock, Ark., 8/11/64, of typhus, malignant fever
Hamilton, John, 35 Jackson, Mo.	2/7/63	Mustered out 10/1/65
Hawkins, Wesley Ft. Scott, Kans.	2/7/63	Deserted Ft. Scott, Kans., 4/25/63
Haywood, Abraham Ft. Scott, Kans.	2/7/63	Deserted Ft. Scott, Kans., 4/27/63
Hedrick, Henry, 23 St. Charles, Mo.	2/7/63	Mustered out 10/1/65
Hill, Edmund Ft. Scott, Kans.	3/9/63	KIA Poison Spring, Ark., 4/18/64
Hoge, Edward Ft. Scott, Kans.	2/7/63	Deserted Ft. Scott, Kans., 4/25/63
Howard, David Ft. Scott, Kans.	3/9/63	KIA Poison Spring, Ark., 4/18/64
Howard, David Ft. Scott, Kans.	2/7/63	Deserted Ft. Scott, Kans., 3/11/63
Howard, John, 40 Ky.	2/7/63	No evidence of muster out on file
Howard, Simeon	9/12/62	No evidence of muster in

Company G

Name, Age, Residence	Joined	Remarks
PRIVATE (CONT.)		
Hunter, Hiram, 35 Butler County, Ky.	2/7/63	Mustered out 10/1/65
Jackson, John Ky.	2/7/63	Died Baxter Springs, C.N., 6/5/63, of congestive chills
Jenkins, Moses, 42 Ky.	2/7/63	Discharged Ft. Scott, Kans., by order of Col. C.W. Blair
Johnson, William, 27 Ky.	2/7/63	Died Ft. Scott, Kans., 8/2/65, of typhus, malignant fever
Lane, James H.	11/25/62	No evidence of muster in
Lewis, Henry	9/2/62	No evidence of muster in
Lindsey, Wilbert, 22 Cooper, Mo.	2/7/63	Mustered out 10/1/65
Lowry, Edward, 34 Cherokee Nation	2/7/63	Deserted Ft. Scott, Kans., 4/27/63
Marshall, Benjamin Fort Scott, Kans.	2/7/63	Discharged Ft. Scott, Ark., 12/4/63, for disability
McWilliams, Doctor, 22 Cass, Mo.	2/7/63	Mustered out 10/1/65
Moody, John, 33 Ala.	2/7/63	Died Little Rock, Ark., 12/28/64, of congestive chills
Muscrow, John Fort Scott, Kans.	2/7/63	Deserted Ft. Scott, Kans., 3/22/63
Over, David Ft. Scott, Kans.	2/7/63	Deserted Ft. Scott, Kans., 3/22/63
Overton, Edward, 26 Lafayette, Ky.	2/7/63	Mustered out 10/1/65
Overton, Rafe, 44 Ala.	2/7/63	Mustered out 10/1/65

Company G

Name, Age, Residence	Joined	Remarks
PRIVATE (CONT.)		
Randolph, David Ft. Scott, Kans.	2/7/63	Died Ft. Smith, Ark., 10/21/63, of disease
Read, David	8/10/62	No evidence of muster in
Reese, John, 30 Va.	2/7/63	Mustered out 10/1/65
Roach, Henry, 23 Cherokee Nation	2/7/63	Mustered out 10/1/65
Sally, Lewis Ft. Scott, Kans.	2/7/63	Died Roseville, Ark., of disease
Saunders, Anderson	8/5/63	Deserted 12/19/63
Scott, William, 21 Platte County, Mo.	2/7/63	Mustered out 10/1/65
Searle, William, 26 Crawford County, Ark.	11/1/63	Deserted 8/9/64
Shepperd, Allen Crawford County, Ark.	11/1/63	Transferred to Co. F, 7/1/63
Simpson, Andy Ft. Scott, Kans.	2/7/63	Mustered out Ft. Scott, Kans., 3/22/63
Simpson, Elias, 25 Tenn.	2/7/63	Mustered out 10/1/65
Simpson, John Ft. Scott, Kans.	2/7/63	Died Ft. Scott, Kans., 3/24/63, of typhoid pneumonia
Simpson, Joseph, 20 Jackson, Mo.	2/7/63	Mustered out 10/1/65
Smith, Horace Ft. Scott	2/7/63	Died Ft. Scott, Kans., 3/18/63, of pneumonia
Starr, Nelson	2/7/63	Died 4/18/63 of pneumonia
Taylor, Nicholas, 28 Ky.	2/7/63	Mustered out 10/1/65
Thomas, Edmund	2/7/63	KIA Poison Spring, Ark., 4/18/64
Thompson, George, 25 Va.	2/7/63	Mustered out 10/1/65

Company G

Name, Age, Residence	Joined	Remarks
PRIVATE (CONT.)		
Thompson, Nelson, 24 Ky.	8/6/62	Mustered out 10/1/65
Trotter, James, 24 Va.	2/7/63	Mustered out 10/1/65
Walker, John, 25 Platt, Mo.	2/7/63	Mustered out 10/1/65
Walker, Joseph Ft. Scott, Kans.	2/7/63	Died Ft. Scott, Kans., 3/11/63, of typhoid fever
Washington, George, 1st, 27 Warren, Mo.	2/7/63	Mustered out 10/1/65
Washington, George, 2nd, 22 Cherokee Nation	2/7/63	Mustered out 10/1/65
Washington, Green, 22 Ky.	2/7/63	Mustered out 10/1/65
Washington, William, 1st Ft. Scott, Kans.	2/7/63	Deserted Ft. Scott, Kans., 4/27/63
Washington, William, 2nd Ft. Scott, Kans.	2/7/63	Transferred to Co. B, 3/10/63
Whitmeyer, Isaac Ft. Scott, Kans.	2/7/63	Deserted Ft. Scott, Kans., 5/5/63
Wood, Harrison, 26 Jackson County, Mo.	2/7/63	Deserted Ft. Scott, Kans., 5/5/63
Wood, James	8/10/62	No evidence of muster in
Wyer, Josiah	10/4/62	No evidence of muster in
ADDITIONAL ENLISTMENTS		
Alston, Ephraim, 40 Mayor County, Mo.	12/26/63	Mustered out 10/1/65
Alston, Jack, 26 Johnston County, Ark.	12/23/63	Mustered out 10/1/65

Company G

Name, Age, Residence	Joined	Remarks
ADDITIONAL ENLISTMENTS (CONT.)		
Brewer, Albert, 18 Johnson County, Ark.	12/20/63	Mustered out 10/1/65
Brewer, Alexander	12/20/63	Died 6/1/64 of wounds from Poison Spring
Brewer, Alfred, 33 Tenn.	12/20/63	Died of disease
Brewer, Daniel, 45 Madison County, Ala.	12/20/63	Mustered out 10/1/65
Buchamp, Emanuel Franklin County, Ark.	11/8/63	Died Ft. Scott, Kans., 1/13/65, of disease
Clayton, Sandy, 24 Marion, Miss.	11/7/63	Mustered out 10/1/65
Culbertson, Silas	8/19/63	KIA Poison Spring, Ark., 4/18/64
Griffin, David, 27 Jackson, Tenn.	11/8/63	Mustered out 10/1/65
Howell, Jefferson, 18 Jackson, Tenn.	11/8/63	Mustered out 10/1/65
Polk, Paul, 18 Madison County, Ark.	11/23/63	Mustered out 10/1/65
Powell, Frederick, 23 Conway County, Ark.	11/26/63	Mustered out 10/1/65
Quail, Finn, 21 Franklin County, Ark.	11/23/63	Mustered out 10/1/65
Quail, Orange, 19 Franklin County, Ark.	11/23/63	Mustered out 10/1/65
Tucker, Andy, 39 Miss.	11/7/63	Mustered out 10/1/65
Ward, Beverly, 18 Johnson County, Ark.	3/1/64	Mustered out 10/1/65
Wallace, Harry	12/23/63	Discharged by surgeon
Wallace, Richmond, 20 Franklin County, Ark.	12/26/63	Mustered out 10/1/65
Walters, Thomas, 21 Ark.	10/21/63	Mustered out 10/1/65

Company G

Name, Age, Residence	Joined	Remarks
ADDITIONAL ENLISTMENTS (CONT.)		
Watson, James	11/25/62	No evidence of muster in
Young, John, 34 La.	10/20/63	Mustered out 10/1/65
Yager, Abraham, 19 Franklin, Ark.	3/26/64	Died Little Rock, Ark., of scrofula

Company H

Name, Age, Residence	Joined	Remarks
CAPTAIN		
Ramson, Ward, 28	5/1/63	Mustered out 10/1/65
FIRST LIEUTENANT		
Coleman, Charles J., 22	5/1/63	KIA Poison Spring, Ark., 4/18/64
Mockett, John H., 25	4/22/65	Mustered out 10/1/65
SECOND LIEUTENANT		
Edgerton, William T., 28 Topeka, Kans.	5/1/63	Resigned 11/14/63
FIRST SERGEANT		
Clark, William, 28 Ray County, Mo.	8/11/62	Mustered out 10/1/65
SERGEANT		
Gilbert, Alexander, 21 Mo.	1/13/63	Mustered out 10/1/65
Jackson, Charles, 24 Ray County, Mo.	3/13/63	Mustered out 10/1/65
Logan, John, 23 Mo.	1/24/63	Mustered out 10/1/65
Richardson, James, 24 Mo.	1/24/63	Mustered out 10/1/65
CORPORAL		
Clark, Austin, 22 Platt County, Mo.	3/18/63	Mustered out 10/1/65

Company H

Name, Age, Residence	Joined	Remarks
CORPORAL (CONT.)		
Gregg, Gratten, 20 Mo.	3/13/63	Mustered out 10/1/65
Jackson, Charles, 24 Ky.	3/13/63	Mustered out 10/1/65
Johnson, John H., 28 Ky.	2/10/64	Mustered out 10/1/65
Landers, Harry, 20 Cherokee Nation	3/25/63	Mustered out 10/1/65
Norman, Louis, 22 Mo.	3/13/63	KIA Poison Spring, Ark., 4/18/64
Sanders, Andrew, 30 Cherokee Nation	3/25/63	Mustered out 10/1/65
Williams, Harrison, 24 Mo.	1/24/63	Mustered out 10/1/65
Wright, Frank, 20 Lafayette, Mo.	1/24/63	Mustered out 10/1/65
PRIVATE		
Abbott, Andrew	10/10/62	No evidence of muster in
Abbott, Charles	10/10/62	No evidence of muster in
Adams, Joseph, 20 Mo.	3/25/63	Mustered out 10/1/65
Allen, Greene, 43 Mo.	1/15/63	KIA Sherwood, Mo., 5/18/63
Allen, Joshua, 18 Lafayette County, Mo.	1/24/63	Mustered out 10/1/65
Anderson, Liberty	9/20/62	No evidence of muster in
Archer, Thomas, 20 Mo.	3/25/63	Mustered out 10/1/65
Baird, George	10/10/62	No evidence of muster in
Baird, William	10/10/62	No evidence of muster in

Company H

Name, Age, Residence	Joined	Remarks
PRIVATE (CONT.)		
Barns, William	8/9/62	No evidence of muster in
Barnet, Nathan	8/25/62	No evidence of muster in
Bass, George, 25 Mo.	3/13/63	Deserted Ft. Scott, Kans., 5/2/63
Bellus, Prior, 19 Lafayette County, Mo.	1/24/63	Mustered out 10/1/65
Booth, John, 36 Mo.	2/10/63	KIA Sherwood, Mo., 5/18/63
Bratcher [Bradshaw], Henry, 18 Mo.	4/1/63	Mustered out 10/1/65
Brookins, Benjamin, 22 Mo.	1/24/63	Mustered out 10/1/65
Brown, Mason, 19 Lafayette County, Mo.	1/24/63	Died Little Rock, Ark., 5/14/65, of consumption
Burton, Matt	9/20/62	No evidence of muster in
Butler, Stanton	8/29/62	No evidence of muster in
Campbell, Alexander, 20 Mo.	3/13/63	Died Ft. Scott, Kans., 5/25/63, of malarial fever
Carson, Robert	8/9/62	No evidence of muster in
Cates, Andrew, 25 Mo.	3/25/63	Deserted Ft. Scott, Kans., 5/4/63
Chandler, Samuel	8/9/62	No evidence of muster in
Clark, Charles, 30 C.N.	3/23/63	Mustered out 10/1/65
Cloud, Charlie	9/20/62	No evidence of muster in
Coldtrain, Sandy, 20 Mo.	1/24/63	Mustered out 10/1/65

Company H

Name, Age, Residence	Joined	Remarks
PRIVATE (CONT.)		
Craig, Allen	10/10/62	No evidence of muster in
Crain, Albert	10/10/62	No evidence of muster in
Davis, George	9/20/62	No evidence of muster in
Davis, John, 19 Pike County, Tex.	3/13/63	Mustered out 10/1/65
Davis, Jonas, 20 Mo.	1/13/63	Died Ft. Smith, Ark., 12/8/63, of smallpox
Davis, Tobias	8/11/62	No evidence of muster in
Dennison, Samuel, 23 Mo.	1/24/63	Mustered out 10/1/65
Dillam, George, 37 Mo.	4/29/63	Died Ft. Smith, Ark., 10/15/63, of diarrhea
Drew, Toby, 35 Mo.	3/25/63	Mustered out 6/7/65
Dyer, John	3/25/63	No evidence of muster in
Field, Edward, 18 Mo.	1/24/63	Mustered out 10/1/65
Fulkerson, Daniel	9/20/62	No evidence of muster in
Fulkerson, Edward	9/20/62	No evidence of muster in
Fulkerson, Henry	9/20/62	No evidence of muster in
Fulkerson, John	9/20/62	No evidence of muster in
Gamble, Frank, 40 Va.	1/24/63	Mustered out Little Rock, Ark., 7/8/65
Garland, Randall, 22 Choctaw Nation	3/13/63	Mustered out 10/1/65
Griffin, Henry, 25 Cherokee Nation	3/25/63	Deserted Ft. Scott, Kans., 5/4/63

Company H

Name, Age, Residence	Joined	Remarks
PRIVATE (CONT.)		
Hawkins, George, 23 Mo.	3/25/63	Mustered out 10/1/65
Hayden, Christopher, 27 Mo.	4/29/63	No evidence of muster out on file
Hayden, Joseph	10/10/62	No evidence of muster in
Henry, James, 18 Mo.	4/1/63	Mustered out 10/1/65
Helm, Fred, 40 Mo.	3/13/63	KIA Poison Spring, Ark., 4/18/64
Hickman, Henry, 25 Mo.	3/13/63	Deserted Ft. Scott, Kans., 5/4/63
Higgins, Charles, 20 Mo.	1/24/63	Mustered out 10/1/65
Hobson, Daniel	10/25/62	No evidence of muster in
Hopkins, Thomas, 32 Mo.	3/13/63	KIA Poison Spring, Ark., 4/18/64
House, Joseph	9/20/62	No evidence of muster in
Houtzer, Charles, 28 Mo.	4/29/63	Mustered out 10/1/65
Jackson, Harrison	10/10/62	No evidence of muster in
Johnson, Andrew, 25 Cherokee Nation	3/25/63	Mustered out 10/1/65
Johnson, Henry, 26 Mo.	3/24/63	Discharged Ft. Scott, Ark., 12/10/63, for disability
Johnson, Israel, 21 Cherokee Nation	3/25/63	Mustered out 10/1/65
Landon, James, 19 Cherokee Nation	3/25/63	Mustered out 10/1/65
Larnum, William	9/20/62	No evidence of muster in

Company H

Name, Age, Residence	Joined	Remarks
PRIVATE (CONT.)		
Lee, Jesse, 37 Mo.	1/24/63	Died Ft. Gibson, C.N., 9/19/63, of flux
Logan, James, 20 Mo.	1/24/63	Mustered out Little Rock, Ark., 7/8/65
Lyon, John, 27 Ky.	1/25/63	Mustered out 10/1/65
Martin, Jackson, 27 Mo.	3/25/63	Mustered out 10/1/65
Mason, John	9/20/62	No evidence of muster in
McCormic, Andrew	8/19/62	No evidence of muster in
McDaniel, Isaac, 22 Mo.	3/25/63	Died Ft. Smith, Ark., 12/26/63, of lung fever
McSpalding, William	8/15/62	No evidence of muster in
Miller, George	8/19/62	No evidence of muster in
Minor, Albert	8/20/62	No evidence of muster in
Minor, Allen, 29 Mo.	4/29/63	Deserted 5/2/63; arrested Leavenworth, Kans.; no evidence of muster out on file
Moore, Samuel, 21 Mo.	3/13/63	Mustered out 10/1/65
Olmstead, Henry, 27 Mo.	1/24/63	Died Baxter Springs, C.N., 5/24/63, of disease
Palmer, Abraham, 32 Mo.	1/24/63	Mustered out 10/1/65
Palmer, Richard, 27 Mo.	1/24/63	Mustered out 10/1/65
Parks, James	5/25/63	Deserted 5/25/63
Pennel, Augustus	8/19/62	No evidence of muster in

Company H

Name, Age, Residence	Joined	Remarks
PRIVATE (CONT.)		
Pennel, Calvin	8/19/62	No evidence of muster in
Pennel, John N.	8/19/62	No evidence of muster in
Pollard, May	9/1/62	No evidence of muster in
Porter, David, 18 Mo.	3/25/63	KIA Poison Spring, Ark., 4/18/64
Price, Otho	10/1/62	No evidence of muster in
Rennick, Joshua, 20 Mo.	1/24/63	Mustered out 10/1/65
Ridings, Jerry	9/20/62	No evidence of muster in
Riley, John	8/9/62	No evidence of muster in
Robinson, Dock	10/10/62	No evidence of muster in
Robinson, George	10/10/62	No evidence of muster in
Robinson, Smith, 22 Mo.	3/25/63	Mustered out 10/1/65
Ross, Franklin, 25 Cherokee Nation	3/25/63	Mustered out 10/1/65
Ruler, Adam	8/19/62	No evidence of muster in
Russell, Charles, 20 Mo.	3/13/63	Mustered out 10/1/65
Sanders, Harvey	8/9/62	No evidence of muster in
Sanders, Nathaniel	8/9/62	No evidence of muster in
Sanders, Squire	4/13/63	No further evidence of service
Simpson, Alexander, 25 Mo.	4/29/63	Deserted 5/25/63; arrested Ft. Leavenworth, Kans.; no evidence of muster out on file

Company H

Name, Age, Residence	Joined	Remarks
PRIVATE (CONT.)		
Smith, James, 18 Mo.	3/13/63	Mustered out Little Rock, Ark., 7/8/65
Smith, William, 18 Mo.	3/13/63	Mustered out 10/1/65
Smith, William J. Mo.	3/25/63	Died Ft. Smith, Ark., 12/23/63, of bilious fever
Sparks, James, 19 Mo.	3/25/63	Mustered out 10/1/65
Stewart, Charlie	10/10/62	No evidence of muster in
Stewart, Samuel	3/13/63	Deserted 3/16/63
Taylor, Benjamin, 27 Mo.	3/13/63	KIA Poison Spring, Ark., 4/18/64
Thompson, Granville	8/9/62	No evidence of muster in
Thompson, John	8/9/62	No evidence of muster in
Todd, Hazel, 30 Mo.	4/29/63	Deserted Ft. Scott, Kans., 12/30/64
Turner, Arthur, 28 Mo.	3/13/63	Mustered out 10/1/65
Waddle, Josiah, 18 Green County, Mo.	3/31/63	Mustered out 10/26/65
Waddle, Thomas, 44 Green County, Mo.	3/31/63	Discharged 4/7/65 for disability
Wadkins, Islam, 19 Lafayette, Mo.	1/24/63	Mustered out 10/1/65
Ward, John	10/10/62	No evidence of muster in
Warren, William	10/10/62	No evidence of muster in
Washington, George, 20 Lafayette, Mo.	1/24/63	Mustered out 10/1/65
Wayne, Robert	10/10/62	No evidence of muster in

Company H

Name, Age, Residence	Joined	Remarks
PRIVATE (CONT.)		
Wesley, John, 18 Lafayette, Mo.	1/24/63	Mustered out 10/1/65
White, Charles, 21 Mo.	3/25/63	KIA Poison Spring, Ark., 4/18/64
White, Isaac, 30 Johnson, Mo.	1/24/63	Mustered out 10/1/65
Whitmire, Dennis	3/25/63	No evidence of muster in
Wiley, James, 20 Mo.	3/15/63	KIA Poison Spring, Ark., 4/18/64
Williams, Armsted	8/25/62	No evidence of muster in
Williams, Louis, 22 Mo.	3/10/63	KIA Poison Spring, Ark., 4/18/64
Wilson, James, 19 Mo.	3/25/63	Mustered out 10/1/65
Winchester, Scipio, 30 Mo.	3/13/63	Mustered out 10/1/65
Wood, Jake	9/20/63	No evidence of muster in
Wood, Wesley, 23 Mo.	3/31/63	Deserted 5/25/63; arrested Ft. Leavenworth, Kans.; no evidence of muster out on file
Wright, George W.	9/20/62	No evidence of muster in
ADDITIONAL ENLISTMENTS		
Adams, Alexander, 27 Ark.	12/21/63	KIA Poison Spring, Ark., 4/18/64
Adams, John, 26 Ark.	12/20/63	Died Ozark, Ark., 2/10/64, of accidental wounds
Adams, William, 18 Ark.	12/20/63	Died Ft. Smith, Ark., 12/10/64, of intermittent fever

Company H

Name, Age, Residence	Joined	Remarks
ADDITIONAL ENLISTMENTS (CONT.)		
Atkinson, Hezekiah	11/1/63	Mustered out 10/1/65
Belt, Benjamin, 21 Ark.	11/16/63	Mustered out 10/1/65
Berry, George, 35 Ark.	10/20/63	Died Little Rock, Ark., 5/17/65, of inflammation of the bowels
Berry, Luke, 18 Ark.	2/10/65	Mustered out 10/1/65
Childs, Rufus, 19 Ark.	12/21/63	Mustered out 10/1/65
Crawford, Andrew, 40 Ark.	11/16/63	Died Waldron, Ark., 11/26/63, of bloody flux
Davis, Charles, 36 Boone County, Ky.	12/21/63	Mustered out 10/1/65
Davis, Richard, 22 Mo.	11/7/63	Died Ft. Smith, Ark., 6/18/64, of bronchitis
Evans, Henry, 20 Ark.	11/7/63	Died Ft. Smith, Ark., 5/18/64, of disease
Harvey, William, 20 Ark.	10/2/63	Mustered out 10/1/65
Hogan, William, 20 Franklin County, Ark.	12/1/63	Mustered out 10/1/65
Jackson, Andrew, 19 Ark.	11/16/63	Mustered out Little Rock, Ark., 7/8/65
Jones, Robert, 18 Cherokee Nation	7/21/63	Mustered out 10/1/65
Lilley, Merritt, 20 Mo.	1/11/64	Mustered out 10/1/65
Marles, Winchester, 18 Waldron, Ark.	11/16/63	Mustered out 10/1/65
Otterbridge, Stephen, 20 Ark.	10/20/63	Died Waldron, Ark., 11/22/63, of remittent fever
Parks, John W., 36 Franklin County, Ark.	12/21/63	Mustered out Little Rock, Ark., 7/8/65

Company H

Name, Age, Residence	Joined	Remarks
ADDITIONAL ENLISTMENTS (CONT.)		
Phillips, Granville, 37 Mo.	12/21/63	Deserted Ft. Smith, Ark., 6/4/64
Rose, John, 18 Johnson County, Ark.	10/3/63	Mustered out 10/1/65
Skinner Jackson, 27 Ark.	11/16/63	Died Ozark, Ark., 2/14/64, of brain fever
Winchester, Charles, 18 N.C.	11/9/63	Mustered out 10/1/65

Company I

Name, Age, Residence	Joined	Remarks
CAPTAIN		
Lewis, Granville M., 22 Elwood, Kans.	2/11/65	Mustered out 10/1/65
Van Horn, Benjamin F., 36	5/1/63	Resigned 1/19/64
FIRST LIEUTENANT		
Harris, Ransom L., 22	6/27/63	Resigned Ft. Smith, Ark., 6/18/64
Hitchcock, Dyer W., 28	4/26/65	Mustered out 10/1/65
SECOND LIEUTENANT		
Johnson, Horace H., 40 Baldwin City, Kans.	12/24/63	Resigned 10/20/64
FIRST SERGEANT		
Berry, Alfred N., 25 Ft. Smith, Ark.	11/8/63	KIA Poison Spring, Ark., 4/18/64
McIntosh, William, 20 Lafayette County, Mo.	3/15/63	Mustered out 10/1/65
SERGEANT		
Alexander, Isaac, 35 Chickasaw Nation	4/10/63	Discharged 6/23/65 for disability
Brown, Jack, 32	4/20/63	Mustered out 10/1/65

Company I

Name, Age, Residence	Joined	Remarks
SERGEANT (CONT.)		
Browning, Henry, 22 Logan, Ky.	3/15/63	Mustered out 10/1/65
Morris, Anderson, 23 St. Louis, Mo.	3/20/63	Mustered out 10/1/65
CORPORAL		
Brady, Saucer, 33 Ala.	4/6/63	Mustered out 10/1/65
Colburn, Gaddis, 33 Sac & Fox Agency	3/20/63	KIA Poison Spring, Ark., 4/18/64
Connell [Kernell], Abraham, 24 Ala.	3/21/63	Mustered out 10/1/65
Connell, Redmond, 32 Ala.	4/6/63	Mustered out 10/1/65
Cudjo, Samuel, 25	3/21/63	Mustered out 10/1/65
Cuttica, Elwis, 25 Sac & Fox Agency	4/19/63	Mustered out 10/1/65
Jennings, Bartlett, 20 Leavenworth, Kans.	3/15/63	KIA Poison Spring, Ark., 4/18/64
Toliver, John, 19 Clay County, Mo.	3/15/63	Mustered out 10/1/65
White, George, 22 Boon, Ky.	3/1/63	Mustered out 10/1/65
Williams, Samuel, 22 Sac & Fox Agency	4/18/63	KIA Poison Spring, Ark., 4/18/64
PRIVATE		
Ards, John, 30 Sac & Fox Agency	4/10/63	Deserted Ft. Scott, Kans., 12/4/63
Battice, John, 28 Sac & Fox Agency	4/10/63	Deserted Ft. Gibson, C.N., 11/25/64
Batts, Alexander, 19 Madison, La.	3/15/63	Mustered out 10/1/65
Batts, John, 21 La.	3/15/63	Mustered out 10/1/65
Bear, Brash, 25 Chickasaw Nation	3/26/63	Discharged Little Rock, Ark., 6/19/65, for mental disabilities

Company I

Name, Age, Residence	Joined	Remarks
PRIVATE (CONT.)		
Bennard, Jacob, 27 Ala.	4/6/63	Mustered out 11/6/65
Bowlegs, George, 25 Chickasaw Nation	4/10/63	Deserted Ft. Gibson, C.N., 12/8/63
Bowlegs, Cyrus, 40 Sac & Fox Agency	4/6/63	Discharged Ft. Smith, Ark., 12/4/63, for disability
Bowlegs, Robert, 27 Sac & Fox Agency	4/15/63	Died Ft. Smith, Ark., 5/26/64, of disease
Brown, Thomas, 50 Prince Edward County, Va.	3/15/63	Discharged Little Rock, Ark., 6/23/65, for disability
Buckner, Charles, 27 Madison, La.	3/26/63	KIA Poison Spring, Ark., 4/18/64
Bruner, William, 27 Creek Nation	4/10/63	Mustered out 10/1/65
Captain, Ned, 27 Sac & Fox Agency	4/10/63	Deserted Baxter Springs, C.N., 6/10/63
Carr, Wilson, 50 Leavenworth, Kans.	3/15/63	Discharged 10/13/63 for disability
Childs, Hambra, 22 Burlingame, Kans.	3/20/63	Died Camden, Ark., 8/21/64, of disease
Coffee, Benjamin, 19 Sac & Fox Agency	3/26/63	KIA Poison Spring, Ark., 4/18/64
Comiger, James, 19 Leavenworth, Kans.	3/15/63	Died Ft. Smith, Ark., 6/14/64, of disease
Connell, Bully, 19 Creek Nation	4/6/63	Sick in hospital Little Rock, Ark., 3/7/65; no evidence of muster out on file
Connell, James, 23 Robinson, Tenn.	4/10/63	Mustered out 10/1/65
Connell, Morris, 28 Ala.	4/6/63	Discharged Little Rock, Ark., 7/4/65, for disability
Daniels, Thomas, 22 Cherokee Nation	4/19/63	Mustered out 10/1/65

Company I

Name, Age, Residence	Joined	Remarks
PRIVATE (CONT.)		
Dunbar, Otha, 18 Lafayette, Mo.	3/15/63	Mustered out 10/1/65
Fife, Joseph, 35 Creek Nation	3/25/63	Discharged Little Rock, Ark., 6/17/65, for disability
Finhulkie, James, 18 Creek Nation	3/20/63	Mustered out 10/1/65
Fondron, William, 22 Leavenworth, Kans.	3/20/63	Died Roseville, Ark., 3/2/64, of disease
Goodin, James, 23 Sac & Fox Agency	4/20/63	Died Camden, Ark., 4/24/64, of wounds received at Poison Spring, Ark.
Gouge, Scipio, 27 Ala.	3/20/63	Mustered out 10/1/65
Hardridge, Elias, 18 Sac & Fox Agency	3/20/63	Discharged Ft. Gibson, C.N., 8/22/63, for disability
Herrod, Thomas, 25 Creek Nation	4/26/63	Mustered out 10/1/65
Island, Billy, 21 Creek Nation	4/10/63	Mustered out 10/1/65
Jackson, Andrew, 23 Ky.	3/15/63	Mustered out 10/1/65
Johnson, Andrew, 25	3/15/63	Discharged Little Rock, Ark., 4/21/65, for disability
Johnson, London, 23	3/15/63	Died
Jonah, George, 18 Creek Nation	3/22/63	Deserted Ft. Smith, Ark., 8/14/64
Kerr, John, 24 Louisville, Ky.	3/15/63	Mustered out 10/1/65
Landrum, Daniel, 35 Creek Nation	3/20/63	Discharged Little Rock, Ark., 6/23/65, for disability
Lewis, Andrew, 23 Creek Nation	4/18/63	Mustered out 10/1/65

Company I

Name, Age, Residence	Joined	Remarks
PRIVATE (CONT.)		
Lewis, Smart, 20 Creek Nation	3/20/63	Mustered out 10/1/65
Lincoln, Thomas, 24 Creek Nation	4/15/63	Died Ft. Smith, Ark., 8/24/64
Lock, Lowry, 19 Steward County, Tenn.	3/15/63	Mustered out 10/1/65
Lynch, Joseph, 23 Cherokee Nation	4/18/63	Mustered out 10/1/65
McAdoo, Jordon, 20 Leavenworth, Kans.	3/15/63	KIA Poison Spring, Ark., 4/18/64
McIntosh, Joseph, 25 Sac & Fox Agency	4/6/63	Deserted Talequah, C.N., 11/5/63
McIntosh, Morris, 25 Sac & Fox Agency	4/6/63	Deserted Baxter Springs, C.N., 5/25/63
McQueen, John, 27 Sac & Fox Agency	4/10/63	Deserted Baxter Springs, C.N., 5/25/63
Mobile, Bankston, 24 Leavenworth, Kans.	4/15/63	Discharged Ft. Smith, Ark., 12/4/63 for disability
Moore, Jack, 19 Sac & Fox Agency	3/20/63	Deserted Ft. Gibson, C.N., 9/14/63
Moore, Jerry, 18 Sac & Fox Agency	3/20/63	Deserted Ft. Gibson, C.N., 9/14/63
Moore, Lewis, 45	3/20/63	Deserted Ft. Smith, Ark., 1/17/65
Noble, Simon, 18	3/20/63	KIA Poison Spring, Ark., 4/28/64
Patent, Robert, 23 Va.	3/15/63	Mustered out 10/1/65
Patterson, Michael, 43 Leavenworth, Kans.	3/15/63	Died Ft. Gibson, C.N., 7/9/63, of disease
Pickens, Manuel, 25 Sac & Fox Agency	4/18/63	KIA Poison Spring, Ark., 4/18/64
Poindexter, Captain, 19 Ala.	3/15/63	Mustered out 10/1/65

Company I

Name, Age, Residence	Joined	Remarks
PRIVATE (CONT.)		
Pope, George, 25 Leavenworth, Kans.	3/15/63	Killed Lawrence, Kans., 8/21/63, by Quantrill's guerrillas
Price, Robert, 20 Lafayette County, Mo	3/15/63	Mustered out 10/1/65
Ransom, Lewis, 32 Williamson County, Tenn.	3/20/63	Mustered out 10/1/65
Ross, Jacob, 20 Lafayette, Mo.	4/15/63	Mustered out 10/1/65
Says, Snow, 23 Creek Nation	4/10/63	Mustered out 10/1/65
Sells, Sampson, 21 Sac & Fox Agency	4/10/63	Died 9/1/65
Sewell, Francis, 51 Toronto, Canada	3/15/63	Discharged Ft. Smith, Ark., 10/13/63, for disability
Shelby, Lafayette, 22 Lafayette, Mo.	3/15/63	Mustered out 10/1/65
Smith, Andrew, 22 Cherokee Nation	4/10/63	Mustered out 10/1/65
Smith, John W., 21 Toronto, Canada	3/15/63	Mustered out 10/1/65
Smith, Monroe, 20 Lafayette, Mo.	3/15/63	Mustered out 10/1/65
Stopp, John, 18 Cherokee Nation	4/6/63	Mustered out 10/1/65
Tiddon, Morris, 23 Ala.	4/10/63	Mustered out 10/1/65
Williams, David, 23 Washington, Miss.	3/15/63	Mustered out 10/1/65
Williams, John, 22 Saline, Mo.	3/15/63	Mustered out 10/1/65
Willis, Curley, 18 Creek Nation	4/10/63	Mustered out 10/1/65

Company I

Name, Age, Residence	Joined	Remarks
ADDITIONAL ENLISTMENTS		
Barnett, Benjamin, 25 Creek Nation	11/21/63	Mustered out 10/1/65
Duly, Zachariah, 18 Camden, Ark.	4/7/64	Mustered out 10/1/65
George, Henry, 19 Clark, Ga.	6/1/63	Mustered out 10/1/65
George, London, 18 Ft. Scott, Kans.	6/1/63	KIA Poison Spring, Ark., 4/18/64
Grayson, Franklin, 30 Creek Nation	7/12/63	Mustered out 10/1/65
Hardridge, Dean	5/10/63	Rejected by surgeon
Hardridge, Nary, 18 Ft. Scott, Kans.	5/10/63	Discharged Ft. Gibson, C.N., 8/22/63, for disability
Harris, Joseph	6/1/13	Rejected by surgeon
Hawkins, Richard, 20 Creek Nation	5/10/63	Mustered out 10/1/65
Jackson, General, 18 Ft. Scott, Kans.	6163	Deserted Ft. Gibson, C.N., 9/14/63
Maye, Robert, 45 Ft. Scott, Kans.	5/10/63	Deserted Ft. Gibson, C.N., 8/23/63
Metter, Jack, 23 Sac & Fox Agency	3/20/63	Died Ft. Gibson, C.N., 9/15/63, of accidental wounds
Reed, Anderson, 18 Cherokee Nation	5/10/63	Mustered out 10/1/65
Robinson, Ashnell, 45 Ft. Scott, Kans.	6/1/63	Died Ft. Gibson, C.N., 4/21/63, of disease
Sanford, John	—	Deserted 5/29/65, not mustered in
Starr, Joseph, 19 Cherokee Nation	6/1/63	Mustered out 10/1/65
Williams, Nathan, 18 Cherokee Nation	6/1/63	Mustered out 10/1/65

Company K

Name, Age, Residence	Joined	Remarks
CAPTAIN		
Sholes, Augustus T. Wyandotte, Kans.	7/21/65	No evidence of muster out on file
Welch, Benjamin W. Ft. Scott, Kans.	3/2/63	Killed Timber Hills, C.N., 11/19/64, in skirmish with guerrillas
FIRST LIEUTENANT		
Sutherland, David M., 20 Lawrence, Kans.	5/2/63	Mustered out 10/1/65
SECOND LIEUTENANT		
Saviers, Albert E. Leavenworth, Kans.	5/2/63	Discharged Ft. Smith, Ark., 2/25/64, for disability
FIRST SERGEANT		
Johnson, Scipio, 26 Ala.	4/1/63	Mustered out 10/1/65
Mitchell, Joseph Leavenworth, Kans.	8/10/62	KIA Poison Spring, Ark., 4/18/64
Montgomery, James, 27 Mason County, Ky.	4/14/63	Mustered out 10/1/65
SERGEANT		
Brown, James Richmond, Va.	4/1/63	Mustered out 10/1/65
Calva, George W., 31 Cooper County, Mo.	4/1/63	Mustered out 10/1/65
Marshall, Harrison, 33 Dinwiddie County, Va.	4/1/63	Mustered out 10/1/65
Wilson, Samuel Richmond, Va.	4/1/63	KIA Flat Rock, C.N., 9/16/64
CORPORAL		
Dixon, John Lafayette County, Mo.	4/1/63	KIA Poison Spring, Ark., 4/18/64
Hays, John Dinwiddie County, Va.	4/1/63	KIA Flat Rock, C.N., 9/16/64

Company K

Name, Age, Residence	Joined	Remarks
CORPORAL (CONT.)		
Lee, James Wyandotte, Kans.	4/1/63	KIA Flat Rock, C.N., 9/16/64
Lightner, Alfred, 21 Lafayette County, Mo.	4/1/63	Mustered out 10/1/65
Shepard, Beverly, 29 Cooper County, Mo.	4/1/63	Mustered out 10/1/65
South, Jesse, 40 Lexington, Ky.	4/1/63	Mustered out 10/1/65
Sweeny, Matthew N.C.	4/1/63	KIA Poison Spring, Ark., 4/18/64
Thomas, John, 22 Franklin County, N.C.	4/1/63	Mustered out 10/1/65
Williams, William, 18 Lafayette, Ky.	4/1/63	Mustered out 10/1/65
Wood, Isom N.C.	4/1/63	Mustered out 10/1/65
MUSICIAN		
Davis, Samuel, 20 Augustine County, Fla.	4/1/63	Mustered out 10/1/65
PRIVATE		
Adams, Henry Augustine County, Fla.	4/1/63	KIA Flat Rock, C.N., 9/16/64
Archy, William	4/1/63	KIA Poison Spring, Ark., 4/18/64
Austin, Charles	4/1/63	KIA Poison Spring, Ark., 4/18/64
Boler, Scott, 49 Spotsylvania County, Va.	4/1/63	Mustered out 10/1/65
Bratcher, Smith, 22 Jefferson County, Ky.	4/1/63	Mustered out 10/1/65
Brown, George	4/1/63	No evidence of muster in

Company K

Name, Age, Residence	Joined	Remarks
PRIVATE (CONT.)		
Caldwell (no first name)	4/1/63	No evidence of muster in
Clark, Gabriel	4/1/63	KIA Flat Rock, C.N., 9/16/64
Clarkson, Perry, 32 Fredrick County, Md.	4/1/63	Mustered out 10/1/65
Collins, Alfred	4/1/63	KIA Flat Rock, C.N., 9/16/64
Connell, Scott	4/1/63	Discharged Ft. Smith, Ark., 10/13/63, for disability
Cresy, Squire	4/1/63	Discharged Ft. Smith, Ark., 12/10/63, for disability
Curry, Hugh	4/1/63	KIA Flat Rock, C.N., 9/16/64
Cussick, Amos	4/1/63	KIA Flat Rock, C.N., 9/16/64
Davis, Edward	4/1/63	Died Ft. Smith, Ark., 11/11/63, of disease
Dixon, George	4/1/63	Charged with murder, sentenced to be hanged by General Court Martial, executed 7/21/65
Duvall, George, 22 Lafayette County, Mo.	4/1/63	Mustered out 10/1/65
Edwards, Lewis	4/1/63	KIA Flat Rock, C.N., 9/16/64
Erving, Charles, 18 Lafayette County, Mo.	4/1/63	Mustered out 10/1/65
Erving, Washington	4/1/63	KIA Flat Rock, C.N., 9/16/64
Erving, Finley	4/1/63	Discharged Ft. Smith, Ark., 12/4/63, for disability

Company K

Name, Age, Residence	Joined	Remarks
PRIVATE (CONT.)		
Gains, John, 21 Ill.	4/1/63	Mustered out 10/1/65
Gifford, Joshua	4/1/63	Died Roseville, Ark., 12/21/63, of disease
Gifford, Spencer	4/1/63	KIA Flat Rock, C.N., 9/16/64
Graham, James	4/1/63	KIA Flat Rock, C.N., 9/16/64
Grandson, Henry	4/1/63	KIA Poison Spring, Ark., 4/18/64
Gross, Montella	4/1/63	Captured at Poison Spring, Ark., 4/18/64
Hamilton, Thomas	4/1/63	KIA Flat Rock, C.N., 9/16/64
Helms, Charles Ark.	4/1/63	Deserted Baxter Springs, C.N., 6/14/63
Helms, Henry	4/1/63	Discharged Ft. Smith, Ark., 12/4/63, for disability
Hill, Edward	4/1/63	KIA Poison Spring, Ark., 4/18/64
Hines, Aaron	4/1/63	Discharged Ft. Smith, Ark., 10/13/63 for disability
Hutchins, James	4/1/63	No evidence of muster
Irvin, Charles, 40 Simpson County, Ky.	4/1/63	Mustered out 10/1/65
Irvin, Martin	4/1/63	KIA Flat Rock, C.N., 9/16/64
Jackson, Clit	4/1/63	Discharged Ft. Smith, Ark., 10/13/63 for disability
Jefferson, Samuel	4/1/63	Died Ft. Gibson, C.N., 10/25/64, of wounds received in action
Johnson, Irvin	4/1/63	Discharged Roseville, Ark., 12/31/63, for disability

Company K

Name, Age, Residence	Joined	Remarks
PRIVATE (CONT.)		
Johnson, John Wyandotte, Kans.	4/1/63	Committed suicide Little Rock, Ark., 6/23/65
Johnson, Newton Wyandotte, Kans.	4/7/63	KIA Flat Rock, C.N., 9/16/64
Johnson, Orange, 27 Cooper County, Mo.	4/1/63	Mustered out 10/1/65
Johnson, Pompey, 21 Franklin County, Mo.	4/7/63	Mustered out 10/1/65
Johnson, Richard Franklin County, Mo.	4/1/63	KIA Flat Rock, C.N., 9/16/64
Kelly, Granville	4/1/63	KIA Poison Spring, Ark., 4/18/64
Lewis, John, 22 Va.	4/1/63	Mustered out 10/1/65
Lindsy, Frank	4/1/63	KIA Flat Rock, C.N., 9/16/64
Link, Hall	4/7/63	KIA Poison Spring, Ark., 4/18/64
Locket, Henry	4/1/63	Died Ft. Gibson, C.N., of disease
Mack, George, 24 Colby County, Md.	4/4/63	Mustered out 10/1/65
McFerley, Mack, 22 Simpson County, Ky.	4/1/63	Mustered out 10/1/65
McFeely, Hannibal	4/1/63	Discharged Ft. Smith, Ark., 12/4/63, for disability
Miller, Jacob	4/4/63	KIA Flat Rock, C.N., 9/16/64
Myers, Elias	4/1/63	KIA Flat Rock, C.N., 9/16/64
Neal, Henry, 24 Lafayette County, Mo.	4/1/63	Mustered out 10/1/65
Nelson, George	4/1/63	KIA Flat Rock, C.N., 9/16/64
Patterson, Isaac, 22 Lafayette County, Mo.	4/4/63	Mustered out 10/1/65

Company K

Name, Age, Residence	Joined	Remarks
	PRIVATE (CONT.)	
Perkins, Jacob	4/1/63	KIA Flat Rock, C.N., 9/16/64
Picket, Reuben	4/1/63	KIA Poison Spring, Ark., 4/18/64
Pinket, Stephen	4/1/63	KIA Flat Rock, C.N., 9/16/64
Polk, James K.	4/4/63	KIA Flat Rock, C.N., 9/16/64
Rankins, Mark, 24 Creek Nation	4/1/63	Mustered out 10/1/65
Richardson, Coleman	4/10/63	KIA Flat Rock, C.N., 9/16/64
Scott, Curly, 33 Casey County, Ky.	4/10/63	Mustered out 10/1/65
Simpson, Peter, 50 Paris, Ky.	4/8/63	Discharged Ft. Smith, Ark., 11/30/64, for disability
Smith, Andrew	4/1/63	Discharged Ft. Smith, Ark., 10/13/63, for disability
Smith, William	4/1/63	KIA Poison Spring, Ark., 4/18/64
Solomon, William, 28 Scott County, Ky.	4/1/63	Mustered out 10/1/65
Straw, Charles	4/1/63	KIA Flat Rock, C.N., 9/16/64
Stratton, Richard	4/1/63	KIA Poison Spring, Ark., 4/18/64
Terrill, Austin	4/1/63	KIA Flat Rock, C.N., 9/16/64
Tibb, George	4/1/63	KIA Flat Rock, C.N., 9/16/64
Thatcher, Henry, 18 Lexington, Ky.	4/1/63	Discharged Little Rock, Ark., 6/16/65 for disability

Company K

Name, Age, Residence	Joined	Remarks
PRIVATE (CONT.)		
Thompson, London, 37 Woodford, Ky.	4/1/63	POW 9/16/64–10/1/65; mustered out 10/1/65
Turpin, Richard	4/1/63	Died Ft. Scott, Kans., 5/19/63, of disease
Vaughn, Jesse	4/1/63	KIA Flat Rock, C.N., 9/16/64
Walker, John	4/1/63	KIA Poison Spring, Ark., 4/18/64
Washington, George, 1st, 38 Frederick County, Va.	4/1/63	Mustered out 10/1/65
ADDITIONAL ENLISTMENTS		
Adams, William, 22 Crawford County, Ark.	2/22/65	Mustered out 10/1/65
Ashby, Allen, 25 Clay County, Mo.	2/25/65	Deserted 4/8/65
Ball, Henry, 25 Crawford County, Ark.	2/24/65	Mustered out 10/1/65
Boyd, Israel, 22 S.C.	2/20/65	Mustered out 10/1/65
Cox, George, 22 St. Louis, Mo.	2/22/65	Mustered out 10/1/65
Flin, Charles, 19 Nashville, Tenn.	3/19/65	Rejected by surgeon
Greenberry, George, 32 Mercer County, Ky.	2/20/65	Mustered out 10/1/65
Jackson, James, 35 Shelby County, Ky.	2/22/65	Mustered out 10/1/65
Lacy, William, 17 Morgan County, Ala.	2/24/65	Mustered out 10/1/65
Lane, William Lincoln, 29 Cooper County, Mo.	2/20/65	Mustered out 10/1/65
Marmaduke, Joseph, 40 Shelby County, Mo.	2/20/65	Mustered out 10/1/65

Company K

Name, Age, Residence	Joined	Remarks
ADDITIONAL ENLISTMENTS (CONT.)		
Mays, Caesar, 26 Greensburgh, Ky.	2/20/63	Mustered out 10/1/65
Nelson, Anderson, 31 Stokes County, N.C.	2/24/65	Mustered out 10/1/65
Parker, William, 40 Simpson County, Ky.	2/20/65	Mustered out 10/1/65
Pee, Charles, 28 Warner County, Tenn.	2/24/65	Mustered out 10/1/65
Peevely, Ephraim, 45 Clay County, Mo.	2/20/65	Died Little Rock, Ark., 8/1/65, of chronic diarrhea
Potter, Harvey, 26 Woodford County, Ky.	2/20/65	Mustered out 10/1/65
Ridings, David, 21 Lafayette County, Mo.	2/23/65	Mustered out 10/1/65
Riley, John, 20 Green County, Mo.	2/24/65	Stopped at St. Louis hospital
Sawyer, David, 43 Washington County, Va.	2/21/65	Mustered out 10/1/65
Smith, Elijah, 27 Stokes County, N.C.	2/20/65	Mustered out 10/1/65
Tyler, Frank, 38 Henry County, Ky.	2/21/65	Mustered out 10/1/65
Van, Gilbert, 36 Cherokee Nation	2/24/65	Mustered out 10/1/65
Washington, George, 2nd, 21 Ky.	2/20/65	Mustered out 10/1/65
Williams, Jacob, 36 Northampton, Va.	2/24/65	Mustered out 10/1/65

Draftees, Substitutes, and Other Individuals
Not Assigned to a Company

Name, Age, Residence	Joined	Remarks
Adams, John	3/14/65	Mustered out 5/12/65
Ball, James, 18 Mo.	2/27/65	Substitute for William Armstrong; mustered out 5/18/65
Barnes, Matterson	3/13/65	Substitute for William Hays; mustered out 5/12/65
Baskville, Hobbs	3/13/65	Mustered out 5/12/65
Bean, Joseph	2/23/65	Mustered out 5/12/65
Biggs, Benjamin, 32 Ky.	3/6/65	Mustered out 5/12/65
Bean, Luther	2/16/65	Substitute for James P. McManus to serve one year; mustered out 5/12/65
Brown, Detroit	2/28/65	Mustered out 5/12/65
Brown, Nelson, 26 Harpers Ferry, Md.	2/23/65	Substitute for E. B. Buck; mustered out 5/12/65
Brown, William, 20 C.N.	3/2/65	Substitute for Whitford Thurber
Bruce, Charles, 24 Ky.	3/1/65	Substitute for Arter Heatherly; mustered out 5/12/65
Cavanaugh, Philip	3/10/65	Substitute for Charles F. Bonnel; mustered out 5/12/65
Clark, Archibald, 45	3/11/65	Substitute for D. C. O. Howel; mustered out 5/12/65
Clark, George	4/29/65	Substitute for John Out; mustered out 5/12/65
Clark, Thomas	3/2/65	Substitute for Michael Branzon; mustered out 5/12/65
Clay, Henry	3/14/65	Substitute for M. L. Inelson

Draftees, Substitutes, and Other Individuals
Not Assigned to a Company

Name, Age, Residence	Joined	Remarks
Collins, Milton	4/29/65	Mustered out 5/12/65
Columbus, Christopher	2/13/65	Substitute for Augustus Shannon; mustered out 5/12/65
Crane, Frank	3/4/65	Substitute for William Crane; mustered out 5/12/65
Daniels, Miles	4/29/65	Substitute for John Barber
Davis, John	4/29/65	Mustered out 5/12/65
Davis, William	3/6/65	Substitute for Ebenezer Disdrow
De Friese, John M.	—	Second Lieutenant, temporarily assigned to regiment from Sixth Kansas Cavalry
Denny, John	2/24/65	Substitute for Solomon Hendburg
Dougherty, Benjamin	6/64	Mustered out 5/19/65
Duncan, Woodford	3/10/65	Substitute for John L. Blair; mustered out 5/12/65
Dunkin, Dee	3/4/65	Mustered out 5/12/65
Edwards, James	5/12/65	Substitute for John Westover; mustered out 5/12/65
Edwards, Mitchell	5/18/65	Mustered out 5/12/65
Estel, Robert	4/29/65	Substitute for William McPherson; mustered out 5/12/65
Farenater, Andrew	3/10/65	Mustered out 5/16/65
Franklin, Benjamin	3/8/65	Mustered out 5/18/65
Gee, Bird	3/10/65	Substitute for Lucius Nutting; mustered out 5/12/65
Gee, Smith	3/10/65	Substitute for Wesley Wood; mustered out 5/12/65

Draftees, Substitutes, and Other Individuals
Not Assigned to a Company

Name, Age, Residence	Joined	Remarks
George, William	3/8/65	Substitute for William Jarrott; mustered out 5/12/65
Gibson, James	2/27/65	Substitute for Oscar Richards; mustered out 5/12/65
Gibson, Robert	6/29/64	No further record of service
Glass, Richard	2/27/65	Mustered out 5/16/65
Golden, David	2/24/65	Substitute for Samuel Loflend; mustered out 5/12/65
Gowans, James N.Mex.	4/29/65	Substitute for Henry Simpson; mustered out 5/12/65
Grandison, Richard	2/10/65	Substitute for Bartley Burris
Grant, Charles	5/18/65	Mustered out 5/18/65
Grant, Henry	3/6/65	No evidence of muster out on file
Gray, Spencer, 43 Mercer County, Ky.	2/21/65	Discharged, no date given
Gray, William	3/2/65	Mustered out 5/18/65
Greenwood, Virgil	3/4/65	Substitute for George Van Starns
Hackwell, Pleasant	3/13/65	Substitute for Benjamin Blackburn; mustered out 5/12/65
Hanks, Samuel	3/2/65	Mustered out 5/18/65
Harris, Ison	2/65	Substitute for William H. Kline; deserted; not mustered out
Harvey, Robert	3/6/65	Substitute for Adam Ernst; mustered out 5/12/65
Hayden, Samuel	2/26/65	Mustered out 5/12/65

Draftees, Substitutes, and Other Individuals
Not Assigned to a Company

Name, Age, Residence	Joined	Remarks
Hazeling, George	3/65	Substitute for Thomas Smith; deserted
Hendspelt, Charles	3/1/65	Unassigned; mustered out 5/18/65
Hill, Ambrose	3/6/65	Mustered out 5/23/65
Hoglin, John	3/4/65	Substitute for Joseph Stoddard
Howard, Elsey	3/8/65	Mustered out 5/12/65
Huffington, William	3/2/65	Mustered out 5/18/65
Jackson, Andrew	3/2/65	Mustered out 5/18/65
Jackson, Andrew (#2)	3/2/65	Mustered out 5/18/65
Jackson, James Andrew	2/21/65	Substitute for Thomas Jones; mustered out 5/12/65
Jackson, Robert, 18	—	Deserted
Jacobs, Tenithus	3/2/65	Mustered out 5/18/65
Jefferson, Alexander	3/10/65	Mustered out 5/18/65
Jefferson, Thomas	3/11/65	Substitute for Donald Carmichael
Johnson, Benjamin	2/17/65	Substitute for John Wilson; mustered out 5/12/65
Johnson, Franklin	2/27/65	No evidence of muster out on file
Johnson, George		
	3/7/65	Substitute for Russell Williams; died in hospital 3/65
Jones, Jonathan	3/8/65	Mustered out 5/18/65
Jordan, Jerd	3/14/65	Substitute for William King; mustered out 5/12/65
Lamb, Jackson	3/14/65	Mustered out 5/12/65
Lewis, Charles	3/3/65	Mustered out 5/16/65
Lewis, Joseph	3/8/65	Mustered out 5/18/65

Draftees, Substitutes, and Other Individuals
Not Assigned to a Company

Name, Age, Residence	Joined	Remarks
Logan, Jeff	3/1/65	Substitute for Christian Thoren; died 5/19/65 of diabetes
Logan, Robert	2/27/65	Substitute for Thurston Lewis; mustered out 5/12/65
Logan, William T.	2/23/65	Substitute for Owen Digan; mustered out 5/12/65
Mallery, Essex	3/13/65	Mustered out 5/12/65
Martin, Ben	3/7/65	Substitute for Samuel Sawyer; mustered out 5/12/65
Martin, John	3/13/65	Substitute for Frederick Back; mustered out 5/12/65
Matthews, John	2/27/65	Substitute for David A. Messer; mustered out 5/12/65
McGinnis, James	3/14/54	Substitute for George G. Engle; mustered out 5/12/65
McKinney, James	3/6/65	Substitute for Orris Fairchild; mustered out 5/12/65
McThompson, Ransom	2/24/65	Substitute for Theodore McMillan; mustered out 5/12/65
Melton, Peter, 35 C.N.	2/20/65	Died Ft. Scott, Kans., 4/1/65, of pneumonia
Miller, Dudley, 18 Kentucky	2/20/65	Substitute for William Carson; mustered out 4/29/65
Monroe, Anthony	2/27/65	Substitute for Norman Chambers; mustered out 5/12/65

Draftees, Substitutes, and Other Individuals
Not Assigned to a Company

Name, Age, Residence	Joined	Remarks
Monroe, James	3/1/65	Substitute for Franklin Weaver; mustered out 5/12/65
Montgomery, William	3/11/65	Substitute for E. M. Gardner; mustered out 5/12/65
Moore, John I.	3/10/65	Substitute for John Arnold; mustered out 5/12/65
Moses, Arnold	3/8/65	Mustered out 5/18/65
Murphy, Richard	3/5/65	Substitute for Albert Lemon; mustered out 5/12/65
Nelson, William	2/20/65	Substitute for John W. Harris; mustered out 5/12/65
Newby, Joseph	4/22/65	Mustered out 10/1/65
Nichols, Thomas F.	4/4/65	Substitute for Ezekial Cox; mustered out 5/12/65
Norman, George	1/26/64	No evidence of muster out on file
Payne, Thomas J.	10/29/64	First Lieutenant, no record of company assignment; mustered out 12/26/64
Preston, Frank	5/18/65	Mustered out 5/18/65
Pryor, Samuel	3/10/65	Substitute for R. S. McCubbin
Randolph, Isaac	5/18/65	Mustered out 5/18/65
Reed, Talbert	3/7/65	No evidence of muster on file
Rice, Henry, 18	2/13/65	Substitute for Elias Woodruff; deserted
Richison, Addison	3/7/65	Substitute for David Sprong
Richison, Henry	3/10/65	Substitute for George Howe; mustered out 5/12/65

Draftees, Substitutes, and Other Individuals
Not Assigned to a Company

Name, Age, Residence	Joined	Remarks
Riley, John Green, Mo.	2/24/65	Mustered out 4/29/65
Roan, Alonzo	3/7/65	Died 4/65 of disease
Rucker, Thomas	3/14/65	Substitute for Marshel Sollars; mustered out 5/12/65
Ruffin, Henry	3/6/65	Mustered out 5/18/65
Samuels, James	5/65	Mustered out 5/18/65
Scales, Andrew	3/11/65	Substitute for John Schwanke; mustered out 5/12/65
Scott, Richard	12/26/64	Mustered out 5/12/65
Shackleford, Samuel	3/14/65	Substitute for William Bayless; mustered out 5/12/65
Sipe, Robert	4/29/65	Mustered out 5/12/65
Six-Killer, John	—	Part of Seaman's Battalion—no company designation listed; KIA Island Mound, Mo., 10/29/62
Smart, Joseph	2/27/65	Substitute for Richard Richards; mustered out 5/12/65
Smart, Martin	2/27/65	Substitute for Robert Young; mustered out 5/12/65
Stewart, Charles R.	3/2/65	Mustered out 5/18/65
Stevison, Samuel	3/6/65	Substitute for William Corlett; mustered out 5/12/65
Stewart, Edward	3/6/65	Mustered out 5/12/65
Strander, Daniel	2/22/65	Mustered out 5/12/65
Sutton, Thomas	2/10/65	Substitute for Henry Hammond; mustered out 5/12/65

Draftees, Substitutes, and Other Individuals
Not Assigned to a Company

Name, Age, Residence	Joined	Remarks
Sylvester, John	2/25/65	Mustered out 5/18/65
Talbott, Greenville	3/14/65	Substitute for William Dunn; mustered out 5/12/65
Taylor, Gibson	3/10/65	Substitute for Patrick Queeny; mustered out 5/12/65
Taylor, John	3/2/65	Mustered out 5/18/65
Thomas, Lewis	2/17/65	Substitute for Fielding Shannon; mustered out 5/12/65
Thompson, Henry	3/6/65	Substitute for James Still; mustered out 5/12/65
Thompson, Montague	3/11/65	Mustered out 5/12/65
Tutt, Robert	3/3/65	Substitute for John P. James
Tyler, Frank Henry County, Ky.	2/65	Mustered out 10/1/65
Vance, James	3/3/65	Mustered out 5/18/65
Ward, Joshua	3/18/65	Mustered out 5/12/65
Warren, Nathan	3/2/65	Mustered out 5/18/65
Weaver, Andy	2/25/65	Mustered out 5/18/65
Weaver, John	2/28/65	Substitute for Augustin Sprague; mustered out 5/12/65
White, Charles Wesley	3/14/65	Substitute for Isaac Nelson Cox; mustered out 5/18/65
White, Moses	3/13/65	Mustered out 5/12/65
Williams, Aleck	3/3/65	Substitute for Comodore Reece; mustered out 5/12/65
Williams, Martin	3/14/65	Substitute for John McDaniel; mustered out 5/12/65

Draftees, Substitutes, and Other Individuals
Not Assigned to a Company

Name, Age, Residence	Joined	Remarks
Williams, Nathan	3/2/65	Mustered out 5/18/65
Willis, Eli	2/18/65	Substitute for John Deal; mustered out 5/12/65
Woodson, Samuel	3/6/65	Substitute for William Hicks; mustered out 5/12/65
Woolridge, Clinton	3/6/65	No evidence of muster out on file
Wright, Jackson	3/7/65	Substitute for Samuel Walters; mustered out 5/12/65
Wright, Joseph	2/22//65	Substitute for James A. Goodman; mustered out 5/12/65
Yancier, Isaac	3/3/65	Mustered out 5/18/65
Young, Dennis	3/11/65	Substitute for James Williams; mustered out 5/12/65

Notes

Prologue

1. *Linn County Republican*, January 3, 1902.
2. Chris Tabor, *The Skirmish at Island Mound, Mo., October 29, 1862* (Independence, Mo.: Blue and Grey Book Shoppe, 2001), 9–11.
3. *New York Times*, November 19, 1862. This account was written by Richard Hinton, the adjutant of the First Kansas Colored. He served as a formal correspondent to the *New York Times* in the fall of 1862.
4. *Official Records of the War of the Rebellion (O.R.)*, ser. 1, vol. 53, 456.
5. *Glory*, dir. Edward Zwick (1989; TriStar Pictures).
6. Allen C. Guelzo, *Lincoln's Emancipation Proclamation: The End of Slavery in America* (New York: Simon & Schuster, 2004), 295.
7. Susan Aud, Mary Ann Fox, and Angelina KewalRamani, *Status and Trends in the Education of Racial and Ethnic Groups* (Washington, D.C.: National Center for Education Statistics, 2010), 8.

Chapter 1

1. *New York Times*, November 5, 1855.
2. *New York Tribune*, July 12, 1856.
3. James M. McPherson, *Battle Cry of Freedom* (New York: Oxford University Press, 1988), 121–23.
4. Lane cited health concerns for his decision not to run. However, his vote for the Kansas-Nebraska Act likely threatened his reelection. See Ian Michael Spurgeon, *Man of Douglas, Man of Lincoln: The Political Odyssey of James Henry Lane* (Columbia: University of Missouri Press, 2008), 35–36.
5. Nicole Etcheson, *Bleeding Kansas: Contested Liberty in the Civil War Era* (Lawrence: University Press of Kansas, 2004), 50–68; James A. Rawley, *Race and Politics: "Bleeding Kansas" and the Coming of the Civil War* (Lincoln: University of Nebraska Press, 1979), 86–95.
6. Perhaps the single best description of northern antislavery attitudes of this time period is Eric Foner's *Free Soil, Free Labor, Free Men: The Ideology of the Republican Party before the Civil War* (New York: Oxford University Press, 1970).
7. Richard B. Sheridan, "From Slavery in Missouri to Freedom in Kansas: The Influx of Black Fugitives and Contrabands into Kansas, 1854–1865," *Kansas History* 12 (Spring 1989): 29.
8. Nicole Etcheson, "Manliness and the Political Culture of the Old Northwest, 1790–1860," *Journal of the Early Republic* 15, no. 1 (Spring 1995): 59–62; Stephen Middleton, *The Black Laws: Race and the Legal Process in Early Ohio* (Athens: Ohio University Press, 2005), 43–44.

9. Robert Atkins Tovey, "A Twelve Months Practical Life in Kansas, Written by an Actual Settler," pp. 64–65, Kansas State Historical Society and University of Kansas, RH MS P186, *Territorial Kansas Online*, http://www.territorialkansasonline.org.
10. Journal, Topeka Constitutional Convention, October 31, 1855, Kansas State Historical Society (KSHS), Topeka.
11. *Herald of Freedom*, September 8, 1855.
12. Rawley, *Race and Politics*, 95; Etcheson, *Bleeding Kansas*, 75.
13. For a description of Lane's experience with the Senate in 1856, see Spurgeon, *Man of Douglas, Man of Lincoln*, 64–83.
14. Thomas J. Marsh to George L. Stearns, Esq., July 24, 1857, John Brown Collection, KSHS.
15. John James Ingalls to Dear Father [Elias T. Ingalls], June 10, 1859, John James Ingalls Collection, KSHS.
16. Sheridan, "From Slavery in Missouri to Freedom in Kansas," 38.
17. Middleton, *The Black Laws*, 43.
18. The episode is known as the Pottawatomie Massacre. Brown would later gain infamy for his failed attempt to spark a slave uprising at Harpers Ferry, Virginia, in 1859. See Thomas Goodrich, *War to the Knife: Bleeding Kansas, 1854–1861* (Lincoln: University of Nebraska Press, 2004), 124–28, 227–47.
19. Etcheson, *Bleeding Kansas*, 31.
20. O. E. L[earnard] to Dear Father, August 10, 1856, Oscar E. Learnard Collection, KSHS.
21. *Cleveland Evening Herald*, June 23, 1856, in Webb Scrapbook, 13:172, KSHS.
22. *Chicago Daily Tribune*, June 2, 1856, in Webb Scrapbook, 13:8, KSHS.
23. Etcheson, *Bleeding Kansas*, 77.
24. Ibid., 178; Spurgeon, *Man of Douglas, Man of Lincoln*, 143.
25. Journal, Leavenworth Constitutional Convention, April 3, 1858, KSHS.
26. *Kansas Weekly Herald*, April 3, 1858.
27. Spurgeon, *Man of Douglas, Man of Lincoln*, 148–49.
28. John E. Stewart to Thaddeus Hyatt, December 29, 1859, Thaddeus Hyatt Collection, KSHS.
29. John Brown to Gents, January 3, 1859, John Brown Collection, KSHS. For more information about this raid see Richard B. Sheridan, ed., *Freedom's Crucible: The Underground Railroad in Lawrence and Douglas County, Kansas, 1854–1865: A Reader* (Lawrence: University Press of Kansas, 2000).
30. William Lee Miller, *Arguing about Slavery: The Great Battle in the United States Congress* (New York: Alfred A. Knopf, 1997), 78.
31. Samuel C. Smith to Dear Doctor [Charles Robinson], December 29, 1858, Charles and Sara Robinson Collection, KSHS.
32. Etcheson, *Bleeding Kansas*, 221; Stephen V. Ash, *Firebrand of Liberty: The Story of Two Black Regiments That Changed the Course of the Civil War* (New York: W. W. Norton, 2008), 94.

33. Sheridan, "From Slavery in Missouri to Freedom in Kansas," 30.
34. Samuel F. Tappan to Thomas W. Higginson, January 24, 1858, printed in Sheridan, *Freedom's Crucible*, 50.
35. John Bowles to F. B. Sandborne, April 4, 1859, printed in Sheridan, *Freedom's Crucible*, 52.
36. Ibid.
37. Theodore Gardner, "The Last Battle of the Border War," in Sheridan, *Freedom's Crucible*, 61, 65.
38. Ibid., 65.
39. Benjamin Van Horn, Autobiographical Letter, January 4, 1909, Misc. Van Horn, B., KSHS.
40. Gary L. Cheatham, "'Slavery All the Time or Not at All': The Wyandotte Constitution Debate, 1859–1861," *Kansas History* 21, no. 3 (Autumn 1998): 172–73. For a contemporary assessment of Democratic opposition to the Wyandotte Constitution, see John J. Ingalls to Dear Father [Elias T. Ingalls], August 14, 1859, John James Ingalls Collection, KSHS.

Chapter 2

1. Jefferson Davis, Message to Congress, April 29, 1861, in *A Compilation of the Messages and Papers of the Confederacy, Including the Diplomatic Correspondence, 1861–1865*, vol. 1, ed. James D. Richardson (Nashville: United States Publishing Company, 1905), 68.
2. Ibid., 68.
3. John Townsend, *The Doom of Slavery in the Union: Its Safety Out of It* (Charleston, S.C.: Evans & Cogswell, 1860), 22, 23.
4. Jabez Lamar Monroe Curry, "The Perils and Duty of the South, . . . Speech Delivery in Talladega, Alabama, November 26, 1860," in *Southern Pamphlets on Secession, November 1860–April 1861*, ed. Jon L. Wakelyn (Chapel Hill: University of North Carolina Press, 1996), 43–44.
5. Joseph E. Brown, Public Letter, December 7, in William W. Freehling and Craig M. Simpson, eds., *Secession Debated: Georgia's Showdown in 1860* (New York: Oxford University Press, 1992), 152–53.
6. St. Louis News article quoted in *Liberty Tribune* (Missouri), November 11, 1860.
7. James M. McPherson, *Battle Cry of Freedom* (New York: Oxford University Press, 1988), 257–58.
8. Ibid., 255.
9. James M. McPherson, *For Cause and Comrades: Why Men Fought in the Civil War* (New York: Oxford University Press, 1997), 16.
10. Bell Irvin Wiley, *The Life of Billy Yank* (Baton Rouge: Louisiana State University Press, 1992), 20.
11. Albert Castel, *Civil War Kansas: Reaping the Whirlwind* (Lawrence: University Press of Kansas, 1997), 39.
12. McPherson, *Battle Cry of Freedom*, 323.
13. *Leavenworth Daily Times*, April 24, 1861.
14. Don E. Fehrenbacher, *The Slaveholding Republic: An Account of the United States Government's Relations to Slavery* (Oxford: Oxford University Press, 2001), 18.

15. Paul H. Smith, ed., *Letters of Delegates to Congress, 1774–1789*, vol. 5 (Washington, D.C.: Library of Congress, 1979), 11.
16. Fehrenbacher, *The Slaveholding Republic*, 19–20.
17. Michael Lee Manning, *The African-American Soldier: From Crispus Attucks to Colin Powell* (New York: Citadel, 2004), 24–25.
18. James M. McPherson, *The Negro's Civil War: How American Blacks Felt and Acted during the War for the Union* (New York: Ballantine Books, 1991), 19, 21.
19. Ibid., 22.
20. Joseph T. Wilson, *The Black Phalanx: African American Soldiers in the War of Independence, the War of 1812, and the Civil War* (New York: Da Capo, 1994), 94n.
21. Benjamin Quarles, *The Negro in the Civil War* (New York: Da Capo, 1989), 32.
22. Ibid., 24–25.
23. *Congressional Globe*, 37th Cong., 1st sess., 257.
24. McPherson, *Battle Cry of Freedom*, 312.
25. Charles B. Haydon, *For Country, Cause and Leader: The Civil War Journal of Charles B. Haydon*, ed. Stephen W. Sears (New York: Ticknor & Fields, 1993), 6.
26. *New York Daily Tribune*, July 8, 1861.
27. James H. Lane to Abraham Lincoln, April 20, 1861, Abraham Lincoln Papers, Library of Congress, Washington, D.C.
28. *Leavenworth Daily Conservative*, April 30, 1861, quoted in Wendell Holmes Stephenson, *The Political Career of General James H. Lane* (Topeka: B. P. Walker, 1930), 105.
29. *Official Records of the War of the Rebellion (O.R.)*, ser. 3, vol. 1, 280–81.
30. T. Harry Williams, *Lincoln and His Generals* (New York: Vintage Books, 2011), 21.
31. *O.R.*, ser. 3, vol. 1, 282.
32. *Lawrence Republican*, June 27, 1861.
33. Bryce Benedict, *Jayhawkers: The Civil War Brigade of James Henry Lane* (Norman: University of Oklahoma Press, 2009), 37.
34. Ibid.
35. McPherson, *Battle Cry of Freedom*, 345–48.
36. Ian Michael Spurgeon, *Man of Douglas, Man of Lincoln: The Political Odyssey of James Henry Lane* (Columbia: University of Missouri Press, 2008), 181.
37. Benedict, *Jayhawkers*, 61.
38. *O.R.*, ser. 1, vol. 3, 469.
39. Ibid., 466–67.
40. *New York Times*, June 2, 1861.
41. *New York Times*, August 6, 1861.
42. William K. Klingaman, *Abraham Lincoln and the Road to Emancipation, 1861–1865* (New York: Viking, 2001), 71.
43. Paul M. Angle and Earl Schenck Miers, eds., *The Living Lincoln: The Man, His Mind, His Times, and the War He Fought, Reconstructed*

from His Own Writings (New York: Barnes & Noble Books, 1992), 432–33.

44. McPherson, *Battle Cry of Freedom*, 353.
45. *O.R.*, ser. 1, vol. 3, 163.
46. Ibid., 164.
47. *O.R.*, ser. 1, vol. 3, 164.
48. Castel, *Civil War Kansas*, 53.
49. *O.R.*, ser. 1, vol. 3, 196; Stephenson, *The Political Career of General James H. Lane*, 111.
50. *Leavenworth Daily Conservative*, September 21, 1861.
51. Benedict, *Jayhawkers*, 61.
52. *Leavenworth Daily Conservative*, October 5, 1861.
53. *Lawrence Republican*, September 26, 1861.
54. Ibid.
55. *O.R.*, ser. 1, vol. 3, 506.
56. Lane blamed the conflagration on artillery shells fired during the skirmish. However, the extent of the damage suggests that much of the fire was intentional. Benedict, *Jayhawkers*, 98–100; *O.R.*, ser. 1, vol. 3, 196; Hildegarde Rose Herklotz, "Jayhawkers in Missouri, 1858–1863," third article, chap. 4, *Missouri Historical Review* 18, no. 1 (October 1923): 68.
57. *Liberty Weekly Tribune*, October 18, 1861.
58. Castel, *Civil War Kansas*, 55.
59. *Congressional Globe*, 37th Cong., 1st sess., 187.
60. Ibid., 190.
61. Benedict, *Jayhawkers*, 104.
62. *Lawrence Republican*, October 17, 1861.
63. Ibid.
64. Ibid.
65. *Lawrence Republican*, November 21, 1861.
66. Ibid.
67. Ibid.
68. Ibid.
69. Ibid.
70. Ibid.
71. Accounts of the total number of refugees ranges from 218 to 256. Stephenson, *The Political Career of General James H. Lane*, 126–27.
72. H. D. Fisher, *The Gun and the Gospel: Early Kansas and Chaplain Fisher* (Chicago: Kenwood, 1896), 155–57.
73. "Extracts from Speech of General Lane, at Tremont Temple, Boston, November 31, 1861," in *Kansas Collected Speeches*, vol. 9, pp. 6–7, Kansas State Historical Society, Topeka.
74. Ibid., 7.
75. *Congressional Globe*, 37th Cong., 2nd sess., 111.
76. Ibid.
77. Ibid.
78. Ibid., 111, 112.
79. *Freedom's Champion* (Atchison, Kans.), February 1, 1862.

80. Ibid.
81. Ibid.
82. Ibid.

Chapter 3

1. James M. McPherson, *The Negro's Civil War: How Black Americans Felt and Acted during the War for the Union* (New York: Ballantine Books, 1991), 164.
2. Edward A. Miller, Jr., *Lincoln's Abolitionist General: The Biography of David Hunter* (Columbia: University of South Carolina Press, 1997), 96.
3. Ibid., 96–97.
4. Dudley Taylor Cornish, *The Sable Arm: Black Troops in the Union Army, 1861–1865* (1956; repr., Lawrence: University Press of Kansas, 1987), 33–36.
5. Ibid., 35.
6. *Official Records of the War of the Rebellion (O.R.)*, ser. 1, vol. 14, 341.
7. *O.R.*, ser. 3, vol. 2, 43.
8. Ibid., 31.
9. Cornish, *The Sable Arm*, 38.
10. Ibid., 43–45.
11. *O.R.*, ser. 3, vol. 2, 346.
12. The 1860 census recorded 625 free blacks and 2 slaves in Kansas territory. Joseph C. G. Kennedy, *Preliminary Report on the Eighth Census: 1860* (Washington, D.C.: Government Printing Office, 1862), 131.
13. *Congressional Globe*, 37th Cong., 2nd sess., pt. 3, 2149.
14. Ibid., pt. 4, 3337.
15. Historian Wendell Stephenson said of Lane's numbers of black refugees in Kansas, "These statements should perhaps be discounted, however, for Lane often exaggerated." Wendell Holmes Stephenson, *The Political Career of General James H. Lane* (Topeka: B. P. Walker, 1930), 127. Richard B. Sheridan, "From Slavery in Missouri to Freedom in Kansas: The Influx of Black Fugitives and Contrabands into Kansas, 1854–1865," *Kansas History* 12 (Spring 1989): 37.
16. Richard J. Hinton, Letter to the Commission, September 4, 1863, American Freedom's Inquiry Commission Collection, bMS Am 702 (48), Houghton Library, Harvard University.
17. Daniel R. Anthony, Letter to the Commission, Leavenworth, Kansas, August 30, 1863, American Freedom's Inquiry Commission Collection, bMS Am 702 (5), Houghton Library, Harvard University.
18. *O.R.*, ser. 3, vol. 2, 959.
19. Albert Castel, *Civil War Kansas: Reaping the Whirlwind* (Lawrence: University Press of Kansas, 1997), 86.
20. *White Cloud Kansas Chief*, July 28, 1864.
21. Castel, *Civil War Kansas*, 87; *O.R.*, ser. 3, vol. 2, 444.
22. *O.R.*, ser. 3, vol. 2, 444.
23. Ibid., 294.
24. Ibid., 959.

25. Ibid., 311.
26. *Congressional Globe,* 37th Cong., 2nd sess., 3337.
27. *O.R.,* ser. 3, vol. 2, 312.
28. John Speer, *Life of Gen. James H. Lane, "The Liberator of Kansas"* (Garden City, Kans.: John Speer, 1897), 261–62.
29. John G. Nicolay and John Hay, *Abraham Lincoln: A History,* vol. 6 (New York: Century, 1917), 445.
30. *O.R.,* ser. 3, vol. 2, 312.
31. Ibid., 445.
32. Ethan Earle, "Journal of Captain Ethan Earle, Company F, First Kansas Colored Volunteer Infantry Regiment," 1873, p. 16, Ethan Earle Collection, New England Historic Genealogical Society, Boston, Mass. Microfilm copy at Kansas State Historical Society (KSHS), Topeka.
33. Ibid., 18.
34. Ibid.
35. Ibid., 19; Ira Berlin, Joseph P. Reidy, and Leslie S. Rowland, eds., *Freedom: A Documentary History of Emancipation, 1861–1867, Selected from the Holdings of the National Archives of the United States,* ser. 2: *The Black Military Experience* (Cambridge: Cambridge University Press, 1982), 69–70.
36. Earle, "Journal of Captain Ethan Earle," 19.
37. *Leavenworth Daily Conservative,* November 9, 1862.
38. For instance, see Christian G. Samito, ed., *Changes in Law and Society during the Civil War and Reconstruction: A Legal History Documentary Reader* (Carbondale: Southern Illinois University Press, 2009), 123.
39. James Montgomery to Charles Robinson, August 3, 1862, Charles Robinson Collection, KSHS.
40. *Leavenworth Daily Conservative,* August 28, 1862.
41. James Montgomery to Charles Robinson, August 3, 1862, Charles Robinson Collection, KSHS.
42. George Hoyt to George Stearns, August 13, 1862, George L. Stearns Collection, KSHS.
43. *Leavenworth Daily Conservative,* August 28, 1862.
44. Ibid., August 6, 1862.
45. Ibid. Subsequent issues also ran side-by-side advertisements.
46. *Leavenworth Daily Conservative,* August 7, 1862. A copy of the order can also be found in Berlin, Reidy, and Rowland, *Freedom,* ser. 2, 68–69.

Chapter 4

1. *Leavenworth Daily Conservative,* August 6, 1862.
2. *Fort Scott Bulletin,* August 16, 1862.
3. *Leavenworth Daily Times,* August 8, 1862.
4. *Leavenworth Daily Conservative,* August 21, 1862.
5. *Fort Scott Bulletin,* September 13, 1862.
6. Slave compensation form for Phillip Dowell, Folder for George Duvall, Compiled Military Service Records, 79th USCT (New), National Archives and Records Administration (NARA), Washington, D.C.

7. Slave compensation form for Samuel Pepper, Folder for Johnson Cooper, Compiled Military Service Records, 79th USCT (New), NARA.

8. James S. Johnson, III, "The Life and Times of George Washington: Slave, Soldier, Farmer," in *Freedom's Crucible: The Underground Railroad in Lawrence and Douglas County, Kansas, 1854–1865: A Reader,* ed. Richard B. Sheridan (Lawrence: University Press of Kansas, 2000), 117–18.

9. William Gordon Deposition, June 7, 1898, William Gordon Pension File, Application 761720, Certificate 907381, NARA.

10. Dock Williams testimony, 1883, in Joseph Bowers Pension File, Application 205507, Certificate 25554, NARA.

11. Deposition of Henry Davis, January 22, 1899; Deposition of Harrison Miller, May 25, 1899; in Henry Davis Pension File, Application 191036, Certificate 782606, NARA.

12. Joseph Sanders Pension File, Mother Application 286560, Certificate 263371, NARA.

13. Case of Ester Payne, widow, Testimony, April 22, 1890, Spencer Payne Pension File, Application 744180, Certificate 698253, NARA.

14. Testimony of Peter Ross and Nancy Grubb, Nelson Lona (alias Nelson Ross) Pension File, Father Application 458729, Certificate 293503, NARA.

15. Jeremiah Fielding Pension File, Application 428960, Widow's Application 504992, Widow's Certificate 327507, NARA.

16. "Claim for Compensation for Enlisted Slave," Allen Minor, Compiled Service Record, 79th USCT (New), NARA.

17. Jackson Donald Pension File, Application 127304, Certificate 186528, NARA.

18. Henry Crittenden Affidavit, July 4, 1895, Henry Crittenden Pension File, Application 763795, Certificate 574087, Widow Application 767258, Certificate 543692, NARA.

19. Freeling Lawson Deposition, June 3, 1907, in Henry (alias Freeling) Lawson Pension File, Application 705557, Certificate 598800, NARA.

20. James W. Wells General Affidavit, November 2, 1905, Silas Hughes (alias James W. Wells) Pension File, Application 1315256, Certificate 1115784, NARA.

21. John Brown Pension File, Application 1061091, Certificate 851546, NARA.

22. To further illustrate the imprecise recording of ages within the regiment, Yaunt was listed as twenty-three years old at enlistment. Within the many pension forms of Yaunt's file, descriptions of his birth date varied from 1834 to 1839. Part of the discrepancy may come from a pension law in 1907 that increased rates for veterans over seventy years old; this law may have contributed to efforts by some veterans to hedge their birth dates in order to qualify. The quote from Yaunt appeared in a 1907 letter attempting to establish his age for a pension increase. Within that letter he also wrote, "I think the Citizens who have known me for many years will bear me out in my claim that I am Seventy

Two Years old or older." Willis Yaunt to J. L. Davenport, November 25, 1907, Willis Yaunt Pension File, Application 514302, Certificate 354577, NARA.

23. General Affidavit, May 29, 1905, William Smith Pension File, Application 763554, Certificate 569755, Minor Application 1083529, Certificate 838379, NARA.

24. Jordan Wood Affidavit, February 12, 1906, Jordan Wood Pension File, Application 810169, Certificate 924765, NARA.

25. Ethan Earle, "Journal of Captain Ethan Earle, Company F, First Kansas Colored Volunteer Infantry Regiment," 1873, p. 20, New England Historic Genealogical Society, Boston, Massachusetts. Microfilm copy at Kansas State Historical Society (KSHS), Topeka; *Report of the Adjutant General of the State of Kansas, 1861–1865*, vol. 1 (Topeka: J. K. Hudson, 1896), 585.

26. *Official Records of the War of the Rebellion (O.R.)*, ser. 1, vol. 13, 619.

27. For instance, see Bertram Wyatt-Brown, "The Mask of Obedience: Male Slave Psychology in the Old South," *American Historical Review* 93, no. 5 (December 1988): 1228–52; and Allan Kulikoff, *Tobacco and Slaves: The Development of Southern Cultures in the Chesapeake, 1680–1800* (Chapel Hill: University of North Carolina Press, 1986), 389–90.

28. Earle, "Journal of Captain Ethan Earle," 19–21.

29. *Leavenworth Daily Times*, August 28, 1862.

30. *White Cloud Kansas Chief*, August 21, 1862.

31. *Leavenworth Daily Conservative*, August 6, 1862.

32. *White Cloud Kansas Chief*, August 28, 1862.

33. Earle, "Journal of Captain Ethan Earle," 21–23; Compiled Service Records, 79th United States Colored Troops (USCT) (New), NARA.

34. Richard. J. Dodge to Br. Gen. L. Thomas, 4 Aug. (1862), Telegrams Collected by the Office of Secretary of War (Bound), RG 107 [L-209], in *Freedom: A Documentary History of Emancipation, 1861–1867, Selected from the Holdings of the National Archives of the United States*, ser. 2: *The Black Military Experience*, ed. Ira Berlin, Joseph P. Reidy, and Leslie S. Rowland (Cambridge: Cambridge University Press, 1982), 67.

35. 79th USCT (New) Infantry Record Books, RG 94, NARA. Residency is not listed for every soldier in the regimental records, and appears to have been recorded well after enlistment and according to the interest of various company officers.

36. The Adjutant General's Report for the State of Kansas lists the men's residency according to their location of enlistment. The actual residency is provided for about half of the men recruited between August 1862 and January 13, 1863, in regimental records in the National Archives in Washington, D.C. Many of the men with no residency listed died during their service, which suggests that the information was not recorded until later in the war. The statistics listed in the text come from 259 men from Companies A through F. 79th USCT (New) Infantry, Regimental Record Book, RG 94, NARA.

37. *Report of the Adjutant General of the State of Kansas, 1861–1865,* vol. I, 570–97.
38. 79th USCT (New) Infantry, Regimental Records, NARA.
39. Michael Fellman, "Emancipation in Missouri," *Missouri Historical Review* 83, no. 1 (October 1988): 38.
40. E. Whitman to G. L. Stearns, September 7, 1862, George L. Stearns Collection, KSHS.
41. *White Cloud Kansas Chief,* August 21, 1862.
42. "The Letters of Samuel James Reader, 1861–1863; Pioneer of Soldier Township, Shawnee County—Concluded," *Kansas Historical Quarterly* 9, no. 2 (May 1940): 155–56.
43. *Leavenworth Daily Times,* August 23, 1862.
44. *Kansas City Daily Journal of Commerce* reprinted in *Lawrence Republican,* August 14, 1862.
45. *Fort Scott Bulletin,* August 16, 1862.
46. *Manhattan Express,* August 19, 1862.
47. *Manhattan Express,* September 23, 1862.
48. *Lawrence Republican,* August 18, 1862.
49. *Leavenworth Daily Conservative,* November 9, 1862.
50. James M. Williams to Gen. T. J. Anderson, Adjutant-General of Kansas, James M. Williams Collection, KSHS.
51. *Linn County Republican,* January 3, 1902.
52. *New York Times,* October 12, 1862.
53. Hamilton Gamble to Abraham Lincoln, September 9, 1862, Abraham Lincoln Papers, Library of Congress, Washington, D.C.
54. Chief of Staff of the Department of the Missouri to the Commander of the Department of Missouri, October 16, 1862, in Berlin, Reidy, and Rowland, *Freedom,* ser. 2, 71; *Linn County Republican,* January 3, 1903.
55. *Leavenworth Daily Times,* August 16, 1862; *New York Times,* October 12, 1862.
56. *Leavenworth Daily Times,* August 15, 1862. Zouaves were French colonial soldiers, distinctive for their unique style of dress, which often included fezzes (with turbans), baggy pantaloons, and colorful waistcoats. Their notable fighting abilities during the Crimean War in Europe, paired with a respect for France's Napoleon-era military prowess, led to the introduction of Zouave-styled units in the United States during the Civil War era. The Zouave reference in this instance, though, focused on the unique ethnic element of the black regiment, rather than their style of dress.
57. Earle, "Journal of Captain Ethan Earle," 21; *Linn County Republican,* January 3, 1902; Chief of Staff of the Department of the Missouri to the Commander of the Department of Missouri, October 16, 1862, in Berlin, Reidy, and Rowland, *Freedom,* ser. 2, 71; *New York Times,* November 19, 1863.
58. Earle, "Journal of Captain Ethan Earle," 21.
59. *New York Times,* November 19, 1863.
60. *Linn County Republican,* January 3, 1903.

61. Chief of Staff of the Department of the Missouri to the Commander of the Department of Missouri, October 16, 1862, in Berlin, Reidy, and Rowland, *Freedom*, ser. 2, 71.
62. *Freedom's Champion*, February 1, 1862.
63. *Leavenworth Daily Conservative*, August 28, 1862.
64. Earle, "Journal of Captain Ethan Earle," 21.
65. Benjamin G. Jones Pension File, Application 256825, NARA.
66. Daniel McFarland Pension File, Application 128, Certification 9552, NARA.
67. The total number of men who served the Union during the course of the war neared 2.1 million, while approximately 900,000 men fought for the Confederacy. Jeffry D. Wert, *The Sword of Lincoln: The Army of the Potomac* (New York: Simon & Schuster, 2003), 4; Russell F. Weigley, *The American Way of War: A History of United States Military Strategy and Policy* (Bloomington: Indiana University Press, 1977), 130.
68. *Leavenworth Daily Conservative*, August 21, 1862.

Chapter 5

1. Horace Greeley to Abraham Lincoln, August 19, 1862, quoted in the *Big Blue Union* (Marysville, Kans.), September 6, 1862; For a good review of Greeley's letter to Lincoln, see Allen C. Guelzo, *Lincoln's Emancipation Proclamation: The End of Slavery in America* (New York: Simon & Schuster, 2004), 147–53.
2. Ira Berlin, Barbara Fields, Thavolia Glymph, Joseph P. Reidy, and Leslie S. Rowland, eds., *Freedom: A Documentary History of Emancipation, 1861–1867*, ser. 1, vol. 1: *The Destruction of Slavery* (New York: Cambridge University Press, 1985), 30.
3. Horace Greeley to Abraham Lincoln, August 19, 1862, quoted in the *Big Blue Union* (Marysville, Kans.), September 6, 1862.
4. Ibid.
5. Printed in *New York Tribune*, August 23, 1862.
6. *New York Times*, August 24, 1862.
7. Ibid.
8. *The Independent* (Oskaloosa, Kans.), September 27, 1862. Emphasis in original.
9. *Freedom's Champion* (Atchison, Kans.), September 13, 1862.
10. Francis Bicknell Carpenter, *Six Months at the White House with Abraham Lincoln: The Story of a Picture* (New York: Hurd and Houghton, 1866), 21.
11. Guelzo, *Lincoln's Emancipation Proclamation*, 131–33.
12. Ibid., 133.
13. Salmon Portland Chase, *The Salmon P. Chase Papers*, vol. 1: *Journals, 1829–1872*, ed. John Niven (Kent, Ohio: Kent State University Press, 1993), 351.
14. Roy P. Basler, ed., *The Collected Works of Abraham Lincoln* (New Brunswick, N.J.: Rutgers University Press, 1953), vol. 5, 336–37.

15. Carpenter, *Six Months at the White House with Abraham Lincoln*, 21.
16. Ibid., 22; Guelzo, *Lincoln's Emancipation Proclamation*, 137.
17. Stephen W. Sears, *George B. McClellan: The Young Napoleon* (New York: Da Capo, 1999), 321.
18. Ibid., 318–19.
19. Guelzo, *Lincoln's Emancipation Proclamation*, 289.
20. Basler, *The Collected Works of Abraham Lincoln*, vol. 7, 18.
21. *The Smoky Hill and Republican Union* (Junction City, Kans.), September 27, 1862.
22. *Freedom's Champion* (Atchison, Kans.), September 27, 1862.
23. James H. Lane to Captain James M. Williams, October 9, 1862, Fort Scott National Park Archives.
24. Ira Berlin, Joseph P. Reidy, and Leslie S. Rowland, eds., *Freedom: A Documentary History of Emancipation, 1861–1867, Selected from the Holdings of the National Archives of the United States*, ser. 2: *The Black Military Experience* (Cambridge: Cambridge University Press, 1982), 70–71.
25. Ibid., 71.
26. Ibid., 71–72.
27. *Official Records of the War of the Rebellion* (*O.R.*), ser. 1, vol. 53, 455–56; *New York Times*, November 19, 1862.
28. Captain Richard Ward's account and the *New York Times* story describe the expedition crossing the Osage River. However, according to modern maps and the historian Chris Tabor's study of the battle at Island Mound, the men likely crossed the Marais des Cygnes River. Chris Tabor, *The Skirmish at Island Mound, Mo., October 29, 1862* (Independence, Mo.: Blue and Grey Book Shoppe, 2001), 10.
29. *Linn County Republican*, January 3, 1902.
30. Ibid.; *Leavenworth Daily Conservative*, November 4, 1862; *O.R.*, ser. 1, vol. 53, 456; Tabor, *The Skirmish at Island Mound*, 10.
31. Tabor, *The Skirmish at Island Mound*, 2.
32. *O.R.*, ser. 1, vol. 53, 456.
33. Ibid.
34. Ibid.
35. Ibid.
36. Ibid.; *Report of the Adjutant General of the State of Kansas, 1861–1865* (Topeka: Kansas State Printing Company, 1896), 574.
37. *O.R.*, ser. 1, vol. 53, 456.
38. Ibid.; *New York Times*, November 19, 1862.
39. *New York Times*, November 19, 1862.
40. *O.R.*, ser. 1, vol. 53, 456; *New York Times*, November 19, 1862.
41. *O.R.*, ser. 1, vol. 53, 456.
42. *New York Times*, November 19, 1862.
43. Ibid.
44. E. Huddleston to F. G. Adams, "The Battle of Island Mound," December 3, 1882, Military History Collection, Kansas State Historical Society (KSHS), Topeka.

45. *Old Settlers' History of Bates County, Missouri* (Amsterdam, Mo.: Tathwell & Maxey, 1897), 187–88.
46. E. Huddleston to F. G. Adams, "The Battle of Island Mound," December 3, 1882, KSHS; *New York Times*, November 19, 1862.
47. Tabor, *The Skirmish at Island Mound*, 14.
48. *New York Times*, November 19, 1862.
49. Ibid.; *O.R.*, ser. 1, vol. 53, 456.
50. E. Huddleston to F. G. Adams, "The Battle of Island Mound," December 3, 1882, KSHS.
51. Edward Curtis Pension File, Application 194359, Certificate 176413, National Archives and Records Administration (NARA), Washington, D.C. While paperwork in Curtis's file does not state exactly when during the battle at Island Mound he sustained these wounds, the number and quick succession of these wounds suggest that they occurred during the intense, swirling clash in the early stages of the October 29 battle.
52. Shelby Bannon Pension File, Application 122564, Certificate 95473, NARA. As with Edward Curtis, the paperwork in the pension file does not specify exactly when during the battle the wounds were sustained. Instead, based on the wounds and events of the battle, I believe Bannon fell wounded during this initial clash.
53. *New York Times*, November 7 and 19, 1862; *Kansas Journal* printed in Frank Moore, *The Rebellion Record*, vol. 6 (New York: G. P. Putnam, 1863), 55.
54. Testimony of Edward Miller, June 5, 1872, Anderson Riley Pension File, Application 168149, Certificate 130823, Minor Application 814240, Certificate 596376, NARA.
55. *Leavenworth Times*, November 7, 1862.
56. *New York Times*, November 19, 1862.
57. *Linn County Republican*, January 3, 1902.
58. *New York Times*, November 19, 1862.
59. *O.R.*, ser. 1, vol. 53, 456; *New York Times*, November 19, 1862; *Kansas Journal* printed in Moore, *The Rebellion Record*, vol. 6, 55.
60. *New York Times*, November 19, 1862.
61. *O.R.*, ser. 1, vol. 53, 456.
62. Ibid.
63. Ibid.
64. Ibid.
65. *New York Times*, November 19, 1862.
66. Ethan Earle, "Journal of Captain Ethan Earle, Company F, First Kansas Colored Volunteer Infantry Regiment," 1873, p. 25, New England Historic Genealogical Society, Boston, Mass. Microfilm copy at Kansas State Historical Society, Topeka.
67. *New York Times*, November 19, 1862.
68. *Leavenworth Daily Conservative*, November 13, 1862; Earle, "Journal of Captain Ethan Earle," 25.
69. *Linn County Republican*, January 3, 1902.

70. Ibid.
71. Ibid.; *New York Times*, November 19, 1862.
72. James M. McPherson, ed., *The Atlas of the Civil War* (New York: Macmillan, 1994), 52, 80.

Chapter 6

1. *Leavenworth Daily Conservative*, November 4 and 9, 1862; *New York Times*, November 8, 1862.
2. *Leavenworth Daily Conservative*, November 4, 1862.
3. Court Martial Case File, LL-580, Trial of Captain Andrew J. Armstrong, Co. D, First Kansas Colored Infantry, 1863, pp. 5–9, RG 153, National Archives and Records Administration (NARA), Washington, D.C.
4. Ibid., 10.
5. Ibid.
6. Ibid., 10–11.
7. Ibid., 11–12.
8. Witness Private Joseph Parker testified that Sergeant Wharfield attacked Captain Martin twice, but Martin's more detailed testimony recounted three separate attacks against him. Court Martial Case File, LL-580, Trial of Captain Andrew J. Armstrong, Co. D, First Kansas Colored Infantry, 1863, pp. 5–6, 12–13, RG 153, NARA.
9. Court Martial Case File, LL-580, Trial of Captain Andrew J. Armstrong, Co. D, First Kansas Colored Infantry, 1863, RG 153, NARA.
10. *Liberty Tribune* (Missouri), October 17, 1862.
11. Letter from Captain James M. Williams, *Leavenworth Daily Conservative*, November 30, 1862.
12. *Leavenworth Daily Conservative*, November 16, 1862; James Williams to Brig. Genl. Blunt, November 24, 1862, James M. Williams Collection, Kansas State Historical Society (KSHS), Topeka (transcription at Fort Scott National Historic Park Archives).
13. James Williams to Brig. Genl. Blunt, November 24, 1862, James M. Williams Collection, KSHS.
14. William D. Matthews testimony, James M. Williams Collection, KSHS (transcription in Fort Scott National Historic Park Archives).
15. According to articles in the *Leavenworth Daily Conservative*, the officers did post bond; see *Leavenworth Daily Conservative*, November 16 and 18, 1862. However, later the newspaper reported that a key point of contention became a disagreement regarding the bond. See below, and *Leavenworth Daily Conservative*, November 20, 1862.
16. *Leavenworth Daily Conservative*, November 16, 1862.
17. James Williams to Brig. Genl. Blunt, November 24, 1862, James M. Williams Collection, KSHS; *Leavenworth Daily Conservative*, November 18, 1862.
18. Ibid.
19. *Leavenworth Daily Conservative*, November 18, 1862.
20. James Williams to Brig. Genl. Blunt, November 24, 1862, James M. Williams Collection, KSHS.

21. *Leavenworth Daily Conservative*, November 18, 1862.
22. James Williams to Brig. Genl. Blunt, November 24, 1862, James M. Williams Collection, KSHS.
23. H. B. Denman to Col. Burns, November 17, 1862, James M. Williams Collection, KSHS (transcription in Fort Scott National Historic Park Archives).
24. *Leavenworth Daily Conservative*, November 18, 1862.
25. *Leavenworth Daily Conservative*, November 20, 1862.
26. Ibid.
27. Ibid., November 18, 1862.
28. *The Independent* (Oskaloosa, Kans.), November 22, 1862.
29. *Leavenworth Daily Times*, December 18, 1862.
30. John R. Graton to Dear Wife, January 10, 1863, John R. Graton Collection, KSHS.
31. Compiled service records for the First Kansas Colored Infantry, filed under the 79th USCT (New) at the National Archives, include a folder for every soldier recorded as having joined the regiment during its service. Within that group of records, 231 men are described as having enlisted in 1862 but failing to be mustered into federal service with the regiment in 1863. According to the federal government, for pension and other recognition purposes, those men were not considered soldiers of the U.S. Army. (It should be noted that a few of these files may be in error due to inconsistent record keeping by company army officials. Several spelling variations for names can be found in company records, which led to the creation within regimental records of multiple folders for single individuals. Generally, previous army officials or archivists later identified these errors and consolidated the records. However, other errors may still exist in a small number of files. For instance, there is a file folder for a "Hazel J. Todd" of Company C who enlisted in October 1862 and was not mustered in; and there is a file folder for a "Hazle Todd" of Company H who enlisted in April 1863 and deserted later during the war. This may be the same individual, with a confusing history within the regiment. Or it may be two different men with the same, unique name, except for a small spelling variation. In any case, according to a government accounting effort of the regiment in the late 1890s, these are two separate men.)
32. Henry Agleston, Compiled Service Records, 79th USCT (New), NARA.
33. Henry Bowles, Compiled Service Records, 79th USCT (New), NARA.
34. Harrison Miller, Compiled Service Record, 79th USCT (New), NARA.

Chapter 7

1. Allen C. Guelzo, *Lincoln's Emancipation Proclamation: The End of Slavery in America* (New York: Simon & Schuster, 2004), 295.
2. Ibid.
3. Ibid.
4. *Congressional Globe*, 37th Cong., 3rd sess., pt. 2, 1442.
5. Ibid.

6. Ibid.
7. Ibid.
8. "The Letters of Samuel James Reader, 1861–1863; Pioneer of Solder Township, Shawnee County—Concluded," *Kansas Historical Quarterly* 9, no. 2 (May 1940): 169.
9. *White Cloud Kansas Chief*, January 1, 1863.
10. *New York Times*, February 15, 1863.
11. *Leavenworth Weekly Inquirer*, February 5, 1863.
12. Ibid.
13. *New York Times*, February 15, 1863.
14. John R. Graton to Dear Wife, January 10, 1863, John R. Graton Collection, Kansas State Historical Society (KSHS), Topeka.
15. John R. Graton to Dear Wife, January 10, 1863, John R. Graton Collection, KSHS.
16. Patrick H. Minor's Compiled Service Record at the National Archives contains only two cards, which note that he had joined the regiment in 1862 and that he was not listed on the muster rolls in 1863. No explanation is given regarding his separation from the unit. P. H. Minor Compiled Service Record, 79th USCT (New), National Archives and Records Administration (NARA), Washington, D.C.
17. Ira Berlin, Joseph P. Reidy, and Leslie S. Rowland, eds., *Freedom: A Documentary History of Emancipation, 1861–1867, Selected from the Holdings of the National Archives of the United States*, ser. 2: *The Black Military Experience* (Cambridge: Cambridge University Press, 1982), 69–70.
18. Ibid.
19. Richard Hinton to Col. Chipman, February 19, 1863, 79th USCT (New) Regimental Order Book, Fort Scott National Park Archives.
20. *Leavenworth Daily Conservative*, January 17, 1863.
21. The First Kansas Colored Infantry was the fourth black regiment to be formally mustered in to federal service during the Civil War. Major General Benjamin Butler, commander of Union forces occupying New Orleans, began organizing the First Regiment of the Native Guards shortly after the First Kansas Colored Infantry began recruiting. On September 27, 1862, the Louisiana unit became the first black regiment to be mustered in to federal service. Two more black Louisiana regiments were mustered in before the Kansas troops were finally sworn in to federal service in January 1863. James G. Hollandsworth, Jr., *The Louisiana Native Guards: The Black Military Experience during the Civil War* (Baton Rouge: Louisiana State University Press, 1995), 17; Dudley Taylor Cornish, *The Sable Arm: Black Troops in the Union Army, 1861–1865* (1956; repr., Lawrence: University Press of Kansas, 1987), 78.
22. United States Military Telegraph, January 28, 1863, RG 94, Entry 360: Letters Received: 1863–88, NARA.
23. *Leavenworth Daily Conservative*, January 17, 1863.
24. Ibid.

25. Newspaper clipping (presumed to be from *Atchison Champion*), James M. Williams Collection, KSHS. A note penciled across the top of this clipping reads: "Clipping supposed to be from Atchison Champion editorials of date about Jan. 20, -1863- This clipping was found immediately following another of the paper and date above, having a notice of Capt. Martin's Co. being mustered and is without doubt from same paper."
26. Newspaper clipping (presumed to be from *Atchison Champion*), James M. Williams Collection, KSHS.
27. *Leavenworth Daily Conservative*, January 17, 1863.
28. Ibid., January 19, 1863.
29. J. M. Williams to Major Henning, January 5, 1863, 79th USCT Regimental Record Books, Fort Scott National Park Archives.
30. Captain Henry C. Seaman, who had been expected to be the regiment's second-in-command, was medically discharged from military service for bronchitis in Leavenworth on January 31, 1863. However, Captain Seaman left the First Kansas Colored Infantry prior to muster, and his discharge records his unit as the Fifth Kansas Cavalry. Report No. 1681, 53rd Cong., 3rd sess., *The Reports of Committees of the House of Representatives* (Washington, D.C.: Government Printing Office, 1895).
31. J. M. Williams to Capt L. A. Thrasher, January 29, 1863, 79th USCT Infantry (New), Regimental Order Book, NARA.
32. Court Martial Case File MM-2035, Trial of Private George True, Company F, 79th USCT, 1865, p. 4, Record Group 153, NARA.
33. Ibid., 3–4.
34. General Order No. 2, N S, January 19, 1863, 79th USCT Infantry (New), Regimental Order Book, NARA.
35. J. M. Williams to Lt. Col. Moonlight, January 29, 1863, 79th USCT Infantry (New), Regimental Order Book, NARA.
36. Statement of Dock Williams [Doc McWilliams], 1883, John Bowers Pension File, Application 205507, Certificate 25554, NARA.
37. Guelzo, *Lincoln's Emancipation Proclamation*, 295.
38. Special Orders No. 11, March 1, 1863, 79th USCT Infantry (New), Regimental Order Book, NARA.
39. This number comes from a review of the individual service records of the First Kansas Colored Infantry at the National Archives. In fact, it represents the minimum number of desertions during that month, as not all desertions were consistently recorded. Compiled Service Records, 79th USCT (New), NARA. (Note: Some of these soldier returned or were later arrested.)
40. Richard Hinton to Col. Chipman, February 19, 1863, 79th USCT, Regimental Order Book, Fort Scott National Park Archives.
41. J. M. Williams to Headquarters, Department of Kansas, April 21, 1863, in Berlin, Reidy, and Rowland, *Freedom*, ser. 2, 72.
42. As before, these numbers come from a review of the individual service records of the First Kansas Colored Infantry at the National Archives.

They represent a minimum number of desertions during that period, as not all desertions were consistently recorded. Some soldiers were arrested or returned to the unit later. Compiled Service Records, 79th USCT (New), NARA.

43. Lt. Col. J. M. Williams to Capt. H. Q. Loring, April 21, 1863, printed in Berlin, Reidy, and Rowland, *Freedom*, ser. 2, 72–73.
44. Deposition of George J. Martin, October 19, 1907, in the Henry Lawson Pension File, Application 705557, Certificate 598800, NARA.
45. Deposition of Freeling (alias Henry) Lawson, November 4, 1907, in the Henry Lawson Pension File, Application 705557, Certificate 598800, NARA.
46. Deposition of George J. Martin, October 19, 1907, in the Henry Lawson Pension File, Application 705557, Certificate 598800, NARA.
47. Compiled Service Records, 79th USCT (New), NARA. For names of deserters who were not returned to the regiment, see *Report of the Adjutant General of the State of Kansas, 1861–1865*, vol. 1 (Topeka: J. K. Hudson, 1896), 574–94, errata.
48. Albert Castel, *Civil War Kansas: Reaping the Whirlwind* (Lawrence: University Press of Kansas, 1997), 114.
49. Abraham Lincoln to James H. Lane, Monday, April 27, 1863, Abraham Lincoln Papers, Library of Congress, Washington, D.C.
50. Castel, *Civil War Kansas*, 114.
51. Christian Isely to Mrs. Eliza Isely, April 24, 1863, Isely Family Papers, Wichita State University Special Collections, Wichita, Kansas.
52. Affidavit of Julia Taylor, December 22, 1906, Nicholas Taylor Pension File, Application 337191, Certificate 305862, Widow Application 857807, Certificate 622606, NARA.
53. *New York Times*, February 15, 1863.
54. Ibid.
55. Autobiographical Letter, January 4, 1909, p. 20, Benjamin Van Horn Collection, KSHS.
56. Ibid.
57. Ibid.
58. Book of Records of Union Volunteer Organizations, Company I, 79th USCT Infantry Descriptive Book, NARA.
59. Statement of William Noble, May 15, 1888, in Cyrus Bowlegs Pension File, Application 495610, Certification 805165, NARA.
60. Alexander, like most of the enlisted men in the regiment, was illiterate, but while applying for a pension in the early 1890s, an agent transcribed Alexander's brief description of his life and service, offering historians a rare first-person account from a First Kansas Colored enlisted man. Pension forms list his year of birth as 1823. Isaac Alexander Pension File, Application 440919, Certificate 670709, NARA.
61. Dudley Taylor Cornish, "Kansas Negro Regiments in the Civil War," *Kansas Historical Quarterly* 20, no. 6 (May 1953), 423.
62. Deposition A, John W. Smith Pension File, Application 1245144, Certificate 1100919, NARA.

63. Autobiographical Letter, January 4, 1909, p. 20, Benjamin Van Horn Collection, KSHS.
64. William J. Hardee, *Rifle and Light Infantry Tactics; For the Exercise and Maneuvres of Troops When Acting as Light Infantry or Riflemen,* vol. 1 (Philadelphia: Lippincott, Grambo & Co., 1855), 40, 41.
65. Claimant's Affidavit, September 9, 1896, Abraham Kernell Pension File, Application 711687, Certificate 548323, NARA.
66. Christian Isely to Henry Isely, April 27, 1863, Microfilm Roll MS 139, KSHS. Emphasis in original.

Chapter 8

1. Jane B. Hewett, ed., *Supplement to the Official Records of the Union and Confederate Armies,* pt. 2, vol. 78 (Wilmington, N.C.: Broadfoot, 1998), 618; *Official Records of the War of the Rebellion (O.R.),* ser. 1, vol. 22, pt. 1, 320–21.
2. Hewett, *Supplement to the Official Records of the Union and Confederate Armies,* pt. 2, vol. 78, 618.
3. James M. Williams to Sir, May 11, 1863, 79th USCT (New) Regimental Order Book, National Archives and Records Administration (NARA), Washington, D.C.
4. Wiley Britton, *The Civil War on the Border,* vol. 2: *1863–1865* (New York: G. P. Putnam's Sons, 1899), 77.
5. *O.R.,* ser. 1, vol. 22, pt. 2, 297.
6. John R. Graton to Dear Wife, May 22, 1863, John R. Graton Collection, Kansas State Historical Society (KSHS), Topeka.
7. Wiley Britton, *Memoirs of the Rebellion on the Border, 1863* (Lincoln: University of Nebraska Press, 1993), 243.
8. Larry Wood, *The Civil War on the Lower Kansas-Missouri Border* (Joplin, Mo.: Hickory, 2000), 60.
9. Wood, *The Civil War on the Lower Kansas-Missouri Border,* 78; Livingston does not give Mrs. Rader's first name in his report and makes no mention of her husband being with his men at the time of this engagement; *O.R.,* vol. 22, pt. 1, 322.
10. Wood, *The Civil War on the Lower Kansas-Missouri Border,* 78.
11. John R. Graton to Dear Wife, May 22, 1863, John R. Graton Collection, KSHS.
12. John Graton wrote to his wife that Livingston's group numbered between 150 and 200 men. Graton was not in the engagement but reported the accounts from the regiment. John R. Graton to Dear Wife, May 22, 1863, John R. Graton Collection, KSHS. For Livingston's report, see *O.R.,* vol. 22, pt. 1, 321–22.
13. John R. Graton to Dear Wife, May 22, 1863, John R. Graton Collection, KSHS.
14. Ibid.; James M. Williams's account of the regiment's history for Adjutant-General of Kansas T. J. Anderson, James M. Williams Collection, KSHS.
15. John R. Graton to Dear Wife, May 22, 1863, John R. Graton Collection, KSHS.

16. Ibid.
17. Ibid.; *O.R.*, vol. 22, pt. 1, 322.
18. Ibid.; James M. Williams's account of the regiment's history for Adjutant-General of Kansas T. J. Anderson, James M. Williams Collection, KSHS.
19. John R. Graton to Dear Wife, May 22, 1863, John R. Graton Collection, KSHS.
20. Ibid.
21. T. R. Livingston to Colonel James M. Williams, May 20, 1863, 79th USCT (New) Regimental Order Book, NARA.
22. Ibid.
23. J. M. Williams to Maj. T. R. Livingston, May 21, 1863, 79th USCT (New) Regimental Order Book, NARA.
24. Ibid.
25. Wood, *The Civil War on the Lower Kansas-Missouri Border*, 81.
26. James M. Williams's account of the regiment's history for Adjutant-General of Kansas T. J. Anderson, James M. Williams Collection, KSHS; see T. R. Livingston to Col. Williams, May 23, 1863, 79th USCT (New) Regimental Order Book, NARA, and R. G. Ward to Maj. T. R. Livingston, May 23, 1863, 79th USCT (New) Regimental Order Book, NARA.
27. J. M. Williams to Maj. T. R. Livingston, May 26, 1863, 79th USCT (New) Regimental Order Book, NARA.
28. Ibid.
29. Ibid.
30. T. R. Livingston to Col. [J. M.] Williams, May 27, 1863, 79th USCT (New) Regimental Order Book, NARA.
31. Ibid.
32. "Military History of the First Kansas (Colored) Volunteer Infantry," in *Report of the Adjutant General of the State of Kansas, 1861–1865*, vol. 1 (Topeka: J. K. Hudson, 1896), 248.
33. *Report of the Adjutant General of the State of Kansas, 1861–1865*, vol. 1, 574–94, errata.
34. Deposition of George J. Martin, October 19, 1907, in the Henry Lawson Pension File, Application 705557, Certificate 598800, NARA.
35. Deposition of Freeling (alias Henry) Lawson, November 4, 1907, in the Henry Lawson Pension File, Application 705557, Certificate 598800, NARA.
36. Hewett, *Supplement to the Official Records of the Union and Confederate Armies*, pt. 2, vol. 78, 619.
37. T. R. Livingston to Col [J. M.] Williams, June 8, 1863, 79th USCT (New) Regimental Order Book, NARA.
38. Ibid.
39. J. M. Williams to T. R. Livingston, June 8, 1863, 79th USCT (New) Regimental Order Book, NARA.
40. *O.R.*, ser. 1, vol. 22, pt. 1, 341–42.
41. Ibid., 342.
42. J. M. Williams to Maj. Genl. Blunt, June 24, 1863, 79th USCT (New) Regimental Order Book, NARA.

43. Thomas Moonlight to Col. J. M. Williams, June 18, 1863, J. M. Williams Collection, KSHS.
44. *O.R.*, ser. 1, vol. 22, pt. 2, 331.
45. Ibid., 337.
46. *O.R.*, ser. 1, vol. 22, pt. 1, 382.
47. J. M. Williams to Maj. Genl Blunt, June 24, 1863, 79th USCT (New) Regimental Order Book, NARA.

Chapter 9

1. Grant Foreman, "Early Trails through Oklahoma," *Chronicles of Oklahoma* 3, no. 2 (June 1925): 117.
2. John Graton to My Dear Wife, July 7, 1863, John R. Graton Collection, Kansas State Historical Society (KSHS), Topeka.
3. *Official Military History of Kansas Regiments during the War for the Suppression of the Great Rebellion* (Leavenworth: W. S. Burke, 1870), 440.
4. *Official Records of the War of the Rebellion (O.R.)*, ser. 1, vol. 22, pt. 1, 382.
5. Wiley Britton, *The Civil War on the Border*, vol. 2: *1863–1865* (New York: G. P. Putnam's Sons, 1899), 95.
6. Ethan Earle, "Journal of Captain Ethan Earle, Company F, First Kansas Colored Volunteer Infantry Regiment," 1873, p. 35, New England Historic Genealogical Society, Boston, Mass. Microfilm copy at KSHS.
7. Ibid.
8. Britton, *The Civil War on the Border*, vol. 2, 95.
9. *O.R.*, ser. 1, vol. 22, pt. 1, 380, 382.
10. John Thomas Howard quoted in Mamie Yeary, comp., *Reminiscences of the Boys in Gray, 1861–1865* (Dallas: Smith & Lamar, 1912), 352.
11. Ibid.
12. Ibid.
13. *O.R.*, ser. 1, vol. 22, pt. 1, 380, 382.
14. The Second Colorado Infantry officially became the Second Colorado Cavalry in November 1863. Williams refers to the Second Colorado as infantry in his report on the battle at Cabin Creek, but someone later inserted the word "cavalry" in brackets behind it in the report in the *Official Records of the War of the Rebellion. O.R.*, ser. 1, vol. 22, pt. 1, 379–81.
15. *O.R.*, ser. 1, vol. 22, pt. 1, 380.
16. Ibid.
17. Britton, *Civil War on the Border*, vol. 2, 95, 97; *O.R.* ser. 1, vol. 22, pt. 1, 379; Bradford K. Felmly and John C. Grady, *Suffering to Silence: 29th Texas Cavalry, CSA Regimental History* (Quanah, Tex.: Nortex, 1975), 75–76.
18. *O.R.*, ser. 1, vol. 22, pt. 1, 380.
19. Luther Dickerson Pension File, Application 502115, Certificate 281394, National Archives and Records Administration (NARA), Washington, D.C. Dickerson's 1886 pension file description of his wound only

gives the private's name as "Smith." Company B had two private Smiths—Isaac Smith and Jerrett (or Jared) Smith. It is as yet unclear which sustained a wound to the hand during the Battle of Cabin Creek. Dickerson's physical description provided by Captain George Martin in an October 19, 1907, deposition in the pension file of Henry Lawson, Application 705557, Certificate 598800, NARA.

20. *O.R.*, ser. 1, vol. 22, pt. 1, 380.
21. Earle, "Journal of Captain Ethan Earle," 38.
22. *O.R.*, ser. 1, vol. 22, pt. 1, 380.
23. Felmly and Grady, *Suffering to Silence*, 79.
24. *O.R.*, ser. 1, vol. 22, pt. 1, 381.
25. Ibid., 379.
26. Ibid., 381.
27. Ezekial Coleman Pension File, Application 196558, Certificate 133741, NARA.
28. *O.R.*, ser. 1, vol. 22, pt. 1, 381.
29. J. M. Williams, "General Orders No. 5," July 12, 1863, 79th USCT (New) Regimental Order Book, NARA.
30. Jonathan D. Martin, *Divided Mastery: Slave Hiring in the American South* (Cambridge, Mass.: Harvard University Press, 2004), 8.
31. Daniel M. Adams to Col. J. M. Williams, July 15, 1863, James M. Williams Collection, KSHS.
32. *United States Statutes at Large*, vol. 12, 599.
33. Confirmation of the payment amount may be found on some muster cards for soldiers of the First Kansas Colored Infantry. For instance, the November and December 1864 muster card for Benjamin Tilton, Company F, has the notation "Paid $7.00 a month from date of enrollment to Jany 30 /64." Benjamin Tilton, Compiled Service Record, 79th USCT (New), NARA.
34. Dudley Taylor Cornish, *The Sable Arm: Black Troops in the Union Army, 1861–1865* (1956; repr., Lawrence: University Press of Kansas, 1987), 184–96.

Chapter 10

1. Combat operations in the far West drew even less attention, but their physical separation from the situation in the East helps explain this disparity.
2. James G. Blunt, "General Blunt's Account of His Civil War Experiences," *Kansas Historical Quarterly* 1, no. 3 (May 1932): 242–43; Kip Lindberg and Matt Matthews, "'To Play a Bold Game,' the Battle of Honey Springs," *North and South* 6, no. 1 (December 2002): 59.
3. James Lane to Sidney Clarke, July 6, 1863, Sidney Clarke Collection, Box 1, Folder 21, Carl Albert Congressional Research and Studies Center Congressional Archives, University of Oklahoma, Norman.
4. Blunt, "General Blunt's Account of His Civil War Experiences," 243; Lindberg and Matthews, "'To Play a Bold Game,'" 60.
5. *Official Records of the War of the Rebellion (O.R.)*, ser. 1, vol. 22, pt. 2, 356–57.

6. Lindberg and Matthews, "'To Play a Bold Game,'" 60.
7. Blunt, "General Blunt's Account of His Civil War Experiences," 244.
8. *O.R.*, ser. 1, vol. 22, pt. 1, 447.
9. Lindberg and Matthews, "'To Play a Bold Game,'" 61.
10. Blunt, "General Blunt's Account of His Civil War Experiences," 244.
11. *O.R.*, ser. 1, vol. 22, pt. 1, 447.
12. Ibid.
13. Ibid., 451.
14. Lindberg and Matthews, "'To Play a Bold Game,'" 60, 61.
15. *O.R.*, ser. 1, vol. 22, pt. 1, 457-58.
16. Ibid., 452.
17. Ibid., 458.
18. Interview of Lucinda Davis in *Slave Narratives: A Folk History of Slavery in Oklahoma from Interviews with Former Slaves: Oklahoma Narratives* (Bedford, Mass.: Applewood Books, 2006), 59.
19. Kip Lindberg and Matt Matthews, eds., "'The Eagle of the 11th Kansas': Wartime Reminiscences of Colonel Thomas Moonlight," *Arkansas Historical Quarterly* 62, no. 1 (Spring 2003): 31.
20. *O.R.*, ser. 1, vol. 22, pt. 1, 447.
21. Ibid.; Ethan Earle, "Journal of Captain Ethan Earle, Company F, First Kansas Colored Volunteer Infantry Regiment," 1873, p. 40, New England Historic Genealogical Society, Boston, Mass. Microfilm copy at Kansas State Historical Society, Topeka.
22. Lindberg and Matthews, "The Eagle of the 11th Kansas," 31.
23. Wiley Britton, *The Union Indian Brigade in the Civil War* (Kansas City, Mo.: Franklin Hudson, 1922), 276-77.
24. *O.R.*, ser. 1, vol. 22, pt. 1, 447.
25. Ibid.
26. Ibid.; Lindberg and Matthews, "'To Play a Bold Game,'" 64.
27. *O.R.*, ser. 1, vol. 22, pt. 1, 456.
28. Ibid., 452-53; Lindberg and Matthews, "'To Play a Bold Game,'" 64.
29. *O.R.*, ser. 1, vol. 22, pt. 1, 459.
30. Ibid.
31. Ibid., 458, 459.
32. Earle, "Journal of Captain Ethan Earle," 40.
33. *O.R.*, ser. 1, vol. 22, pt. 1, 449.
34. Ibid.; Lieutenant Colonel John Bowles reported the strength of the regiment at Honey Springs, including officers, to be five hundred. *O.R.*, ser. 1, vol. 22, pt. 1, 450.
35. James M. Williams to Gen. T. J. Anderson, J. M. Williams Collection, Kansas State Historical Society (KSHS), Topeka.
36. Colonel Otis Welch, 29th Texas Cavalry, CSA, letter to the *Clarksville Standard*, September 12, 1863.
37. James M. Williams to Gen. T. J. Anderson, J. M. Williams Collection, KSHS.
38. Captain Benjamin Van Horn of Company I later wrote, "Our main line marched out with 52 yards (I stepped the ground afterwards) of where their main line was laying concealed in the brush and high grass, then

both ranks fired apparently precisely at the same time." Benjamin Van Horn Autobiographical Letter, January 4, 1909, Benjamin Van Horn Collection, KSHS.

39. Lindberg and Matthews, "'To Play a Bold Game,'" 66; Robert McDermott to Dear Wife, July 22, 1863, Twentieth Texas Collection, Texas Historical Research Center, Hill College, Hillsboro.

40. O.R., ser. 1, vol. 22, pt. 1, 449–50.

41. James M. Williams to Gen. T. J. Anderson, J. M. Williams Collection, KSHS.

42. O.R., ser. 1, vol. 22, pt. 1, 450.

43. Lindberg and Matthews, "'To Play a Bold Game,'" 66.

44. "Report of Lieut. Col. John Bowles, First Kansas Colored Infantry, Judson's brigade," July 20, 1863, 79th USCT (New) Book Records of Volunteer Union Organizations, RG 94: Records of the Adjutant General's Office, National Archives and Records Administration (NARA), Washington, D.C.; 79th USCT (New) Carded Medical Records, RG 94: Records of the Adjutant General's Office, Entry 534, NARA.

45. O.R., ser. 1, vol. 22, pt. 1, 450.

46. Ibid.

47. Robert McDermott to Sis, July 22, 1863, Twentieth Texas Collection, Texas Historical Research Center, Hill College, Hillsboro.

48. O.R., ser. 1, vol. 22, pt. 1, 450.

49. Ibid., 459.

50. Clarksville Standard, September 12, 1863.

51. O.R., ser. 1, vol. 22, pt. 1, 450, 459; Earle, "Journal of Captain Ethan Earle," 41.

52. O.R., ser. 1, vol. 22, pt. 1, 459.

53. Lucinda Davis in Slave Narratives, 61.

54. Earle, "Journal of Captain Ethan Earle," 41.

55. Lindberg and Matthews, "'The Eagle of the 11th Kansas,'" 32.

56. O.R., ser. 1, vol. 22, pt. 1, 460.

57. Ibid., 448.

58. "Proof of Disability," Testimony of George Washington and Jack Boss, October 26, 1885, Andrew J. Glenn (alias Andrew Jackson) Pension File, Application 541566, Certificate 339737, Widow Application 738196, Certificate 538153, NARA.

59. O.R., ser. 1, vol. 22, pt. 1, 448.

60. Lucinda Davis in Slave Narratives, 61.

61. O.R., ser. 1, vol. 22, pt. 1, 448; Lindberg and Matthews, "'To Play a Bold Game,'" 68; Robert McDermott to Dear Wife, July 22, 1863, Twentieth Texas Collection, Texas Historical Research Center, Hill College, Hillsboro.

62. Earle, "Journal of Captain Ethan Earle," 41; O.R., ser. 1, vol. 22, pt. 1, 448, 460.

63. Lieutenant Colonel John Bowles's after-action report claims that thirty men were wounded, but a comparison of his casualty list and the regiment's medical cards shows a few discrepancies. Thus some wounded

men may not have been listed on Bowles's account, while a few from his list with light wounds may not have been admitted to a federal hospital. "Report of Lieut. Col. John Bowles, First Kansas Colored Infantry, Judson's brigade," July 20, 1863, 79th USCT, Book Records of Volunteer Union Organizations, RG 94: Records of the Adjutant General's Office, NARA; 79th USCT Carded Medical Records, RG 94: Records of the Adjutant General's Office, Entry 534, NARA.

64. *Clarksville Standard,* September 12, 1863.
65. Earle, "Journal of Captain Ethan Earle," 41.
66. *O.R.*, ser. 1, vol. 22, pt. 1, 448.
67. Earle, "Journal of Captain Ethan Earle," 43.

Chapter 11

1. For instance, Companies B, E, G, and I camped on the Verdigris River some eight miles northwest of Fort Blunt. Janet B. Hewett, ed., *Supplement to the Official Records of the Union and Confederate Armies,* pt. 2—*Record of Events,* vol. 78, serial 90 (Wilmington, N.C.: Broadfoot, 1998), 620.
2. Edwin C. Bearss and A. M. Gibson, *Fort Smith: Little Gibraltar on the Arkansas* (Norman: University of Oklahoma Press, 1969), 266–67.
3. General James G. Blunt to Major H. Z. Curtis, August 10, 1863, Thomas Moonlight Papers, Kansas State Historical Society (KSHS), Topeka.
4. Ibid.
5. Hewett, *Supplement to the Official Records,* pt. 2, vol. 78, ser. 90, 629, 634, 639; Bearss and Gibson, *Fort Smith,* 267, 268; *Official Records of the War of the Rebellion (O.R.),* ser. 1, vol. 22, pt. 1, 597–98, 599–600.
6. Bearss and Gibson, *Fort Smith,* 268–69.
7. American Freedmen's Inquiry Commission Form, Daniel R. Anthony, Letter to the Commission, Leavenworth, Kansas, August 30, 1863, American Freedom's Inquiry Commission Collection, bMS Am 702(5), Houghton Library, Harvard University, Cambridge, Mass.
8. According to the *Preliminary Report on the Eighth Census,* of the 31.4 million people in the United States in 1860, approximately 4.43 million were African American. Joseph C. G. Kennedy, *Preliminary Report on the Eighth Census: 1860* (Washington, D.C.: Government Printing Office, 1862), 5; *New York Times,* April 5, 1860.
9. Daniel R. Anthony, Letter to the Commission, Leavenworth, Kans., August 30, 1863, American Freedom's Inquiry Commission Collection, bMS Am 702(5), Houghton Library, Harvard University, Cambridge, Mass. Anthony answered yes to the question regarding intellectual differences between blacks and mulattoes.
10. James M. Williams, Letter to the Commission, November 14, 1863, bMS Am 702 (121), American Freedom's Inquiry Commission Collection, Houghton Library, Harvard University, Cambridge, Mass.
11. William A. Phillips, Letter to the Commission, October 10, 1863, bMS Am 702 (81), American Freedom's Inquiry Commission Collection, Houghton Library, Harvard University, Cambridge, Mass.

12. Ibid.
13. A good description of the challenges facing runaway slaves can be found in John Hope Franklin and Loren Schweninger, *Runaway Slaves: Rebels on the Plantation* (New York: Oxford University Press, 1999), 49–74.
14. General Orders Number 3, September 18, 1863, Richard J. Hinton Collection, KSHS.
15. Special Orders 56 [attached to General Orders No. 3, September 18, 1863], Richard J. Hinton Collection, KSHS.
16. According to company records, the regiment arrived at Fort Smith in at least two sections over the course of two days. Hewett, *Supplement to the Official Records*, pt. 2, vol. 78, serial 90, 619–41 errata. Ethan Earle, "Journal of Captain Ethan Earle, Company F, First Kansas Colored Volunteer Infantry Regiment," 1873, p. 44, New England Historic Genealogical Society, Boston, Mass. Microfilm copy at KSHS.
17. S. H. Melcer to Headquarters of Department of Missouri, October 6, 1863, First Kansas Colored Record Book, Fort Scott National Park Archives.
18. John David Smith, "Let Us All Be Grateful That We Have Colored Troops That Will Fight," in *Black Soldiers in Blue: African American Troops in the Civil War Era*, ed. John David Smith (Chapel Hill: University of North Carolina Press, 2002), 41.
19. Numbers quoted come from those deaths recorded to specific dates. *Report of the Adjutant General of the State of Kansas, 1861–1865*, vol. 1 (Topeka: J. K. Hudson, 1896), pp. 574–97 errata. Descriptions of death from disease vary in available regimental records and many fail to provide diagnoses of medical condition or date of death. Other records, such as the Carded Medical Records, 79th USCT (New) at the National Archives and Records Administration (NARA), Washington, D.C., provide basic information for many hospital admissions, but generally do not cover deaths.
20. S. H. Melcer to Headquarters of Department of Missouri, October 6, 1863, First Kansas Colored Record Book, Fort Scott National Park Archives.
21. Ibid.
22. Earle, "Journal of Captain Ethan Earle," 43
23. *Report of the Adjutant General of the State of Kansas, 1861–1865*, vol. 1 (Topeka: J. K. Hudson, 1896), 575–97 errata.
24. Technically, Schofield's promotion to major general had not been confirmed by the Senate. At one point, Blunt claimed credit for pulling political strings to deny the confirmation. See *Official Records of the War of the Rebellion* (hereafter O.R.), ser. 1, vol. 22, pt. 2, 742; Albert Castel, *Civil War Kansas: Reaping the Whirlwind* (Lawrence: University Press of Kansas, 1997), 162; Bearss and Gibson, *Fort Smith*, 273.
25. *Report of the Adjutant General of the State of Kansas, 1861–1865*, vol. 1, 575.

26. Ibid., 578.
27. *Fort Smith New Era*, January 30, 1864. The regimental roster does not list a Jacob Hill. This individual may be Jacob Hall of Company B, who died of illness on January 12, 1864. *Report of the Adjutant General of the State of Kansas, 1861–1865*, vol. 1, 578.
28. *O.R.*, ser. 1, vol. 22, pt. 2, 690–91.
29. Ibid., 691.
30. Ibid., 692.
31. Some companies were sent to surrounding locations. Companies A and E were at Bower's Mill, and Company H collected supplies at Ozark, Arkansas. Hewett, *Supplement to the Official Records*, pt. 2, vol. 78, serial 90, 620.
32. *O.R.*, ser. 1, vol. 22, pt. 2, 728.
33. Hewett, *Supplement to the Official Records*, pt. 2, vol. 78, serial 90, 620.
34. *O.R.*, ser. 1, vol. 22, pt. 2, 682.
35. Ibid., 690.
36. Ibid., 728.
37. James G. Blunt, "General Blunt's Account of His Civil War Experiences," *Kansas Historical Quarterly* 1, no. 3 (May 1932): 249.
38. *O.R.*, ser. 1, vol. 22, pt. 2, 728.
39. Blunt, "General Blunt's Account of His Civil War Experiences," 249.
40. *Fort Smith New Era*, December 12, 1863.
41. Ibid.
42. Ibid.
43. Ibid.
44. Champion Vaughan to James M. Williams, December 10, 1863, J. M. Williams Collection, KSHS.
45. John R. Graton to Wife, January 27, 1864, John R. Graton Collection, KSHS. Graton appears to have written the letter over a period of some days. The section in which he referred to the regiment's location at Roseville is under a section dated December 28.
46. Tom Wing, ed., *"A Rough Introduction to This Sunny Land": The Civil War Diary of Private Henry A. Strong, Co. K, Twelfth Kansas Infantry* (Little Rock: Butler Center for Arkansas Studies, 2006), 20.
47. John R. Graton to Wife, January 27, 1864, John R. Graton Collection, KSHS.
48. James M. Williams to Brigadier General [John] McNeil, January 4, 1864, 79th USCT (New) Infantry, Regimental Order Book, NARA.
49. John R. Graton to Wife, January 27, 1864, John R. Graton Collection, KSHS.
50. Ibid.
51. Special Orders No. 5, January 13, 1864, 79th USCT (New) Infantry, Regimental Order Book, NARA.
52. Earle, "Journal of Captain Ethan Earle," 45.
53. E. Bowland to Col. Williams, December 30, 1863; J. M. Williams to E. Bowland, Esq., January 4, 1864, 79th USCT (New) Infantry, Regimental Order Book, NARA.

54. James M. McPherson, *Battle Cry of Freedom* (New York: Oxford University Press, 1988), 698–99.
55. Carl H. Moneyhon, *The Impact of the Civil War and Reconstruction on Arkansas: Persistence in the Midst of Ruin* (Fayetteville: University of Arkansas Press, 2002), 159–60.
56. Earle, "Journal of Captain Ethan Earle," 45.
57. Moneyhon, *The Impact of the Civil War and Reconstruction on Arkansas*, 160.
58. *Fort Smith New Era*, January 16, 1864.
59. Thomas D. Morris, *Southern Slavery and the Law, 1619–1860* (Chapel Hill: University of North Carolina Press, 1996), 31–32.
60. *Fort Smith New Era*, January 16, 1864.
61. Moneyhon, *The Impact of the Civil War and Reconstruction on Arkansas*, 138.
62. Court Martial of Captain Andrew J. Armstrong, 1864, Court Martial Case File, LL-2107, pp. 7–9, Record Group 153, NARA.
63. Ibid., 3–6.
64. Ibid., 9–13.
65. Ibid., 16.
66. Ibid., 27–28.
67. Ibid., 43. After the war, Captain Earle wrote of a combined effort among company officers to expel the colonel. "When in Roseville the company officers for the second time preferred charges against Col. Williams," Earle explained. "He was charged with about every crime which could disgrace an officer and render him unfit and unworthy of holding an office in the Army. These charges were signed by nearly every Company officer in the Regiment, with a request to have the Col. arraigned and tried by Court Martial." No details have emerged from this reported incident, nor do unit records at the National Archives and Kansas State Historical Society show opposition to the regiment's commander. Earle complained that this effort "like the others was unnoticed except to land the officer who headed it, to Fort Gibson for three months a prisoner." The reason, he sardonically noted: "Col. Williams was too valuable a link in the 'Army Ring' to take him out." Earle, "Journal of Captain Ethan Earle," 44.
68. Earle, "Journal of Captain Ethan Earle," 44.
69. John Bowles to Colonel J. M. Williams, October 25, 1863, John Bowles Compiled Service Record, 79th USCT (New), NARA.
70. Surgeon Certificate, October 30, 1863, John Bowles Compiled Service Record, 79th USCT (New), NARA.
71. J. H. Lane to Maj. Gen. Curtis, January 11, 1864, John Bowles Compiled Service Record, 79th USCT (New), NARA.
72. John R. Graton to Dear Wife, November 27, 1864, John R. Graton Collection, KSHS.
73. *United States Service Magazine*, vol. 3 (New York: Charles R. Richardson, 1865), 188.

74. Bowles was mustered out on June 1, 1865, by Special Order No. 335, War Department. *Report of the Adjutant General of the State of Kansas, 1861–1865*, vol. 1 (Topeka: J. K. Hudson, 1896), 574.
75. In his analysis of the Camden Expedition, Michael J. Forsyth called Shreveport the "de facto Confederate capital of the Trans-Mississippi Department." Michael J. Forsyth, *The Camden Expedition of 1864 and the Lost Opportunity by the Confederacy to Change the Civil War* (Jefferson, N.C.: McFarland & Company, 2003), 6.
76. Ibid., 7; *O.R.*, ser. 1, vol. 34, 657.
77. *O.R.*, ser. 1, vol. 34, 659.
78. Forsyth, *The Camden Expedition of 1864*, 71–72.
79. Hewett, *Supplement to the Official Records*, pt. 2, vol. 78, serial 90, 621.
80. Wing, *"A Rough Introduction to This Sunny Land,"* 33.
81. Gregory J. W. Urwin, "'We Cannot Treat Negroes . . . as Prisoners of War': Racial Atrocities and Reprisals in Civil War Arkansas," in *Black Flag over Dixie: Racial Atrocities and Reprisals in the Civil War*, ed. Gregory J. W. Urwin (Carbondale: Southern Illinois University Press, 2004), 141.

Chapter 12

1. Tom Wing, ed., *"A Rough Introduction to This Sunny Land": The Civil War Diary of Private Henry A. Strong, Co. K, Twelfth Kansas Infantry* (Little Rock: Butler Center for Arkansas Studies, 2006), 34.
2. *Official Records of the War of the Rebellion (O.R.)*, ser. 1, vol. 34, pt. 1, 673.
3. Wing, *"A Rough Introduction to This Sunny Land,"* 34.
4. Michael J. Forsyth, *The Camden Expedition of 1864 and the Lost Opportunity by the Confederacy to Change the Civil War* (Jefferson, N.C.: McFarland & Company, 2003), 89–90.
5. Ibid., 93.
6. Ibid., 91, 94, 95–96; Wiley Britton, *The Civil War on the Border*, vol. 2, *1863–1865* (New York: G. P. Putnam's Sons, 1899), 263.
7. Forsyth, *The Camden Expedition of 1864*, 998–99; Janet B. Hewett, ed., *Supplement to the Official Records of the Union and Confederate Armies*, pt. 2—Records of Events, vol. 78 (Wilmington, N.C.: Broadfoot, 1998), 621.
8. *O.R.*, ser. 1, vol. 34, pt. 1, 680.
9. Ibid., 682.
10. Edwin C. Bearss, *Steele's Retreat from Camden and the Battle of Jenkins Ferry* (Little Rock: Pioneer, 1995), 5–6.
11. *O.R.*, ser. 1, vol. 34, pt. 1, 743.
12. *Topeka Daily Capital*, March 13, 1886.
13. Ibid.
14. *O.R.*, ser. 1, vol. 34, pt. 1, 743; Gregory J. W. Urwin, "'Cut to Pieces and Gone to Hell': The Poison Spring Massacre," *North and South* 2, no. 6 (August 2000): 47.
15. *Topeka Daily Capital*, February 28, 1886.

16. Ibid., March 13, 1886.
17. *O.R.*, ser. 1, vol. 34, pt. 1, 743.
18. Ibid., 847.
19. Ibid., 744.
20. Gregory J. W. Urwin, "'We Cannot Treat Negroes . . . as Prisoners of War': Racial Atrocities and Reprisals in Civil War Arkansas," in *Black Flag over Dixie: Racial Atrocities and Reprisals in the Civil War*, ed. Gregory J. W. Urwin (Carbondale: Southern Illinois University Press, 2004), 138.
21. Ibid., 138.
22. *O.R.*, ser. 1, vol. 34, pt. 1, 744.
23. Ibid., 818–19; Urwin, "'Cut to Pieces and Gone to Hell,'" 47.
24. *O.R.*, ser. 1, vol. 34, pt. 1, 819.
25. Ibid., 841; Urwin, "'Cut to Pieces and Gone to Hell,'" 51.
26. *O.R.*, ser. 1, vol. 34, pt. 1, 744, 819.
27. Ibid., 819.
28. Ibid.; Urwin, "'Cut to Pieces and Gone to Hell,'" 48.
29. *O.R.*, ser. 1, vol. 34, pt. 1, 744.
30. *Topeka Daily Capital*, February 28, 1886.
31. *O.R.*, ser. 1, vol. 34, pt. 1, 744, 750.
32. Ibid., 842.
33. *Clarksville Standard*, April 30, 1864.
34. *O.R.*, ser. 1, vol. 34, pt. 1, 846.
35. Ibid., 744.
36. Ibid.
37. Ibid.; *Clarksville Standard*, April 30, 1864.
38. *O.R.*, ser. 1, vol. 34, pt. 1, 752.
39. Ibid.; *Topeka Daily Capital*, February 28, 1886.
40. *O.R.*, ser. 1, vol. 34, pt. 1, 752, 791; Urwin, "'Cut to Pieces and Gone to Hell,'" 50.
41. Britton, *The Civil War on the Border*, vol. 2, 284–85; *O.R.*, ser. 1, vol. 34, pt. 1, 752.
42. *Clarksville Standard*, April 30, 1864.
43. *O.R.*, ser. 1, vol. 34, pt. 1, 847.
44. Ibid., 755.
45. Ibid., 744.
46. Ibid.
47. Wing, "*A Rough Introduction to This Sunny Land*," 41.
48. *Fort Smith New Era*, May 7, 1864.
49. *O.R.*, ser. 1, vol. 34, pt. 1, 847.
50. Ibid., 848.
51. Ibid., 753.
52. Ibid., 754.
53. Ibid., 752.
54. Ibid., 847; Urwin, "'Cut to Pieces and Gone to Hell,'" 50.
55. *O.R.*, ser. 1, vol. 34, pt. 1, 748, 750, 751, 849.
56. Ibid., 752.

57. George Washington, "Deposition A," August 17, 1896, George Washington Pension File, Application 266875, Certificate 180670, Widow Application 666120, Certificate 493549, National Archives and Records Administration (NARA), Washington, D.C.
58. Wiley Britton, *The Union Indian Brigade in the Civil War* (Kansas City, Mo.: Franklin Hudson, 1922), 367.
59. *O.R.*, ser. 1, vol. 34, pt. 1, 744, 754.
60. Ibid., 752.
61. Ibid., 744; *Topeka Daily Capital*, March 13, 1886.
62. *O.R.*, ser. 1, vol. 34, pt. 1, 744.
63. *O.R.*, ser. 1, vol. 34, pt. 1, 744, 753.
64. Ibid., 828.
65. Ibid., 842.
66. Ibid., 755.
67. Ibid.
68. Ibid., 753.
69. Ibid.
70. Ibid., 756.
71. Anonymous to Dear Sallie, April 20, 1864, in Mark Christ, ed., *"All Cut to Pieces and Gone to Hell": The Civil War, Race Relations, and the Battle of Poison Spring* (Little Rock: August House, 2003), 100.
72. *Fort Smith New Era*, May 7, 1864; *O.R.*, ser. 1, vol. 34, pt. 1, 754.
73. *O.R.*, ser. 1, vol. 34, pt. 1, 745.
74. Ibid., 745, 749, 757.
75. Ibid., 849. The historian Gregory Urwin writes that the Choctaw soldiers did break formation to pillage the train. Urwin, "'Cut to Pieces and Gone to Hell,'" 53; *O.R.*, ser. 1, vol. 34, pt. 1, 847.
76. *O.R.*, ser. 1, vol. 34, pt. 1, 828.
77. *Topeka Daily Capital*, March 13, 1886.
78. *O.R.*, ser. 1, vol. 34, pt. 1, 849.
79. Ibid., 842.
80. Deposition of William Gordon, November 22, 1899, William Gordon Pension File, Application 761720, Certificate 907381, NARA.
81. *O.R.*, ser. 1, vol. 34, pt. 1, 842.
82. Ibid.
83. Britton, *The Civil War on the Border*, vol. 2, 291.
84. Urwin, "'Cut to Pieces and Gone to Hell,'" 54.
85. Ibid., 53.
86. Roman J. Zorn, ed., "Campaigning in Southern Arkansas: A Memoir by C. T. Anderson," *Arkansas Historical Quarterly* 8 (Autumn 1949): 242–43.
87. *Washington Telegraph*, May 11, 1864.
88. *Confederate Veteran* 9, no. 6 (June 1901): 276.
89. Urwin, "We Cannot Treat Negroes . . . as Prisoners of War," 143.
90. Ibid., 140.
91. Anonymous to Dear Sallie, April 20, 1864, printed in Christ, *"All Cut to Pieces and Gone to Hell,"* 100. The historian Mark Christ persuasively

argues that the letter was written by Alfred G. Hearn of the Tenth Arkansas Cavalry. Hearn was married to Sallie, and the couple did own two male slaves. Christ, "*All Cut to Pieces and Gone to Hell,*" 103. The identity of the two former slaves mentioned by name in the letter, "Dr. Rowland's Clabe and Kyle's Berry," is unclear. No soldier named "Clabe" (or any similar variation) was listed in the regimental roster as killed at Poison Spring. The only "Berry" recorded as killed at the battle was Company I's First Sergeant Alfred Berry. First Sergeant Berry was from Arkansas—he enlisted at Fort Smith in December 1863—but there is, as of yet, no information to prove he was the man referred to in the letter.

92. *Fort Smith New Era*, May 7, 1864.
93. Ibid.
94. *New York Times*, May 14, 1864.
95. Jesse Brown Pension File, Application 128405, Certificate 93714, NARA.
96. Frank Grayson Pension File, Application 441021, Certificate 424857, Widow Application 525234, Certificate 471437, Minor Application 642652, Certificate 471438, NARA.
97. Amos Adair Pension File, Application 435098, Certificate 661495, NARA. Based on the 79th USCT (New) carded medical records, other soldiers reported to have sustained wounds to multiple parts of the body at Poison Spring are Jesse Brown, Henry Clay, Richard Davis, James Mattox, Eberle Q. Macey, Peter Mathews, Gum Ridings, David Sanders, and Dock Scott. These carded medical records do not provide a complete accounting of wounds or illnesses within the regiment, and some cards are duplicates. Furthermore, discrepancies exist among some of the duplicates. The soldiers mentioned above appeared to have sustained distinctly separate wounds at Poison Spring. Carded Medical Records, 79th USCT (New), NARA.
98. Samuel Jefferson, Carded Medical Records, 79th USCT (New), NARA.
99. *Topeka Daily Capital*, March 13, 1886.
100. O.R., ser. 1, vol. 34, pt. 1, 746.
101. Wing, "*A Rough Introduction to This Sunny Land,*" 41.
102. Ibid.
103. *Fort Smith New Era*, May 7, 1864.
104. *New York Times*, May 14, 1864.
105. O.R., ser. 1, vol. 34, pt. 1, 754.
106. William F. Fox, *Regimental Losses in the American Civil War, 1861–1865* (Albany, N.Y.: Albany Publishing, 1889), 24–25.
107. The total number of casualties for Shiloh and Gettysburg listed in the text only accounts for wounded and killed; it does not include captured or missing in action. According to Fox, Union forces suffered 1,754 killed, 8,408 wounded, and 2,885 captured or missing at Shiloh and 3,063 killed, 14,492 wounded, and 5,435 captured or missing at Gettysburg. Fox, *Regimental Losses in the American Civil War*, 23.

108. Immediate reports after the battle recorded 117 men killed. However, at least 4 men reported as killed had been captured and held alive. Because Confederates held the field, Union officers could not take an accurate accounting of dead, and concluded that those not safe in Union lines were dead. Except for the handful of wounded and captured spared from execution, the assumption was generally correct. The Kansas Adjutant General's Report of the First Kansas Colored Infantry, compiled after the war, lists 110 men killed at Poison Spring. *Report of the Adjutant General of the State of Kansas, 1861–1865*, vol. 1 (Topeka: J. K. Hudson, 1896), 574–97.

109. Fox, *Regimental Losses in the American Civil War*, 17.

110. Urwin, "'Cut to Pieces and Gone to Hell,'" 54.

111. *O.R.*, ser. 1, vol. 34, pt. 1, 751.

112. Joseph Frankovic, Jeremy Lynch, Julie Northrip, and Sam Trisler, "Prairie D'Ane and Poison Spring from a Southern Perspective," *Journal of the Fort Smith Historical Society* 31, no. 1 (April 2007): 38.

113. Ibid., 43–44.

114. *Fort Smith New Era*, June 18, 1864.

115. *Topeka Daily Capital*, February 28, 1886.

116. Company C Muster Out Roll, 79th USCT (New) Company Record Books, NARA.

117. Urwin, "'Cut to Pieces and Gone to Hell,'" 54.

118. *O.R.*, ser. 1, vol. 34, pt. 1, 848.

119. Ibid., 819, 842, 848.

120. *Missouri Republican*, November 12, 1885.

Chapter 13

1. Amos Adair Pension File, Application 435098, Certificate 661495, National Archives and Records Administration (NARA), Washington, D.C.

2. Green Washington (alias Green Ward) Pension File, Application 210152, Certificate 143402, NARA.

3. Giles Green's pension file contains some contradictory information about his neck injury and actions during the Camden Expedition. Pension officials learned that regimental records listed him absent due to sickness during the spring and early summer of 1864. They also suspected that scars on his neck came from noncombat injuries or ailments. A couple of accounts from his comrades also suggested that he had problems with his neck prior to Poison Spring. However, multiple interviews with other people—including his company commander, his former owner's son, the doctor who attended to him as a slave, and other enlisted veterans of the regiment—corroborated his story of being wounded during the Camden Expedition. See files in Giles Green Pension Application 150047, Certificate 524424, Widow Application 1624875, Certificate a2-21-29, NARA.

4. A. F. Sperry, *History of the 33d Iowa Infantry Volunteer Regiment 1863–6*, ed. Gregory J. W. Urwin and Cathy Kunzinger Urwin (Fayetteville: University of Arkansas Press, 1999), 91.

5. *Official Records of the War of the Rebellion (O.R.)*, ser. 1, vol. 34, pt. 1, 682.

6. Tom Wing, ed., *"A Rough Introduction to This Sunny Land": The Civil War Diary of Private Henry A. Strong, Co. K, Twelfth Kansas Infantry* (Little Rock: Butler Center for Arkansas Studies, 2006), 41.

7. Ibid., 42.

8. *O.R.*, ser. 1, vol. 34, pt. 1, 663; Edwin C. Bearss, *Steele's Retreat from Camden and the Battle of Jenkins Ferry* (Little Rock: Pioneer, 1995), 44–45; Gregory J. W. Urwin, "'Cut to Pieces and Gone to Hell,'" *North and South* 2, no. 6 (August 2000): 54.

9. Steele's army had numbered around twelve thousand during the height of the campaign. However, battlefield losses and the reassignment of three cavalry regiments to other areas by April 22 had reduced that number. *O.R.*, ser. 1, vol. 34, pt. 1, 663.

10. Ibid.

11. Ethan Earle, "Journal of Captain Ethan Earle, Company F, First Kansas Colored Volunteer Infantry Regiment," 1873, p. 54, New England Historic Genealogical Society, Boston, Mass. Microfilm copy at Kansas State Historical Society, Topeka.

12. *O.R.*, ser. 1, vol. 34, pt. 1, 664–66; Bearss, *Steele's Retreat from Camden*, 55–79.

13. Earle, "Journal of Captain Ethan Earle," 54.

14. Cynthia DeHaven Pitcock and Bill J. Gurley, "'I Acted from Principle': William Marcellus McPheeters, Confederate Surgeon," *Missouri Historical Review* 89, no. 4 (July 1995): 396.

15. Wiley Britton, *The Civil War on the Border*, vol. 2, *1863–1865* (New York: G. P. Putnam's Sons, 1899), 304–305.

16. Bearss, *Steele's Retreat from Camden*, 143; Urwin, "'Cut to Pieces and Gone to Hell,'" 55.

17. John H. Lewis quoted in Mamie Yeary, comp., *Reminiscences of the Boys in Gray, 1861–1865* (Dallas: Smith & Lamar, 1912), 352.

18. David S. Williams quoted ibid., 799.

19. J. R. Jones quoted ibid., 390.

20. *Fort Smith New Era*, August 6, 1864.

21. Urwin, "'Cut to Pieces and Gone to Hell,'" 56.

22. *Fort Smith New Era*, August 6, 1864.

23. Ibid., June 18, 1864. Hayes reported that all nine black soldiers were killed in the field hospital.

24. Bearss, *Steele's Retreat from Camden*, 161.

25. Wing, *"A Rough Introduction to This Sunny Land,"* 39–40.

26. Ibid., 34, 35, 43, 44.

27. Ibid., 34.

28. Sperry, *History of the 33d Iowa Infantry Volunteer Regiment*, 110.

29. Janet B. Hewett, ed., *Supplement to the Official Records of the Union and Confederate Armies*, pt. 2—*Records of Events*, vol. 78 (Wilmington, N.C.: Broadfoot, 1998), 621.

30. John R. Graton to Dear Wife, May 6, 1864, John R. Graton Collection, Kansas State Historical Society (KSHS), Topeka.
31. Christian Isely to My own Dearest Wife & Darling Eliza, May 5, 1864, Isely Family Papers, Special Collections, Wichita State University, Wichita, Kans.
32. Ephraim Alston and Amanda Alston, Pension File, Widow Application 444603, Certificate 328280, NARA.
33. *New York Times*, May 6, 1864.
34. Christian Isely to My own Dearest Wife & Darling Eliza, May 5, 1864, Isely Family Papers, Special Collections, Wichita State University, Wichita, Kans.
35. *Leavenworth Daily Times*, May 21, 1864.
36. Earle, "Journal of Captain Ethan Earle," 54.
37. John R. Graton to Dear Wife, May 6, 1864, John R. Graton Collection, KSHS.
38. Earle, "Journal of Captain Ethan Earle," 56; Hewett, *Supplement to the Official Records of the Union and Confederate Armies*, pt. 2—*Records of Events*, vol. 78, 622.
39. Britton, *Civil War on the Border*, vol. 2, 341; Edwin C. Bearss and A. M. Gibson, *Fort Smith: Little Gibraltar on the Arkansas* (Norman: University of Oklahoma Press, 1969), 281; *O.R.*, ser. 1, vol. 34, pt. 4, 84.
40. *Fort Smith New Era*, July 9, 1864.
41. *Washington Telegram*, August 4, 1858, quoted in Orville W. Taylor, *Negro Slavery in Arkansas* (Little Rock: University of Arkansas Press, 2000), 256; Thomas D. Morris, *Southern Slavery and the Law, 1619–1860* (Chapel Hill: University of North Carolina Press, 1999), 31–32.
42. *Congressional Globe*, 38th Cong., 1st sess., pt. 1, 640.
43. Ibid., 481–83.
44. Ibid., 640.
45. Ibid.

Chapter 14

1. In a letter to his wife, Captain John Graton noted that six companies were around Fort Gibson in early September. After the war, former cavalryman and Civil War historian Wiley Britton wrote that Graton escorted the wagon train with five companies of the First Kansas Colored Infantry in late August. The discrepancy may be a mistake by Britton; or perhaps a sixth company arrived at Fort Gibson before Graton's letter. John Graton to Dear Wife, September 29, 1864, John R. Graton Collection, Kansas State Historical Society (KSHS), Topeka; Wiley Britton, *The Civil War on the Border*, vol. 2: *1863–1865* (New York: G. P. Putnam's Sons, 1899), 244.
2. Tom Wing, ed., *"A Rough Introduction to This Sunny Land": The Civil War Diary of Private Henry A. Strong, Co. K, Twelfth Kansas Infantry* (Little Rock: Butler Center for Arkansas Studies, 2006), 55–56.
3. Estimates of the number of First Kansas Colored men at Flat Rock vary. Captain Barker spoke of thirty-seven black soldiers in his detail. His claim is the most specific reference to the number of men, closely matches up with the regimental casualty statistics, and is most credible

given his role as overall commander of the hay-gathering party. *Official Records of the War of the Rebellion* (*O.R.*), ser. 1, vol. 41, pt. 1, 772.

4. *O.R.*, ser. 1, vol. 41, pt. 1, 771–72.
5. See Britton, *The Civil War on the Border*, vol. 2, 244.
6. *Clarksville Standard*, October 15, 1864.
7. *O.R.*, ser. 1, vol. 41, pt. 1, 789.
8. Ibid., 785; *Clarksville Standard*, October 15, 1864. Charles DeMorse was the owner of the *Clarksville Standard* and frequently sent letters of his regiment's exploits to the newspaper during the war. As in this case, he occasionally signed them "Private." Bradford K. Felmly and John C. Grady, *Suffering to Silence: 29th Texas Cavalry, CSA Regimental History* (Quanah, Tex.: Nortex, 1975), 166.
9. *O.R.*, ser. 1, vol. 41, pt. 1, 789.
10. Ibid., 771–72.
11. *O.R.*, ser. 1, vol. 41, pt. 1, 772; Mamie Yeary, comp., *Reminiscences of the Boys in Gray, 1861–1865* (Dallas, Tex.: Smith & Lamar, 1912), 684.
12. *O.R.*, ser. 1, vol. 41, pt. 1, 772.
13. Ibid., 772, 785.
14. Ibid., 785.
15. *Clarksville Standard*, October 15, 1864.
16. *O.R.*, ser. 1, vol. 41, pt. 1, 785, 789.
17. Britton, *The Civil War on the Border*, vol. 2, 246.
18. *Clarksville Standard*, October 15, 1864.
19. W. David Baird, ed., *A Creek Warrior for the Confederacy: The Autobiography of Chief G. W. Grayson* (Norman: University of Oklahoma Press, 1991), 95–96.
20. *Clarksville Standard*, October 15, 1864.
21. Baird, *A Creek Warrior for the Confederacy*, 96.
22. *Clarksville Standard*, October 15, 1864.
23. Yeary, *Reminiscences of the Boys in Gray*, 46.
24. Baird, *A Creek Warrior for the Confederacy*, 96.
25. *O.R.*, ser. 1, vol. 41, pt. 1, 789.
26. Yeary, *Reminiscences of the Boys in Gray*, 684.
27. *O.R.*, ser. 1, vol. 41, pt. 1, 772, 785, 789.
28. Ibid., 789.
29. Ibid., 772.
30. Baird, *A Creek Warrior for the Confederacy*, 96.
31. *Report of the Adjutant General of the State of Kansas, 1861–1865*, vol. 1 (Topeka: J. K. Hudson, 1896), 594, 595, 596. The adjutant general's report about the regiment does not list Lieutenant David Sutherland among those captured at Flat Rock, but his capture is confirmed by other sources. See John R. Graton to Dear Wife, September 29, 1864, John R. Graton Collection, KSHS.
32. Britton, *The Civil War on the Border*, vol. 2, 246.
33. *Report of the Adjutant General of the State of Kansas, 1861–1865*, vol. 1, 596.
34. Yeary, *Reminiscences of the Boys in Gray*, 684.

35. *Clarksville Standard*, October 15, 1864; *O.R.*, ser. 1, vol. 41, pt. 1, 789.
36. *O.R.*, ser. 1, vol. 41, pt. 1, 789–90.
37. Ibid., 789.
38. *Clarksville Standard*, October 15, 1864.
39. *O.R.*, ser. 1, vol. 41, pt. 1, 789.
40. Ibid., 790.
41. John Graton to Dear Wife, September 29, 1864, John R. Graton Collection, KSHS.
42. Ibid.
43. Ibid.; *O.R.*, ser. 1, vol. 41, pt. 1, 765.
44. James C. Hazlett, Edwin Olmstead, and M. Hume Parks, *Field Artillery Weapons of the Civil War* (Chicago: University of Illinois Press, 2004), 109.
45. John Graton to Dear Wife, September 29, 1864, John R. Graton Collection, KSHS.
46. *O.R.*, ser. 1, vol. 41, pt. 1, 791.
47. Ibid., 765.
48. John Graton to Dear Wife, September 29, 1864, John R. Graton Collection, KSHS.
49. Britton, *The Civil War on the Border*, vol. 2, 252.
50. *O.R.*, ser. 1, vol. 41, pt. 1, 791.
51. Ibid.

Chapter 15

1. Captain John Graton to Dear Wife, November 27, 1864, John R. Graton Collection, Kansas State Historical Society (KSHS), Topeka.
2. Ibid.
3. Ibid.
4. Letter of John R. Graton to Dear Wife, January 5, 1865, John R. Graton Collection, KSHS.
5. Letter of John R. Graton, January 15, 1865, John R. Graton Collection, KSHS.
6. Ibid.
7. Letter of John R. Graton to Dear Wife, November 27, 1864, John R. Graton Collection, KSHS.
8. Testimony of Eliza Tyler, Joseph Carris Pension File, Application 418714, Certificate 230304, National Archives and Records Administration (NARA), Washington, D.C.
9. 79th USCT Carded Medical Records, Record Group 94: Records of the Adjutant General's Office, Entry 534, NARA.
10. "David Barbour," "Andy Breedlove," "Jeff Burns," 79th USCT Carded Medical Records, Record Group 94: Records of the Adjutant General's Office, Entry 534, NARA.
11. Giles Gully Affidavit April 1888, Giles Gully Pension Application, Application 650177, Certificate 594776, NARA.
12. John Speaker was accidentally shot in the finger; William St. Clair received a scalp laceration from a stone; William Selectman was accidentally shot

410 NOTES TO PAGES 246–49

by a sentinel; Austin French and James Brown each punctured a foot on separate occasions; Samuel Davis, General Dudley, Anderson Johnson, and Wilbur Lindsey were treated for burns; 79th USCT Carded Medical Records, Record Group 94: Records of the Adjutant General's Office, Entry 534, NARA. Sipio Dandridge cut his leg on a branch, which led to a serious infection; Sipio Dandrige Pension File, Application 523254, NARA.

13. "Early [Hurley] O'Bannon," 79th USCT Carded Medical Records, Record Group 94: Records of the Adjutant General's Office, Entry 534, NARA.

14. Isaac Alexander Testimony, May 25, 1895, Isaac Alexander Pension File, Application 440919, Certificate 670709, NARA.

15. Isaac Alexander Testimony, May 25, 1895, Isaac Alexander Pension File, Application 440919, Certificate 670709, NARA.

16. Willis Yaunt Affidavit, August 4, 1896, Willis Yaunt Pension File, Application 514302, Certificate 354577, NARA.

17. John Smith Pension File, Application 119699, Certificate 88816, NARA.

18. *Report of the Adjutant General of the State of Kansas, 1861–1865*, vol. 1 (Topeka: J. K. Hudson, 1896), 597–99.

19. The compiled service records of these men include the original substitution agreement forms. Compiled Service Records, 79th USCT (New), NARA.

20. Substitute Volunteer Enlistment Form, Compiled Service Record of James T. P. Ball, Compiled Service Records, 79th USCT (New), NARA.

21. *Report of the Adjutant General of the State of Kansas, 1861–1865*, vol. 1, 597.

22. Orders No. 27, December 13, 1864, 79th USCT, Regimental Order Book, Record Group 94: Book Records of Volunteer Union Organizations, NARA.

23. Joseph T. Glatthaar, *Forged in Battle: The Civil War Alliance of Black Soldiers and White Officers* (Baton Rouge: Louisiana State University Press, 2000), xii.

24. William A. Dobak, *Freedom by the Sword: The U.S. Colored Troops, 1862–1867* (Washington, D.C.: Center of Military History, 2011), 308.

25. Paul M. Angle and Earl Schenck Miers, eds., *The Living Lincoln: The Man, His Mind, His Times, and the War He Fought, Reconstructed from His Own Writings* (New York: Marboro Books, 1992), 212.

26. Doris Kearns Goodwin, *Team of Rivals: The Political Genius of Abraham Lincoln* (New York: Simon & Schuster, 2005), 686.

27. Angle and Miers, *The Living Lincoln*, 630.

28. Clayton E. Jewett and John O. Allen, *Slavery in the South: A State-by-State History* (Westport, Conn.: Greenwood, 2004), 182.

29. John G. Nicolay and John Hay, *Abraham Lincoln: A History*, vol. 10 (New York: Century, 1917), 85.

30. *Congressional Globe*, 38th Cong., 2nd sess., 531.

31. Alexander Tsesis, *The Thirteenth Amendment and American Freedom: A Legal History* (New York: New York University Press, 2004), 47, 48.
32. John R. Graton to Dear Wife, April 16, 1865, John R. Graton Collection, KSHS.
33. Ibid.
34. Section 5, "An Act to amend the several Acts heretofore passed to provide for the Enrolling and Calling out the National Forces, and for other purposes," *Appendix to the Congressional Globe*, March 3, 1865, 38th Cong., 2nd sess., 134.
35. The signatories included James M. Williams, Richard G. Ward, John K. Graton, Elkanah Huddleston, Bethuel Hitchcock, Benjamin G. Janes, Daniel M. Sutherland, Ransom Ward, Andrew J. Armstrong, and Luther A. Thrasher. Ira Berlin, Joseph P. Reidy, and Leslie S. Rowland, *Freedom: A Documentary History of Emancipation, 1861–1867, Selected from the Holdings of the National Archives of the United States*, ser. 2: *The Black Military Experience* (Cambridge: Cambridge University Press, 1982), 405.
36. Ibid., 404–405.
37. Ibid., 405.
38. Total includes field and staff and company personnel. *Report of the Adjutant General of the State of Kansas, 1861–1865*, vol. 1 (Topeka: J. K. Hudson, 1896), 574–97.
39. The number 1,505 comes from my review and comparison of the regimental roster published in the *Report of the Adjutant General of the State of Kansas* and the compiled service records of the 79th USCT (New) at the National Archives. The number includes 232 men who were reported to have enlisted in 1862 but, for unknown reasons, failed to muster in with the regiment in 1863. It also includes draftees and substitutes who were not assigned to the regiment in the field. There may be discrepancies among some files due to inconsistent record keeping, poor handwriting (which resulted sometimes in multiple files being created for single individuals), and unknown omissions. I used discretion to eliminate duplications. In some cases, individuals were listed in the adjutant general's report but did not have a file in the compiled service records, and vice versa. *Report of the Adjutant General of the State of Kansas, 1861–1865*, vol. 1, 574–99, errata; Compiled Service Records, 79th USCT (New), NARA.
40. All numbers are based on regimental roster in the *Report of the Adjutant General of the State of Kansas, 1861–1865*, vol. 1, 574–99, errata. The roster lists 165 men killed in action after muster. I then added the nine men reported killed at Island Mound before muster, which raised the total to 174.
41. As noted before, the adjutant general's report does not record those men who died, were killed, or deserted before muster in January 1863. If such information became available, the number of deaths from disease may be higher than combat deaths. However, until such information can be found, the adjutant general's report combined with battle

reports from Island Mound provide the most substantial accounting of personnel.

42. John David Smith, "Let Us All Be Grateful That We Have Colored Troops That Will Fight," in *Black Soldiers in Blue: African American Troops in the Civil War Era*, ed. John David Smith (Chapel Hill: University of North Carolina Press, 2002), 41; Dudley Taylor Cornish, *The Sable Arm: Black Troops in the Union Army, 1861–1865* (1956; repr., Lawrence: University Press of Kansas, 1987), 288.

43. Desertion statistics are somewhat deceiving. Numbers listed above cover only desertions that resulted in the permanent loss of the soldier. Compiled service records of soldiers in the First Kansas Colored Infantry reveal that at least 129 soldiers were recorded as deserters at some point between January 1863 and October 1865. The adjutant general's roster only provides the final disposition of the soldier. Thus if the deserter returned to the regiment, either voluntarily or forcibly, his desertion was not recorded in the roster.

44. *Report of the Adjutant General of the State of Kansas, 1861–1865*, vol. 1, 574–99, errata.

45. *Christian Recorder* (Philadelphia, Pa.), December 23, 1865.

46. Roger D. Cunningham, "Welcoming 'Pa' on the Kaw: Kansas's 'Colored' Militia and the 1864 Price Raid," *Kansas History* 25, no. 2 (Summer 2002): 93.

47. *Christian Recorder* (Philadelphia, Pa.), December 23, 1865.

48. Ibid.

49. Ibid.

50. Ibid.

51. Eric Foner, *Reconstruction: America's Unfinished Revolution, 1863–1877* (New York: HarperCollins, 2002), 199–200.

52. *Christian Recorder* (Philadelphia, Pa.), December 23, 1865.

53. Ibid.

54. Ibid.

Epilogue

1. Historians have vigorously debated the aspect of matrilineal or matriarchal society in American slave communities. This book does not argue that slave families developed vastly different gender roles than white American families. Instead, it highlights the South's practice of tying slave children to the mother rather than the father. For a good discussion of slave family development in the South, see Ann Patton Malone, *Sweet Chariot: Slave Family and Household Structure in Nineteenth-Century Louisiana* (Chapel Hill: University of North Carolina Press, 1992), and Brenda E. Stevenson, *Life in Black and White: Family and Community in the Slave South* (New York: Oxford University Press, 1996).

2. Elizabeth R. Varon, *Disunion! The Coming of the American Civil War, 1789–1859* (Chapel Hill: University of North Carolina Press, 2008), 18; Kevin R. Johnson, *Mixed Race America and the Law: A Reader* (New York: New York University Press, 2003), 24–26.

3. Ethan Earle, "Journal of Captain Ethan Earle, Company F, First Kansas Colored Volunteer Infantry Regiment," 1873, p. 20, New England Historic Genealogical Society, Boston, Mass. Microfilm copy at Kansas State Historical Society, Topeka.

4. Julia Taylor Testimony, Nicholas Taylor Pension File, Application 337191, Certificate 305862, Widow Application 857807, Certificate 622606, National Archives and Records Administration (NARA), Washington, D.C.

5. Catherine Carter Widow Pension Application, December 4, 1902, Benjamin Carter Pension File, Application 748862, Widow Application 623259, Certificate 433717, NARA.

6. Testimony of Millie Young, December 4, 1902, Catherine Carter Widow Pension Application, Benjamin Carter Pension File, Application 748862, Widow Application 623259, Certificate 433717, NARA.

7. Deposition D, James Markham, August 26, 1891, Jeffrey Markham Pension File, Widow Application 493569, Certificate 306367, NARA.

8. General Affidavit for Harriet Markham, August 10, 1892, Jeffrey Markham Pension File, Widow Application 493569, Certificate 306367, NARA.

9. Susan Newby Widow Pension File (widow of Silas Newby), Application 205602, Certificate 163364, NARA.

10. Isaac Miller Testimony, February 12, 1895, Annie Jenkins Widow Pension File, Widow Application 488749, Certificate 423614, NARA.

11. Company G's roster in the Adjutant General's Report of Kansas lists Moses Jenkins as forty-two years old. However, his discharge papers from April 1865 note that he was fifty-nine years old. Such age discrepancies are common among records of the First Kansas Colored Infantry soldiers, particularly for the middle-aged men. *Report of the Adjutant General of the State of Kansas, 1861–1865*, vol. 1 (Topeka: J. K. Hudson, 1896), 589; Certificate of Discharge, April 14, 1865, Moses Jenkins Pension File, Application 554768, Widow App 488749, Certificate 423614, NARA.

12. Annie Jenkins Testimony, 12 February 1895, Annie Jenkins Widow Pension File, Widow Application 488749, Certificate 423614, NARA.

13. Ibid.

14. Maria Craig, "Deposition A," February 11, 1896, Green Craig Pension File, Application 342481, Certificate 485738, Widow Application 604381, Certificate 420734, NARA.

15. Alfred Alexander Pension File, Application 823586, Certificate 997247, NARA.

16. Squire Creecy's first wife's name is recorded different ways in his pension file—as Clarinda and Marinda. Squire Creecy Pension File, Application 232396, Widow Application 425914, Certificate 334825, NARA.

17. Henry Johnston, "Deposition B," May 19, 1892, Squire Creecy Pension File, Application 232396, Widow Application 425914, Certificate 334825, NARA.

18. Mariah Richardson, "Deposition E," May 19, 1892, Squire Creecy Pension File, Application 232396, Widow Application 425914, Certificate 334825, NARA.
19. Margaret Creecy, "Deposition A," May 18, 1892, Squire Creecy Pension File, Application 232396, Widow Application 425914, Certificate 334825, NARA.
20. Letty Shields Affidavit, June 29, 1909, George W. Shields Pension File, Application 400032, Certificate 923334, Widow Application 920577, Certificate 299282, NARA.
21. Deposition A, Henry Davis, January 30, 1899, Henry Davis Pension File, Application 191036, Certificate 782606, Widow Application 1085559, NARA.
22. Henry Davis Pension File, Application 191036, Certificate 782606, Widow Application 1085559, NARA.
23. Daniel Campbell Pension File, Application 1137082, Certificate 899780, NARA; Joseph Simpson Pension File, Application 1076179, Certificate 894088, NARA; Edward Clark Pension File, Application 943308, Certificate 747856, NARA; Charles Houston Pension File, Application 548407, Certificate 329221, Widow Application 656501, NARA; Adam Spencer Pension File, Application 894744, Certificate 629415, NARA.
24. Silas Hughes, alias James W. Wells, Pension File, Application 1315256, Certificate 1115784, Widow Application 1163427, Certificate 903560, NARA.
25. Deposition D, James Markham, August 26, 1891, Jeffrey Markham Pension File, Widow Application 493569, Certificate 306367, NARA.
26. Affidavit, April 19, 1888, Giles Gully Pension File, Application 650177, Certificate 594776, NARA; Samuel Miller Pension File, Application 748996, Certificate 591656, NARA.
27. Harrison Miller Pension File, Application 775396, Certificate 910937, Widow Application 953338, Certificate 716078, NARA.
28. Lawrence is in Douglas County, Kansas. Jeremiah Fielding Pension File, Application 428960, Widow Application 504992, Certificate 327507, NARA.
29. Philip Dudley Pension File, Application 659795, Certificate 445269, Minor Application 832656, NARA.
30. Jackson Donald, alias Jackson Gorl, Application 127304, Certificate 186528, NARA.
31. Affidavit of Simon Lynch, 1886, in John Bean Pension File, Application 373992, Certificate 361573, Widow Application 531128, Certificate 572475, NARA.
32. Deposition of William Gordon, June 7, 1898, William Gordon Pension File, Application 761720, Certificate 907381, NARA.
33. Joseph Bowers Deposition, November 15, 1886, Joseph Bowers Pension File, Application 205507, Certificate 25554, NARA.
34. Dock Williams Testimony, 1883, Joseph Bowers Pension File, Application 205507, Certificate 25554, NARA.
35. Hiram Hunter Testimony, Joseph Bowers Pension File, Application 205507, Certificate 25554, NARA.

36. John Smith Declaration for Invalid Pension, July 31, 1866, John Smith Pension File, Application 119699, Certificate 88816, NARA.

37. Brief in case of John Smith, n.d., John Smith Pension File, Application 119699, Certificate 88816, NARA.

38. Isaac Alexander Testimony, May 25, 1895, Isaac Alexander Pension File, Application 440919, Certificate 670709, NARA.

39. Jack Costin Pension File, Application 411312, Certificate 247141, NARA.

40. Harrison Miller Pension File, Application 775396, Certificate 910937, NARA.

41. Deposition A, William Turner, July 31, 1897, William Turner Pension File, Application 775586, Certificate 949406, NARA.

42. Deposition A, Cyrus Bowlegs Pension File, Application 495610, Certificate 805165, NARA.

43. Testimony of William Noble, Sr., May 15, 1888, Cyrus Bowlegs Pension File, Application 495610, Certificate 805165, NARA.

44. E. G. Macy to Hon. Wm E. McLean, August 4, 1886, Shebua Creps Pension File, Application 556703, Certificate 379090, Widow Application 357880, Certificate 238910, NARA.

45. Shebua Creps, Widow Pension Application 357880, Certificate 238910, NARA.

46. Glenna R. Schroeder-Lein, *The Encyclopedia of Civil War Medicine* (New York: M. E. Sharpe, 2008), 17.

47. Michael A. Dreese, *The Hospital on Seminary Ridge at the Battle of Gettysburg* (Jefferson, N.C.: McFarland & Company, 2002), 134.

48. Randolph Morgan, Compiled Service Record, 79th USCT (New), NARA.

49. Charles Anderson Pension File, Application 719430, National Archives and Records Administration, Washington, D.C.

50. Medical Card for Fox Holt, 79th USCT Carded Medical Records, Record Group 94: Records of the Adjutant General's Office, Entry 534, NARA.

51. Wilbert Lindsey, "Deposition A," June 17, 1892, Wilbert Lindsey Pension File, Application 840706, Certificate 797013, NARA.

52. Ibid.

53. Wilbert Lindsey Pension File, Application 840706, Certificate 797013, NARA.

54. The exceptions involved men who remained in hospitals or the care of others due to complete disability, such as John Smith of Company C, who sustained severe burns on his legs from boiling brine and entered a military soldier's home after discharge.

55. George Washington Pension File, Application 266875, Certificate 180670, Widow Application 666120, Certificate 493549, NARA.

56. Henry Holmes Pension File, Application 882922, Certificate 834959, NARA.

57. Testimony of Medora Renfro, Edmund Prater Pension File, Application 576528, Certificate 400602, Widow Application 550941, Certificate 341031, and Minor Application 613162, Certificate 440207, NARA.

58. Joseph Bowers Testimony, Joseph Bowers Pension File, Application 205507, Certificate 25554, NARA.
59. Hiram Hunter Testimony, Joseph Bowers Pension File, Application 205507, Certificate 25554, NARA.
60. Carr Taylor Pension File, Application 902966, Certificate 1018615, NARA.
61. John W. Smith Pension File, Application 1245144, Certificate 1100919, NARA.
62. Deposition of William Gordon, June 7, 1898, William Gordon Pension File, Application 761720, Certificate 907381, NARA.
63. Moses Holt Pension File, Application 345844, Certificate 496893, NARA.
64. Samuel Davis Pension File, Application 1152242, Certificate 865749, Widow Application 685236, Certificate 499745, NARA.
65. Several compiled service record files of First Kansas Colored Infantry officers include petitions dated in the summer of 1865 for "examination of Officers who wish to be retained in the military service of the United States." Compiled Service Records, 79th USCT (New), NARA.
66. Funeral Card for James M. Williams, James M. Williams Collection, Kansas State Historical Society (KSHS), Topeka. Also see Robert W. Lull, *Civil War General and Indian Fighter James M. Williams: Leader of the 1st Kansas Colored Volunteer and the 8th U.S. Cavalry* (Denton: University of North Texas Press, 2013), 155–222.
67. Testimonies of General Dudley, Andrew Jones Pension File, Application 619198, Certificate 421609, NARA.
68. Cyrus Bowlegs Pension File, Application 495610, Certificate 805165, NARA.
69. Bully Cornell (Connell) Pension File, Application 211572, Certificate 820641, Widow Application 823152, Certificate 607418, NARA.
70. Diane Mutti Burke, *On Slavery's Border: Missouri's Small Slaveholding Households, 1815–1865* (Athens: University of Georgia Press, 2010), 367 n. 42.
71. John Burton Compiled Service Record, 79th USCT (New), NARA.
72. Isaac Peace Slave Compensation Application, Gabriel Clark Compiled Service Record, 79th USCT (New), NARA.
73. Edward Dobson Slave Compensation Application, Manuel Dobson Compiled Service Record, 79th USCT (New), NARA.
74. Harrison Miller Compiled Service Record, 79th USCT (New), NARA.
75. Thomas Cheek Compiled Service Record, 79th USCT (New), NARA.
76. Burke, *On Slavery's Border*, 367 n. 42.
77. By 1890, James Lane, the Kansas senator and creator of the First Kansas Colored Infantry, had long since died: he committed suicide in 1866. See Ian Michael Spurgeon, *Man of Douglas, Man of Lincoln: The Political Odyssey of James Henry Lane* (Columbia: University of Missouri Press, 2008), 261–63.

78. Report No. 3157, Bill S. 2471, House of Representatives, 51st Cong., 1st sess., Congressional Edition, vol. 2816 (Washington, D.C.: U.S. Government Printing Office, 1891).
79. *Statutes of the United States of America Passed at the Second Session of the Fifty-First Congress, 1890–1891* (Washington, D.C.: Government Printing Office, 1891), 316.
80. *Leavenworth Times,* October 8, 1890.
81. Ibid.
82. Ibid.
83. Ibid.
84. Ibid.
85. Ibid.

Appendix A

1. Henry Steele Commager, ed., *The Blue and the Gray: The Story of the Civil War as Told by Participants,* vol. 1 (Indianapolis: Bobbs-Merrill, 1950), xxi.
2. Randall C. Jimerson, *The Private Civil War: Popular Thought during the Sectional Conflict* (Baton Rouge: Louisiana State University Press, 1988), 3.
3. Dudley Taylor Cornish, *The Sable Arm: Black Troops in the Union Army, 1861–1865* (1956; repr., Lawrence: University Press of Kansas, 1987), vii.

Bibliography

Manuscript Collections

Kansas State Historical Society
Abbott, James, Collection
Brown, George Washington, Papers, 1855–1914
Brown, John, Collection
Connelley, William, Collection
Foster, Charles, Collection
Goodnow, Isaac, Collection
Hyatt, Thaddeus, Collection
Ingalls, John J., Collection
Kansas Biographical Scrapbook
Lane, James H., Collection
Learnard, Oscar, Collection
Montgomery, James, Collection
Robinson, Charles, Collection
Rodgers, James, Collection
Van Horn, Benjamin, Collection
Webb Scrapbook
Williams, James Monroe, Papers
Wood, Samuel N., Collection

Houghton Library, Harvard University
American Freedom's Inquiry Commission Collection

Library of Congress
Lincoln, Abraham, Papers

New England Historic Genealogical Society, Boston
Earle, Ethan, Collection

Texas Historical Research Center, Hill College
Twentieth Texas Collection

University of Kansas: Spencer Research Library
Lane, James H., Papers
Lane Scrapbook

University of Oklahoma: Carl Albert Congressional Research and Studies Center Congressional Archives
Clarke, Sidney, Collection

Newspapers
Big Blue Union
The Christian Recorder
Fort Scott Bulletin
Freedom's Champion
Herald of Freedom
The Independent
Kansas Daily Tribune
Kansas Freeman
Kansas Free State
Kansas Weekly Herald
Lawrence Republican
Leavenworth Daily Conservative
Lecompton Union
Liberty Weekly Tribune
Missouri Republican
National Democrat
New York Times
The Smoky Hill and Republican Union
Topeka Daily Capital
Weekly Indiana State Sentinel
White Cloud Kansas Chief

Published Primary Sources
Angle, Paul M., and Earl Schenck Miers, eds. *The Living Lincoln: The Man, His Mind, His Times, and the War He Fought, Reconstructed from His Own Writings.* New York: Marboro Books, 1992.
Basler, Roy P., ed. *The Collected Works of Abraham Lincoln.* Vols. 5 and 7. New Brunswick, N.J.: Rutgers University Press, 1953.
Berlin, Ira, Barbara Fields, Thavolia Glymph, Joseph P. Reidy, and Leslie S. Rowland, eds. *Freedom: A Documentary History of Emancipation, 1861–1867,* ser. 1, vol. 1: *The Destruction of Slavery.* New York: Cambridge University Press, 1985.
Berlin, Ira, Joseph P. Reidy, and Leslie S. Rowland, eds. *Freedom: A Documentary History of Emancipation, 1861–1867,* ser. 2: *The Black Military Experience.* Cambridge: Cambridge University Press, 1982.
Chase, Samon Portland. *The Salmon P. Chase Papers,* vol. 1: *Journals, 1829–1872,* ed. John Niven. Kent, Ohio: Kent State University Press, 1993.
Dobak, William A., ed. "Civil War on the Kansas-Missouri Border: The Narrative of Former Slave Andrew Williams." *Kansas History* 6, no. 4 (Winter 1983): 237–42.

Freehling, William W., and Craig M. Simpson, eds. *Secession Debated: Georgia's Showdown in 1860*. New York: Oxford University Press, 1992.

Haydon, Charles B. *For Country, Cause, and Leader: The Civil War Journal of Charles B. Haydon*. Edited by Stephen W. Sears. New York: Ticknor & Fields, 1993.

Kennedy, Joseph C. G. *Preliminary Report on the Eighth Census: 1860*. Washington, D.C.: Government Printing Office, 1862.

Langsdorf, Edgar, ed. "The Letters of Joseph H. Trego, 1857–1864, Linn County Pioneer," pt. 2: "1861, 1862." *Kansas Historical Quarterly* 19, no. 3 (August 1951): 287–309.

Lovejoy, Julia Louisa. "Letters of Julia Louisa Lovejoy, 1856–1865," pt. 1: "1856." *Kansas Historical Quarterly* 15, no. 2 (May 1947): 127–42.

———. "Letters of Julia Louisa Lovejoy, 1856–1865," pt. 5: "1860–1864—Concluded." *Kansas Historical Quarterly* 16, no. 2 (May 1948): 175–211.

Murray, Donald M., and Robert M. Rodney, eds. "The Letters of Peter Bryant, Jackson County Pioneer," pt. 1. *Kansas Historical Quarterly* 27, no. 3 (Autumn 1961): 320–52.

Official Military History of Kansas Regiments during the War for the Suppression of the Great Rebellion. Leavenworth: W. S. Burke, 1870.

The Official Records of the War of the Rebellion (also known as *The War of the Rebellion: A Compilation of the Official Records of the Union and Confederate Armies*). Washington: Government Printing Office, 1880.

Old Settlers' History of Bates County, Missouri. Amsterdam, Mo.: Tathwell & Maxey, 1897.

Reader, Samuel James. "The Letters of Samuel James Reader, 1861–1863; Pioneer of Soldier Township, Shawnee County—Concluded." *Kansas Historical Quarterly* 9, no. 2 (May 1940): 155–69.

Redkey, Edwin S., ed. *A Grand Army of Black Men: Letters from African-American Soldiers in the Union Army, 1861–1865*. Cambridge: Cambridge University Press, 1992.

Report of the Adjutant General of the State of Kansas, 1861–1865. Vol. 1. Topeka: J. K. Hudson, 1896.

Richardson, James D., ed. *A Compilation of the Messages and Papers of the Confederacy, Including the Diplomatic Correspondence, 1861–1865*. Vol. 1. Nashville: United States Publishing, 1905.

Rollins, C. B., ed. "Letters of George Caleb Bingham to James S. Rollins," pt. 5: "January 22, 1862–November 21, 1871." *Missouri Historical Review* 33, no. 1 (October 1938): 45–78.

Slave Narratives: A Folk History of Slavery in Oklahoma from Interviews with Former Slaves: Oklahoma Narratives. Bedford, Mass.: Applewood Books, 2006.

Smith, Paul H., ed. *Letters of Delegates to Congress, 1774–1789*. Vol. 5. Washington, D.C.: Library of Congress, 1979.

Sperry, A. F. *History of the 33d Iowa Infantry Volunteer Regiment 1863–6.* Edited by Gregory J. W. Urwin and Cathy Kunzinger Urwin. Fayetteville: University of Arkansas Press, 1999.

Sumner, Charles. *Charles Sumner: His Complete Works.* With introduction by George Frisbie Hoar. Boston: Lee and Shepard, 1900.

"The Topeka Movement." *Collections of Kansas State Historical Society* 16 (1923–25): 125–249.

Townsend, John. *The Doom of Slavery in the Union: Its Safety Out of It.* Charleston, S.C.: Evans & Cogswell, 1860.

United States Service Magazine. Vol. 3. New York: Charles R. Richardson, 1865.

Wakelyn, Jon, ed. *Southern Pamphlets on Secession.* Chapel Hill: University of North Carolina Press, 1996.

"When Kansas Became a State." *Kansas Historical Quarterly* 27, no. 1 (Spring 1961): 1–21.

Wing, Tom, ed. *"A Rough Introduction to This Sunny Land": The Civil War Diary of Private Henry A. Strong, Co. K, Twelfth Kansas Infantry.* Little Rock: Butler Center for Arkansas Studies, 2006.

Zorn, Roman J., ed. "Campaigning in Southern Arkansas: A Memoir by C. T. Anderson." *Arkansas Historical Quarterly* 8 (Autumn 1949): 240–44.

Secondary Sources

Ash, Stephen V. *Firebrand of Liberty: The Story of Two Black Regiments That Changed the Course of the Civil War.* New York: W. W. Norton, 2008.

Aud, Susan, Mary Ann Fox, and Angelina KewalRamani. *Status and Trends in the Education of Racial and Ethnic Groups.* Washington, D.C.: National Center for Education Statistics, 2010.

Bailey, Anne J., and Daniel E. Sutherland, eds. *Civil War Arkansas: Beyond Battles and Leaders.* Fayetteville: University of Arkansas Press, 2000.

Baird, W. David, ed. *A Creek Warrior for the Confederacy: The Autobiography of Chief G. W. Grayson.* Norman: University of Oklahoma Press, 1991.

Bearss, Edwin C. *Steele's Retreat from Camden and the Battle of Jenkins Ferry.* Little Rock: Pioneer, 1995.

Bearss, Edwin C., and A. M. Gibson. *Fort Smith: Little Gibraltar on the Arkansas.* Norman: University of Oklahoma Press, 1969.

Benedict, Bryce. *Jayhawkers: The Civil War Brigade of James Henry Lane.* Norman: University of Oklahoma Press, 2009.

Blunt, James G. "General Blunt's Account of His Civil War Experiences." *Kansas Historical Quarterly* 1, no. 3 (May 1932): 211–65.

Bogue, Allan G. *The Earnest Men: Republicans of the Civil War Senate.* Ithaca, N.Y.: Cornell University Press, 1981.

Bown, David Warren. *Andrew Johnson and the Negro.* Knoxville: University of Tennessee Press, 1989.

Brigham, Johnson. *James Harlan.* Iowa City: Iowa State Historical Society, 1913.

Bright, John D., ed. *Kansas: The First Century*. New York: Lewis Historical, 1956.

Brinkerhoff, Fred W. "The Kansas Tour of Lincoln, the Candidate." *Kansas Historical Quarterly* 13, no. 1 (February 1944): 294–307.

Britton, Wiley. *The Civil War on the Border*. Vol. 1, *1861–1862*. New York: G. P. Putnam's Sons, 1899.

———. *The Civil War on the Border*. Vol. 2, *1863–1865*. New York: G. P. Putnam's Sons, 1899.

———. *Memoirs of the Rebellion on the Border, 1863*. Lincoln: University of Nebraska Press, 1993.

———. *The Union Indian Brigade in the Civil War*. Kansas City, Mo.: Franklin Hudson, 1922.

Burke, Diane Mutti. *On Slavery's Border: Missouri's Small Slaveholding Households, 1815–1865*. Athens: University of Georgia Press, 2010.

Butler, Pardee. *Personal Recollections of Pardee Butler with Reminiscences by His Daughter Mrs. Rosetta B. Hastings*. Cincinnati: Standard, 1889.

Carpenter, Francis Bicknell. *Six Months at the White House with Abraham Lincoln: The Story of a Picture*. New York: Hurd and Houghton, 1866.

Castel, Albert. "Civil War, Kansas, and the Negro." *Journal of Negro History* vol. 51, no. 2 (April 1966): 125–38.

———. *Civil War Kansas: Reaping the Whirlwind*. Lawrence: University Press of Kansas, 1997. Originally published as *A Frontier State at War: Kansas, 1861–1865*. Ithaca, N.Y.: Cornell University Press, 1958.

———. "Jim Lane of Kansas." *Civil War Times Illustrated* 12, no. 1 (April 1973): 22–28.

———. "Order No. 11 and the Civil War on the Border." *Missouri Historical Review* 57, no. 4 (July 1963): 357–68.

Cecil-Fronsman, Bill. "'Advocate the Freedom of White Men, as Well as, That of Negros': *The Kansas Free State* and Anti-Slavery Westerners in Territorial Kansas." *Kansas History* 20, no. 2 (Summer 1997): 102–15.

Cheatam, Gary L. "'Slavery All the Time or Not at All': The Wyandotte Constitution Debate 1859–1861." *Kansas History* 21, no. 3 (Autumn 1998): 168–87.

Chesnut, Mary. *A Diary from Dixie*. Edited by Isabella D. Martin and Myrta Lockett Avary. 1905. Reprint, New York: Gramercy Books, 1997.

Christ, Mark, ed. *"All Cut to Pieces and Gone to Hell": The Civil War, Race Relations, and the Battle of Poison Spring*. Little Rock: August House, 2003.

———, ed., *Rugged and Sublime: The Civil War in Arkansas*. Fayetteville: University of Arkansas Press, 1994.

Clark, John G. "Mark W. Delahay: Peripatetic Politician." *Kansas Historical Quarterly* 25, no. 3 (Autumn 1959): 301–13.

Clugston, W. G. *Rascals in Democracy*. New York: Richard R. Smith, 1940.

Commager, Henry Steele, ed. *The Blue and the Gray: The Story of the Civil War as Told by Participants*. Vol. 1. Indianapolis: Bobbs-Merrill, 1950.

Connelley, William Elsey. *An Appeal to the Record*. Topeka: William Connelley, 1903.

———. *James Henry Lane: The "Grim Chieftain" of Kansas*. Topeka: Crane & Co., 1899.

———. "The Lane Trail." *Collections of Kansas State Historical Society* 13 (1913–14): 268–79.

———. *A Standard History of Kansas and Kansans*. Vol. 1. Chicago: Lewis, 1918.

Corder, Eric. *Prelude to Civil War: Kansas-Missouri 1854–61*. London: Crowell-Collier, 1970.

Cornish, Dudley Taylor. "Kansas Negro Regiments in the Civil War." *Kansas Historical Quarterly* 20, no. 6 (May 1953): 417–29.

———. *The Sable Arm: Black Troops in the Union Army, 1861–1865*. 1956. Reprint, Lawrence: University Press of Kansas, 1987.

Cunningham, Roger D. "Welcoming 'Pa' on the Kaw: Kansas's 'Colored' Militia and the 1864 Price Raid." *Kansas History* 25, no. 2 (Summer 2002): 87–101.

Davis, Kenneth S. *Kansas: A History*. New York: W. W. Norton, 1984.

Davis, William C. *"A Government of Our Own": The Making of the Confederacy*. New York: Free Press, 1994.

———. *Lincoln's Men: How President Lincoln Became Father to an Army and a Nation*. New York: Free Press, 1999.

DeBlack, Thomas A. *With Fire and Sword: Arkansas, 1861–1874*. Fayetteville: University of Arkansas Press, 2003.

Dobak, William A. *Freedom by the Sword: The U.S. Colored Troops, 1862–1867*. Washington, D.C.: Center of Military History, 2011.

Dorris, Jonathan Truman. *Pardon and Amnesty under Lincoln and Johnson: The Restoration of the Confederates to Their Rights and Privileges, 1861–1898*. Chapel Hill: University of North Carolina Press, 1953.

Dreese, Michael A. *The Hospital on Seminary Ridge at the Battle of Gettysburg*. Jefferson, N.C.: McFarland & Company, 2002.

Eldridge, Shalor Winchell. *Recollections of Early Days in Kansas*. Topeka: Kansas State Printing Plant, 1920.

Etcheson, Nicole. *Bleeding Kansas: Contested Liberty in the Civil War Era*. Lawrence: University Press of Kansas, 2004.

———. "Manliness and the Political Culture of the Old Northwest, 1790–1860." *Journal of the Early Republic* 15, no. 1 (Spring 1995): 59–77.

Fehrenbacher, Don E. *The Slaveholding Republic: An Account of the United States Government's Relations to Slavery*. Oxford: Oxford University Press, 2001.

Fellman, Michael. "Emancipation in Missouri." *Missouri Historical Review* 83, no. 1 (October 1988): 36–56.

Felmly, Bradford K., and John C. Grady. *Suffering to Silence: 29th Texas Cavalry, CSA Regimental History*. Quanah, Tex.: Nortex, 1975.

Fisher, H. D. *The Gun and the Gospel: Early Kansas and Chaplain Fisher*. Chicago: Kenwood, 1896.

Foner, Eric. *Forever Free: The Story of Emancipation and Reconstruction*. New York: Alfred A. Knopf, 1995.

———. *Free Soil, Free Labor, Free Men: The Ideology of the Republican Party before the Civil War*. New York: Oxford University Press, 1970.

———. *Reconstruction: America's Unfinished Revolution, 1863–1877*. New York: HarperCollins, 2002.

Foreman, Grant. "Early Trails through Oklahoma." *Chronicles of Oklahoma* 3, no. 2 (June 1925): 99–119.

Forsyth, Michael J. *The Camden Expedition of 1864 and the Lost Opportunity by the Confederacy to Change the Civil War*. Jefferson, N.C.: McFarland & Company, 2003.

Fox, William F. *Regimental Losses in the American Civil War, 1861–1865*. Albany, N.Y.: Albany Publishing, 1889.

Franklin, John Hope. *Reconstruction after the Civil War*. Chicago: University of Chicago Press, 1961.

Franklin, John Hope, and Loren Schweninger. *Runaway Slaves: Rebels on the Plantation*. New York: Oxford University Press, 1999.

Frankovic, Joseph, Jeremy Lynch, Julie Northrip, and Sam Trisler. "Prairie D'Ane and Poison Spring from a Southern Perspective." *Journal of the Fort Smith Historical Society* 31, no. 1 (April 2007): 35–44.

Glatthaar, Joseph T. *Forged in Battle: The Civil War Alliance of Black Soldiers and White Officers*. Baton Rouge: Louisiana State University Press, 2000.

Gleed, Charles S. ed. *The Kansas Memorial: A Report of the Old Settlers' Meeting Held at Bismarck Grove, Kansas, September 15th and 16th, 1879*. Kansas City: Press of Ramsey, Millett & Hudson, 1880.

Goodrich, Thomas. *Black Flag: Guerrilla Warfare on the Western Border, 1861–1865*. Indianapolis: Indiana University Press, 1995.

———. *Bloody Dawn: The Story of the Lawrence Massacre*. Kent, Ohio: Kent State University Press, 1991.

———. *War to the Knife: Bleeding Kansas, 1854–1861*. Lincoln: University of Nebraska Press, 2004.

Goodwin, Doris Kearns. *Team of Rivals: The Political Genius of Abraham Lincoln*. New York: Simon & Schuster, 2005.

Gresham, Luveta W. "Colonization Proposals for Free Negroes and Contrabands during the Civil War." *Journal of Negro Education* 16, no. 1 (Winter 1947): 28–33.

Guelzo, Allen C. *Lincoln's Emancipation Proclamation: The End of Slavery in America*. New York: Simon & Schuster, 2004.

Hardee, William J. *Rifle and Light Infantry Tactics: For the Exercise and Maneuvres of Troops When Acting as Light Infantry or Riflemen*. Vol. 1. Philadelphia: Lippincott, Grambo & Co., 1855.

Harrell, David Edwin, Jr. "Pardee Butler: Kansas Crusader." *Kansas Historical Quarterly* 34, no. 4 (Winter 1968): 386–408.

Hart, Charles Desmond. "The Natural Limits of Slavery Expansion: Kansas-Nebraska, 1854." *Kansas Historical Quarterly* 35, no. 1 (Spring 1968): 32–50.

Hauptman, Laurence M. *Between Two Fires: American Indians in the Civil War*. New York: Simon & Schuster, 1996.

Hazlett, James C., Edwin Olmstead, and M. Hume Parks. *Field Artillery Weapons of the Civil War*. Urbana: University of Illinois Press, 2004.

Herklotz, Hildegarde Rose. "Jayhawkers in Missouri, 1858–1863." First article, chap. 1. *Missouri Historical Review* 17, no. 3 (April 1923): 266–84.

———. "Jayhawkers in Missouri, 1858–1863." Third article, chap. 4. *Missouri Historical Review* 18, no. 1 (October 1923): 64–101.

Hewett, Jane B., ed., *Supplement to the Official Records of the Union and Confederate Armies*. Pt. 2, vol. 78. Wilmington, N.C.: Broadfoot, 1998.

Hollandsworth, James G., Jr. *The Louisiana Native Guards: The Black Military Experience during the Civil War*. Baton Rouge: Louisiana State University Press, 1995.

Holt, Michael F. *Political Parties and American Political Development from the Age of Jackson to the Age of Lincoln*. Baton Rouge: Louisiana State University Press, 1992.

Ingalls, John James. "John Brown's Place in History." *North American Review* 138 (February 1884): 138–50.

———. "Kansas 1541–1891." *Harper's Magazine* 86 (April 1893): 697–713.

Isely, W. H. "The Sharp's Rifle Episode in Kansas History." *American Historical Review* 12, no. 3 (April 1907): 546–66.

Jewett, Clayton E., and John O. Allen. *Slavery in the South: A State-by-State History*. Westport, Conn.: Greenwood, 2004.

Jimerson, Randall C. *The Private Civil War: Popular Thought during the Sectional Conflict*. Baton Rouge: Louisiana State University Press, 1988.

Johnson, Kevin R. *Mixed Race America and the Law: A Reader*. New York: New York University Press, 2003.

Johnson, Samuel A. *The Battle Cry of Freedom: The New England Emigrant Aid Company in the Kansas Crusade*. Westport, Conn.: Greenwood, 1977.

Joiner, Gary D. *Through the Howling Wilderness: The 1864 Red River Campaign and Union Failure in the West*. Knoxville: University of Tennessee Press, 2006.

Josephy, Alvin M., Jr. *The Civil War in the American West*. New York: Alfred A. Knopf, 1991.

Kelly, Orr, and Mary Davies Orr. *Dream's End: Two Iowa Brothers in the Civil War*. New York: Kodansha International, 1998.

Klein, Maury. *Days of Defiance: Sumter, Secession, and the Coming of the Civil War*. New York: Vintage Books, 1997.

Klingaman, William K. *Abraham Lincoln and the Road to Emancipation, 1861–1865.* New York: Viking, 2001.

Kolchin, Peter. *American Slavery, 1619–1877.* New York: Hill and Wang, 1993.

Krug, Mark M. "The Republican Party and the Emancipation Proclamation." *Journal of Negro History* 48, no. 2 (April 1963): 98–114.

Kulikoff, Allan, *Tobacco and Slaves: The Development of Southern Cultures in the Chesapeake, 1680–1800.* Chapel Hill: University of North Carolina Press, 1986.

Lause, Mark A. *Race and Radicalism in the Union Army.* Urbana: University of Illinois Press, 2009.

Lindberg, Kip, and Matt Matthews, eds. "'The Eagle of the 11th Kansas': Wartime Reminiscences of Colonel Thomas Moonlight." *Arkansas Historical Quarterly* 62, no. 1 (Spring 2003): 1–41.

———. "'To Play a Bold Game': The Battle of Honey Springs." *North and South* 6, no. 1 (December 2002): 56–69.

Lull, Robert W. *Civil War General and Indian Fighter James Williams: Leader of the 1st Kansas Colored Volunteer Infantry and the 8th U.S. Cavalry.* Denton: University of North Texas Press, 2013.

Luthin, Reinhard H. "Some Demagogues in American History." *American Historical Review* 57 (October 1951–July 1952): 22–46.

Mallam, William D. "Lincoln and the Conservatives." *Journal of Southern History* 28, no. 1 (February 1969): 31–45.

Malone, Ann Patton. *Sweet Chariot: Slave Family and Household Structure in Nineteenth-Century Louisiana.* Chapel Hill: University of North Carolina Press, 1992.

Manning, Michael Lee. *The African-American Soldier: From Crispus Attucks to Colin Powell.* New York: Citadel, 2004.

Martin, Jonathan D. *Divided Mastery: Slave Hiring in the American South.* Cambridge, Mass.: Harvard University Press, 2004.

Mayer, Henry. *All on Fire: William Lloyd Garrison and the Abolition of Slavery.* New York: St. Martin's, 1998.

McPherson, James M., ed. *The Atlas of the Civil War.* New York: Macmillan, 1994.

———. *Battle Cry of Freedom.* New York: Oxford University Press, 1988.

———. *For Cause and Comrades: Why Men Fought in the Civil War.* New York: Oxford University Press, 1997.

———. *The Negro's Civil War: How American Blacks Felt and Acted during the War for the Union.* New York: Ballantine Books, 1991.

Means, Howard. *The Avenger Takes His Place: Andrew Johnson and the 45 Days That Changed the Nation.* Orlando: Harcourt, 2006.

Middleton, Stephen. *The Black Laws: Race and the Legal Process in Early Ohio.* Athens: Ohio University Press, 2005.

Mildfelt, Todd. *The Secret Danites: Kansas' First Jayhawkers.* Richmond, Kans.: Todd Mildfelt, 2003.

Miller, Edward A., Jr. *Lincoln's Abolitionist General: The Biography of David Hunter.* Columbia: University of South Carolina Press, 1997.

Miller, William Lee. *Arguing about Slavery: The Great Battle in the United States Congress.* New York: Alfred A. Knopf, 1997.

Miner, Craig. "Lane and Lincoln: A Mysterious Connection." *Kansas History* 24, no. 3 (Autumn 2001): 186–99.

Mink, Charles R. "General Orders, No. 11: The Forced Evacuation of Civilians during the Civil War." *Military Affairs* 34, no. 4 (December 1970): 132–37.

Monaghan, Jay. *Civil War on the Western Border, 1854–1865.* Lincoln: University of Nebraska Press, 1955.

Moneyhon, Carl H. *The Impact of the Civil War and Reconstruction on Arkansas: Persistence in the Midst of Ruin.* Fayetteville: University of Arkansas Press, 2002.

Moore, Frank. *The Rebellion Record.* Vol. 6. New York: G. P. Putnam, 1863.

Morris, Thomas D. *Southern Slavery and the Law, 1619–1860.* Chapel Hill: University of North Carolina Press, 1996.

Mullis, Tony R. *Peacekeeping on the Plains: Army Operations in Bleeding Kansas.* Columbia: University of Missouri Press, 2004.

Nicolay, John G. *The Outbreak of Rebellion.* New York: Scribner's Sons, 1881. Reprint, New York: Da Capo, 1995.

Nicolay, John G., and John Hay. *Abraham Lincoln: A History.* 10 vols. New York: Century, 1917.

Oates, Stephen B. *To Purge This Land with Blood: A Biography of John Brown.* New York: Harper & Row, 1970.

Oertel, Kristen Tegtmeier. "'The Free Sons of the North' vs. 'The Myrmidons of Border-Ruffianism': What Makes a Man in Bleeding Kansas." *Kansas History* 25, no. 3 (Autumn 2002): 174–89.

Patrick, Rembert W. *The Reconstruction of the Nation.* London: Oxford University Press, 1967.

Pitcock, Cynthia DeHaven, and Bill J. Gurley. "'I Acted from Principle': William Marcellus McPheeters, Confederate Surgeon." *Missouri Historical Review* 89, no. 4 (July 1995): 384–405.

Plummer, Mark A. *Frontier Governor: Samuel J. Crawford of Kansas.* Lawrence: University Press of Kansas, 1971.

———. "Governor Crawford's Appointment of Edmond G. Ross to the United States Senate." *Kansas Historical Quarterly* 28, no. 2 (Summer 1962): 145–53.

Quarles, Benjamin. *The Negro in the Civil War.* New York: Da Capo, 1989.

Rawley, James A. *Race and Politics: "Bleeding Kansas" and the Coming of the Civil War.* Lincoln: University of Nebraska Press, 1979.

———. *Secession: The Disruption of the American Republic, 1844–1861.* Malabar, Fla.: Robert E. Krieger, 1990.

Report of the Adjutant General of the State of Kansas, 1861–1865. Vol. 1. Topeka: J. K. Hudson, 1896.

Robinson, Charles. *The Kansas Conflict.* Lawrence: Journal Publishing, 1898.

———. "Topeka and Her Constitution." *Transactions of the Kansas State Historical Society* 6 (1897–1900): 291–316.

Royster, Charles. *The Destructive War: William Tecumseh Sherman, Stonewall Jackson, and the Americans*. New York: Alfred A. Knopf, 1991.

Samito, Christian G., ed., *Changes in Law and Society during the Civil War and Reconstruction: A Legal History Documentary Reader*. Carbondale: Southern Illinois University Press, 2009.

Sanborn, F. B., ed. *The Life and Letters of John Brown, Liberator of Kansas and Martyr of Virginia*. New York: Negro Universities Press, 1969.

Schroeder-Lein, Glenna R. *The Encyclopedia of Civil War Medicine*. New York: M. E. Sharpe, 2008.

Scott, Otto J. *The Secret Six: John Brown and the Abolitionist Movement*. New York: Times Books, 1979.

Sears, Stephen W. *George B. McClellan: The Young Napoleon*. New York: Da Capo, 1999.

Shaffer, Donald A. *After the Glory: The Struggles of Black Civil War Veterans*. Lawrence: University Press of Kansas, 2004.

Shannon, Fred A. "The Federal Government and the Negro Soldier, 1861–1865." *Journal of Negro History* 11, no. 4 (October 1926): 563–83.

Sheridan, Richard B., ed. *Freedom's Crucible: The Underground Railroad in Lawrence and Douglas County, Kansas, 1854–1865: A Reader*. Lawrence: University Press of Kansas, 2000.

———. "From Slavery in Missouri to Freedom in Kansas: The Influx of Black Fugitives and Contrabands into Kansas, 1854–1865." *Kansas History* 12 (Spring 1989): 28–47.

Smith, John David, ed. *Black Soldiers in Blue: African American Troops in the Civil War Era*. Chapel Hill: University of North Carolina Press, 2002.

Speer, John. *Life of Gen. James H. Lane, "The Liberator of Kansas."* Garden City, Kans.: John Speer, 1897.

Spring, Leverett W. "The Career of a Kansas Politician." *American Historical Review* 4 (October 1898–July 1899): 80–104.

———. *Kansas: The Prelude to the War for the Union*. Boston: Houghton Mifflin, 1885.

Spurgeon, Ian Michael. *Man of Douglas, Man of Lincoln: The Political Odyssey of James Henry Lane*. Columbia: University of Missouri Press, 2008.

Stampp, Kenneth M. *And the War Came: The North and the Secession Crisis, 1860–1861*. 1970. Reprint, Baton Rouge: Louisiana State University Press, 1990.

———. ed. *The Causes of the Civil War*. 1959. Reprint, Englewood Cliffs, N.J.: Prentice-Hall, 1974.

———. *The Imperiled Union: Essays on the Background of the Civil War*. New York: Oxford University Press, 1990.

Stephenson, Wendell Holmes. *The Political Career of General James H. Lane*. Topeka: B. P. Walker, 1930.

———. "The Transitional Period in the Career of General James H. Lane." *Indiana Magazine of History* 25, no. 2 (June 1929): 75–91.

Stevenson, Brenda E. *Life in Black and White: Family and Community in the Slave South.* New York: Oxford University Press, 1996.

Stoddard, William Osborn. *Inside the White House in War Times.* New York: C. L. Webster & Co., 1890.

Tabor, Chris. *The Skirmish at Island Mound, Mo., October 29, 1862.* Independence, Mo.: Blue and Grey Book Shoppe, 2001.

Taylor, Orville W. *Negro Slavery in Arkansas.* Little Rock: University of Arkansas Press, 2000.

Tovey, Robert Atkins. "A Twelve Months Practical Life in Kansas, Written by an Actual Settler." Kansas State Historical Society and University of Kansas, RH MS P186, *Territorial Kansas Online,* http://www.territorialkansasonline.org.

Townsend, John. *The Doom of Slavery in the Union: Its Safety Out of It.* Charleston, S.C.: Evans & Cogswell, 1860.

Trefousse, Hans L. *The Radical Republicans: Lincoln's Vanguard for Racial Justice.* New York: Alfred A. Knopf, 1969.

Trudeau, Noah Andre. *Like Men of War: Black Troops in the Civil War, 1862–1865.* New York: Little, Brown, 1998.

Tsesis, Alexander. *The Thirteenth Amendment and American Freedom: A Legal History.* New York: New York University Press, 2004.

Urwin, Gregory J. W., ed. *Black Flag over Dixie: Racial Atrocities and Reprisals in the Civil War.* Carbondale: Southern Illinois University Press, 2004.

———. "'Cut to Pieces and Gone to Hell': The Poison Spring Massacre." *North and South* 2, no. 6 (August 2000): 45–57.

Varon, Elizabeth R. *Disunion! The Coming of the American Civil War, 1789–1859.* Chapel Hill: University of North Carolina Press, 2008.

Villard, Oswald Garrison. *John Brown, 1800–1859.* Boston: Houghton Mifflin, 1910.

Wakelyn, Jon L., ed. *Southern Pamphlets on Secession, November 1860–April 1861.* Chapel Hill: University of North Carolina Press, 1996.

Watts, Dale E. "How Bloody Was Bleeding Kansas: Political Killings in Kansas Territory 1854–1861." *Kansas History* 18, no. 2 (Summer 1995): 116–29.

Weigley, Russell F. *The American Way of War: A History of United States Military Strategy and Policy.* Bloomington: Indiana University Press, 1977.

Welch, G. Murlin. *Border Warfare in Southeastern Kansas, 1856–1859.* Pleasanton, Kans.: Linn County, 1977.

Wert, Jeffry D. *The Sword of Lincoln: The Army of the Potomac.* New York: Simon & Schuster, 2003

Wilder, Daniel C. *The Annals of Kansas.* Topeka: Geo. W. Martin, Kansas Publishing House, 1875.

Wiley, Bell Irvin. *The Life of Billy Yank.* Baton Rouge: Louisiana State University Press, 1992.

Williams, T. Harry. *Lincoln and His Generals*. New York: Vintage Books, 2011.

Wilson, Joseph T. *The Black Phalanx: African American Soldiers in the War of Independence, the War of 1812, and the Civil War*. New York: Da Capo, 1994.

Wood, Larry. *The Civil War on the Lower Kansas-Missouri Border*. Joplin, Mo.: Hickory, 2000.

Wyatt-Brown, Bertram. *Honor and Violence in the Old South*. New York: Oxford University Press, 1986.

———. "The Mask of Obedience: Male Slave Psychology in the Old South." *American Historical Review* 93, no. 5 (December 1988): 1228–52.

Yeary, Mamie, comp. *Reminiscences of the Boys in Gray, 1861–1865*. Dallas: Smith & Lamar, 1912.

Zarefsky, David. *Lincoln, Douglas and Slavery: In the Crucible of Public Debate*. Chicago: University of Chicago Press, 1990.

Zornow, William Frank. *Kansas: A History of the Jayhawk State*. Norman: University of Oklahoma Press, 1957.

———. "The Kansas Senators and the Reelection of Lincoln." *Kansas Historical Quarterly* 19, no. 2 (May 1951): 133–44.

Index

Illustrations are indicated with italicized page numbers.

abolitionists: and African
　Americans, 17, 19–20, 49;
　on black military service,
　26, 44, 48, 51, 70; and black
　soldiers, 59; on Emancipation
　Proclamation, 108–109; and
　Lincoln, criticism of, 33; in
　territorial Kansas, 9–16
Adair, Amos, 216, 221
Adams, Daniel, 156
Adams, John, president, 26
Aggleston, Henry, 104, 105
Alexander, Alfred, 260–61
Alexander, Isaac, 121, 246–47,
　264–65
Alston, Ephraim, 226
American Freedmen's Inquiry
　Commission, 178–80
Anderson, Charles, 266
Anderson, R. C., 118
Anthony, Daniel R., 53
Antietam, battle of, 83, 97
Appomattox Courthouse, 249–50
Armstrong, Andrew: at Island
　Mound, 87–89, 90, 94–95; at
　Poison Spring, 219–20; and
　Wharfield, shooting of, 99, 100;
　and Williams, dispute with,
　219–20
atrocities, 139–40, 212, 214–16,
　223–25, 235–36

Ball, James, 247
Banks, Nathaniel P., 193, 222
Bannon, Shelby, 91–92
Barber, Marion, 95
Barker, Edgar A., 231–34, 236–37
Battice, John, 120
Baxter Springs, 136, 144, 145–46,
　148

Bean, John, 263
Biddle, Nicholas, 27–28
Bishop, John, 140
Black Codes, 254–55
black exclusion: in Arkansas, 189,
　228; in Kansas, 10, 12, 13, 15,
　16, 21, 52
"black law." *See* black exclusion
Blair, Charles, 136
Blunt, James G.: and black soldiers
　for manual labor, 85; as
　commander of District of
　Kansas, 39, 53; on desertion,
　113; discharges soldiers,
　121; on First Kansas Colored
　Infantry, 109–10, 176; and
　First Kansas Colored Infantry,
　command of, 118; at Fort
　Gibson, 145, 146; at Fort
　Smith, 184–85; at Honey
　Springs, 158–76; and Kansas,
　shortage of soldiers in, 138;
　and Leavenworth incident,
　102, 103; and northeastern
　Indian Territory, 177–78;
　photograph of, *126*; and
　recruitment of black soldiers,
　56, 119–20; relieved of
　command, 182
Bowers, Joseph, 63, 115, 264, 268
Bowlegs, Cyrus, 120, 265, 269
Bowles, Henry, 104, 105
Bowles, John, 18, 98, 170–72,
　192–93
Brant, R. C., 100
Braze, Jefferson, 235
Britton, Wiley, 137, 164–65
Brown, George W., 12
Brown, James, 237
Brown, Jesse, 216

433

Dobson, Jacob, 26–27
Dobson, Manual, 95, 270
Dodd, Theodore H., 151
Dodge, Richard, 69
Donald (Donnell), Jackson, 64, *132*, 262–63
Donnell, Robert, 263
Douglas, Stephen, 10, 14
Douglass, Frederick, 6, 42, 48–49
Dowell, Philip, 62
Dry Wood Creek, battle of, 34
DuBois, John V., 181
Dudley, General, 269
Dudley, Philip, 262
Duncan, William M., 202, 206, 207–208
Duvall, George, 62, 234, 237

Eakin, John, 215
Earle, Ethan: and black soldiers, 56–58, 60, 66–67; and John Bowles, court-martial of, 192; and Cabin Creek, on Confederate position at, 149; and Cabin Creek, wounded at, 153; on Camden, 222, 223; and Company F, command of, 111; and cotton operations in Arkansas, 187; on Honey Springs, battle at, 168, 173, 175; on Clement Johnson, 258; on muskets, 77; on Poison Spring, 227; and Second Kansas Colored Infantry, reaction to, 182; on Unionists in Arkansas, 188; and white soldiers, change in attitude of, 176; and James Williams, 68
Ehle, M. M., 136, 138
Eighteenth Iowa Infantry, 183, 185, 194, 196, 198, 201, 202, 206, 207–208, 210, 212, 216, 219
Eighteenth Texas Infantry, 224
Eighth United States Cavalry, 268
Eleventh United States Colored Troops, 184, 231

emancipation: in Arkansas, 188, 189; and James H. Lane, 40, 46, 60; and Abraham Lincoln, discussed by, 82; in Missouri, 32; opposition to, 43; in South Carolina, 50; through Thirteenth Amendment, 248–49
Emancipation Proclamation, 6, 82–84, 106–107, 108–109, 116, 178, 215, 248
Ewing, Thomas, 158

Fagan, James F., 200
Fielding, Jeremiah, 64, 262
Fielding, Sanford, 64
Fields, Joseph F., 62
Fifth Kansas Cavalry, 59, 77, 78, 86
Fifth New York Infantry, 219
Fifth Texas Partisans, 173, 233
Fifteenth New Jersey Infantry, 219
Fifty-Fourth Massachusetts Infantry, 5–6
Fifty-Fourth United States Colored Troops, 231
First Arkansas Infantry (Union), 183, 196
First Arkansas Light Artillery, 231
First Cherokee Mounted Regiment, 166, 232, 234
First Choctaw and Chickasaw Regiment, 162, 166 168, 173
First Choctaw Regiment, 200, 213
First Creek Regiment, 168
First Indian Home Guard, 149, 161, 166, 172
First Kansas Colored Infantry, 5, 6, 7; at Cabin Creek, 149–54; daily schedule of, 115; and desertions, 104, 113–15, 117; discipline within, 98–100, 104–105, 116, 117; and 1890 reunion of, 270–71; equipment of, 75–78; and federal service, mustered in, 110–13; and federal service, mustered out,

www.ingramcontent.com/pod-product-compliance
Lightning Source LLC
Chambersburg PA
CBHW032119011225
36123CB00048B/433